DK COLLECTOR'S GUIDES

ART NOUVEAU

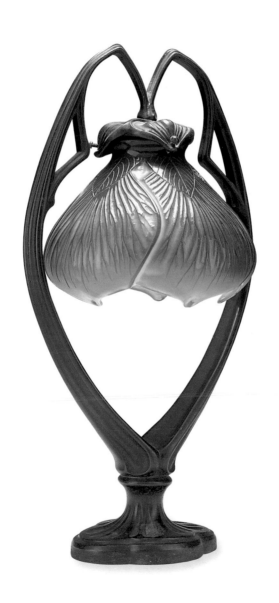

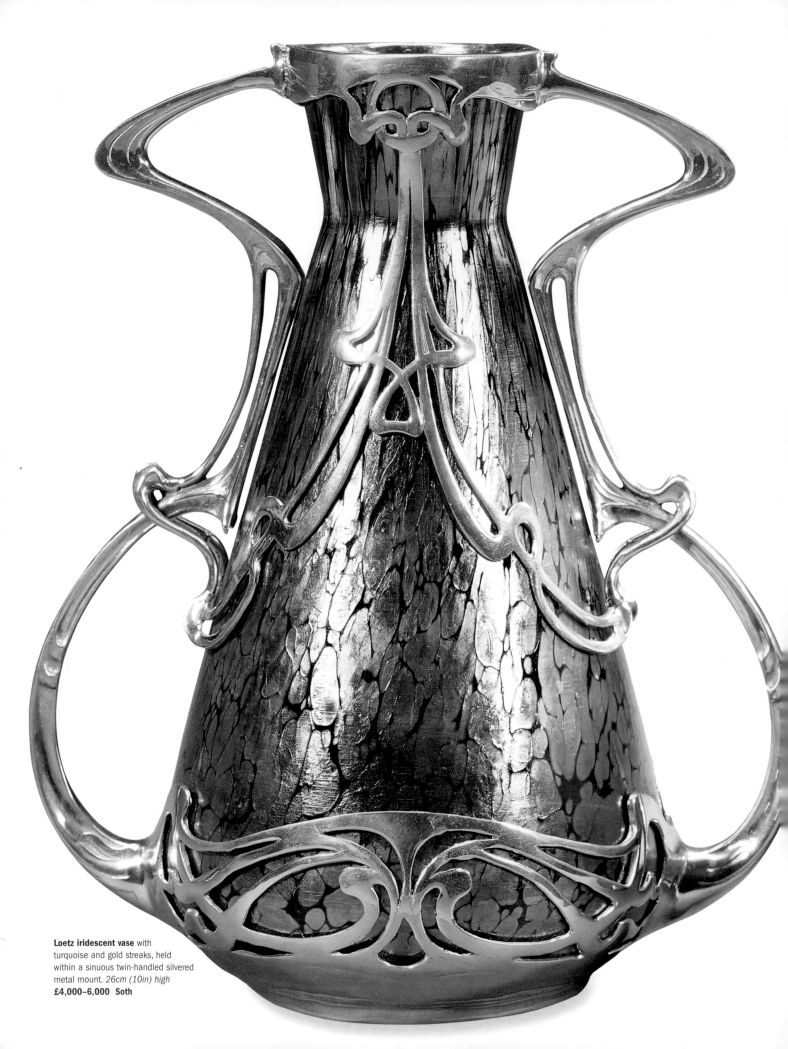

Loetz iridescent vase with
turquoise and gold streaks, held
within a sinuous twin-handled silvered
metal mount. *26cm (10in) high*
£4,000–6,000 Soth

DK COLLECTOR'S GUIDES

ART NOUVEAU

JUDITH MILLER

with Jill Bace, David Rago,
and Suzanne Perrault

A Dorling Kindersley Book

Project Art Editor Kelly Meyer
Editorial Assistant Kathryn Wilkinson
Design Assistant Anna Plucinska
Managing Editor Julie Oughton
Managing Art Editor Heather McCarry
Art Director Carole Ash
Category Publisher Jackie Douglas
Production Rita Sinha, Luca Frassinetti
DTP Designer Mike Grigoletti
Picture Research Sarah Duncan

Sands Publishing Solutions
Editors David & Sylvia Tombesi-Walton
Art Editor Simon Murrell

THE PRICE GUIDE COMPANY LIMITED
Publishing Manager Julie Brooke
Managing Editor Claire Smith
Editorial Assistants Jessica Bishop, Dan Dunlavey
Consultant Keith Baker
Contributors John Wainwright,
Nicholas Lowry (Swann Galleries, New York),
John Mackie (Lyon & Turnbull)

While every care has been taken in the compilation of this guide, neither the authors nor the publishers accept any liability for any financial or other loss incurred by reliance placed on the information contained in DK Collector's Guides: Art Nouveau.

First published in 2004 by
Dorling Kindersley Limited
80 Strand, London WC2R 0RL

A Penguin Company

The Price Guide Company (UK) Ltd
info@thepriceguidecompany.com

2 4 6 8 10 9 7 5 3 1

A CIP catalogue record for this book is available from the British Library.

ISBN 1 4053 0251 8

Colour reproduction by GRB, Italy
Printed and bound by L.E.G.O., Italy

Discover more at
www.dk.com

Contents

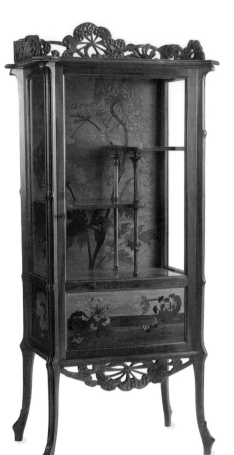

Emile Gallé walnut vitrine, p.26

Furniture 20

Textiles 60

Glass 68

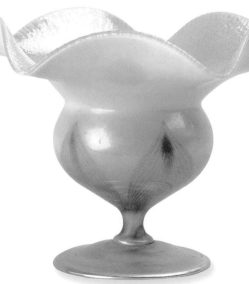

Tiffany floriform vase, p.97

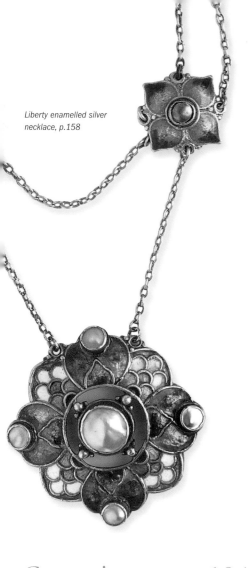

Liberty enamelled silver necklace, p.158

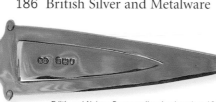

Edith and Nelson Dawson silver bookmark, p.186

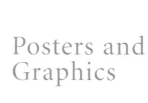

Alphonse Mucha lithographic poster, p.214

How to use this book

DK Collector's Guides: Art Nouveau is divided into eight chapters: furniture, textiles, glass, ceramics, jewellery, silver and metalware, sculpture, and posters and graphics. Each section opens with an introductory overview that discusses the historical background to the medium, and its place in Art Nouveau. This is followed by profiles of the most important Art Nouveau designers and factories from Britain, Europe, and the United States, and examples of their work. Highlighted sidebars provide an at-a-glance list of the key features for each designer or factory, and cornerstone pieces are expertly selected and carefully annotated to show what makes them icons of Art Nouveau design. Every item is briefly and concisely described, given an up-to-date price, and, where possible, dated.

Key Features
Lists the particular characteristics, influences, motifs, and marks for each designer and factory.

Cornerstone Pieces
Selects, annotates, and highlights the features that make the piece stand out as an icon of Art Nouveau style.

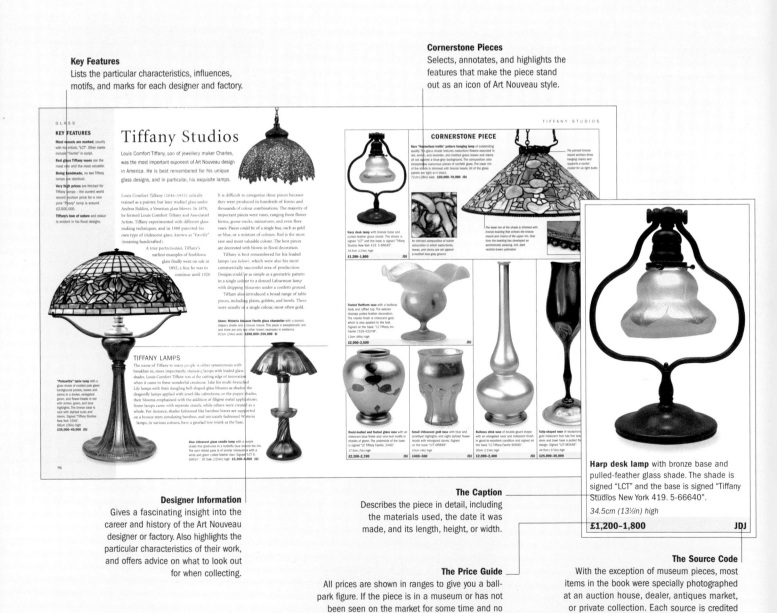

Designer Information
Gives a fascinating insight into the career and history of the Art Nouveau designer or factory. Also highlights the particular characteristics of their work, and offers advice on what to look out for when collecting.

The Caption
Describes the piece in detail, including the materials used, the date it was made, and its length, height, or width.

The Price Guide
All prices are shown in ranges to give you a ball-park figure. If the piece is in a museum or has not been seen on the market for some time and no price is available, the letters NPA will be used.

The Source Code
With the exception of museum pieces, most items in the book were specially photographed at an auction house, dealer, antiques market, or private collection. Each source is credited here. See pp.230–232 for full listings.

Foreword

From the first time I visited the Willow Tea Rooms in Glasgow and saw the uniquely contrasting "light feminine" and "dark masculine" themes of the interior, I was fascinated by how Charles Rennie Mackintosh's design theory fitted with the organic, sinuous, and asymmetric Art Nouveau that had sprung up at the same time in France. Then, on a visit to Paris, I caught sight of Hector Guimard's majestic cast-iron Métro entrances and visited the Musée Carnavalet to see the atmospheric interior of the Café de Paris by Henri Sauvage. More recently, in 1986, the opening of the Musée d'Orsay in the city brought some of the best work by craftsmen such as Emile Gallé, Victor Horta, and Louis Majorelle to mass attention.

In the United States, the glorious Art Nouveau interiors Louis Comfort Tiffany created for the Mark Twain house in Hartford, Connecticut, showed me how American designers had taken the "New Art" and made it their own.

What impressed me most was the diversity of the Art Nouveau style, and the variety of beautiful pieces available to collectors. Too often thought of as purely inspired by nature, it was in fact a complex reaction to the previous decades' heavy and overly ornate styles. Art Nouveau came about when a group of disparate artists, designers, and craftsmen felt the need to dictate a new design rationale, as the 20th century dawned, rather than simply rework the designs of the past. It encompassed the organically inspired Emile Gallé, René Lalique, and Louis Comfort Tiffany, and also the rectilinear and geometric styles of Josef Hoffmann, Charles Rennie Mackintosh, and Gustav Stickley.

While many pieces by the masters of the genre are out of almost everyone's reach, it is still possible to collect contemporary pieces by factories such as W.M.F. and Moorcroft on a modest budget. So, while you may fall in love with a Majorelle cabinet, like me you can probably only dream of owning one. However, don't despair. The style can be achieved by getting your "eye in" and searching for the many beautiful pieces copied from, or based on, the works of the masters.

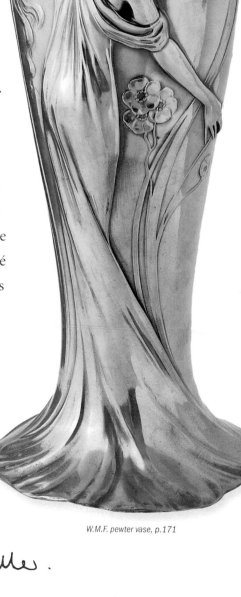

W.M.F. pewter vase, p.171

Judith Miller.

7

What is Art Nouveau?

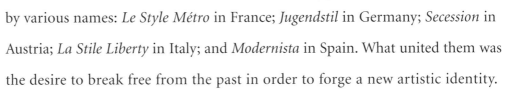

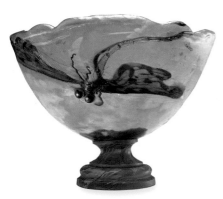

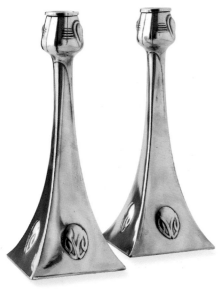

The style known as Art Nouveau, which emerged around 1890 and lasted until about 1914, completely transformed the decorative arts. Genuinely international, it had a profound influence on an astonishing variety of art forms in many different countries. At the heart of this dramatic change lay the desire to be rid of the stifling historicism and confusion of period styles that defined late 19th-century interiors. Art Nouveau presented a refreshing, modern solution that broke the stranglehold of established traditions and offered exciting new forms of expression.

No single artist or designer personified the Art Nouveau style. Across Europe, the movement was interpreted in many different ways, reflecting the individual character of each country, and hence it was known by various names: *Le Style Métro* in France; *Jugendstil* in Germany; *Secession* in Austria; *La Stile Liberty* in Italy; and *Modernista* in Spain. What united them was the desire to break free from the past in order to forge a new artistic identity.

The Industrial Revolution and the growing dependence on the machine were catalysts for this radical change. The mass production of everything, from furniture to textiles, in order to meet growing demands was blamed by artist-craftsmen for sustaining the taste for revivalism, as well as for the decline in the quality of furnishings. It was William Morris in England who first challenged the decline in values brought about by the proliferation of shabby, mass-produced wares. His condemnation of the machine and his efforts to bring about reform gave birth to a movement that celebrated the art of the medieval craftsman. His innovative designs drew on a decorative vocabulary rooted in the natural world, and his veneration of hand-craftsmanship paved the way for the evolution of Art Nouveau.

Emile Gallé cameo glass hanging lamp.
The pinkish body is overlaid with brown acid-etched foliage. *c.1910. 38cm (15in) high*
£3,000–5,000 Soth

W.M.F. pair of pewter candlesticks.
Decorated with foliate oval panels at the sconces and near the spreading square bases. The design is attributed to Albin Muller. *c.1905. 23cm (9in) high* **£700–800 TO**

Emile Gallé "La Libellule" *marqueterie-sur-verre* coupe, with carved detail of a dragonfly in flight. *c.1904. 14.5cm (5¾in) high*
£200,000–250,000 CHR

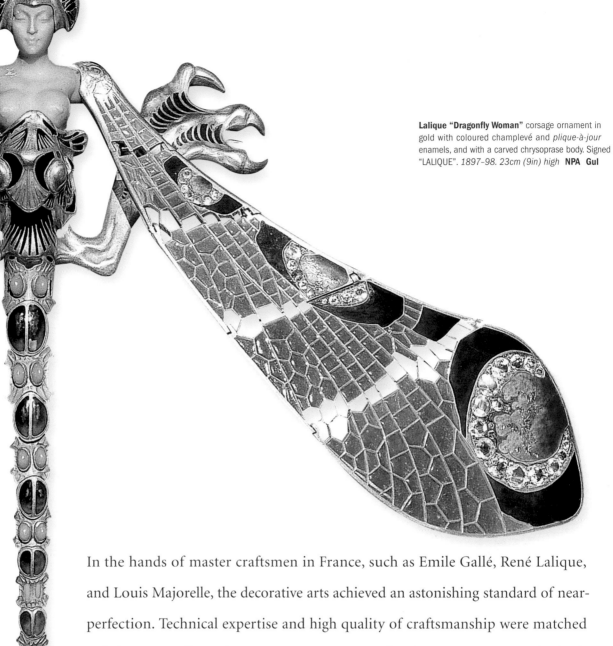

Lalique **"Dragonfly Woman"** corsage ornament in gold with coloured champlevé and *plique-à-jour* enamels, and with a carved chrysoprase body. Signed "LALIQUE". *1897–98. 23cm (9in) high* **NPA Gul**

In the hands of master craftsmen in France, such as Emile Gallé, René Lalique, and Louis Majorelle, the decorative arts achieved an astonishing standard of near-perfection. Technical expertise and high quality of craftsmanship were matched only by extraordinary imagination, creativity, and vision. But sustaining this high level of artistic integrity proved difficult, and what had begun as a revolutionary, dynamic, modern movement began to lose its way after a mere 15 years.

What drove the success of the Art Nouveau movement was also ultimately responsible for its relatively brief life and subsequent decline. For it was a style fuelled by the independent achievements of a number of brilliant, individual artists, rather than by a cohesive philosophy based on a canon of stylistic continuity. The fundamental principle of good design – that the decoration of an object should be second to function – and the fresh naturalistic motifs that had once captivated the public's imagination gradually gave way to repetition and clichéd images.

A diverse movement

During its brief lifespan, Art Nouveau left its mark on architecture, furniture, ceramics, textiles, posters, glass, and jewellery. It can be seen in the sinuous contours of Victor Horta's houses in Brussels, in the dazzling glasswork of Tiffany, Loetz, and Daum, and in Hector Guimard's swirling cast-iron entranceways for Paris métro stations. A more angular version of it is apparent in the geometric designs of the Wiener Werkstätte and Charles Rennie Mackintosh. The rectilinear footprint of the "New Art" was expressed in the United States by the work of the Stickleys, Limbert, and the Roycrofters.

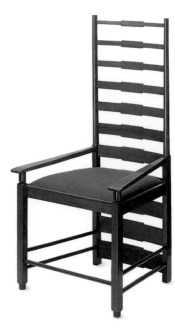

Charles Rennie Mackintosh mahogany armchair for Basset-Locke's business friend Horstmann, based on "Derngate" originals. *1917. 103.5cm (40¾in) high* **NPA V&A**

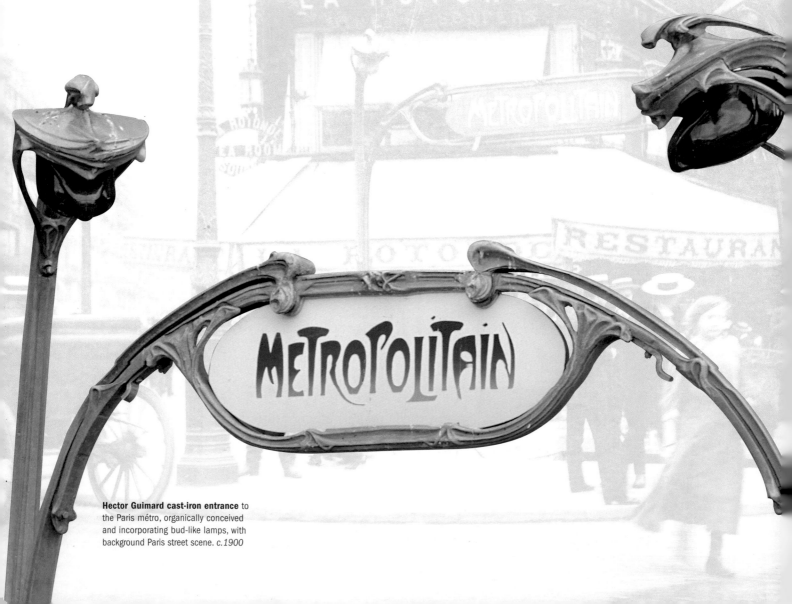

Hector Guimard cast-iron entrance to the Paris métro, organically conceived and incorporating bud-like lamps, with background Paris street scene. *c.1900*

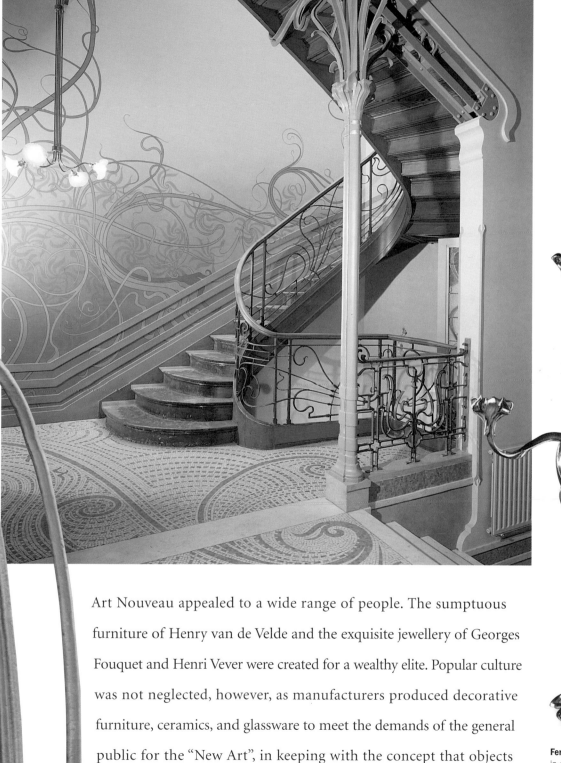

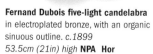

Art Nouveau appealed to a wide range of people. The sumptuous furniture of Henry van de Velde and the exquisite jewellery of Georges Fouquet and Henri Vever were created for a wealthy elite. Popular culture was not neglected, however, as manufacturers produced decorative furniture, ceramics, and glassware to meet the demands of the general public for the "New Art", in keeping with the concept that objects in the home should be aesthetically pleasing as well as functional.

Fernand Dubois five-light candelabra in electroplated bronze, with an organic sinuous outline. *c.1899* *53.5cm (21in) high* **NPA Hor**

Origins and influences

A huge variety of diverse influences helped foster the development of Art Nouveau. In view of the impressive work that came out of Nancy and Paris – the roots for Art Nouveau architecture laid down in the writings of Viollet-le-Duc, the innovations in glass by Emile Gallé, the furniture designs of Majorelle and Guimard, the jewellery of Lalique and Fouquet, and the innovations in ceramics credited to Theodore Deck – one can be forgiven for assuming that the Art Nouveau movement originated in France.

But it is Britain that must take credit for laying the foundations for change, beginning with William Morris, writer and craftsman, who promoted the virtues of hand-craftsmanship over the industrial machine, and then by the talented architect Arthur Heygate Mackmurdo. Although fellow artists such as C.F.A. Voysey and Charles Robert Ashbee held fast to the simple, understated style adopted by the Arts and Crafts and Aesthetic movements, it was the linear simplicity, flowing, asymmetrical compositions, abstract plant motifs, and undulating movement of Mackmurdo's designs that paved the way for the European interpretation of Art Nouveau.

Japanese art was another pivotal influence. The opening-up of Japan to western traders in the mid 19th century led to a host of exotic artifacts flooding into Europe, including fans, enamelware, prints, vases, and lacquerware. Japanese art was characterized by simple design, and, in particular, by the use of asymmetric forms and undulating lines. It was also inspired by a deep reverence for nature. Motifs such as cherry blossom, waterlilies, irises, and dragonflies recur and were adopted in turn by many Art Nouveau artists. Siegfried Bing in Paris and Arthur Lasenby Liberty in London displayed Japanese pieces in their popular emporia, and from 1888 to 1891, Bing even published a journal called *Le Japon Artistique*, which took a close look at the styles and techniques used in Japanese art.

Arthur Heygate Mackmurdo mahogany chair with fretwork panel pierced with sinuous foliage and painted detail. *1882* 97.2cm (38¼in) high **NPA V&A**

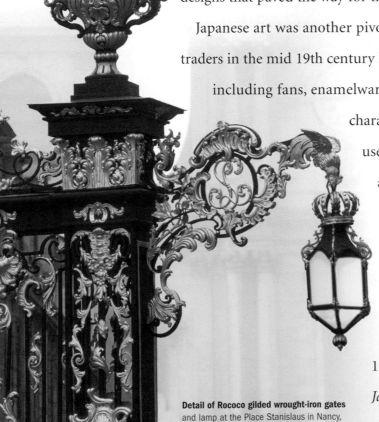

Detail of Rococo gilded wrought-iron gates and lamp at the Place Stanislaus in Nancy, Lorraine, France. *18th century*

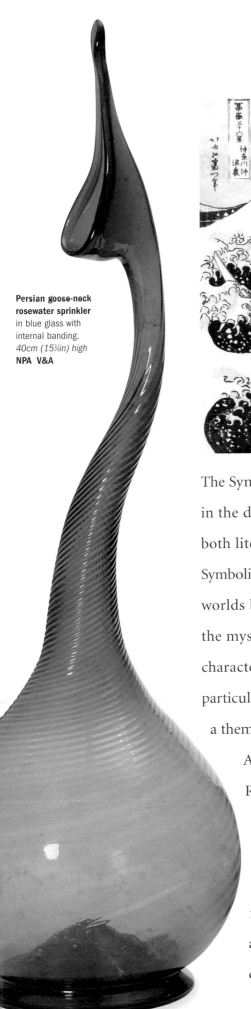

Persian goose-neck rosewater sprinkler in blue glass with internal banding. *40cm (15¾in) high* **NPA V&A**

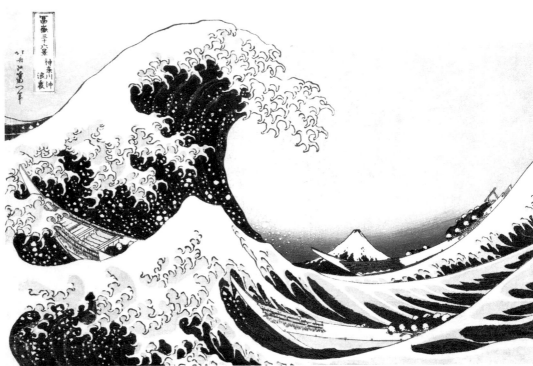

"The Great Wave of Kanagawa" colour woodblock print, from the "36 Views of Mount Fuji" series (*Fugakku sanjuokkei*), published by Nishimura Eijudo. *1831 37cm (14½in) high* **NPA BRI**

The Symbolist movement also played a significant role in the development of the Art Nouveau style. Using both literature and painting as forms of expression, Symbolists sought to reconcile the spiritual and material worlds by looking to the sensuous, the poetic, and the mystical for inspiration. Their work was often characterized by disturbing, dream-like imagery, in particular by images of mysterious, sensuous women, a theme taken up by many Art Nouveau designers.

Art Nouveau also drew inspiration from the Rococo style, which flourished in 18th-century France during the reign of Louis XV. The Rococo taste for nature and fantasy took form in asymmetry, swirling lines, and stylized plants, flowers, insects, and shells. Art Nouveau designers adopted many of these themes and stylistic characteristics and interpreted them anew.

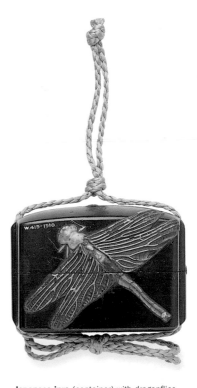

Japanese inro (container) with dragonflies in relief decoration of lacquer and porcelain. Signed "Mochizuki Hanzan". *1775–1800 7.9cm (3in) wide* **NPA V&A**

The early years

In the 1890s, Art Nouveau became a recognizable style, with Europe, Britain, and the United States all developing their own unique interpretations. The flowing, sinuous designs of Mackmurdo, the illustrations of Aubrey Beardsley that paid homage to Japanese printmaking techniques, the Hotel Tassel in Brussels by Victor Horta – a tour de force of imaginative architecture with coiling, sinuous decorative ornament (*see p.11*) – and Hermann Obrist's wall hangings embroidered with curling whiplash patterns, these were all individual expressions of Art Nouveau.

In Nancy in eastern France, the imaginative glasswork of Gallé and Daum and the curvaceous furniture in precious woods by Louis Majorelle were at the forefront of this new style of art. In Glasgow and Vienna, on the other hand, the style was shaped by the visionary designs of Charles Rennie Mackintosh and his fellow designers, and by Josef Hoffmann and Joseph Olbrich, whose expressions of the "New Art"

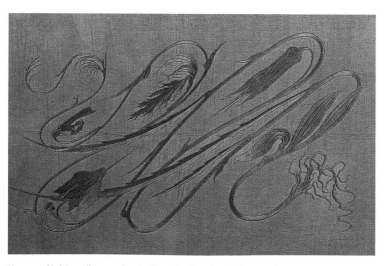

Hermann Obrist woollen panel embroidered in silk with a wildly energetic whiplash plant form motif. *c.1895. 183cm (72in) wide* **NPA Stad**

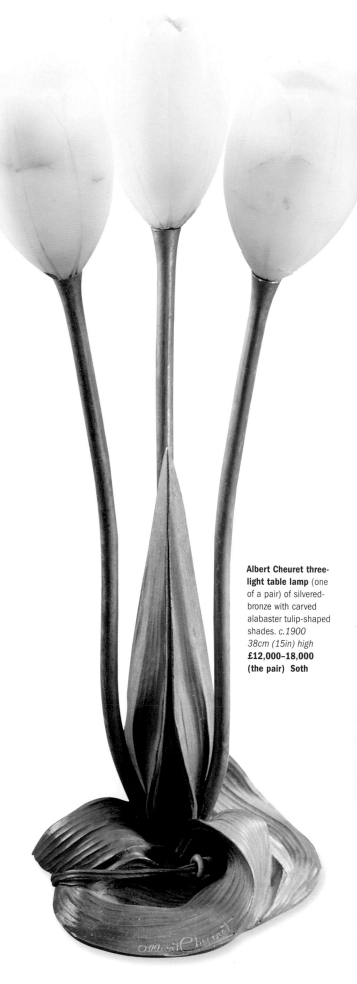

Albert Cheuret three-light table lamp (one of a pair) of silvered-bronze with carved alabaster tulip-shaped shades. *c.1900 38cm (15in) high* **£12,000–18,000 (the pair) Soth**

took form in elegant, rectilinear pieces that were widely admired for their radical simplicity and restraint. Rejecting William Morris's exhortations to serve the interests of the common man, Hoffmann and his peers at the Wiener Werkstätte created furniture, ceramics, metalwork, sculpture, jewellery, and textiles that catered to the sophisticated demands of a wealthy, educated, and cosmopolitan audience.

Along with influential art publications, such as *Jugend*, *La Revue des Art Décoratifs*, *Pan*, *The Studio*, and *Deutsche Kunst und Dekoration*, which made the Art Nouveau style known to a wide audience across Europe, the most important forums for showcasing the new movement were Siegfried Bing's shop, L'Art Nouveau, and the gallery La Maison Moderne operated by Julius Meier-Graefe in Paris. Bing even forged a business partnership with the American Louis Comfort Tiffany in an effort to bring him to the attention of Europeans.

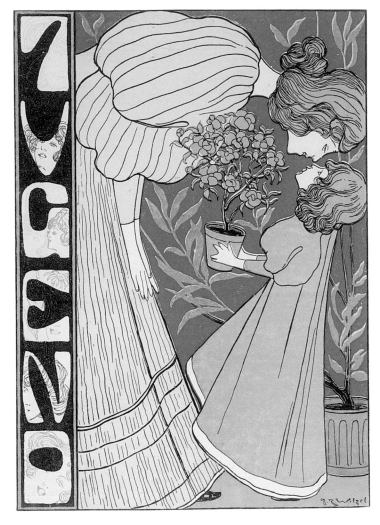

J.R. Witzel chromolithographic title page from the German *Jugend* magazine, dated 3 October 1896, issue number 40. **NPA AKG**

Henri and Paul Vever gold butterfly brooch picked out in coloured translucent enamels and punctuated with diamonds. *c.1900. 6.7cm (2¾in) high* **£7,000–8,000 Soth**

Other important venues for bringing Art Nouveau to a public hungry for a new and modern vision were the international exhibitions, where designers and retailers displayed their innovative wares. A turning point was the 1900 Universal Exposition in Paris, which, to much acclaim, assembled the innovative designs of artists and craftsmen from Britain, Europe, and the United States. Art Nouveau had well and truly made its mark.

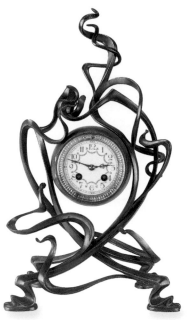

Victor Horta bronze clock, the dial between wildly sinuous foliate stems that extend as supports. *c.1895. 45.7cm (18in) high* **£50,000–70,000 CHR**

The sinuous line

There were two main strands in the development of Art Nouveau, but they were merely contrasting parts of the same movement. A reverent awe of nature lay at the heart of the sinuous, flowing style that made up the strand prevalent in France and Belgium. The mystery and poetry embodied in the natural world were an inspiration to designers, especially to the Symbolists. The smallest detail evocative of nature's beauty – a tiny flower bud, a graceful corolla or stem, the flowing roots of a voluptuous plant, the wings of a dragonfly – was translated into art by skilled designers and craftsmen.

W.M.F. plated-metal fruit or sweet dish with three linked bowls and a curved, branch-like handle enclosing a classical maiden in diaphanous robes. Stamped with the maker's marks. *c.1905 18.5cm (7¼in) high* **£150–200 DN**

Alphonse Mucha poster advertising "Job" cigarette papers, with sinuous treatment to the model's hair and cigarette smoke. *1896 52cm (20in) high* **£4,000–8,000 AKG**

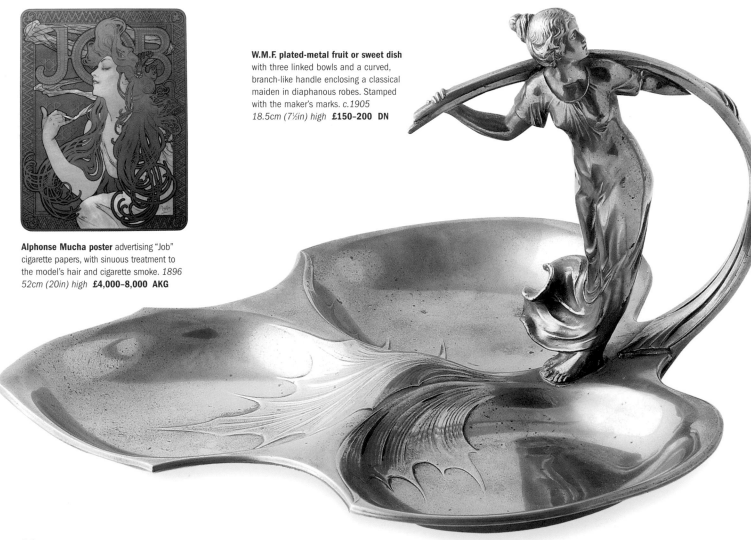

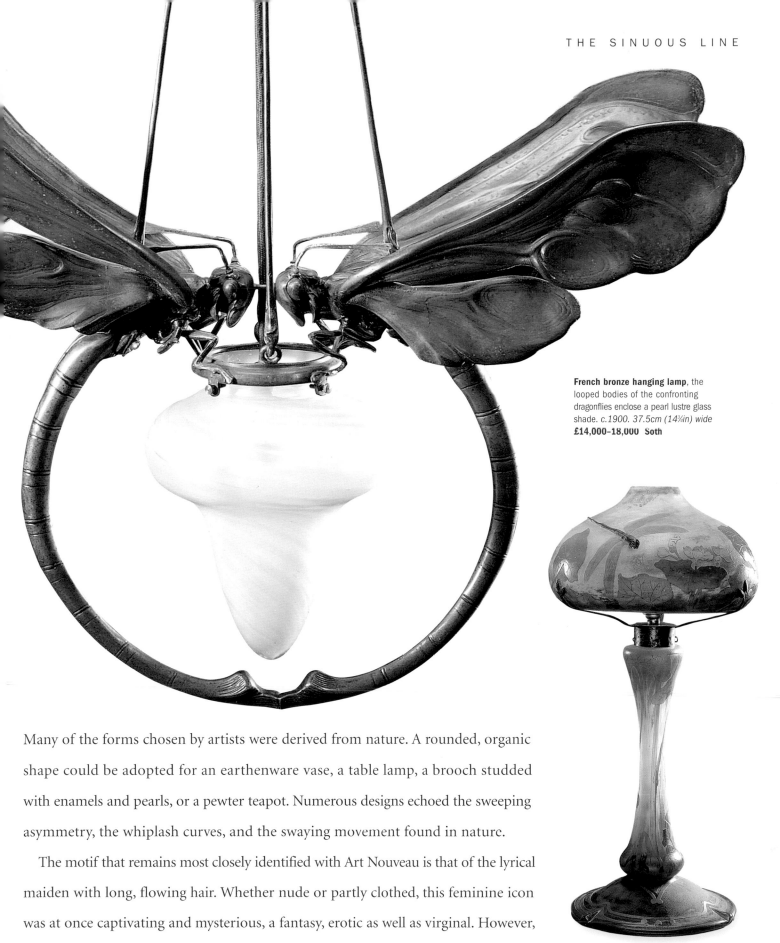

French bronze hanging lamp, the looped bodies of the confronting dragonflies enclose a pearl lustre glass shade. *c.1900. 37.5cm (14¾in) wide* **£14,000–18,000 Soth**

Many of the forms chosen by artists were derived from nature. A rounded, organic shape could be adopted for an earthenware vase, a table lamp, a brooch studded with enamels and pearls, or a pewter teapot. Numerous designs echoed the sweeping asymmetry, the whiplash curves, and the swaying movement found in nature.

The motif that remains most closely identified with Art Nouveau is that of the lyrical maiden with long, flowing hair. Whether nude or partly clothed, this feminine icon was at once captivating and mysterious, a fantasy, erotic as well as virginal. However, over time, the appetite for decorative household objects celebrating the beauty of the female form waned, as it became reduced to an overexposed, hackneyed cliché.

Daum Frères cameo table lamp, the multicoloured overlay is acid-etched with marshplants, and the shade has a dragonfly in relief. *c.1905* **£18,000–20,000 Soth**

Branching out

As the sinuous strand of Art Nouveau developed in France and Belgium, it was taken up by designers in other countries and interpreted in a variety of different ways. Exotic Arabic influences coupled with fantasy animated the extraordinary designs of Carlo Bugatti in Milan, and Antoní Gaudí in Barcelona. Nature still provided the inspiration for the style, but in the work of these designers, natural forms were twisted and moulded into quixotic shapes with a quirky appeal.

Art Nouveau was transformed into yet another contrasting idiom in the hands of designers such as Charles Rennie Mackintosh in Glasgow, Joseph Maria Olbrich in Darmstadt in Germany, and Josef Hoffmann at the Wiener Werkstätte in Vienna. It was the geometry found in the natural world that held their attention and informed their art. From the Art Nouveau credo that architecture, decoration, and furniture should be united into a cohesive whole, they developed a spare, linear style that

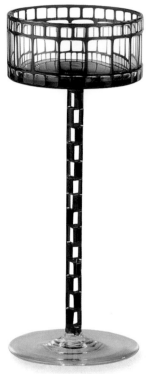

Otto Prutscher blue-flashed wine glass, with geometrically cut decoration, produced by Meyrs Neffe. *c.1912. 21cm (8¼in) high* **£8,000–10,000 CHR**

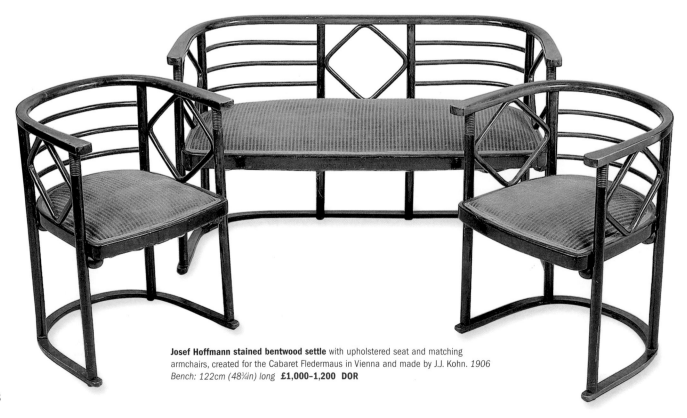

Josef Hoffmann stained bentwood settle with upholstered seat and matching armchairs, created for the Cabaret Fledermaus in Vienna and made by J.J. Kohn. *1906 Bench: 122cm (48¾in) long* **£1,000–1,200 DOR**

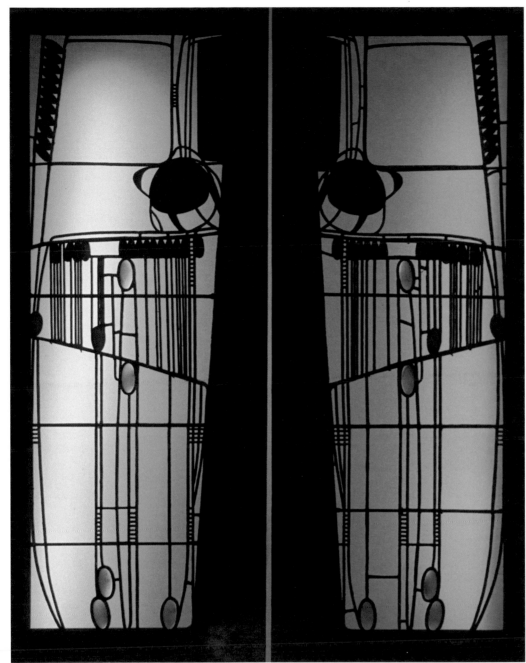

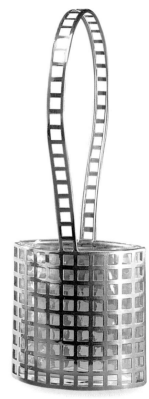

Wiener Werkstätte basket in white metal, pierced with squares and a loop-handle, by Josef Hoffman. *c.1910. 30cm (12in) high* **£2,000–3,000 Soth**

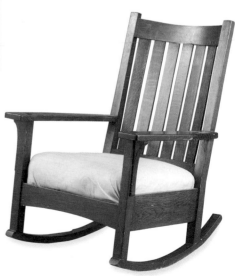

L. & J.G. Stickley oak open-arm rocker with vertical back slats and drop-in seat cushion, and original finish. *c.1910 101.5cm (40in) high* **£1,200–1,800 CR**

rejected the sensuous interpretation of nature in favour of simple, elegant shapes and geometric patterns. In the United States, designer-craftsmen such as Gustav Stickley embraced a similar ethic, creating furniture that relied on beautiful materials, simplicity of design, and excellent craftsmanship in the Arts and Crafts tradition in order to create their own interpretation of the "New Art".

As the popularity of Art Nouveau began to wane, it was the simpler, more geometric strand of design that endured, transformed during the 1920s into the linear, graphic style that formed the foundations of Art Deco and Modernism.

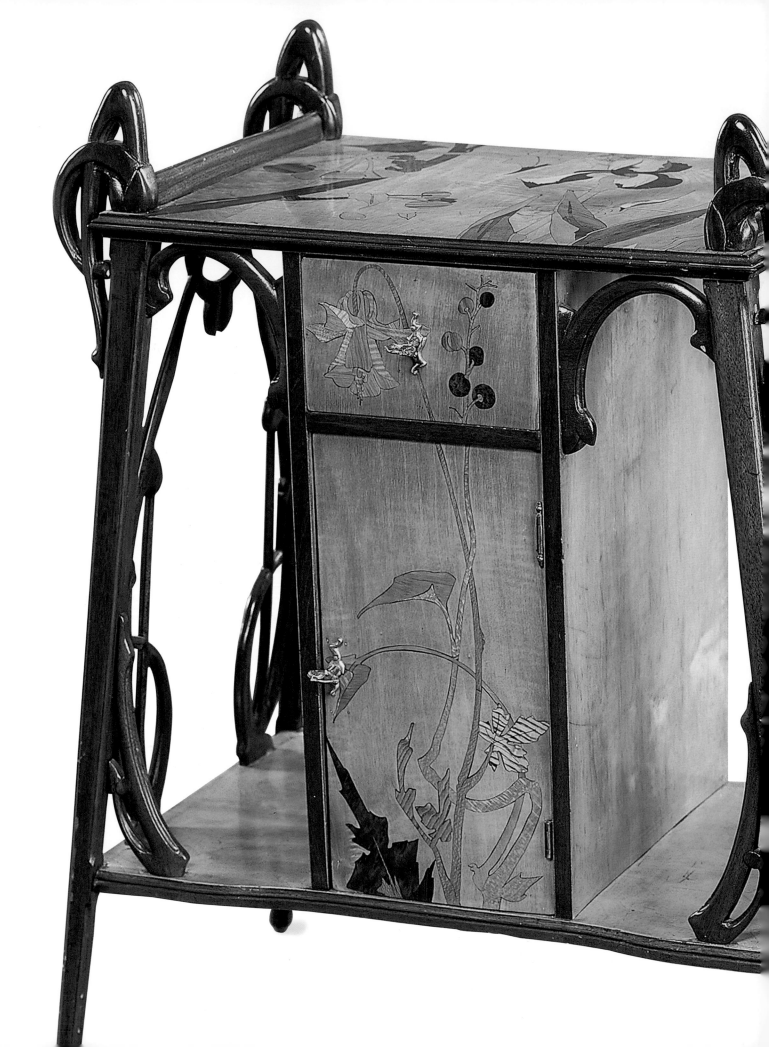

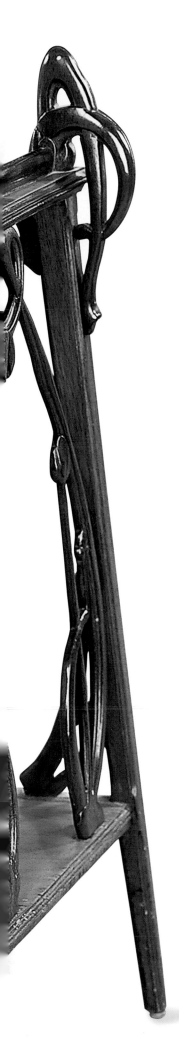

Furniture

During most of the 19th century, furniture makers throughout Europe looked back to earlier styles for inspiration. As a result, furniture design was lacking in both innovation and imagination until the birth of Art Nouveau at the turn of the century brought a powerful injection both of ornamental exuberance and geometric simplicity.

It was architects who provided the catalyst for change, embracing the Art Nouveau style and charting a new direction for furniture design. Buildings that had exteriors with whiplash organic contours now had interiors to match. The eclectic 19th-century interior, typified by a motley array of furniture in a variety of styles, gave way in the 1890s to the concept of room furnishings designed as an integrated whole. The traditional ideal that furniture should be well-made and functional was turned on its head as decorative features took precedence. A table embellished with sculpted flowers or dragonflies, for example, might take the form of a flowering tree, with feet resembling branches or roots.

SUMPTUOUS DESIGNS
But such excesses ignored the quiet, beautifully crafted and sumptuous designs using luxurious materials created by masters such as Louis

Majorelle, Victor Horta, and Emile Gallé. And while nature lay at the heart of Art Nouveau furniture design, the new style was interpreted in a very different manner by some designers who created simpler, more abstract pieces.

FURNITURE FOR ALL
In Britain, furniture designers shared some of the decorative themes of French Art Nouveau, but explored them in a more understated way, while in the United States, furniture makers looked back to the Arts and Crafts movement for inspiration and produced simple, undecorated pieces.

By 1905, mass-produced furniture created by designers in Germany, Austria, and the Low Countries had begun to replace the one-off masterpieces by the most gifted furniture designers. The French refused to compromise quality but tempered their designs in response to the need for less expensive furniture.

Mahogany and mixed wood marquetry side table by Leon Benouville. The top, inlaid with floral decoration, sits above a short drawer and cupboard inlaid with a daffodil. The table has four supports embellished with sinuous tendrils, and handmade brass fittings. *c.1902. 63.5cm (25in) long* **NPA CALD**

THE PURE FRENCH STYLE

As with other disciplines in the decorative arts, the Art Nouveau style first made itself felt in French furniture design. At the heart of this progressive international style was the School of Nancy, where an astonishing band of talented cabinetmakers and designers created lyrical, visionary furniture in sumptuous materials that celebrated the skills of the craftsman. Working alongside the designer, was a host of artisans dedicated to providing exquisite finishing touches, using textiles, glass, leather, and metalwork.

Without question Louis Majorelle stood head and shoulders above all others as the doyen of Art Nouveau furniture makers. At once a superb designer and a highly skilled technician, he created exquisite masterpieces of breathtaking luxury and unrivalled quality, using sumptuous timbers embellished with extravagant materials, including gilt bronze and glass. Second only to Majorelle was the multi-talented Emile Gallé, who added to his glassworks a cabinetmaking

Louis Majorelle blonde mahogany and marquetry cabinet with a mirrored back and inlaid geometric decoration. It has pierced side panels, a frieze drawer with bronze goosehead drawer pulls, and cupboards inlaid with exotic woods showing a gaggle of geese. c.1900 155cm (61in) wide **NPA CALD**

workshop that produced sophisticated furniture designs highlighted with marquetry decoration.

In Paris, the annual Salons – L'Art Nouveau of Siegfried Bing, and Julius Meier-Graefe's La Maison Moderne – provided the opportunities for furniture designers to exhibit their latest creations. Among the large band of cabinetmakers working in the French capital, the furniture designed by Hector Guimard – the creator of the distinctive wrought-iron entrances for the Paris Métro (see p.10) – stands apart as being the most innovative and progressive.

Architecture played a significant role in Art Nouveau furniture design, especially in Brussels, where the pioneering architects Victor Horta, Henry van de Velde, and Gustave Serrurier-Bovy were instrumental in developing the style in Belgium. Between them, they designed furniture with curvaceous lines and floral exuberance to complement the interiors of their buildings.

GERMAN AND AUSTRIAN AUSTERITY

Germany responded to the new style with restraint, rejecting the florid Art Nouveau taste of the French and Belgian furniture makers in favour of design that valued function over superficial decoration. Exceptions can be found in the work of a few German designers who flirted with the Art Nouveau style, including Richard Riemerschmid, Peter Behrens, and August Endell. Their furniture – while in restrained shapes – occasionally borrow from the organic vocabulary for sculpted ornament or decorative details.

In Austria, the Viennese Secessionists drew inspiration from the bold, architectural furniture

DEFINITIVE STYLES

Art Nouveau furniture design is extremely varied and often typical of its country of origin. Mainly inspired by nature, French and Belgian pieces are characterized by sinuous whiplash curves, tendrils, and stylized interpretations of plant forms. German and Austrian Secessionist designs and most Scottish pieces are rectilinear and graphic in form. American furniture designers generally produced austere, but well-made pieces that drew inspiration from the Arts and Crafts movement.

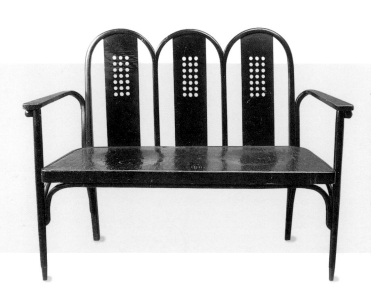

J. & J. Kohn dark stained beech settle, in the style of Josef Hoffmann, with three back splats pierced with circular holes held within an arched framework. The solid seat has curved armrests secured with spheres on tapering supports. The brass capped front feet are united by curved strengthening supports. c.1906 125.5cm (49in) wide **£900–1,100 VZ**

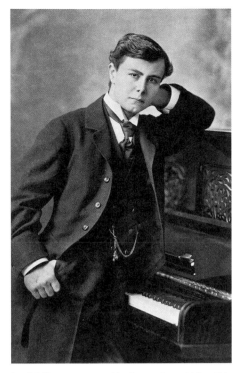

Josef Hoffmann was one of Art Nouveau's most influential furniture designers, paving the way for the more restrained yet functional strand of the design movement.

ANGLO-SAXON DESIGN

With the exception of Charles Rennie Mackintosh's bold designs, British furniture remained largely static, and firms clung to the sturdy forms developed by William Morris. However, some furniture designers, including C.F.A. Voysey, employed decorative scrolling metalwork motifs characteristic of the Art Nouveau style.

In the United States, furniture craftsmen failed to be seduced by the opulent Art Nouveau fashions. Instead, the solid, simple furniture by designers such as Frank Lloyd Wright, the Greene Brothers, and Gustav Stickley were more of an interpretation of the British Arts and Crafts movement.

MEDITERRANEAN OPULENCE

Two figures of unmatched creativity stand apart in the realm of Art Nouveau furniture. The Spanish architect Antoní Gaudí created eccentric and highly original furniture for the interiors of his buildings. Rendered primarily in oak, they exhibit exceptional vitality and imagination.

In Italy, Carlo Bugatti's unconventional interpretation of the Art Nouveau style combined a variety of sumptuous, incongruous materials and a fresh mixture of influences to create an astonishing range of furniture designs.

of Scotland's Charles Rennie Mackintosh, whom they much admired. Josef Hoffmann took up the baton for the new decorative aesthetic, producing elegant, uncluttered furniture that was both useful and beautiful: stools, chairs, cabinets, and tables exemplified his desire for simple, geometric form. This innovative style of furniture design was championed by other artist-craftsmen working for the Wiener Werkstätte, including Koloman Moser and Josef Olbrich.

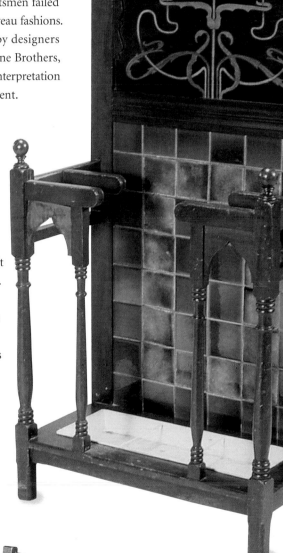

Mahogany hall stand, possibly by Shapland & Petter. The shaped back with shelf displays coloured marquetry thistle motifs above a panel of coloured glazed tiles. *c.1890* *128cm (50½in) high* **£700–1,000 DN**

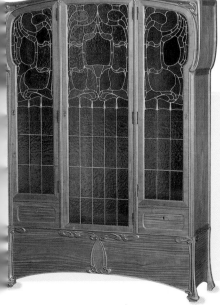

Edward Colonna lemonwood and satinwood glazed bookcase of shaped outline with carved whiplash detailing. The three clear glass doors are decorated with leaded panels of coloured glass leaves and have two drawers. Probably sold by Siegfried Bing for the Bibliothèque Victor Hugo. *c.1900. 145cm (57in) wide* **NPA CALD**

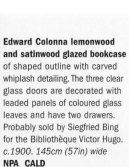

Gustav Stickley stained oak ladderback rocking chair, solidly constructed, with a scooped crest rail, plain broad armrests with revealed tenons, and a black leather upholstered seat. Displays a newly finished surface and bears a red decal (label) mark. *84cm (33in) high* **£1,200–1,800 CR**

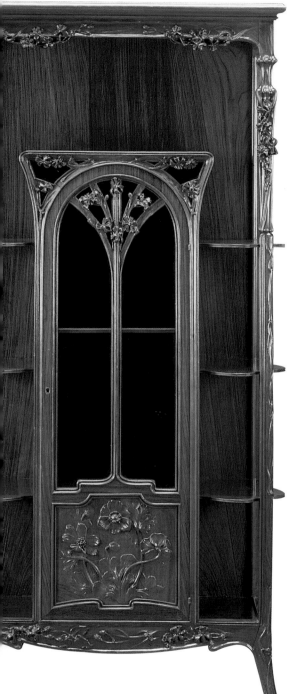

SCULPTURAL FORMS

Throughout Europe, nature remained the greatest source of inspiration for furniture design, although a variety of talented craftsmen interpreted the Art Nouveau style in a number of different and highly original ways.

In France, the two main centres of Art Nouveau furniture production – the Nancy School and the Paris School – pioneered the fashion for curvilinear, organic furniture designs that looked first and foremost to nature for inspiration. Yet the giant talents generally credited for bringing about this incredibly rich and fertile period of furniture design – Louis Majorelle and Emile Gallé at Nancy and Hector Guimard in Paris – each drew from nature in decidedly different ways.

Furniture created by Gallé, Majorelle, and other craftsmen at the Nancy School embraced nature with joyful exuberance. Finely-crafted cabinets, tables, and chairs in highly imaginative and sculptural organic forms were

Louis Majorelle "Clematite" mahogany display cabinet, with central glazed compartment. The fenestration and panel are carved with clematis blooms, flanked by a series of shelves. The superstructure is also carved with clematis flowers and leaves. c.1900. 189cm (74½in) high
£8,000–10,000 Soth

lavishly decorated with veneers of exotic woods, inlays of mother-of-pearl, and gilt bronze mounts shaped as waterlilies or dragonflies. Other distinctive decorative features include panels of intricate marquetry, added to embellish sinuous supports, and mouldings in naturalistic or zoomorphic shapes. Botanical motifs – scrolling plants and flower blossoms, fruits and vegetables, insects and crustaceans – were faithfully rendered.

By contrast, the furniture designed by Hector Guimard was highly charged, while his contemporaries working in Paris tended to be more stylized and restrained. Graceful, sculptural forms crafted mainly in fruitwoods feature nature-inspired decoration – the whiplash curve is a common theme – but in general are far less florid than the furniture made at Nancy.

In Belgium, the influential Victor Horta designed furniture with an energetic, scrolling, whiplash style that emphasized fluidity and movement. Henry van de Velde's restrained sculptural forms with little or no decoration, on the other hand, echoed the more symmetrical design typical of the Paris School.

GEOMETRIC STYLE

Beyond France and Belgium, finely-crafted Art Nouveau furniture was made in many other European cities, and in each country the interpretation of the style varied. German and Austrian furniture design took a more linear approach, with

FORM AND DECORATION

Furniture makers working in the Art Nouveau style created pieces with a nature-inspired theme that was borne out either in the form or the decoration of the piece. French furniture makers such as Majorelle, produced pieces with flowing lines and decorative detail, often featuring stylized plant-form motifs. In contrast, furniture in innovative, organic shapes, such as Bugatti's "Cobra" chair, and in striking, geometric styles, like Charles Rennie Mackintosh's writing cabinet, was also produced.

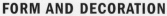

Louis Majorelle mahogany dining chair. The top rail is carved with tendrils and foliage above a slender back rest with moulded sides, inlaid with floral motifs. The stuff-over seat has a carved apron and is raised on carved tapering supports. 93cm (36½in) high
£6,000–8,000 Soth

Right: Charles Rennie Mackintosh ebonized mahogany writing cabinet, opened to reveal the insides of the doors inlaid with mother-of-pearl squares, and pigeon holes flanking a leaded glass panel probably by Margaret Macdonald. On an open-fronted support with mauve ceramic detail. Designed for Hill House, Helensburgh.
£1,000,000+ CHR

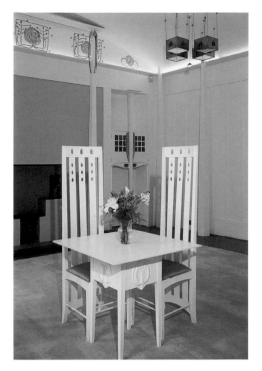

Charles Rennie Mackintosh interior featuring Art Nouveau white, geometric high-backed chairs and table, in the House for an Art Lover, Glasgow, Scotland.

forms of the French school. Austria was also the birthplace of the revolutionary bentwood technique created by the innovative furniture designer Michael Thonet.

LAVISH AND EXOTIC

Still another thread of Art Nouveau furniture design was taken up in Italy with the imaginative creations of Carlo Bugatti. His inventive cabinets, tables, and chairs are distinguished by the lavish use of sumptuous materials – ivory, brass, and pewter inlays and vellum upholstery, for example – which looked not only to nature for inspiration but to Egyptian, Moorish, and Japanese art. In a similar vein, Barcelona's Antoní Gaudi created exotic furniture that embraced nature with twisting, sculptural shapes decorated with floral motifs.

Carlo Bugatti "Cobra" chair of fluid outline. The wooden carcase is covered with vellum and delicately painted with highly stylized winged insect motifs. The circular back support has an embossed and pierced copper panel. Made as part of the furnishing of the "Snail Room" at the Turin Exhibition of 1902. *97cm (38in) high* **NPA RdM**

Secessionist furniture generally more sober and disciplined. Austrian designers, in particular, pioneered a purer, more abstract version of Art Nouveau furniture led by the Wiener Werkstätte architect and designer Josef Hoffmann, and influenced by the linear, geometric tables and chairs produced by the Scottish architect Charles Rennie Mackintosh. Decoration consisting of rectangles and square shapes could not be more different from the curving plant

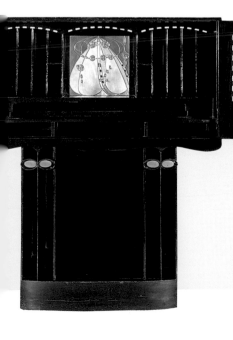

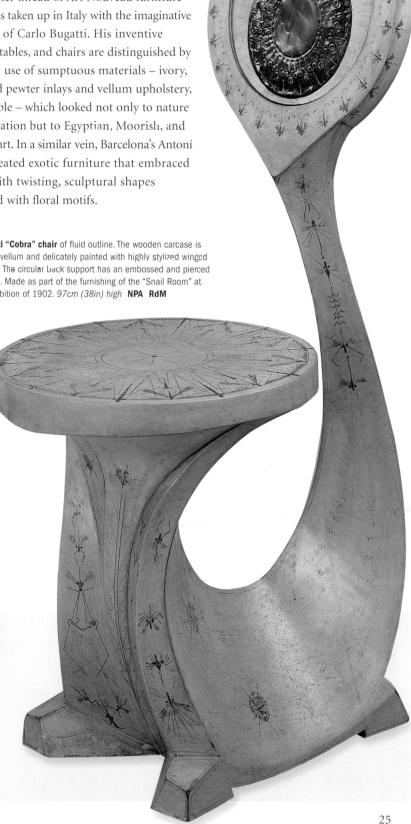

Curving, sinuous shapes, reminiscent of the 18th century and the reign of Louis XV, appear in Gallé's furniture designs.

Exotic and colourful wood veneers and marquetry decoration feature insects, flowers, fruits, and animals.

Inspired by nature, furniture supports are shaped into dragonfly wings, bronze mounts appear as insects, and drawer handles are modelled after flora and fauna.

Sophisticated decorations combine sumptuous materials, such as inlaid or veneered exotic woods, colourful carved glass, and mother-of-pearl.

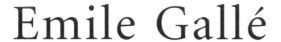

Emile Gallé

Although glassware is most closely identified with the prolific career of Emile Gallé, this enterprising French designer from Nancy also created some of Art Nouveau's most exquisite furniture.

As an innovative artist and designer, Emile Gallé frequently ignored the long-established traditions of furniture construction, preferring to experiment with new ways of realizing his imaginative designs. Tables and cabinets rendered in a variety of exotic or richly coloured woods were fashioned in sinuous, scrolling shapes echoing Louis XV forms. Many of Gallé's decorative features pay tribute to his love of nature: tables stand on dragonfly-wing supports; decorative bronze mounts resemble insects; drawer handles take the form of grapes, corn, barley, or snails; and carved frogs, bats, and moths add a humourous touch to a cabinet.

Much of Gallé's furniture, dominated by the extravagant and organic decoration, was enriched with the sumptuous and expensive technique of marquetry (*see*

below). Lavish wood veneers featuring delicate asymmetrical fruit, flower, foliage, insect, and animal motifs cover the tops of occasional tables, cupboards, headboards, chairs, buffets, vitrines, and firescreens.

In 1885, Gallé added a cabinetmaking and marquetry workshop to his glassworks factory at Nancy. There, useful furniture such as screens, tea tables, nests of tables, and guéridons were produced. After 1890, however, Gallé turned his attention to creating larger, more sophisticated furniture for an exclusive market.

After his death in 1904, furniture continued to be produced in Gallé's workshop, but, in general, these pieces tended to be in more traditional styles and lacked the imaginative, decorative details that characterized his highly unique designs.

Above: Two-tier étagère in walnut with boldly carved C-scroll supports for the upper tier, and curvaceous cabriole legs for the lower. It is decorated with a fine-quality daffodil motif and fruitwood marquetry. Signed "Gallé". *81cm (31½in) high* **£12,000–19,000 MACK**

MARQUETRY

Marquetry was first practised in Germany and the Low Countries before being introduced to France in the early 17th century. It was a fashionable and expensive technique whereby a veneer composed of shaped pieces of subtly shaded exotic woods or other materials – commonly ivory, bone, mother-of-pearl, brass, or pewter – was applied to the furniture carcase to form a mosaic in a decorative floral, figural, or arabesque pattern. The technique differs from inlay, in which a variety of materials – wood, ivory, horn, or metal – is inset into the solid wood carcase. Marquetry was perfected by Emile Gallé, who embellished many of his pieces with decorative veneers that brought flowers and animals to life with much delicacy and charm.

Fine walnut vitrine with carved and pierced cresting and an apron of Japanese cherry flowers. The glazed door and sides enclose an asymmetrically stepped two-tier interior, and bird's-eye maple and exotic wood leaf marquetry. *148cm (57¾in) high* **£23,000–38,000 MACK**

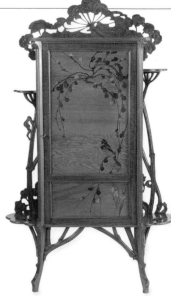

Rear of a cabinet with floral cresting, stepped shelves with tree supports and branch stretchers, and ash, oak, and calamander marquetry panels. *156cm (60¾in) high* **£30,000–45,000 MACK**

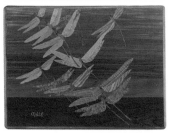

Insects, and in particular dragonflies, are a recurring form of decoration in Gallé's designs.

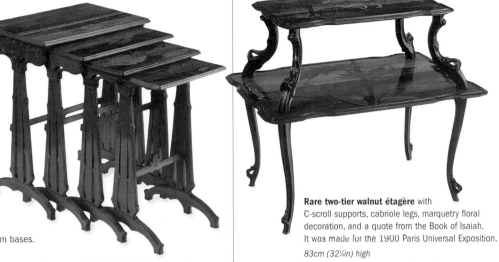

Nest of four tables, each with fruitwood marquetry decoration displaying dragonflies in a wetland setting. The tables have stretchered end-supports of stylized, lyre-like form on curved platform bases.

Largest: 58cm (22⅞in) wide

£12,000–15,000   **MACK**

Rare two-tier walnut étagère with C-scroll supports, cabriole legs, marquetry floral decoration, and a quote from the Book of Isaiah. It was made for the 1900 Paris Universal Exposition.

83cm (32¼in) high

£23,000–30,000   **MACK**

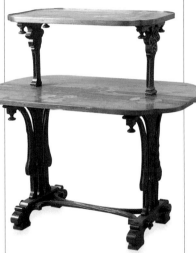

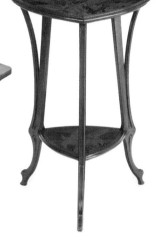

Two-tier étagère on stepped and stretchered platform bases. Elongated hexagonal, walnut tops decorated with marquetry of blossoming branches, foliage, and grasshoppers. *c.1900*

87.5cm (34½in) wide

£3,500–3,800   **VZ**

Two-tier occasional table in rosewood. The shield-like tiers have floral marquetry decoration. With three out-splayed supports and scroll legs with carved hoof feet.

77cm (30in) high

£12,000–19,000   **MACK**

CORNERSTONE PIECE

Walnut and rosewood vitrine. The enclosed upper section has glazed doors with carved leaf and branch surrounds extending down to a central support to form a heart motif. Below, shelves are set in moulded supports, against a back with leaf-form marquetry. It has a carved, pierced root-form apron, scroll legs, and hoof feet.
158cm (61½in) high **£23,000–38,000 MACK**

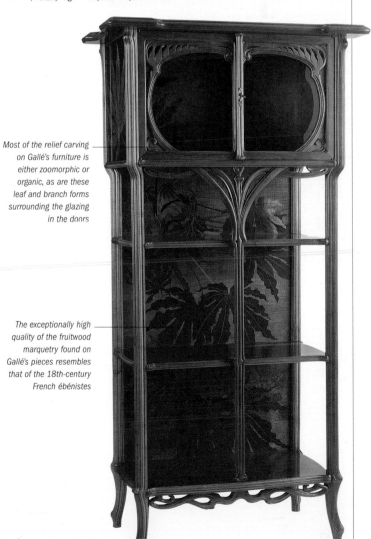

Most of the relief carving on Gallé's furniture is either zoomorphic or organic, as are these leaf and branch forms surrounding the glazing in the doors

The exceptionally high quality of the fruitwood marquetry found on Gallé's pieces resembles that of the 18th-century French ébénistes

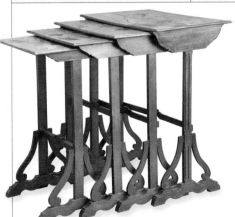

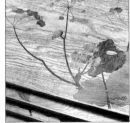

Gallé's blossom and branch imagery was partly inspired by Japanese art.

Nest of four mahogany tables with fruitwood marquetry of blossoming branches and foliage. Stretchered end-supports have S-scroll braces on serpentine-shaped platform bases. *c.1900*

Largest: 72.25cm (28½in) high

£2,400–2,800   **VZ**

KEY FEATURES

Dark, exotic hardwoods, including mahogany and rosewood, feature decorative inlays, using mother-of-pearl and metals such as pewter or brass.

Furniture shapes remain traditional with graceful, gently curving lines.

Fine-quality veneers and marquetry designs incorporate floral or chicory-leaf motifs.

Organic forms – waterlilies and orchids – are incorporated in the gilt-bronze decoration.

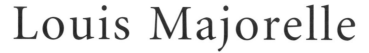

Louis Majorelle

At the Ecole de Nancy, the richly ornamented furniture created by the accomplished cabinetmaker Louis Majorelle complemented and contrasted with the nature-inspired, visionary Art Nouveau designs of Emile Gallé.

Having studied painting in Paris, and upon his father's death in 1879, Louis Majorelle (1859–1926) assumed control of his family's cabinetmaking workshop in Nancy, France, which produced reproduction furniture in the 18th-century style. Influenced by Emile Gallé, Majorelle guided the family firm towards the Art Nouveau style that looked to nature for inspiration.

Majorelle's training as a cabinetmaker served him well. With a sound knowledge of wood and veneers, a superb design sense, and technical virtuosity, he refused to abandon the celebrated principles of fine French craftsmanship. Despite the fact that much of his furniture was made using some machine-made parts, the quality of Majorelle's pieces often challenged the works of the great 18th-century cabinetmakers. In an effort to reach a wide audience, he established several workshops,

where craftsmen produced numerous versions of a single furniture design. Specializing in whole suites of furniture – produced in assembly-line fashion – rather than in one-off exhibition pieces, Majorelle's expertise as a furniture maker really found its voice between 1898 and 1908 with richly ornamented designs of breathtaking quality.

After 1908, when it was decided to industrialize the workshops, the quality of Majorelle's furniture dropped sharply. In the push to reach commercial goals, aesthetic quality and innovation were the unfortunate victims. The luxuriance of furniture embellished with gilt-bronze mounts was replaced by a broad range of lightly sculptured furniture designed to appeal to a wider public.

Above: Mahogany elbow chair with foliage marquetry to the splat, spiral-turned spindles to back and sides, U-shaped crinoline arms with duck-head terminals, and a stuff-over seat on tapering legs. *107.5cm (40in) high* **£13,000–17,000 MACK**

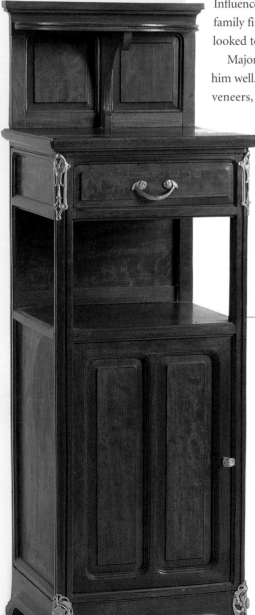

GILT-BRONZE DETAILS

Majorelle initially favoured marquetry panels in veneers of precious woods to embellish his furniture. Later, he abandoned this labour-intensive method and turned his attention instead to the design of finely-worked decorative mounts made of gilt bronze or wrought iron. Majorelle's decorative schemes looked back to the Rococo preference for warm, lustrous woods enhanced by elegant, nature-inspired mounts in luminous gilt bronze. Flower buds, waterlilies, and orchids were lavishly applied to the feet, legs, handles, and keyholes of cabinets, desks, and tables.

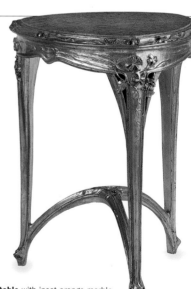

Mahogany and tamarind bedside cabinet (one of a pair), with shelves above and below a small drawer, fielded-panel cupboard doors, and gilt-bronze corner mounts, handle, and catch. *c.1908. 113cm (44in) high* **£26,000–40,000 (the pair) CALD**

Gilt wood side table with inset orange marble top, within a carved leaf and berry motif moulding, above a wavy frieze. It has three moulded tapering legs, united by arched stretchers, with carved and pierced floral tops. *78cm (30½in) high* **£10,000–17,000 MACK**

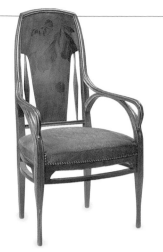

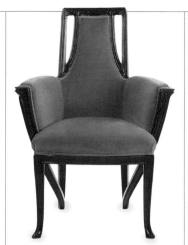

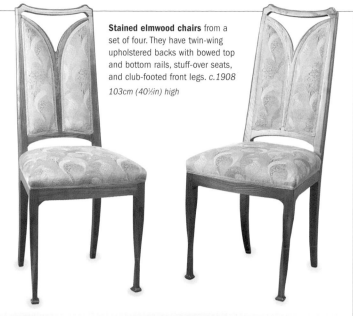

Stained elmwood chairs from a set of four. They have twin-wing upholstered backs with bowed top and bottom rails, stuff-over seats, and club-footed front legs. *c.1908*

103cm (40½in) high

"Marrons d'Inde" armchair (one of a pair) with a back splat with exotic wood marquetry, bent and carved arms, tapering legs, and a stuff-over upholstered seat. *1905–10*

103cm (40½in) high

£10,000–11,000 (the pair)   MACK

Mahogany frame chair (one of a pair) with a back with padded splat, stuff-over arms on sweeping, reverse-curved supports, and stuff-over seat on moulded legs.

103cm (40½in) high

£13,000–26,000 (the pair)   MACK

£1,500–2,000 (the set)   VZ

Leaf and berry motif handles.

Mahogany writing desk with a raised back and two central drawers flanked by open shelves. It has a tooled skiver, two frieze drawers, carved and tapering legs on block feet, and gilt-bronze leaf and berry handles.

312cm (121½in) wide

£20,000–27,000 (with matching chair)

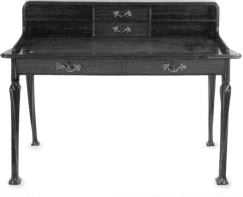

MACK

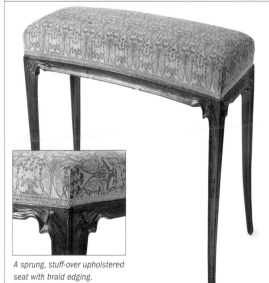

A sprung, stuff-over upholstered seat with braid edging.

Carved walnut stool finely carved with floral decoration in relief on the corners of the frame and the tops of the long, tapering legs. The Art Nouveau pattern cover of the stuff-over upholstered seat is a later replacement. *c.1905*

104cm (40½in) wide

£4,500–5,500   CALD

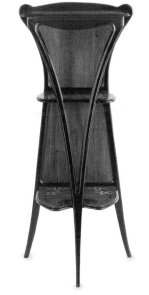

Three-tier mahogany étagère with Y-shaped front support. The serpentine-shaped tiers have ash and satinwood floral marquetry.

125cm (48¾in) high

£12,000–15,000   MACK

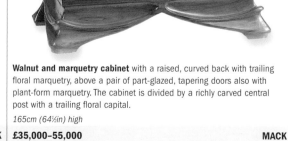

Walnut and marquetry cabinet with a raised, curved back with trailing floral marquetry, above a pair of part-glazed, tapering doors also with plant-form marquetry. The cabinet is divided by a richly carved central post with a trailing floral capital.

165cm (64½in) high

£35,000–55,000   MACK

KEY FEATURES

Solid, sculptural forms with little applied decoration were favoured for van de Velde's furniture.

Curved lines of nature are apparent in his pieces.

Spartan yet elegant, van de Velde's finely crafted furniture designs feature light-coloured native timbers, such as walnut, oak, and beech.

Outward-curving legs, slender splats, and upholstery held in place by studwork are typical of van de Velde chairs.

Henry van de Velde

After he turned his attention to architecture and the decorative arts, the Antwerp-born Impressionist painter Henry van de Velde (1863–1957) wore the mantle of Belgium's chief designer working in the Art Nouveau style.

Influenced by the writings of William Morris, the highly original designs of pioneer Henry van de Velde won attention with the house he built for himself – Bloemenwerf – near Brussels in 1894, and for which he created the furniture, silver, cutlery, and decorative fixtures. His preoccupation with a harmonious organic environment, and the influence of the English architect and designer C.F.A. Voysey, can be detected in the clean lines of his undecorated chairs, tables, and cabinets.

Samuel Bing was so impressed that in 1896 he commissioned van de Velde to design rooms for his celebrated Paris shop L'Art Nouveau, which brought him much acclaim throughout Europe. He then worked as a designer of furniture, metalwork, ceramics, textiles, and bookbinding, and in 1897, founded the Société van de Velde, with workshops for producing furniture and metalwork.

A champion of the role of the artist over the machine in the Arts and Crafts tradition, van de Velde travelled widely, creating elegant furniture for the very rich and becoming director of the School of Arts and Crafts in Weimar in 1908. The function of his furniture remains paramount, and any decoration applied to the restrained sculptural forms is spare. Chairs in light-coloured native woods, such as beech, walnut, and oak, tend to boast slender splats, legs that curve outwards, rush seats, or upholstery – leather or batik – fixed in place with studwork.

The sweeping, energetic lines of his early furniture later gave way to a more restrained interpretation of Art Nouveau. Eventually, van de Velde abandoned furniture design in order to concentrate on architecture and theory.

Above: Mahogany dining chair with curved top rail, vertical back slats, and a padded support for the lower back. With a drop-in seat, on curved and tapering supports. *1896 87.8cm (34½in) high* **NPA RdM**

NATURAL LINES

Henry van de Velde believed that art should always follow organic form, and this theory provided the basis for his furniture designs. He embraced the curved lines of nature in his work, avoiding applied, inlaid, or any elaborate ornamental decoration. He believed natural lines perfectly complemented the wood he used and that this combination had the greatest impact for his pieces of furniture. Despite his theories on producing radical designs, van de Velde's pieces remain functional, with a nod to traditional design conventions. However, they represented a new way of thinking, which he went on to develop in architectural designs later in his career.

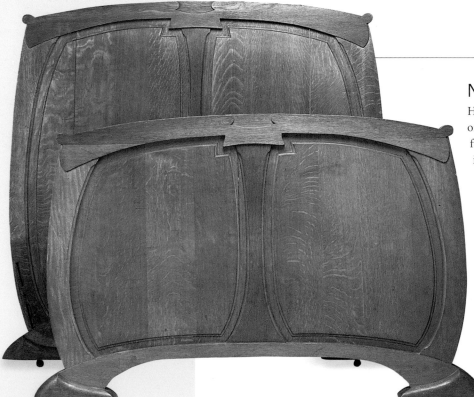

Stained oak bed of bold, curvilinear form. The head and footboards have bowed and arched profiles and pairs of raised and fielded, shield-shape panels. Set on splayed feet with brass castors. *1897–98 203.5cm (80in) wide* **£7,500–9,500 Qu**

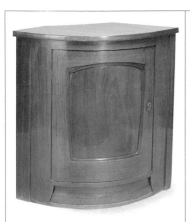

Mahogany corner cupboard from a suite. Its overhanging top has a chamfered edge, above a bowed door with arch-topped centre panel and brass escutcheon. The side panels are bowed, and the base scooped. *1903*

76.5cm (30in) high

£3,500–4,500   Qu

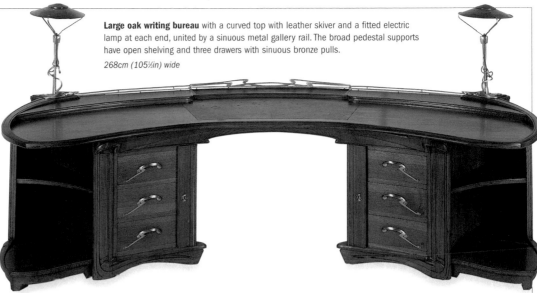

Large oak writing bureau with a curved top with leather skiver and a fitted electric lamp at each end, united by a sinuous metal gallery rail. The broad pedestal supports have open shelving and three drawers with sinuous bronze pulls.

268cm (105½in) wide

NPA   RdM

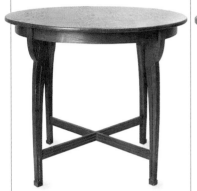

Oak occasional table in the style of Henry van de Velde. It has a circular top overhanging a plain apron, curved corbels, and gently bowed legs with stepped X-frame stretchers. *c.1903*

79.5cm (31¼in) high

£1,700–2,200   VZ

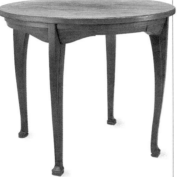

Walnut occasional table with overhanging circular top, above an arched apron, and gently curving cabriole-style legs, terminating in stylized animal-paw feet. *c.1916*

69.5cm (27¼in) high

£9,000–£10,000   Qu

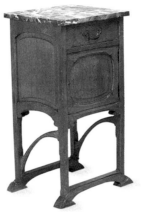
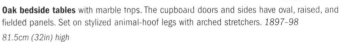

Oak bedside tables with marble tops. The cupboard doors and sides have oval, raised, and fielded panels. Set on stylized animal-hoof legs with arched stretchers. *1897–98*

81.5cm (32in) high

£600–1,000   Qu

Victor Horta

A pioneer of the Art Nouveau style was the Belgian architect and designer Victor Horta (1861–1947), who was celebrated for his harmonious, integrated environments that included door-frames, wall panelling, and metalwork fixtures. His energetic, sinuous style was highly influential – in particular on Parisian designers such as Hector Guimard – although he spent most of his life in his native Belgium designing furniture for his own buildings. A hallmark of Horta's Art Nouveau designs for interiors was the exuberant whiplash curve, which married various decorative features throughout a house, from tile floors to ironwork door fittings. For his furniture Horta favoured maple, mahogany, and fruitwoods embellished with luxurious, opulent upholstery such as velvet and silk.

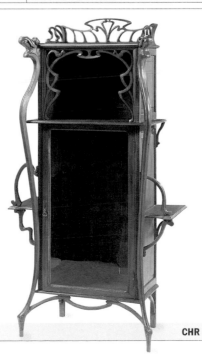

Mahogany cabinet attributed to Victor Horta with a rectangular tiled top with sinuous carved surround, open recess, and a glazed door. Also with small side shelves and shaped legs.

90cm (35in) wide

£3,000–5,000   CHR

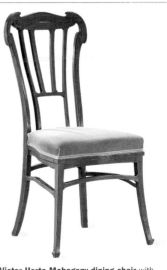

Victor Horta Mahogany dining chair with flared, open back and a sinuous outline. The stuff-over seat is on splayed supports. *c.1901*

95.2cm (37½in) high

£7,000–9,000   CHR

French and Belgian Furniture

Due to a lively interchange between France and its northern neighbour Belgium, the Art Nouveau furniture produced by both countries had much in common. The Paris School led by Hector Guimard (1867–1942) shared with the renowned Belgian architect and designer Henry van de Velde (*see pp.30–31*) a taste for restrained sculptural forms bearing little applied decoration. Both sold furniture at Samuel Bing's shop in Paris, L'Art Nouveau. The bold, energetic, whiplash style of the furniture from Belgium was widely influenced by the Parisian designers, including Hector Guimard.

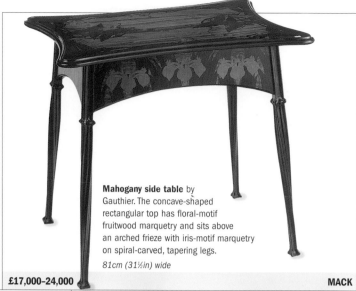

Mahogany side table by Gauthier. The concave-shaped rectangular top has floral-motif fruitwood marquetry and sits above an arched frieze with iris-motif marquetry on spiral-carved, tapering legs.
81cm (31½in) wide

£17,000–24,000 MACK

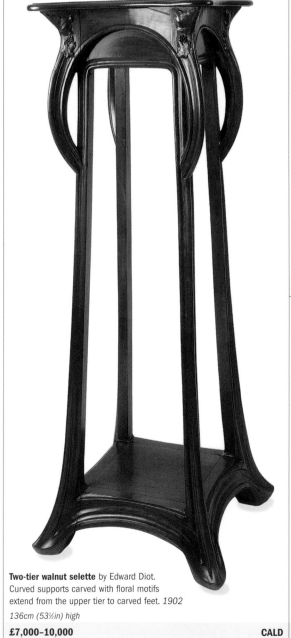

Two-tier walnut selette by Edward Diot. Curved supports carved with floral motifs extend from the upper tier to carved feet. *1902*
136cm (53½in) high

£7,000–10,000 CALD

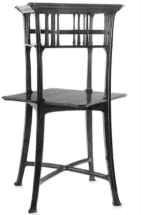

Mahogany library selette by Tony Selmersheim, with a bookshelf compartment above an off-set lower tier, on out-splayed legs.
90cm (35in) wide

£12,000–£17,000 MACK

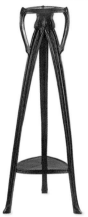

Two-tier mahogany selette by Emile André, with curved triangular tiers, three arched, pierced supports, and tapering legs.
131cm (51in) high

£12,000–17,000 MACK

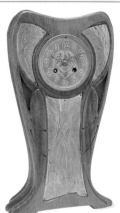

Mahogany mantel clock with a gold-plated brass dial. The case is by Maurice Dufrêne and the mechanism by L. Marti & Cie. *c.1900*
39.25cm (15½in) high

£3,300–3,800 Qu

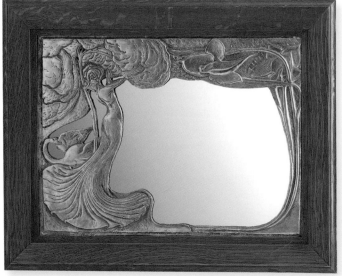

Oak-framed wall mirror by Georges de Feure for the 1900 Paris Universal Exposition, with a silver-plated, relief-moulded scene of a young woman in a stylized landscape.
45cm (17½in) wide

£10,000–17,000 MACK

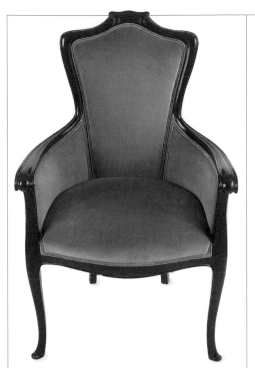

Mahogany-frame elbow chair by Edward Colonna. Part of a suite including a settee and side-chair exhibited at the 1900 Paris Universal Exposition.

110cm (43in) high

£20,000–33,000 MACK

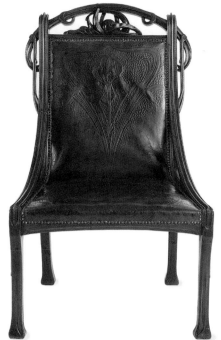

Walnut-frame chair by Eugène Gaillard, with pierced plant-form carving to the back, embossed leather upholstery, and bronze mounts to the tops of the legs.

107.5cm (42in) high

£10,000–17,000 MACK

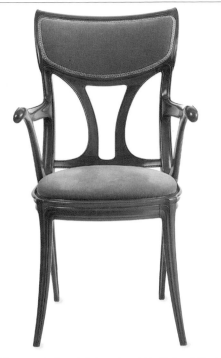

Cherry-wood elbow chair (one of a pair) by Eugène Gaillard, with padded back above curved slats, cantilevered supports to the arms, stuff-over seat, and out-splayed legs.

107.5cm (42in) high

£20,000–34,000 (the pair) MACK

Jallot

One of the new generation of rational and restrained furniture designers, Leon Jallot (1874–1967) reacted against the early "macaroni" style of Art Nouveau – with heavily moulded woodwork – that was championed by pioneering artist-craftsmen such as Hector Guimard and Louis Majorelle. Like many of his contemporaries, Jallot preferred a style characterized by plain lines, pure forms, and a more precise sense of proportion. Luxurious woods were used alone or in subtle combinations to create simple, practical furniture that was soundly constructed. His work saw florid carved Art Nouveau plant motifs replaced with restrained ornament comprised of ivory inlays or pierced decoration.

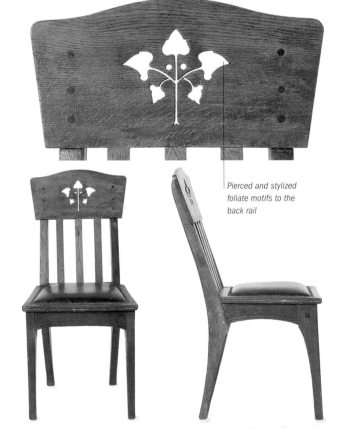

Pierced and stylized foliate motifs to the back rail

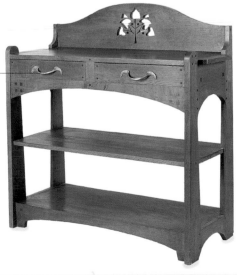

Brass handles terminating in stylized leaf motifs

Jallot oak and purpleheart server with an arched, raised back that has pierced, stylized leaf motifs above two frieze drawers and two open shelves. On tapering legs.

122.5cm (47¾in) wide

£8,000–10,000 CALD

Jallot oak and purpleheart chair (from a set of six), with pierced, stylized leaf decoration to the top rail. The tapering legs each have visible purpleheart tenons. *c.1908*

107.5cm (42cm) high

£8,000–10,000 (the set) CALD

KEY FEATURES

Lavish inlay materials, such as ivory, brass, pewter, mother-of-pearl, and ebony are used.

Imaginative combinations of woods and metals are embellished with materials including leather, vellum, silk, and metal.

Furniture often combines elements, such as tables with cabinets or chairs with integral lamps.

Bugatti's signature sometimes appears painted in vellum panels or as a pewter inlay.

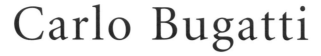

Carlo Bugatti

In Italy, Art Nouveau was known as *La Stile Liberty*, and chief among its furniture designers was Carlo Bugatti. His highly imaginative designs were inspired by a wide variety of sources.

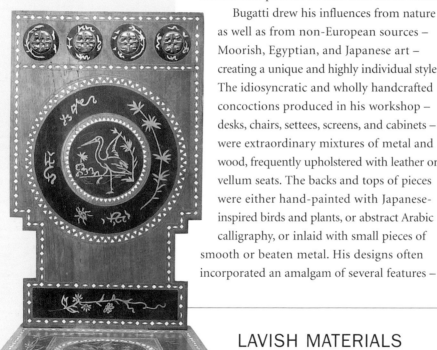

Bugatti was a fascinating and highly individual furniture designer who established his workshops in Milan in 1888. His work is completely without precedent and laced with a dose of fantasy. Neither very functional nor well constructed, his designs nonetheless possess a rustic and exotic charm.

Bugatti drew his influences from nature as well as from non-European sources – Moorish, Egyptian, and Japanese art – creating a unique and highly individual style. The idiosyncratic and wholly handcrafted concoctions produced in his workshop – desks, chairs, settees, screens, and cabinets – were extraordinary mixtures of metal and wood, frequently upholstered with leather or vellum seats. The backs and tops of pieces were either hand-painted with Japanese-inspired birds and plants, or abstract Arabic calligraphy, or inlaid with small pieces of smooth or beaten metal. His designs often incorporated an amalgam of several features –

tables had built-in cabinets, and chairs boasted integral lamps, for example.

Bugatti created furniture for particular settings, such as the Moorish interior he designed for the Italian Pavilion at the 1902 International Exhibition of Modern Decorative Arts in Turin. This caused a furore and won him a prestigious first prize. The influence of North Africa can be observed in his subdued colours, tasselled fringes, and decorative strips of beaten or pierced metal. Other features, such as shield backs, crescent legs, and minaret-shaped sections, add to the exotic, Islamic flavour of his pieces. Bugatti's early style, characterized by busy decoration, eventually gave way to more restrained furniture, featuring serpentine curves and lighter colours that point to the influence of the Parisian Art Nouveau designers.

Above: Mahogany occasional table with the top inlaid in pewter and bone with circular parquetry, the sides with stylized florets and roundels. The legs feature embossed bronzed coverings. *40cm (15¾in) high* **£1,200–1,500 L&T**

LAVISH MATERIALS

Among the highlights of Bugatti's work is the wide range of lavish materials applied as decoration. A favoured fabric, vellum – a parchment made of calfskin commonly used for manuscripts and bindings – was used to upholster chairs and cover tabletops and boxes. Inlays used a variety of rich and expensive materials, including metals – brass, pewter, and copper – ebony, bone, and mother-of-pearl to create sumptuous and intricate patterns. Metals were also applied to furniture in imaginative ways: copper might be wrapped around the uprights of chairs, or strips of smooth, beaten, or pierced metals used to enhanced the already-exotic appearance of a walnut armchair or cabinet. Other luxurious fabrics ornamenting Bugatti's designs include leather and knotted silk tassels.

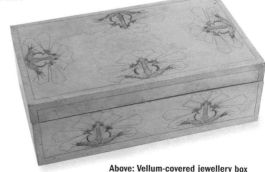

Above: Vellum-covered jewellery box decorated with stylized frogs on lily pads picked out in soft colours. The interior is lined with velvet. Signed "Bugatti" in red on the underside. *34cm (13½in) wide* **£6,000–9,000 MACK**

Left: Mahogany chair with the back featuring an ebony roundel with inlaid pewter stork and foliage, and a row of copper and ebony roundels above. The seat is similarly decorated, while the legs have inlays and embossed copper banding. *c.1895. 104cm (41in) high* **£1,800–2,200 VZ**

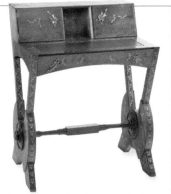

Walnut, brass, and pewter strung desk. The two cupboards and frieze drawer have gilt-bronze dragonfly handles and floral motifs. With characteristic wheel-segment supports.

69.5cm (23½in) wide

£30,000–45,000   **MACK**

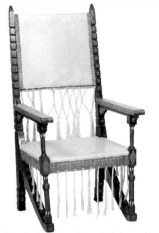

Dark-stained nut-wood armchair (one of a pair) with inlaid pewter decoration and embossed copper banding. Upholstered in natural leather with woollen tassels. *c.1900*

118.5cm (46¾in) high

£5,000–6,000 (the pair)   **DOR**

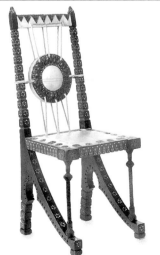

Ebonized-wood chair with turned uprights inlaid with ivory. The seat is vellum and the back a vellum and copper roundel. Embossed copper banding covers the front legs. *c.1888*

110cm (43¼in) high

£1,500–2,000   **VZ**

CORNERSTONE PIECE

Inlaid sideboard with a hinged, vellum-covered, drop-down door on the rectangular upper section, enclosing shelving and small drawers. Further vellum-covered doors are in the base. The whole is contained within four turned and blocked supports, with overall brass, silver, ebony, and ivory inlays. *c.1900. 154.5cm (60in) wide* **£35,000–45,000 VZ**

Upper section shown open to reveal shelves and drawers, possibly for flatware

Applied with embossed brass banding and woollen tassels

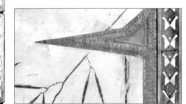

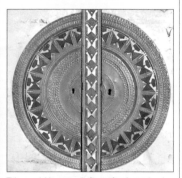

This elaborate, embossed-brass ornamental hinge is applied to the vellum surface as a foil to the spare and simple nature of the painted oriental-style foliage.

This roundel is a tour de force of embossed and inlaid metalware. The centre and outer banding in embossed brass encloses a geometric pattern resembling winged insects in a pale wood, ebony, silver, ivory, and brass inlay.

Antoní Gaudí

The Art Nouveau style was championed in Spain by a small group of Catalan architects led by Antoní Gaudí in Barcelona. Rejecting tradition, his idiosyncratic furniture designs boldly embrace asymmetry. The ethic of nature is manifest in Gaudí's frequent use of floral motifs and curving, organic shapes. Gaudí's designs in his preferred timber of oak often play a number of practical roles, with display cabinets harbouring cupboards and mirrors and sofas incorporating small tables. Much of his furniture was created for his vigorous, sculptural buildings, such as Barcelona's magnificent Guell Palace.

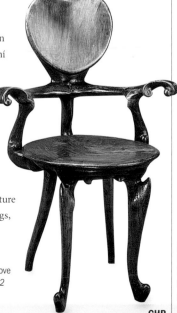

Antoní Gaudí rare carved padouk wood armchair, of sculptural organic form. The back rest is heart-shaped above scrolling ribbon-like arm supports, with a solid seat. *1902*

98cm (38½in) high

£80,000–120,000   **CHR**

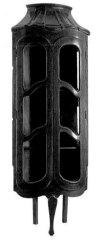

Antoní Gaudí glazed display corner cabinet, fashioned in oak with a fluted top and twin doors on plain and sinuous supports. *1904–05*

230cm (90½in) high

£150,000–200,000   **RdM**

Hoffmann designs owe much to the elegant, linear style of the Scottish designer Charles Rennie Mackintosh, whose work was much praised in Vienna.

Austrian Biedermeier pieces, made earlier in the century, also influenced Hoffmann's work.

A stark, functional style was embraced by Hoffmann, leaving behind the fluid, curvilinear designs typical of the French strain of Art Nouveau.

Geometric patterns featuring open-centred rectangles and squares, circles, and spheres decorate tables and chairs in limed oak, mahogany, and beechwood.

Josef Hoffmann

Unlike the sumptuous confections of the French Art Nouveau artisans, the timeless furniture designs being created in Vienna by the illustrious Secessionist Josef Hoffmann looked to a new and very modern future.

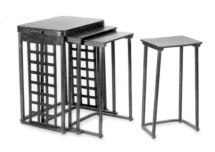

A co-founder of the Wiener Werkstätte – modelled after Charles Robert Ashbee's Guild of Handicraft in Britain – the Moravian-born Josef Hoffmann (1870–1956) was a pioneer of functional design. His early Art Nouveau belief in the unity of architecture, furniture, and decoration found him ultimately embracing a style that was stark, functional, and decidedly opposed to the florid, curvilinear Art Nouveau fashion promoted by his French contemporaries.

Although Hoffmann's first designs bore the fluid lines typical of French Art Nouveau, by 1900 he had fallen under the spell of Charles Rennie Mackintosh, who was widely admired in Vienna.

But Hoffmann went beyond aesthetic principles to embrace a philosophy that saw functional furniture take on elegance and restraint. His most celebrated designs include those for Vienna's Purkersdorf Sanatorium and the Palais Stoclet in Brussels.

Hoffmann favoured beechwood, limed oak, mahogany, and other ebonized woods. He was one of the premier designers for the firm set up by Michael Thonet, whose great success was attributed to the invention of the bentwood technique.

Above: Nest of four tables (model number 968) in mahogany-stained beech, manufactured by J. & J. Kohn and with remnants of the original paper label. *1905.*
Largest: 75.5cm (29¾in) high **£1,800–2,200 Qu**

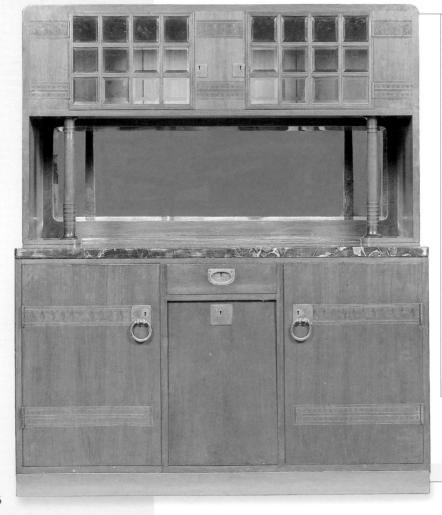

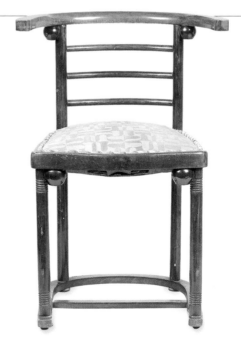

"Cabaret Fledermaus" chair in beechwood with ebony ball brackets under the back rail and a drop-in seat pad. Made by Thonet. *c.1907*
75cm (29½in) high

£2,000–2,600	DOR

Walnut-veneered sideboard by the School of Josef Hoffmann. Spindle supports raise cupboards over a marble-topped base with cupboards and a drawer, all with patterned inlay and brass hardware. *c.1902*
178cm (70in) high

£10,000–12,000	DOR

Koloman Moser

A founder of the Vienna Secession and, later, the Wiener Werkstätte with Josef Hoffmann, Moser designed furniture that was frequently embellished with stylized ornament, which flattered the otherwise severe rectilinear design.

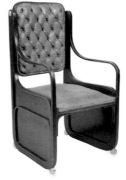

Koloman Moser (1868–1918) was the multi-talented Austrian architect and designer of a broad range of decorative arts that included jewellery, metalwork, glass, and textiles. From the 1890s, he conceived furniture in severely geometric but refined rectilinear shapes that were richly decorated and far more colourful than much of the furniture being made by his Viennese contemporaries.

Furniture designed by Moser often saw lavish decoration take precedence over form, with luxurious timbers such as rosewood and maple used for veneers, and decorative patterns inlaid with opulent materials such as exotic woods or mother-of-pearl.

Moser held the prestigious post of professor at the School of Applied Arts from 1899 until his untimely death nearly 20 years later.

Along with the designs produced by his Wiener Werkstätte colleague Josef Hoffmann, Moser's finely crafted furniture tended to be exclusive and expensive and largely depended on the patronage of wealthy clients.

Above: "Fauteuil No. 413" manufactured by J. & J. Kohn in dark mahogany-stained beech with brass rivets. The seat and buttoned back are in dark brown leather. *1901* *99cm (39in) high* **£5,000–6,000 DOR**

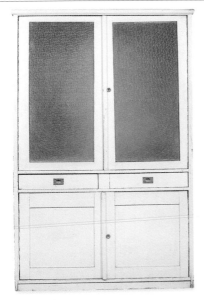

Painted softwood cupboard with shelves behind glazed double doors. Below are two drawers and a double-door cupboard. Painted in white, with brass hardware. From Koloman Moser's flat in Vienna. *c.1902* *213.5cm (84in) high*

£20,000–25,000   **DOR**

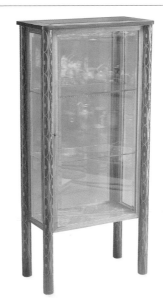

Display cabinet by the School of Koloman Moser. The four stained hardwood legs are cylindrical with inlaid geometric motifs. The door, side panels, and centre shelves are glass. *1905* *183cm (72in) high*

£1,800–2,200   **HERR**

Exotic music cabinet, the design attributed to Moser and manufactured by Ludwig Schmidt. The rosewood surface is inlaid with light wood roundels, flanking a narrow rectangular panel of a girl wearing an exotic costume of inlaid abalone, ebony, and polychrome-stained fruitwoods. *1900–05* *134.5cm (53in) high*

NPA   **Soth**

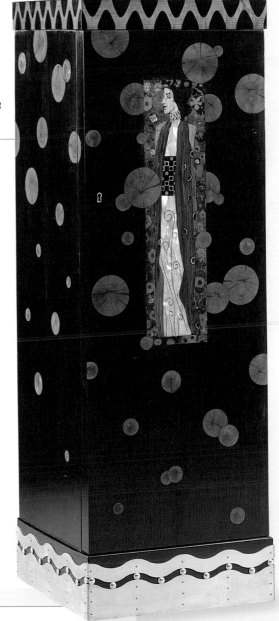

Sinuous, curving shapes made from solid or laminated wood that has been steamed and bent, is a hallmark of Thonet's furniture.

Thonet's bentwood chairs are reminiscent of the 18th-century Rococo style, where asymmetrical curves replaced the linear, angular, and architectural style of the Baroque.

Decorative ornament is lacking on Thonet's bentwood furniture.

Thonet

The development of Art Nouveau furniture in Austria owes much to the pioneering bentwood designs of the innovative German designer Michael Thonet, who established his furniture workshop in 1819.

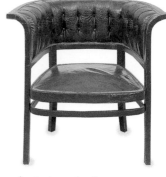

Like many entrepreneurial craftsmen, Thonet (1796–1871) began to experiment with laminated wood. The success of his groundbreaking bentwood chairs – which looked back to the curves of the Rococo style – saw Thonet move to Vienna under the patronage of Prince Metternich of Austria.

In Vienna, Thonet was granted a patent for a process that involved steaming or boiling solid or laminated wood so that it could be bent into different shapes. Chair frames were formed of long curved rods, replacing hand-carved corner joints with gentle, flowing curves. Light, flexible, and inexpensive, Thonet's bentwood furniture was nonetheless remarkably durable.

By 1853, Thonet had given the factory over to his five sons. Six years later, the sinuous curves – that would later be associated with the Art Nouveau style – featured heavily in the first catalogue advertising the remarkable bentwood furniture produced by the Viennese firm that was now known as Gebrüder Thonet.

At the beginning of the 20th century, the firm employed a number of forward-looking designers, including Josef Hoffmann (*see p.36*).

Above: Beech armchair by Marcel Kammerer, produced by Thonet, Vienna. The frame is stained mahogany in colour and upholstered with a greeny-brown leather cover, fixed with copper rivets. Original punch stamp. *c.1910. 81.5cm (32in) high* **£800–1,000 DOR**

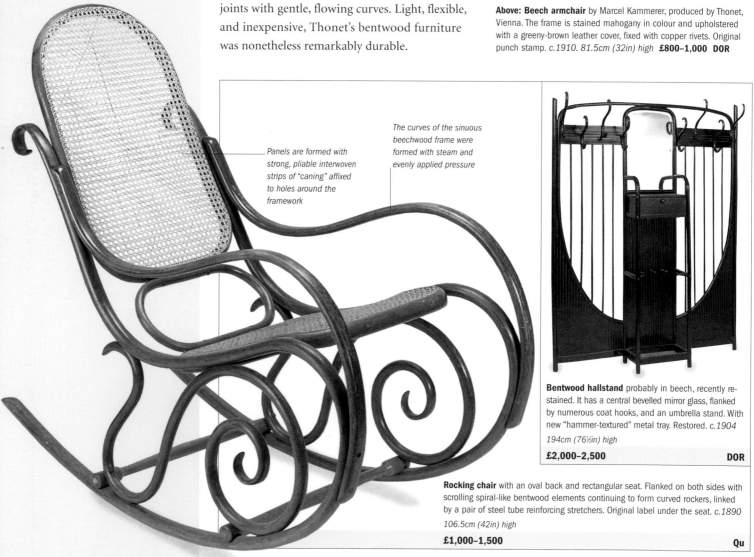

Panels are formed with strong, pliable interwoven strips of "caning" affixed to holes around the framework

The curves of the sinuous beechwood frame were formed with steam and evenly applied pressure

Bentwood hallstand probably in beech, recently re-stained. It has a central bevelled mirror glass, flanked by numerous coat hooks, and an umbrella stand. With new "hammer-textured" metal tray. Restored. *c.1904 194cm (76½in) high*

£2,000–2,500   **DOR**

Rocking chair with an oval back and rectangular seat. Flanked on both sides with scrolling spiral-like bentwood elements continuing to form curved rockers, linked by a pair of steel tube reinforcing stretchers. Original label under the seat. *c.1890 106.5cm (42in) high*

£1,000–1,500   **Qu**

Richard Riemerschmid

The development of the internationally acclaimed Munich Style of Art Nouveau owes much to the versatile and prolific German designer and architect Richard Riemerschmid (1868–1957), whose career as a furniture designer began in 1895.

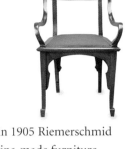

Riemerschmid's earliest designs look to both historical and Arts and Crafts sources for inspiration, with a nod to contemporary Art Nouveau in carving, brasswork, and inlays.

For the Glaspalast Exhibition in 1897, he designed a buffet in yew wood with iron mounts, receiving praise for its materials and simplicity. The following year, he helped establish the Munich Vereinigte Werkstätten für Kunst im Handwerk (the United Workshops for Art and Handicraft), encouraging designers and manufacturers to work for the common man's benefit. A music-room chair shown in Dresden in 1899 cemented Riemerschmid's reputation.

Allied with the Deutscher Werkbund, in 1905 Riemerschmid designed his first machine-made furniture – *Maschinenmöbel* – for the Dresden workshops founded by his cabinetmaker brother-in-law Karl Schmidt. Schmidt's atelier identified with the principles of William Morris and the Arts and Crafts movement but differed in its acceptance of practical machinery. This furniture was functional, simple, and inexpensive.

Above: Mahogany elbow chair with broad, shaped top rail, sinuous arm rests, and drop-in seat (newly upholstered). On tapering supports, with block feet. Produced by Wenzel Till, Munich. *84.5cm (33¼in) high* **£2,300–2,800 VZ**

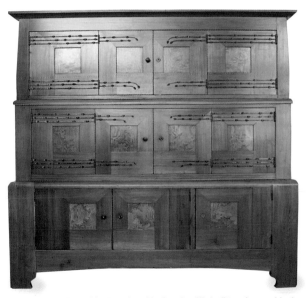

Richly coloured pine cabinet produced by Dresdner Werkstätten. Arranged in three sections: the upper two have central cupboard doors with extraordinary wrought-iron applied bands and hinges of organic form; the lower section has cupboards with double doors and a single door. With the original locks and key. *1902*
211cm (83in) wide
£6,500–8,500   **VZ**

Dark-stained beech elbow chair with pierced motifs on a back slat that extends to the floor. It has curved armrests, a solid seat, and square supports united by stretchers. Produced by J. Fleischauer's Söhne. *1900*
85.5cm (33¼in) high
£1,300–1,800   **VZ**

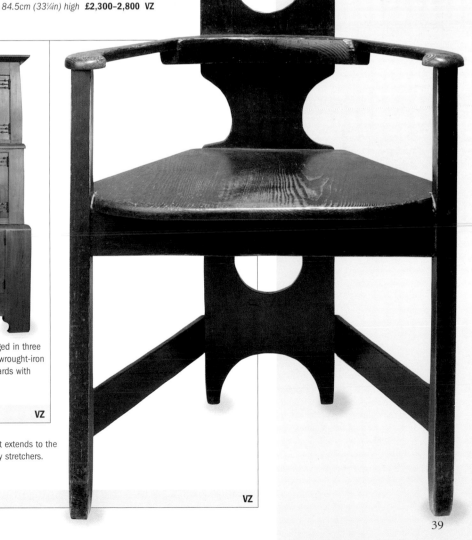

German and Austrian Furniture

Furniture designers in Germany and Austria rejected the richly poetic marquetry confections of Emile Gallé and the florid naturalism of Hector Guimard in favour of bold, timeless, and functional designs produced in radical new materials such as aluminium, plywood, and bent beechwood. The distinctive furniture designers of the Vienna Secession and the Wiener Werkstätte (including Josef Hoffmann and Koloman Moser) and the quiet, restrained designs of the progressive Munich- and Dresden-based Jugendstil revolutionaries (Peter Behrens and Richard Riemerschmid) charted unexplored territory to produce fresh and innovative furniture for a new century.

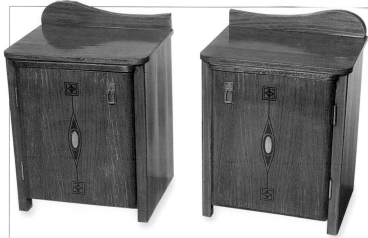

Austrian Secessionist nightstands in mahogany, with fruitwood and mother-of-pearl inlay. They are part of a suite also comprising a bed and an armoire. *c.1900*

61cm (24in) wide

£3,500–4,000 (the pair)　　　　　　　　　　　　　**FRE**

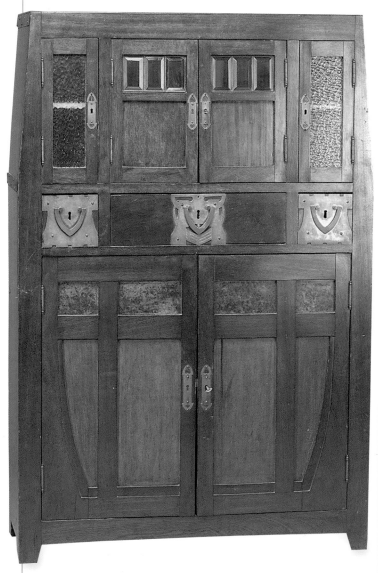

German display cabinet with glazed and panelled doors and three drawers. In mahogany with selective fruitwood panelling and brass handles and escutcheons. *1900–05*

138.5cm (54½in) high

£2,300–2,600　　　　　　　　　　　　**Qu**

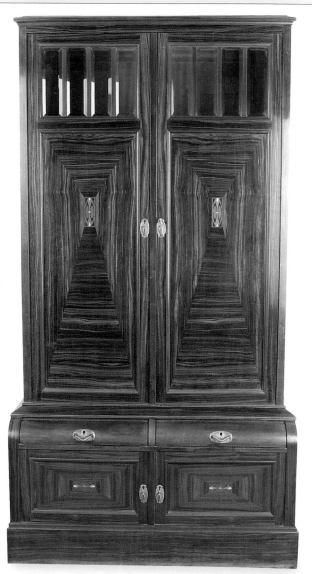

German display cabinet by J. Groschklus. In dark- and light-stained mahogany with six cupboards and two drawers; the upper cupboard doors each have four panes of glass.

188.5cm (74¼in) high

£1,400–1,800　　　　　　　　　　　　**VZ**

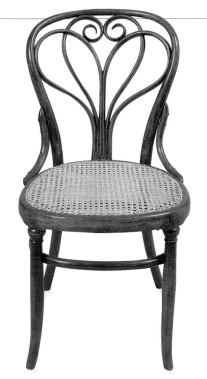

Bentwood armchair "No.25" made by Mundus of Vienna. In dark brown stained beech, with an open back slat of stylized, scrolling plant stems and a canework seat. *c.1910*

91.5cm (36in) high

£600–800   **DOR**

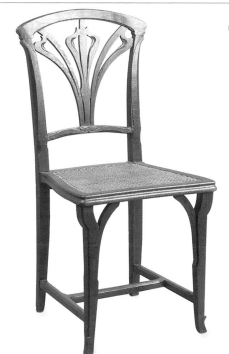

German oak chair stained dark brown with a canework seat and a partly pierced back slat of three stylized leaf forms in the French Art Nouveau style.

92cm (36¼in) high

£250–300   **VZ**

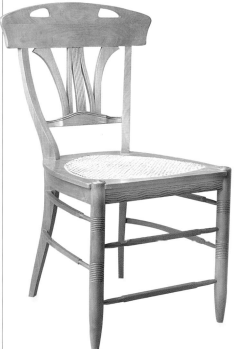

Vereinigte Werkstätten chair designed by Bernhard Pankok, in nutwood with a canework seat. The back slat features highly stylized plant stems; the top rail, leaf-motif piercings.

34cm (19in) wide

£2,800–3,200   **VZ**

Joseph Maria Olbrich

A founding member of the Vienna Secession, the prolific architect and designer of metalwork, textiles, and graphics Joseph Maria Olbrich (1867–1908) created few, but distinctive, furniture designs. Following travels in Rome and Africa, Olbrich worked alongside Josef Hoffman in Otto Wagner's workshop. Together with Koloman Moser and others, Olbrich and Hoffman broke from the conservative Künstlerhaus in 1897 to form the Vienna Secession, for which Olbrich designed the premises. By 1899, Olbrich had moved to the Artists' Colony at Darmstadt, designing a room in restrained taste for the Darmstadt exhibit at the 1900 Paris Universal Exposition. Clear-cut forms rather than ornamentation define his furniture.

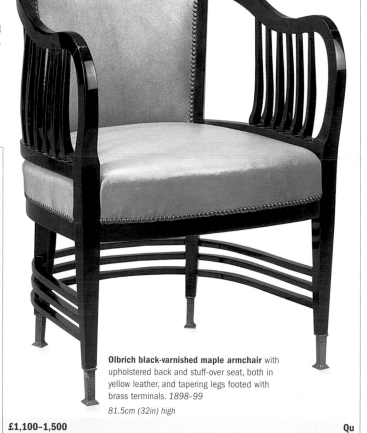

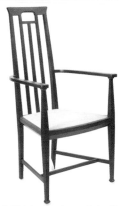

Olbrich high-back oak armchair with vertical back slats, curved arms, turned and tapering legs with turned stretchers, and an upholstered drop-in seat pad.

108cm (42½in) high

£1,000–1,500   **WW**

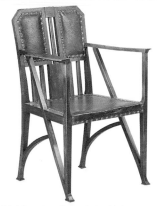

Olbrich nutwood armchair with brown-leather seat, diagonal and arched supports to the arms and legs, and vertical back slats augmented with two leather pads. *c.1900*

95.5cm (37¼in) high

£1,800–2,500   **DOR**

Olbrich black-varnished maple armchair with upholstered back and stuff-over seat, both in yellow leather, and tapering legs footed with brass terminals. *1898–99*

81.5cm (32in) high

£1,100–1,500   **Qu**

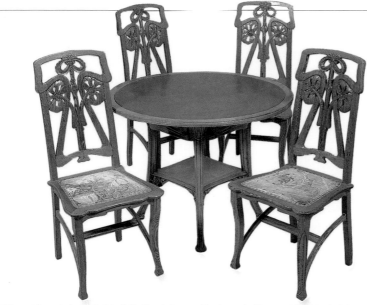

Table and four chairs by Portois & Fix. The chairs are of larch wood with carved floral back slats and have upholstered seats; the table is nutwood with a leather skiver and floral carving to the legs. *1900–05*

Table: 106.5cm (42in) high

£2,500–3,000 DOR

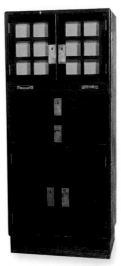

Cupboard by Adolf Loos, in black-painted and varnished softwood with twin two-over-three glazed doors and brass hardware. *c.1908*

142.5cm (56in) high

£20,000–25,000 WKA

Austrian display cupboard in mahogany-veneered softwood, with a glazed and a panelled door and nickel and silver hardware. *c.1900*

164cm (68½in) high

£1,800–2,200 DOR

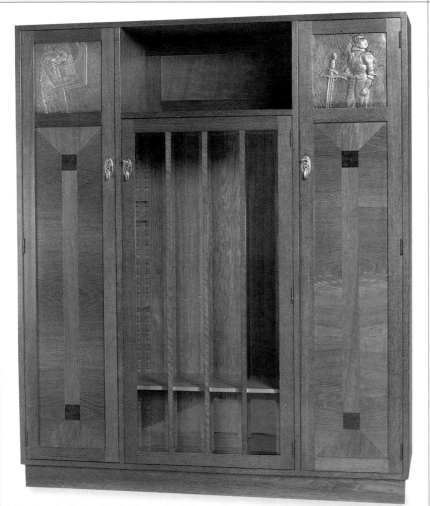

Oak and maple display cabinet with geometrically banded flat panels, bevelled glass central doors, and brass panels embossed with a harpist and a knight. Influenced by Gustav Klimt's "Beethoven Frieze" and probably worked on by his brother Georg. *1905–10*

183cm (72in) high

£6,000–8,000 Qu

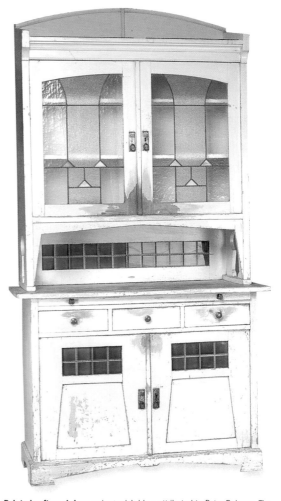

Painted softwood dresser in greyish-blue, attributed to Peter Behrens. The leaded glass doors of the top cupboard have pale blue triangular highlights. The base doors and splashback have dark blue ceramic tiles. *c.1902*

231cm (91in) high

£2,000–2,500 Qu

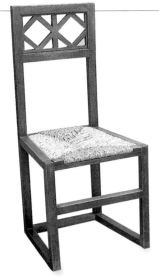

Austrian oak chair by Hans Ofner, with a drop-in rushwork seat and a high back with trellis-like supports under the top rail. Unsigned. *1904*

106cm (41¾in) high

£800-1,000　　　　　　　　　　**HERR**

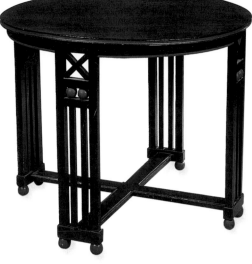

Austrian Secessionist ebonized table with a round top. The four slatted supports have spherical spacers and X-panels and are joined by moulded cross-stretchers on spherical feet.

92cm (36¼in) wide

£300-500　　　　　　　　　　**L&T**

Austrian Secessionist card table with a circular top that has radiating walnut veneers above four pull-out wells with brass-capped attendant supports, on a hammered, brass-domed base.

74cm (29in) high

£1,500-2,000　　　　　　　　　　**L&T**

J. & J. Kohn

The firm established in Vienna by Jacob and Josef Kohn was renowned in the late 19th century for the production of good-quality but simple, modest furniture aimed at a middle-class clientele. Kohn's output included furniture that reflected the widely celebrated artistic tradition of the early 19th-century Biedermeier period, but the company also specialized in the creation of bentwood furniture, made popular by Thonet. Kohn's reputation was considerably enhanced by its successful collaboration with Wiener Werkstätte artist Josef Hoffmann, manufacturing a number of his designs, including the bentwood dining chair of laminated beechwood for Vienna's fashionable Purkersdorf Sanatorium, and an adjustable armchair and chairs for the bar of the Cabaret Fledermaus in Vienna.

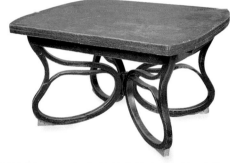

J. & J. Kohn rare extending table in black-stained beech. The rectangular top has rounded ends and is set on sinuously curved and fluted supports of stylized organic form with brass feet. *1901*

133.5cm (52½in) wide

£8,000-10,000　　　　　　　　　　**DOR**

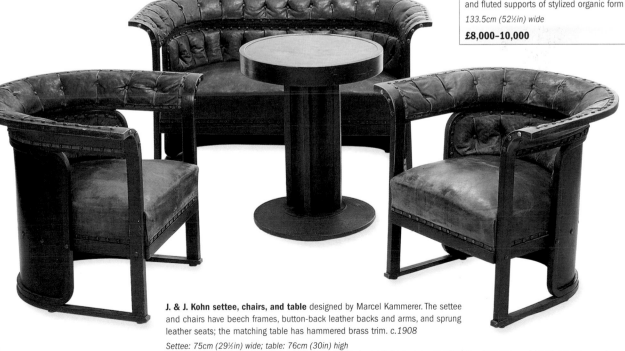

J. & J. Kohn settee, chairs, and table designed by Marcel Kammerer. The settee and chairs have beech frames, button-back leather backs and arms, and sprung leather seats; the matching table has hammered brass trim. *c.1908*

Settee: 75cm (29½in) wide; table: 76cm (30in) high

£8,000-10,000　　　　　　　　　　**WKA**

Straight lines are combined with gentle curves.

Geometric shapes – rectangles and squares – form Mackintosh's important decorative elements.

Chairs typically have high, attenuated backs; tables feature spindly supports; and cupboards have broad projecting cornices.

Wood may be coloured in dark, masculine tones – grey and olive – but is frequently painted white or in pale, pastel shades.

Charles Rennie Mackintosh

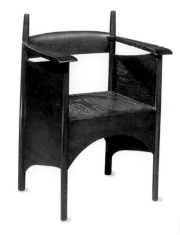

A leading figure of the international Art Nouveau movement, Charles Rennie Mackintosh was hailed as one of the most talented architects and designers of furniture, textiles, and interiors of his generation.

Born and educated in Glasgow, Charles Rennie Mackintosh (1868–1928) practised architecture from 1889 for the prestigious firm of John Honeyman and Keppie, rising to partner in 1901. Demonstrating an interest in both Scottish and Gothic architecture, he rejected the widely-held affection for the classical tradition. His early success as a student earned him a number of prizes, including the prestigious Alexander Thomson Travelling Scholarship, which took him to France, Belgium, and Italy.

THE GLASGOW FOUR

Influenced by the widely acclaimed and groundbreaking journal *The Studio*, which celebrated the work of the most advanced artists and designers, Mackintosh developed a decorative, abstract, rectilinear Art Nouveau style. Encouraged by the director of the renowned Glasgow School of Art Francis H. Newbery, and his wife Jessie, Mackintosh and his fellow artist J.H. MacNair teamed up with Margaret and Frances Macdonald, to form an alliance known as "The Four". Together they developed a common style for decorative designs that included furniture, posters, and metalwork.

ARCHITECT AND DESIGNER

Among his most notable architectural achievements was the design and furnishing of a new building for the Glasgow School of Art in 1897, a number

Above: Charles Rennie Mackintosh dark stained oak armchair, for the Argyle Street Tearooms, Glasgow, with spreading arm supports and filled inside panels and apron, raised on circular supports. **£5,000-10,000 CHR**

GLASGOW AND VIENNA

Whilst in most parts of Britain furniture making was dominated by the Arts and Crafts style, a new design movement flourished in Glasgow. Mackintosh developed designs that were striking for their bold, straight lines and minimal decoration. When Mackintosh exhibited his furniture at the 8th Secessionist Exhibition in 1900 in Vienna, he left a lasting impression on his contemporary Austrian furniture designers, most notably Koloman Moser and Josef Hoffmann. Inspired by Mackintosh's strong, rectilinear forms and highly stylized motifs, the Secessionists developed their own furniture designs that clearly incorporated these bold influences (*see pp.36–37*).

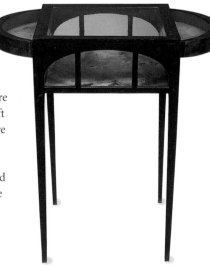

Bijouterie table cabinet by James Herbert MacNair. In stained beech with a glazed, hinged top, and sliding demi-lune display boxes. *c.1901* 77cm (30½in) high **£8,000-10,000 L&T**

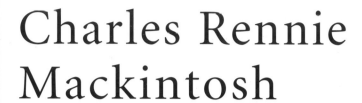

Charles Rennie Mackintosh stained oak, high-backed dining chair, for the Argyle Street Tearooms in Glasgow, with pierced oval top, two broad back splats flanked by tapering uprights, and drop-in seat on tapering supports. *136.5cm (53¾in) high* **NPA V&A**

MISS CRANSTON'S TEAROOMS

The success achieved by Charles Rennie Mackintosh in a number of decorative areas was second only to his pioneering schemes for buildings with interiors that were beautifully integrated into a single cohesive theme. One of the finest examples of this architectural *chefs d'oeuvre* was the chain of tearooms he created in Glasgow between 1896 and 1917 for Miss Kate Cranston. In addition to his rectilinear designs for chairs produced for the Argyle Street Tearooms, Mackintosh made his mark with his unified decorative schemes for tearooms in Ingram Street and at The Willow in Sauchiehall Street. Here, architecture and interior design worked together to create a serene atmosphere that saw furniture restrained in both form and decoration, and which exhibited his signature "light-feminine" and "dark-masculine" colour schemes.

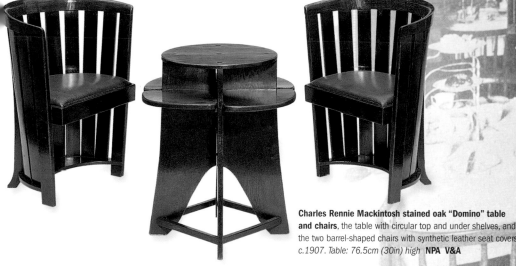

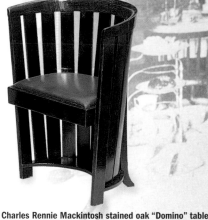

Charles Rennie Mackintosh stained oak "Domino" table and chairs, the table with circular top and under shelves, and the two barrel-shaped chairs with synthetic leather seat covers. *c.1907. Table: 76.5cm (30in) high* **NPA V&A**

of tearooms in Glasgow for Miss Kate Cranston in collaboration with the decorator George Walton, and several private houses for which he created integrated furniture and interiors.

Mackintosh designed furniture for his own use, and provided designs for the Glasgow furniture-makers Guthrie and Wells. For Miss Cranston's tearoom in Argyle Street he provided the furniture, which included the first examples of his signature high-backed chairs – in this instance boasting a distinctive oval top rail (*see left*).

A LASTING INFLUENCE

Mackintosh cared little for the details associated with fine craftsmanship or for the natural beauty of wood that so preoccupied the Arts and Crafts designers, preferring instead sparsely-decorated woodwork painted in pale colours. Prominent straight lines combined with gentle curves characterize his sophisticated furniture designs: chairs boast tall, attenuated backs; cupboards are mounted with wide projecting cornices; and tables have long and slender supports. Mackintosh's

choice of style was decidedly at odds with the sensual spirit of the French Art Nouveau and the robust masculinity of Arts and Crafts furniture.

Although Mackintosh's later rectilinear style found little favour in England or in his native Scotland, it was widely admired in continental Europe, and had enormous influence, especially on artists in Germany and Austria, such as Josef Hoffmann (*see opposite*). The refinement and imagination of his schemes for the Scottish section of the Vienna Secession Exhibition of 1900 confirmed his place in the pantheon of pioneering, highly influential designers working in the "New Art", and he remains celebrated today as a harbinger of the Modern Movement.

Oak side chair (one of a pair). It has a serpentine-profile top rail with cut-out handle, drop-in upholstered seat, arched seat rails, and square, tapering legs with double-spindle stretchers. *1897 99.5cm (38¾in) high* **£7,000–12,000 (the pair) L&T**

THE GLASGOW SCHOOL

Charles Rennie Mackintosh and his contemporaries paved the way for a movement in Scotland that paralleled the contemporary French Art Nouveau style. Among the innovative pioneers that gave voice to the Glasgow School were the Macdonald sisters, Frances and Margaret, who worked with textiles, embroidery, metalwork, watercolour, and stained glass. Another innovator was the architect and designer J. Herbert MacNair, who created quiet schemes for furniture and interiors. Also included in this group was the gifted and versatile Ernest Archibald Taylor, renowned for muted, elegant, and highly polished designs in the Mackintosh style; George Walton with his delicate and refined confections for textiles, furniture, and glass; and the accomplished designer of stained glass, metalwork, and furniture, Talwin Morris.

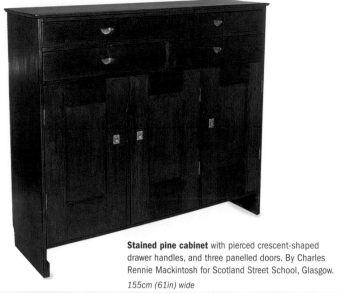

Stained pine cabinet with pierced crescent-shaped drawer handles, and three panelled doors. By Charles Rennie Mackintosh for Scotland Street School, Glasgow.

155cm (61in) wide

£4,000–6,000　　　　L&T

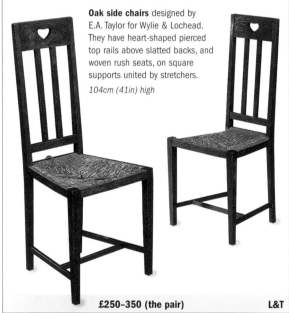

White painted oak table with two stacked drawers, a waved apron, and stretchered, supports. By Charles Rennie Mackintosh for Windyhill house, Kilmalcolm. *1901*

77cm (30in) high

£10,000–15,000　　　　L&T

Oak side chairs designed by E.A. Taylor for Wylie & Lochead. They have heart-shaped pierced top rails above slatted backs, and woven rush seats, on square supports united by stretchers.

104cm (41in) high

£250–350 (the pair)　　　　L&T

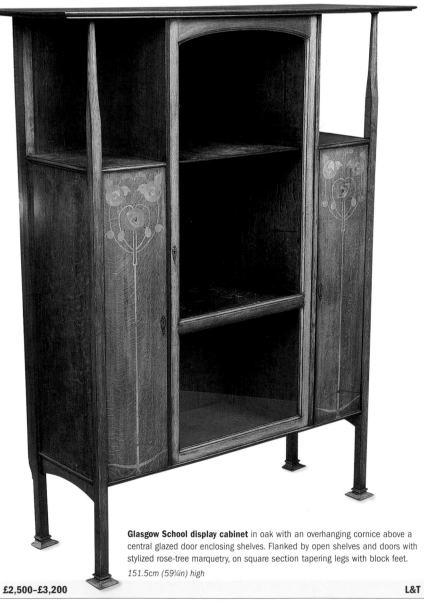

Glasgow School display cabinet in oak with an overhanging cornice above a central glazed door enclosing shelves. Flanked by open shelves and doors with stylized rose-tree marquetry, on square section tapering legs with block feet.

151.5cm (59¾in) high

£2,500–£3,200　　　　L&T

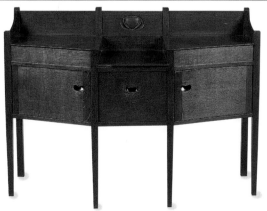

Oak sideboard by George Walton & Co. Ltd. The ledge back has an oval panel of stained and leaded glass with a brass heart centre. The canted top is above a central frieze drawer flanked by cupboards. *c.1900*

135cm (53in) wide

£2,500–3,500　　　　L&T

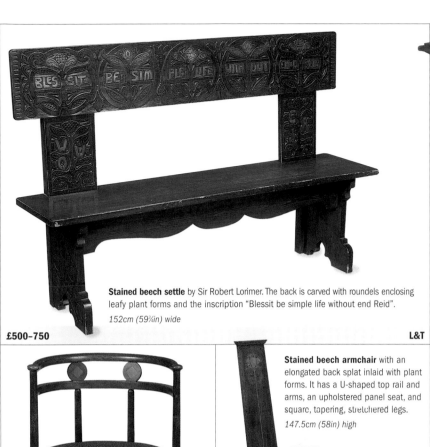

Stained beech settle by Sir Robert Lorimer. The back is carved with roundels enclosing leafy plant forms and the inscription "Blessit be simple life without end Reid".

152cm (59¾in) wide

£500–750   L&T

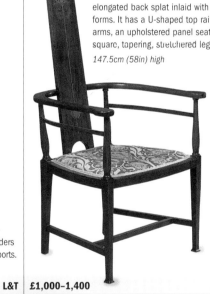

Stained beech armchair with an elongated back splat inlaid with plant forms. It has a U-shaped top rail and arms, an upholstered panel seat, and square, tapering, stretchered legs.

147.5cm (58in) high

Stained beech armchair by Wylie & Lochead. The double-curved top rail has lozenge-inlaid disc dividers and turned spindles; the seat is on stretchered supports.

94cm (37in) high

£300–500   L&T   £1,000–1,400   L&T

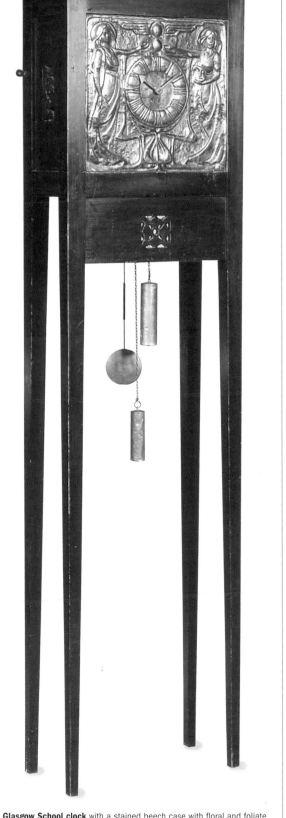

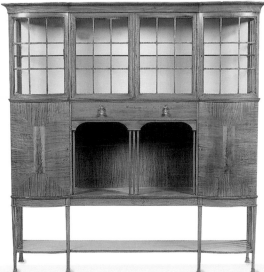

Satinwood display cabinet in George Walton style. It has a projecting cornice above twin-glazed doors, with applied astragals, bowed, glazed, and panelled doors, an open shelf with drawer above, and square, tapering supports.

168cm (66¼in) wide

£3,000–4,000   L&T

Glasgow School clock with a stained beech case with floral and foliate piercings. Its brass dial, by Margaret Thomson Wilson, has two female figures touching a stylized hour glass. *c.1900*

206cm (80½in) high

£7,000–9,000   L&T

KEY FEATURES

Oak was the usual choice for C.F.A. Voysey furniture, and it was admired for its visual beauty.

Chairs frequently boast rush seats with vertical, tapering supports.

Favourite decorative motifs include cut-out vertical panels and minimal, pierced heart-shaped patterns.

Large, metal strap hinges with Art Nouveau motifs tend to feature on simple, abstract-shaped cabinets.

C.F.A. Voysey

A disciple of William Morris and A.H. Mackmurdo, Charles Francis Annesley Voysey (1857–1941) was one of Britain's most innovative furniture designers during the Art Nouveau period.

Although many of the recognizable features of Arts and Crafts style can be directly attributed to Voysey, this talented English architect and designer was to develop an engaging and highly personal approach in his designs for furniture, textiles, and metalwork that typically boasted much greater lightness and elegant simplicity. Far from the sophisticated urban creations produced by the Glasgow School (*see pp.46–47*) Voysey's graceful, abstract, stylized furniture relied heavily on the beauty and visual qualities of the wood. Finely crafted cabinets of pale oak with elaborate metal strap hinges, and rush-seated chairs with tapering, vertical uprights and heart-shaped decorative cut-outs in their high backs have an appealing, rustic-farmhouse quality that matches the style of his architecture.

Voysey used decoration sparingly, but occasionally added an elaborate touch with metal mounts or appliqués. These motifs are often of flowing, organic design, which is clearly influenced by the naturalistic French Art Nouveau style.

Above: Oak dining chair with a broad back splat pierced with a heart motif, tapering arm rests, drop-in leather seat, and tapering supports. *c.1902.* 100cm (39½in) high **£5,000–10,000 BRI**

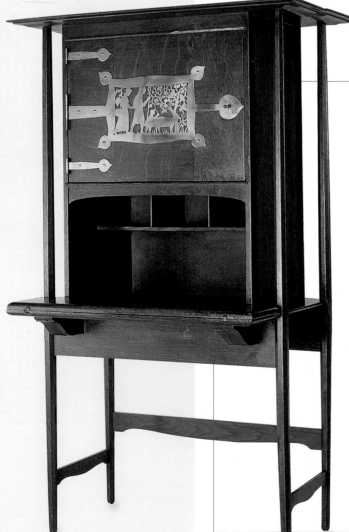

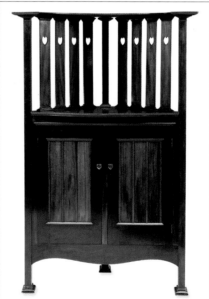

Mahogany corner cabinet with vertical slats pierced with heart motifs. On three block-ended supports, the twin doors enclose shelving. *1898*

175cm (69in) high

£100,000+   **CHR**

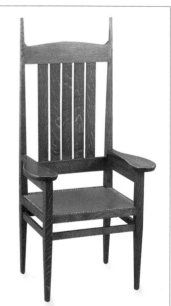

Rare oak hall chair with vertical back slats, paddle arms, tapering legs, and leather seat (replaced). With a dark finish. *1895*

139.7cm (55in) high

£9,000–11,000   **CR**

Important oak writing desk on hexagonal section supports that extend to form feet. The door to the upper section has elaborate copper hinges and a panel pierced with figures in a rural setting, above an open recess with pigeon holes and an extending work surface.

167.6cm (66in) high

NPA   **V&A**

Liberty & Co.

Less expensive but no less innovative than the exclusive furniture created by the Arts and Crafts and Art Nouveau designers was that produced by commercial companies such as Liberty & Company on London's Regent Street.

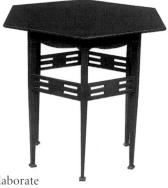

By 1883, Liberty & Co. – already celebrated for its Art Nouveau fabrics and a broad selection of imported wares from India, Japan, and the Middle East – had established a Furnishing and Decoration Studio that offered a wide variety of styles, including a line of Art Nouveau furniture known as "Quaint".

Liberty championed the work of the most progressive designers of British "New Art" furniture, such as Charles Rennie Mackintosh and C.F.A. Voysey, and produced commercial imitations in this highly popular style. High-backed chairs with cut-out patterns and simply constructed cabinets boasting painted- or stained-glass panels and elaborate hinges of beaten copper were created in an effort to respond to the demand for fashionable but affordable furniture. The designs commissioned for oak chairs, tables, and cupboards by E.G. Punnett and Leonard F. Wyburd are among the most widely recognized items of Liberty furniture.

Above: Hexagonal occasional table with the moulded top raised above square tapering legs that are linked by pierced stretchers and have pad feet. *73cm (28¾in) high* **£550–650 L&T**

KEY FEATURES

Oak and mahogany was the favoured timber for commercially produced furniture by Liberty's.

Simple construction, symmetrical design, and the restrained application of decorative motifs are among the most typical features of Liberty furniture.

Decorative features include pierced or cut-out patterns, painted or stained-glass panels, and elaborate hinges in hand-beaten copper.

Commonly marked "Liberty & Co." on rectangular ivorine plaques.

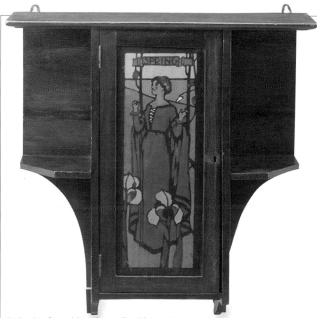

Stained softwood hanging wall cabinet with extended top and side shelving. The door is stencilled with a polychrome panel entitled "Spring" featuring a pre-Raphaelite maiden with irises. It is refinished, and has an ivorine Liberty retail tag.

58.5cm (23in) high

£1,200–1,800   **CR**

Walnut armchair designed by G. Walton and made by William Birch of High Wycombe. The top rail has inlaid panels of abalone shell, with slender curved vertical splats, curved arms, and further slats to the sides. A drop-in upholstered seat is on tapering supports united by stretchers. *c.1899*

NPA   **V&A**

British Furniture

A decline in the quality of 19th-century British furniture led craftsmen to seek new ways to reform styles and methods of manufacture. Designers such as William Morris and Arthur Mackmurdo produced simple oak furniture alongside more elaborate pieces in mahogany, satinwood, or walnut. Furniture designed by architect Ernest Gimson – with inlays of ivory, silver, abalone shell, or fruitwoods – illustrates the dichotomy between luxury and simplicity. Notable among the innovators are C.F.A. Voysey, Charles Robert Ashbee, and Charles Rennie Mackintosh. The firm of Shapland & Petter also took up the mantel and produced quality furniture, often with fine inlays.

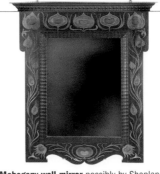

Mahogany wall mirror possibly by Shapland & Petter. The shaped outline is decorated in marquetry with stylized blooms and foliage resembling peacock feathers. *c.1900*

87cm (34¼in) high

£850–1,000   **VZ**

Mahogany and stained-glass firescreen by Shapland & Petter in the style of the Glasgow School. With embossed copper plaques and a glass panel.

99cm (39in) high

£900–1,100   **DN**

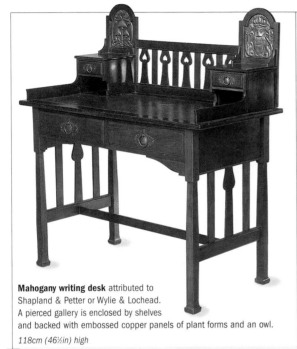

Mahogany writing desk attributed to Shapland & Petter or Wylie & Lochead. A pierced gallery is enclosed by shelves and backed with embossed copper panels of plant forms and an owl.

118cm (46½in) high

£1,700–1,900   **L&T**

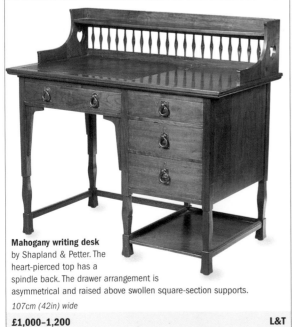

Mahogany writing desk by Shapland & Petter. The heart-pierced top has a spindle back. The drawer arrangement is asymmetrical and raised above swollen square-section supports.

107cm (42in) wide

£1,000–1,200   **L&T**

CORNERSTONE PIECE

Mahogany and marquetry display cabinet by Shapland & Petter. The central glazed section has a decorative cornice above an openwork plated-metal panel of stylized snowdrops and is flanked by open shelves and cupboards. The doors and frieze drawer are inlaid with stylized lilies and butterflies in fruitwoods and mother-of-pearl and have sinuous plated-metal door furniture. *c.1900. 197.5cm (77¾in) high* **£5,000–6,000 VZ**

This high-quality wood and mother-of-pearl marquetry is typical of Shapland & Petter Art Nouveau furniture

The workmanship and design of this panel and other metal details support and complement the marquetry decoration

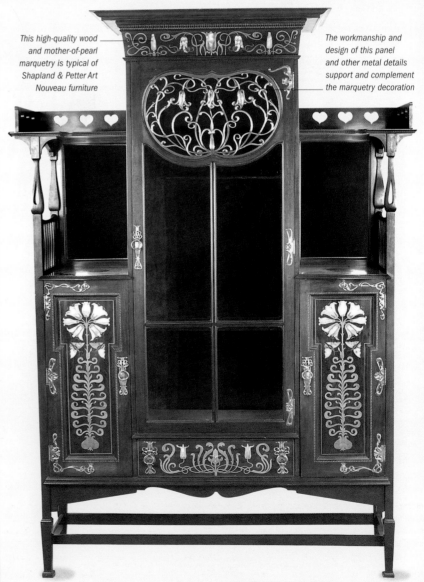

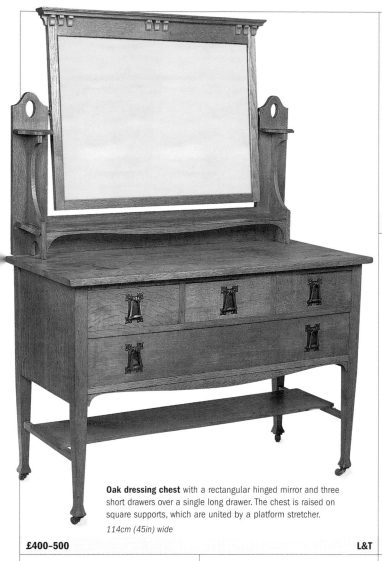

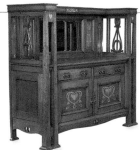

Oak and marquetry mirrored sideboard. The back panels are inlaid with stylized plants; the sides are carved and pierced with stylized tulips. The base has two inlaid panel doors.

169cm (66½in) high

£700–1,000   **L&T**

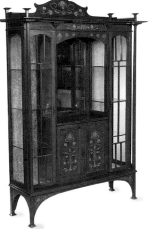

Mahogany and marquetry display cabinet, inlaid with copper, pewter, and wood with stylized flowers and tendrils. The square legs have decorative supports.

207cm (81½in) high

£2,000–2,500   **L&T**

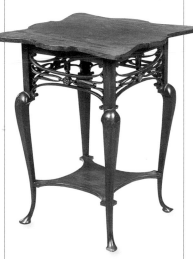

Oak dressing chest with a rectangular hinged mirror and three short drawers over a single long drawer. The chest is raised on square supports, which are united by a platform stretcher.

114cm (45in) wide

£400–500   **L&T**

Mahogany jardinière stand with a square top on canted square tapering supports, which are united by two further tiers and decorative bracket supports.

120cm (47¼in) high

£120–180   **L&T**

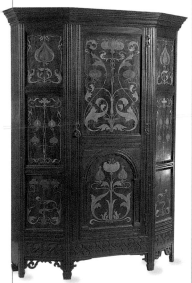

Mahogany and inlaid cupboard possibly by J.S. Henry. The panelled door is inlaid with stylized plant forms and flanked by similarly inlaid panels. Moulded cornice at the top.

210cm (82¾in) high

£1,200–1,800   **L&T**

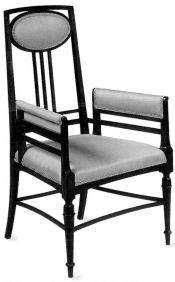

Mahogany single armchair by G.M. Ellwood. The back has a tapering rectangular outline with an oval upholstered panel, and the turned legs have tassel-carved feet.

94cm (37in) high

£600–800   **L&T**

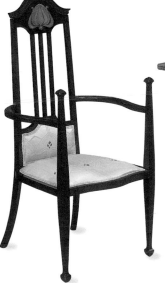

Mahogany armchair attributed to G.M. Ellwood for J.S. Henry. The arched back is inlaid with a stylized flower-head above open slats and the seat is raised on square supports.

102cm (40in) high

£600–800   **L&T**

Mahogany occasional table by J.S. Henry. The shaped top sits above an elaborate fretwork frieze on cabriole legs, which are united by an under tier. Bears the maker's label.

72cm (28¼in) high

£600–800   **L&T**

Gustav Stickley

Gustav Stickley was the father of the American Arts and Crafts Movement. The eldest of five Stickley brothers who all became influential furniture designers, Gustav was the forerunner of the American "New Art" in furniture design.

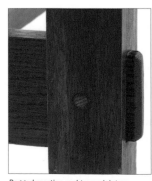

Born in Wisconsin, Gustav Stickley (1858–1942) was a furniture builder by trade. He worked at first for his uncle in Pennsylvania and later with his brothers, Charles and Albert, making and selling furniture in New York. Gustav travelled to Europe in 1898 where he was influenced by the Art Nouveau furniture designs he saw. Upon his return to the United States, he embarked on a new line of household furniture, which eschewed the turned legs and heavy ornament that had been so popular during the Victorian era. He successfully exhibited his work at a 1900 furniture trade show in Grand Rapids, Michigan, and produced his first illustrated catalogue, showing clear influences from English designs.

After a period of association with furniture makers Tobey Furniture Company, Stickley decided to maintain control over the production of his own designs. He established his own "Craftsman" showroom in Syracuse, New York, where he began to design and sell his new range of furniture.

CRAFTSMAN PRINCIPLES

The workshop championed handcrafted work based on honest materials and solid construction, principles he set out in his *Craftsman* magazine from 1901 (*see opposite*). Stickley adopted the Dutch motto, *Als ik kan* (As best I can), which had also been used by English Arts and Crafts designer William Morris, and chose a joiner's compass as his trademark.

By 1902, Stickley hit his stride and began producing furniture that would set the standard for all Period American designers. Typified by

Above: Drop-leaf sewing stand by Harvey Ellis. Its maple-veneered softwood has inlaid copper and fruitwood Jugendstil-style motifs to the leaves and drawers, and circular wooden pulls. *c.1902–10* *45.5cm (18in) wide* **£4,500–5,000 CR**

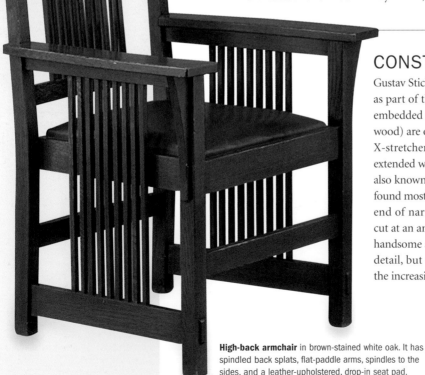

High-back armchair in brown-stained white oak. It has spindled back splats, flat-paddle arms, spindles to the sides, and a leather-upholstered, drop-in seat pad. *115cm (48in) high* **£2,500–3,300 CR**

CONSTRUCTION TECHNIQUES

Gustav Stickley and other Period makers used elements of construction as part of the design. The most common device is a "pin", or a flush, embedded dowel holding a joint together. Corbels (arched pieces of wood) are often found beneath a flat arm and the top of a leg upright. X-stretchers are usually notched into each other unevenly, with an extended wooden dowel, locking the "X" into place. Chamfered boards, also known as "V" boards, were used on some early pieces. These are found mostly on the backs, where each end of narrow vertical boards was cut at an angle, forming a "V". It is a handsome and elegant construction detail, but was soon phased out by the increasing cost of labour.

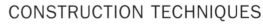

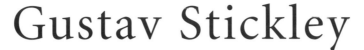

Pegged mortise-and-tenon joint on a Stickley oak side table.

COMPLETE HOME DESIGN

Gustav Stickley designed homes to complement his furniture, and his interiors are marked by the use of natural materials, and the harmony between all elements of the room. Colours are usually earthy, with tones of brown, ochre, and green, and wood and brick is revealed on the floor and walls rather than covered with carpet or paper.

Natural light was very important to Stickley, and he designed rooms with an abundance of windows to allow the sunlight to pour in and become part of the environment. Stickley's best interiors integrate all aspects of the decorative arts, including furniture, ceramics, textiles, woodblock prints, and wrought-iron metalware. The overriding principle was that the design should be practical, as Stickley himself wrote in his *Craftsman* magazine: "We have planned houses from the first that are based on the big fundamental principles of honesty, simplicity, and usefulness."

Lounge room, designed by Gustav Stickley, where a pleasing ambience is achieved by the harmonization of various elements including furniture, textiles, lamps, and art pottery.

thick pieces of heavy, quartered oak, his furniture was constructed by hand, and covered with fumed dark finishes that were imparted through a chemical reaction with the wood rather than by a stain applied to the wood.

A LIGHTER TOUCH

In 1903, Gustav recruited designer Harvey Ellis. They worked together for only seven months until Ellis's untimely death, but Ellis became an important influence on Gustav's work. Ellis had a lighter approach to his designs and his subtle touches can be seen in Gustav's later work.

Stickley's mature period started around 1905, and he changed his production standards to include smaller pieces of oak, which were covered with lighter brown finishes. What these pieces lacked in scale they compensated for with a cleaner, more consistent vision of Period oak. These modifications allowed for a more affordable product, and one that was more available to the middle classes who, according to Stickley's principles, were supposed to benefit from his efforts.

His last period of any consequence was from about 1910 until 1916, when he was forced to close his factory. These pieces bear lighter finishes and the mass and scale of such furnishings are comparatively light. It is the greatest irony that the interest he sparked in the "New Art" resulted in

no fewer than 50 furniture companies nationwide competing for market share. This competition, combined with the changing tastes of the American public, pushed Stickley into bankruptcy.

Mahogany tabouret table with a pentagonal top. On pierced and flared legs of stylized organic form, united by a star-shaped stretcher. *51cm (20in) high* **£1,800–3,000 CR**

PRINCIPLES

Considered the father of the American Arts and Crafts, Stickley's magazine, which was published from 1901 to 1916, became the voice of the movement. The Craftsman bought Stickley's principles of honesty, simplicity, and hand-craftsmanship to a wide readership across the United States.

THE CRAFTSMAN MAGAZINE

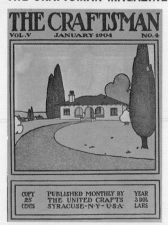

The Craftsman – which also included articles by painters, poets, and authors – contained blueprints on how to make your own furniture. Gustav Stickley's ideal was to encourage people to become craftsmen and to "make their own", so as to enjoy the fruits of having created unique pieces for themselves. While this potentially cost Stickley sales of his own furniture, it cemented his place as the leader in his field – both as an expert furniture maker and as the leading proponent of Arts and Crafts in the United States.

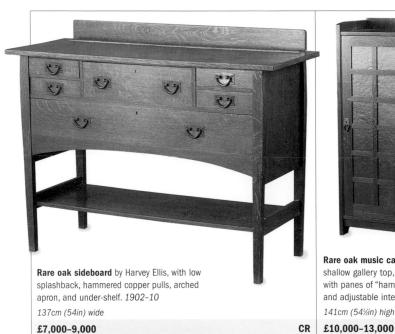

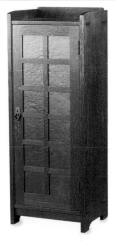

Rare oak sideboard by Harvey Ellis, with low splashback, hammered copper pulls, arched apron, and under-shelf. *1902–10*

137cm (54in) wide

£7,000–9,000 CR

Rare oak music cabinet with a shallow gallery top, a single door with panes of "hammered" glass, and adjustable interior shelves.

141cm (54½in) high

£10,000–13,000 CR

Rare cheval mirror with oak-framed mirror glass on wishbone legs, arched stretcher under-shelf, and iron hardware.

175.25cm (69in) high

£14,000–18,000 CR

Oak armchair with horizontal back splat and inverted-"V" cresting rail. With stretchered, flaring legs, and a leather-upholstered seat. *c.1900*

95.25cm (37½in) high

£12,000–18,000 CR

Fine cube chair in brown-stained white oak, with slatted back and sides, chamfered legs, and a leather back-squab and upholstered seat pad.

72.5cm (29in) wide

£5,500–6,500 CR

Rare blanket chest in a rich brown-stained white oak. It has square and rectangular panelled hinged top and sides, set on square post feet, and with rectangular and arched wrought-iron straps and hinges. Maker's mark stamped in red. *1902–03*

88.25cm (34¾in) wide

£20,000–25,000 CR

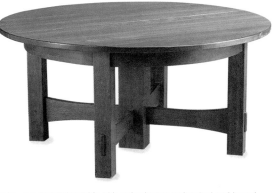

Split-pedestal dining table with a circular top and arched and bowed stretchers tenoned through square post legs (has eight additional leaves).

152.5cm (60in) wide

£8,000–12,000 CR

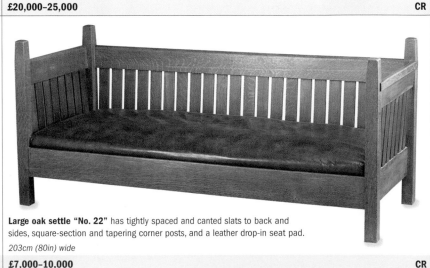

Large oak settle "No. 22" has tightly spaced and canted slats to back and sides, square-section and tapering corner posts, and a leather drop-in seat pad.

203cm (80in) wide

£7,000–10,000 CR

L. & J.G. Stickley

Leopold (1869–1957) and John George (1871–1921) Stickley were two of Gustav's younger brothers and were both astute businessmen. Leopold had initially worked with Gustav, but branched out on his own in 1904 under the name Onondaga Shops. Meanwhile John George had been working for brother Albert in Michigan *(see box below)*. In 1904, Leopold and John George united to establish L. & J.G. Stickley in Fayetteville, New York (renamed Handcraft in 1906 and later, from 1912, called The Work of L. & J.G. Stickley). In contrast to Gustav's handcrafted techniques, the brothers favoured highly efficient, mechanical production methods. Their style, however, did reflect the influence of their older brother in their simple, Arts and Crafts-inspired designs.

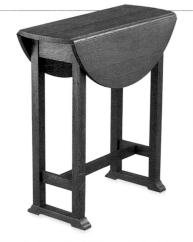

Drop-leaf occasional table in stained oak. Its top is circular when raised, set on square-section legs with concave-profile stretchers and moulded feet.
71cm (28in) wide
£500–650   **CR**

Mahogany Onondaga Shop armchair with scooped cresting rail above vertical back slats, flat-paddle arms, arched apron, and chamfered legs.
88.5cm (34¾in) high
£700–900   **CR**

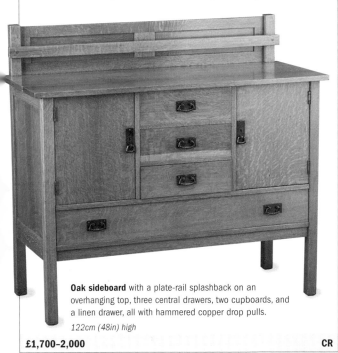

Oak sideboard with a plate-rail splashback on an overhanging top, three central drawers, two cupboards, and a linen drawer, all with hammered copper drop pulls.
122cm (48in) high
£1,700–2,000   **CR**

Mahogany hall bench with columnar vertical slats, a hinged seat compartment, square-section corner posts, and with arched corbels under the rectangular apron.
106.5cm (42in) wide
£4,500–£5,500   **CR**

The Stickley Brothers

The Stickley Brothers company name was adopted by John George and younger brother Albert (1862–1928) in Grand Rapids, Michigan, in 1891. It referred to the name Albert and Charles had used when they worked with Gustav in New York.

John George left the firm to work with Leopold *(see above)*, but Albert continued the business under the family name. He often worked in a different vein to his brothers, incorporating more decorative elements into his furniture. He called his style "Quaint" and pieces are marked with this logo. Albert had a strong affinity with the designs of England and Scotland and had his own showroom in London until 1902.

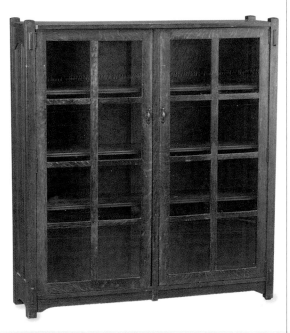

"Quaint" oak bookcase with panelled sides through-tenoned to square-section corner posts, and with a pair of "two-over-eight" faux-mullion glazed doors enclosing a shelved interior.
122cm (48in) wide
£2,000–3,000   **CR**

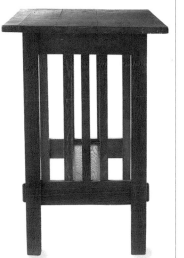

"Quaint" oak side table with a quarter-sawn, five-plank square top on vertical slatted sides and square-section legs, with side rails and a rectangular under-shelf.
67cm (26in) high
£3,000–3,500   **CALD**

KEY FEATURES

Darker finished woods were often utilized in Limbert furniture.

An authenticating brand mark is generally found on Limbert pieces.

Cut-out decorative designs of squares and hearts are characteristics to look out for.

Dutch furniture-design influences can be seen in Limbert's work. Many of the workers in his Michigan factory were Dutch settlers.

Limbert

One of the most popular producers of American "New Art" furniture was Charles P. Limbert's Limbert Furniture Company, which produced well-crafted pieces that were influenced by the rectilinear Scottish Art Nouveau style.

While the furniture produced by Limbert was not as well crafted as that produced in Gustav Stickley's factory in Eastwood, New York, his company offered a broad range of good-quality Mission oak pieces. As with Stickley, Limbert's earliest production, from around 1902 to 1907, is the most interesting and desirable to collectors, even though it was often extremely derivative of European precedents. These pieces are typified by cut-out squares, clearly influenced by the Glasgow School designers (*see pp.44–47*). Such pieces include lamp tables, desks, Morris chairs, and even coatstands.

During this early period, Limbert tended to use darker finishes, much in the fashion of Stickley's fumed oak. Most Limbert production is found in medium- to medium-dark brown colours. As is often the rule with Mission oak, darker is usually better. Rarities include early pieces decorated with stylized inlays of metal and fruitwood.

The Limbert Furniture Company's middle period, from around 1908 to 1915, is marked by the production of solid pieces of furniture of average weight, usually with an excellent tiger-grained oak. Again, while lacking the mass of similar examples by other makers such as Stickley, these pieces possess an attractive balance of line and scale.

Later pieces of Limbert furniture – those made around and after World War I – are often spindly in form, offering only a watered-down interpretation of the bulk that marked the best work of the Art Nouveau period. Since Limbert pieces were nearly always marked with a large rectangular brand, they retain the company designation even after refinishing.

Above: Oak magazine stand with five graduated shelves secured to flaring sides with mortise-and-tenon joints. Each of the sides has two trapezium-shaped cut-outs. With maker's mark. *c.1910* *101.5cm (40in) high* **£2,500–3,000 CR**

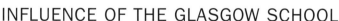

INFLUENCE OF THE GLASGOW SCHOOL

European influences had a strong impact on Limbert's designs, and he was particularly interested in the work of the Glasgow School and Charles Rennie Mackintosh in Scotland. Mackintosh's work was widely publicized in journals at the time and was displayed at many of the key exhibitions showcasing the new style. Limbert made use of square cut-outs in some of his designs – a particularly strong sign of the Mackintosh style. Influences of the rectilinear lines of the Secessionist designs coming out of Austria and Germany are also echoed in Limbert's furniture.

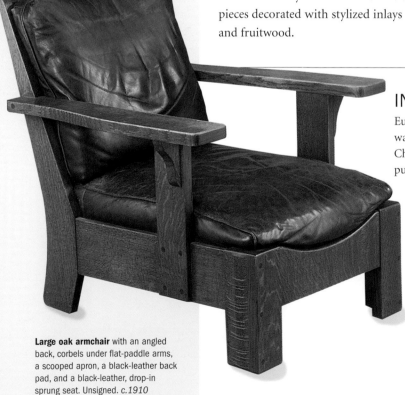

Large oak armchair with an angled back, corbels under flat-paddle arms, a scooped apron, a black-leather back pad, and a black-leather, drop-in sprung seat. Unsigned. *c.1910* *84cm (33in) high* **£3,300–3,700 CR**

Oak-frame armchair with two vertical back slats, flat-paddle arms, four leg stretchers, and a brown leather-covered seat cushion. With maker's mark. *c.1910* *106.5cm (42in) high* **£750–1,100 CR**

CORNERSTONE PIECE

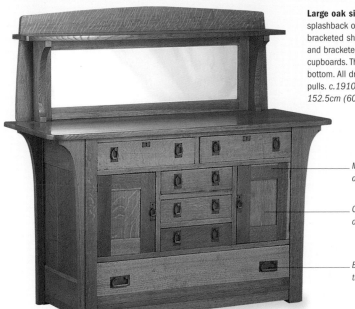

Large oak sideboard with a mirrored splashback on the upper section, set beneath a bracketed shelf. The base has an overhanging and bracketed top above a set of drawers and cupboards. There is a large linen drawer at the bottom. All drawers and doors have brass drop-pulls. *c.1910*

152.5cm (60in) wide **£3,000–4,500 CR**

Mortise-and-tenoned door frames

Contrasting lighter and darker staining

Brass drop-pulls on the drawers

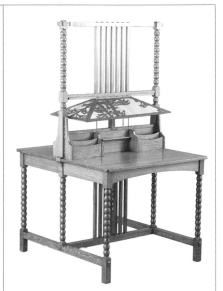

Rare double desk with a letter-slot divider beneath a slatted partition and a copper, brass, and ivory glass shade. There are ball-turned posts throughout. Made for the Yellowstone National Park hotel.

166.5cm (65½in) high

£6,000–10,000 **CR**

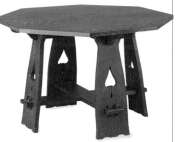

Octagonal chalet table in stained oak, with cross-stretchers mortised to spade-shaped legs with keyed-through tenons and inverted-heart cut-outs. Marked "No.120". *c.1910*

114.5cm (45in) wide

£2,750–3,500 CR

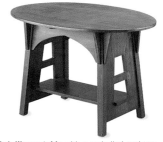

Oak library table with a corbelled oval top, two arched and two square-cut aprons, and a rectangular lower shelf. With maker's mark. *c.1910*

114.5cm (45in) wide

£2,000–2,800 CR

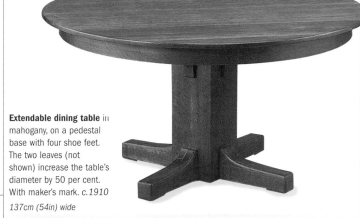

Extendable dining table in mahogany, on a pedestal base with four shoe feet. The two leaves (not shown) increase the table's diameter by 50 per cent. With maker's mark. *c.1910*

137cm (54in) wide

£1,300–2,000 **CR**

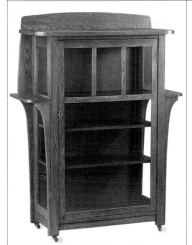

Oak china cabinet with three shelves, a single, three-over-one glazed door, glass side panels, open shelves to the sides, and castor feet. With maker's mark. *c.1910*

150cm (59in) high

£3,500–6,500 CR

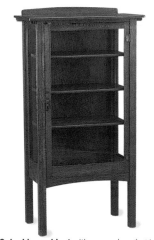

Oak china cabinet with an overhanging top, a glass panel in the sides and the single door, stile legs, and three adjustable shelves. With maker's mark. *c.1910*

75.5cm (29¾in) high

£1,700–2,000 CR

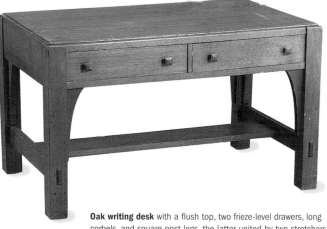

Oak writing desk with a flush top, two frieze-level drawers, long corbels, and square-post legs, the latter united by two stretchers supporting an under-shelf. With maker's mark. *c.1910*

122cm (48in) wide

£1,200–1,500 **CR**

American Furniture

On the surface, Mission oak furniture seems diametrically opposed to Art Nouveau. However, in the United States at least, the Arts and Crafts are a curious, powerful Art Nouveau hybrid. The designers substituted a straightforward use of natural materials for the curvilinear naturalism employed by the Europeans. In some cases – as with stylized inlays of metal and wood – the connection is clear. American adherents stressed a simplicity of design, with materials and elements of construction serving as all the decoration needed; a carved lion's paw on the foot of a chair was an anathema to them. American Mission furniture was simple yet bold, decorative but unexcessive, and basic but robust.

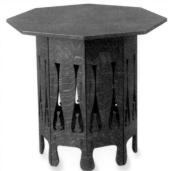

Octagonal table by Charles Rohlfs, in dark oak with pierced panels, a cabinet door with stamped hinges and a latch, and two interior shelves.

73cm (28¾in) high

£3,000–3,500   CR

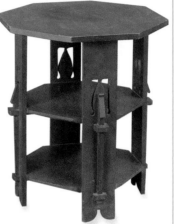

Octagonal-top table by Charles Rohlfs, in dark oak, with two lower shelves secured with mortise-and-tenon joints to four pierced legs. Incised "CR". *c.1902*

73.5cm (29in) high

£5,000–6,500   CR

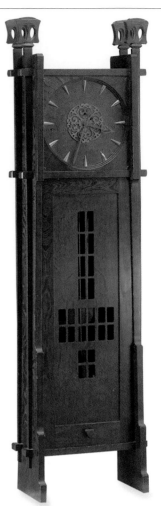

Rare longcase clock by Charles Rohlfs, in black-stained oak with carved and pierced posts and door, and a circular dial with copper hands and numerals. Signed "CR".

218cm (85½in) high

£40,000–55,000   CR

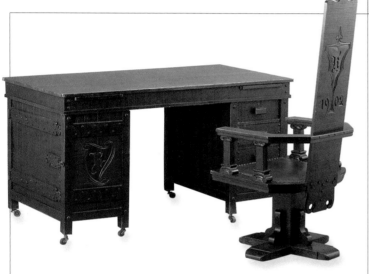

Rare double-pedestal desk with chair by Charles Rohlfs, in stained black oak with carved "R" medallions. The swivel chair has a *fleur-de-lys* finial and red leather seat. Carved "CR". *1902*

Desk: 152.5cm (60in) wide; chair: 150cm (59in) high

£18,000–26,000   CR

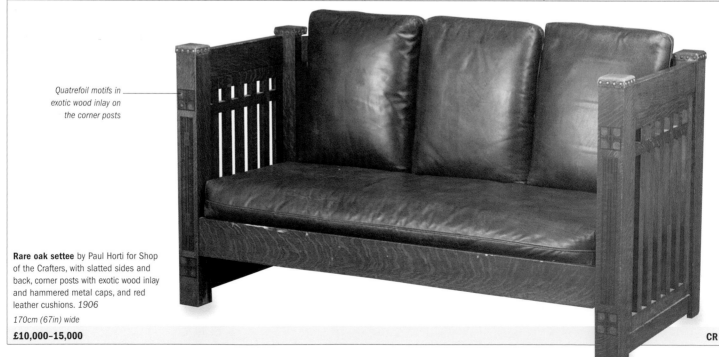

Quatrefoil motifs in exotic wood inlay on the corner posts

Rare oak settee by Paul Horti for Shop of the Crafters, with slatted sides and back, corner posts with exotic wood inlay and hammered metal caps, and red leather cushions. *1906*

170cm (67in) wide

£10,000–15,000   CR

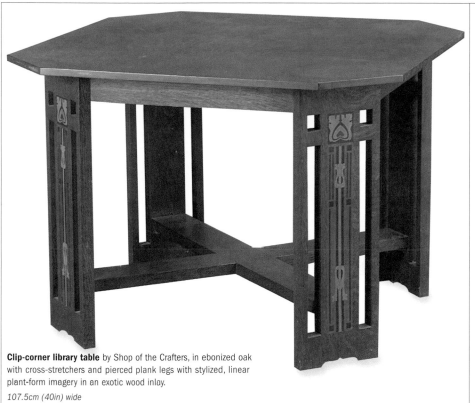

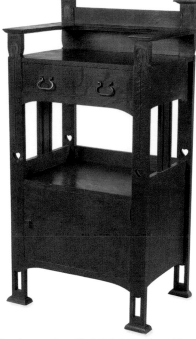

Clip-corner library table by Shop of the Crafters, in ebonized oak with cross-stretchers and pierced plank legs with stylized, linear plant-form imagery in an exotic wood inlay.

107.5cm (40in) wide

£4,500–5,000   CR

Oak and marquetry cabinet attributed to Shop of the Crafters and in the style of C.F.A. Voysey. With pierced heart motifs and wrought-iron handles.

113cm (44in) high

£3,500–7,000   CALD

Life-Time

The name Life-Time refers to a line of furniture, sometimes also called The Cloisters Style, produced by The Grand Rapids Bookcase and Chair Company in Michigan. The designs were simple and unornamented, with references to the styles of exclusive American designers of the time, such as the Stickleys. They created a more affordable and accessible market for many Americans at the turn of the 20th century. This was a successful, highly commercial company interested in efficient processes that produced long-lasting pieces. Much of the construction of Life-Time furniture was carried out by machine, but the work was well finished and high-quality woods were used.

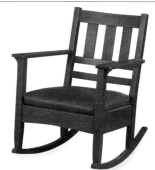

Life-Time rocking chair in oak with three short, vertical back slats, open arms, and a leather-upholstered, sprung-seat cushion. Numbered "624" and with original paper label.

85.5cm (33¾in) high

£300–450   CR

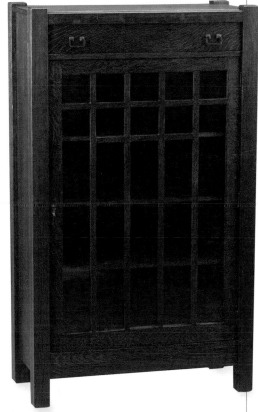

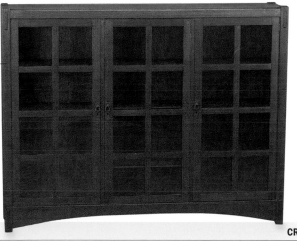

Oak is the favoured wood of Life-Time furniture

Life-Time three-door oak bookcase with flush top, arched base, and interior shelves. Each door has eight-pane, faux-mullion latticework and copper hardware.

157.5cm (62in) wide

£4,750–5,250   CR

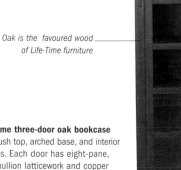

Life-Time oak bookcase on stile feet with a single drawer, a faux-mullion latticework door, and three interior shelves. With the remnants of the original paper label.

81cm (32in) wide

£1,800–2,500   CR

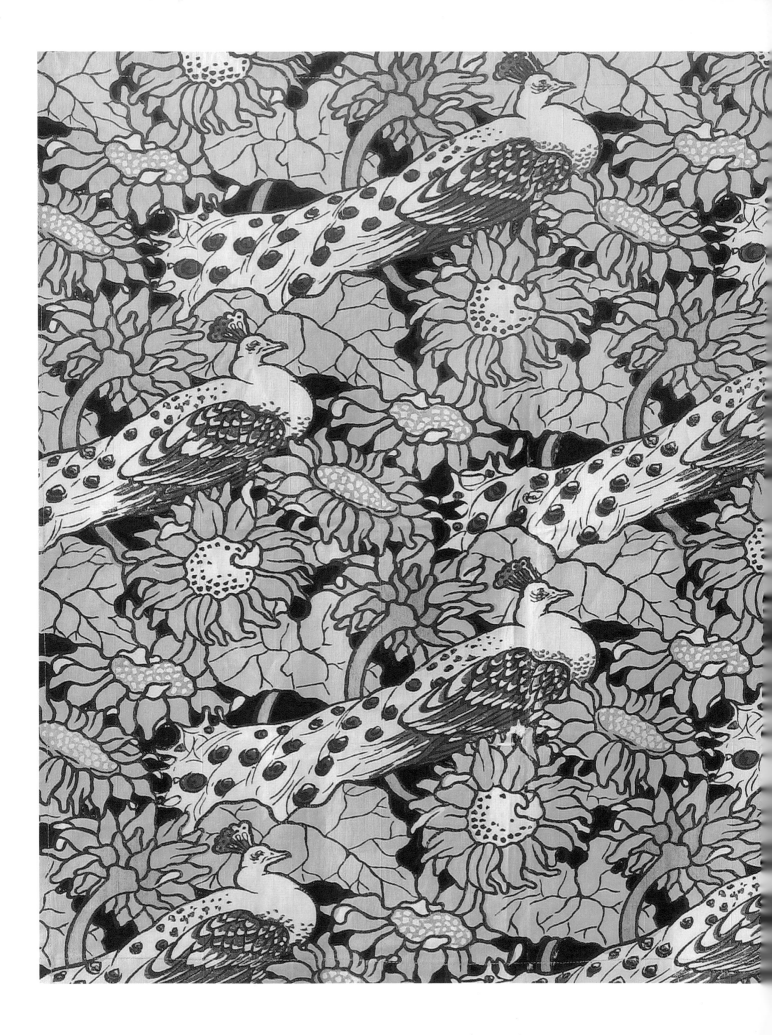

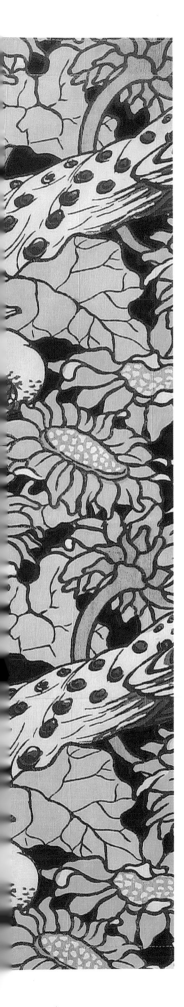

Textiles

Although few examples have survived, textiles played an important part in the creation of the integrated interior, which was key to the philosophy of Art Nouveau designers, adding colour, pattern, and texture to the furnishings. From machine-woven or printed silks and linens to embroidered panels and hand-woven tapestries, they embraced a wide range of materials and influences.

The revival of interest in historic patterns and their translation into new designs were key features of textile design during the second half of the 19th century. Eventually, traditional patterns were replaced by a new style of design that looked to the past for inspiration but reinterpreted it in a modern form.

NEW STYLE OF NEEDLEWORK

One of the most iconic examples of Art Nouveau is in fact a piece of needlework: Hermann Obrist's celebrated *Peitschenhieb* (Whiplash) embroidery (*see p.14*), exhibited at the Arts and Crafts Exhibition in London in 1896. Obrist's design shows tortured roots, stems, and flower-heads scrolling across the fabric, depicted in the finest embroidery stitches. His embroidery was revolutionary in using traditional methods to represent a new attitude to design.

NATIONAL CHARACTERISTICS

There was, however, no continuous line of development in Art Nouveau textiles. In Britain and across Europe, from France and Belgium to Hungary and Scandinavia, there were strong geographical differences. Most countries also produced work with strong national or regional characteristics, often drawing on local folklore and traditions for inspiration. There were also many different types of manufacture. Nonetheless, a common trend emerged, as designers strove to create a new form of expression using traditional skills and methods of manufacture.

The Art Nouveau textiles that graced interiors at the turn of the century included wall hangings and woven carpets, as well as furnishing fabrics for curtains, table and bedcovers, chairs and settees, wall panels, and firescreens, all designed as part of an integrated interior.

Printed cotton panel (*one of a pair*) graphically depicting a formalized repeat pattern of peacocks nestling amid sunflowers and foliage in soft colours against a red field. *c.1900*
86.5cm (34in) long **£600–900 (the pair) Wrob**

LEADING THE WAY

At the forefront of the new style of textiles was the influential William Morris, who objected to the poor design and mass production of poorly made textiles commonplace in Victorian Britain. A brilliant designer, Morris fused medieval and naturalistic motifs in his textiles and wallpapers and championed a revival of the role of the craftsman-designer.

A.H. Mackmurdo's textile designs featuring abstract, curving forms of birds and animals based on botanical studies were created for the group known as "The Century Guild". Mackmurdo's designs foreshadowed the Art Nouveau style and were highly influential among the new generation of British designers. C.F.A. Voysey is often credited with being the first artist to design repeating patterns for textiles and wallpapers, featuring stylized birds, flowers, and animals in bright colours outlined with black. His influence was widespread among Art Nouveau designers in Europe.

THE LURE OF THE EAST

The Japanese influence that pervaded all aspects of design in the 1870s and 80s was adopted by Liberty & Company in London, which imported Japanese fabrics and adopted the peacock motif as its unofficial trademark. Textiles were printed with synthetic dye colours, and new graphic themes and styles were introduced to reflect Japanese style and its textile traditions. By the 1890s, however, Liberty had moved on and was

William Morris "Seaweed" pattern designed by John Henry Dearle, depicting a dense repeat image of feathery plant forms and foliage of graduating size, punctuated with florets. **NPA BRI**

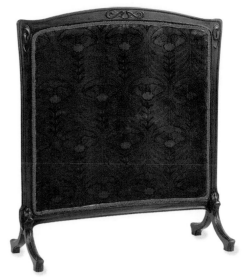

Edward Colonna rosewood framed firescreen, retaining original fabric depicting a repeat image of stylized flower-heads and foliage in soft colours. The frame is carved with delicate scrolling floral detail. 70cm (27½in) wide **£9,000–14,000 MACK**

commissioning textiles in the Art Nouveau style designed by artists such as Voysey, Walter Crane, and the Silver Studio. These Liberty textiles received widespread international acclaim, so much so, that Art Nouveau became known in Italy as *La Stile Liberty* (The Liberty Style) The designers of the Silver Studio, in particular, were influenced by contemporary French and Belgian textiles and created repeating designs featuring wild flowers, seed pods, and poisonous plants, such as hemlock.

STYLIZED FLORAL PATTERNS

Although many of the foundations of the Art Nouveau style were first established in Britain, European countries played a key role in the later development of textiles. The sinuous, swirling patterns developed in France and Belgium, for

DEFINITIVE DESIGN

The repeated pattern in textiles, popularized by William Morris, lent itself beautifully to Art Nouveau designs. It allowed cascading images of foliage and flowers or stylized birds nestling in trees. The more rectilinear approach tended to abstract natural forms until they were no longer recognized as specific plants but only as a series of geometric shapes. The designs of graphic artists, such as Mucha, were also transferred to textiles.

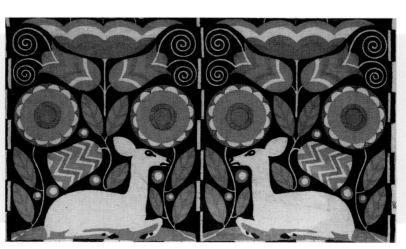

Carl Otto Czeschka "Waldidyll" (Forest Idyll) printed cotton sample, possibly retailed through the Wiener Werkstätte. It shows, in autumnal colours, a pair of white deer crouching amid highly stylized flowering plants with circular and bell-shaped blooms and spiralling stamens, and with linear detailing, against a black field. It is framed and glazed. 1910–11 21.5cm (8½in) long **£800–1,000 Wrob**

example, were adapted for both woven and printed fabrics. The Belgian architect Henry van de Velde, best known for his Brussels interiors and furniture, designed some of the most striking Art Nouveau textiles. His work ranged from abstract and oriental motifs to stylized floral patterns and Gauguin-like pictorial wall hangings, composed of bold coloured blocks of appliqué. Georges De Feure and Edward Colonna created dramatic patterns using strong contrasting colours, as well as single-coloured textiles on backgrounds with a watered effect reminiscent of opalescent glass.

REVIVAL OF HANDMADE CRAFTS

Handmade textiles also played an important part in defining the "New Art". Many designers in Hungary and Scandinavia turned to folk art for inspiration, reviving traditional skills such as tapestry and embroidery, but using them to create pieces in the Art Nouveau style. British designers, on the other hand, preferred the style promoted by the Glasgow School of Art. Jessie Newbery, Ann Macbeth, and Jessie M. King produced furnishings embroidered with simple linear designs featuring flowers, especially roses. Scandinavian designers like Gerhard Munthe and Frida Hansen created innovative tapestries characterized by strong, graphic design and bold areas of flat colour.

MOVING ON

Austrian and German designers, such as Josef Hoffmann and Richard Riemerschmid, designed distinctive, nature-inspired textiles in which the geometric aspects became more and more dominant. Ultimately, this style grew away from Art Nouveau and had many of the characteristics typical of Art Deco and Modernism later on in the century.

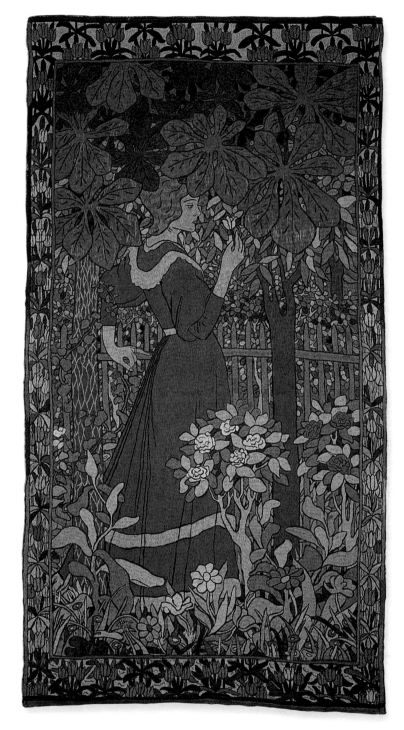

Right: Joszef Rippl-Ronai "Dame en robe rouge" wool tapestry, woven by the artist's wife, Lazarine Boudrion. It shows a woman beneath a horse-chestnut tree and surrounded by flowering shrubs within a floral border. *1898. 230cm (90½in) high* **NPA AKG**

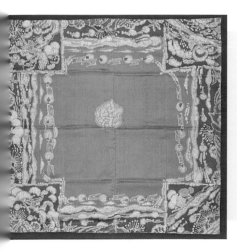

Liberty & Co. silk batik square scarf, designed by Jessie M. King. It is decorated in the corners with square panels of stylized aquatic foliage, and linked by bands of seagulls in flight above clouds with fish and anemones. It has a central organic motif in white against a cornflower blue background. It is framed and glazed. *84cm (33in) wide* **£800–1,200 L&T**

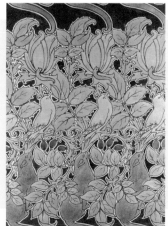

C.F.A. Voysey "Let us Prey" pattern, amusingly based on life's food chain. It shows a grey cat considering the unsuspecting bird perched above it as the next meal, enclosed within a canopy of dense foliage punctuated with stylized yellow tulip blooms and red rosehips. *1909* **NPA AA**

European Textiles

Textiles formed an ideal vehicle for the expression of the Art Nouveau style – from brightly coloured carpets and draperies, to wall hangings and screens, bed and table covers, and upholstery fabrics for chairs and sofas. In Britain and throughout Europe, silk, printed and woven cottons, linens, and wools were called upon to display a host of themes redolent of the Art Nouveau taste for sinuous, exotic flower blooms, scrolling foliage, fruits, birds, and animals rendered in stylized patterns or geometric interpretations in a range of warm, sumptuous colours.

Key exponents of Art Nouveau textiles in Britain and Europe include the London firm of Liberty & Co. and members of the Wiener Werkstätte in Austria, whose output included creations designed by its co-founder Josef Hoffmann.

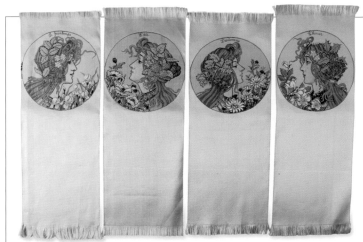

Four silk panels by Arpad Basch, in pastel yellow, pink, blue, and green, each with a medallion portrait of the head and shoulders of a young woman with flowers in her hair. Together, the set represents the four seasons.

39cm (15½in) long

£200–300   **MEN**

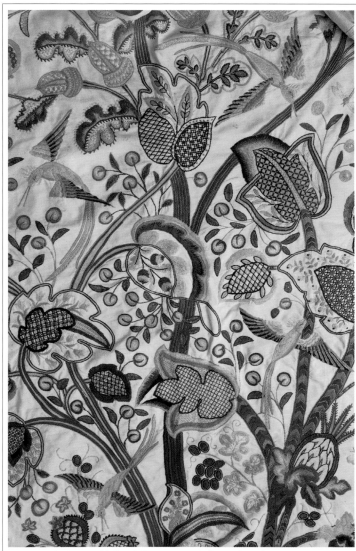

Crewelwork bed cover with densely interwoven exotic flowers, fruits, foliage, and birds stitched in worsted yarns on an off-white cotton ground. The stylized forms display an Art Nouveau aesthetic, but the overall composition is inspired by 17th-century Jacobean "Tree of Life" crewelwork designs. *c.1900*

250cm (98½in) wide

£450–550   **ATL**

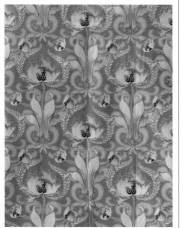

English printed cotton made for curtains or upholstery, with a formalized flower-and-foliage pattern in pink, red, and beige. *c.1890*

305cm (120in) long

£500–750   **Wrob**

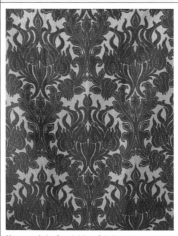

Heavyweight furnishing fabric with a repeat stylized flower-and-leaf pattern woven in cotton and wool, in reddish-brown on a pink ground. *c.1895*

183cm (72in) long

£280–320   **Wrob**

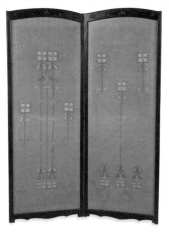

Bi-fold draught-screen in the Glasgow style. The mahogany frames are carved with buds; the linen panels are decorated with stylized plant forms embroidered in silk and wool.

181cm (71in) high

£2,500–3,000   **L&T**

Mahogany-frame firescreen with eliptical and square piercings on carved bracket supports. Encloses a woven silk panel with two figures under a fruit tree. *c.1900*

99cm (39in) high

£100–150   **L&T**

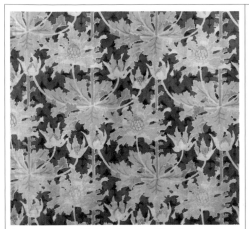

Cotton furnishing fabric attributed to Silver Studios, with a printed repeat flower-and-leaf pattern in shades of brown and grey on a black ground. *c.1900*

432cm (170in) long

£800–1,200   **Wrob**

WILLIAM MORRIS TEXTILE DESIGNS

A dislike for contemporary commercial textile production prompted William Morris to look to the past and master old-fashioned techniques that reflected the importance of the craftsman in decorative art. Establishing Morris & Company in 1875, he turned his hand to embroideries, wallpapers, printed and woven textiles, carpets, and tapestries. He developed a recognizable style with an imaginative vocabulary of flat, carefully balanced, and closely integrated patterns of flowers and foliage in rich, luxuriously intertwined hues. For his fabric and carpet designs, Morris looked to other epochs and cultures for inspiration but he was never imitative. His impressive creations in turn influenced many Art Nouveau textile designers.

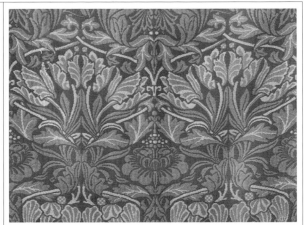

William Morris furnishing fabric, with a woven repeat "Tulip and Rose" pattern in shades of red and pale yellow. Designed in the late 1870s but registered in the early 20th century.

94cm (37in) long

£500–700   **Wrob**

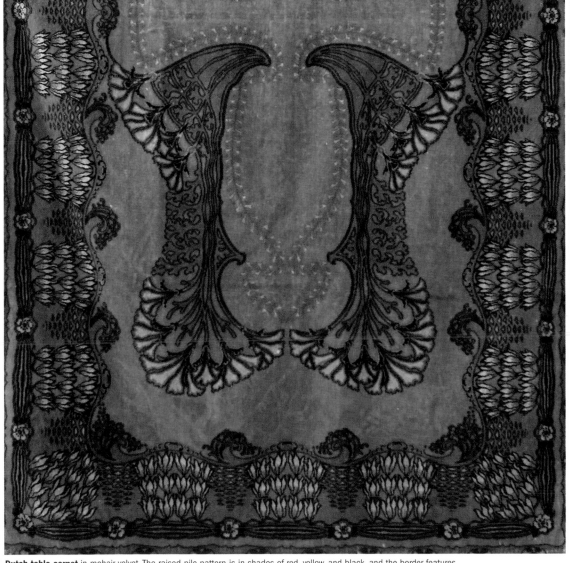

Dutch table carpet in mohair velvet. The raised-pile pattern is in shades of red, yellow, and black, and the border features single, scrolled, and clustered flower-heads linked with foliage. The centre pattern is of bouquets and chains of flowers. *1900–05*

290cm (114in) long

£500–800   **Wrob**

Cotton furnishing fabric by Silver Studios, with a repeat flower-and-scrolling-leaf pattern printed in red and pink on a black ground. *1890s*

228.5cm (90in) long

£600–700   **Wrob**

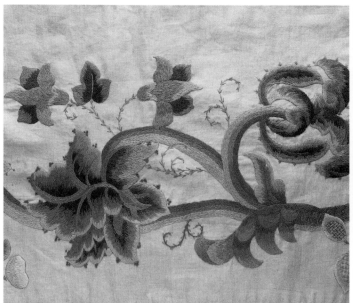

English crewelwork runner with a stylized plant-form pattern, comprising blooming flowers and scrolling leaves, stems, and branches. Woven in pink-, green-, and brown-dyed worsted yarns on a mottled, pale-brown linen ground. *c.1900*

250cm (98½in) long

£350–400 ATL

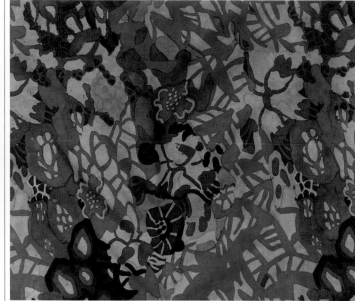

Printed cotton dress fabric by Gustav Kalhammer of the Wiener Werkstätte, with trailing flowers in shades of brown, yellow, red, green, mauve, grey, and black above stylized leaf forms in shades of red on a pink ground. *1910–12*

117cm (46in) wide

£400–600 Wrob

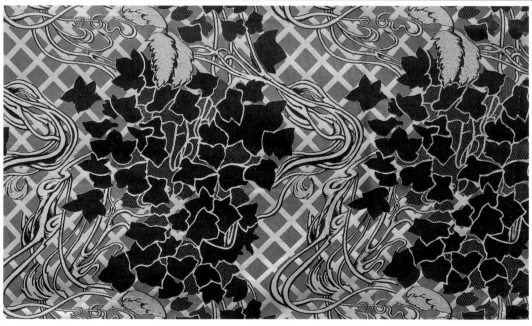

French woven silk panel with a stylized ivy pattern. The leaves and sinuously curved and whiplash stems are rendered in shades of black and brown on silver trelliswork against a pinkish-red ground. *c.1895*

162.5cm (64in) long

£700–1,000 Wrob

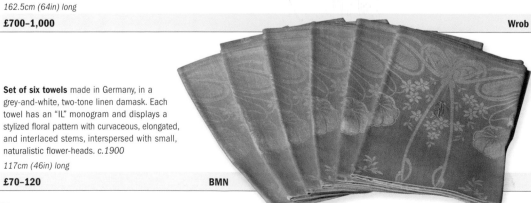

Set of six towels made in Germany, in a grey-and-white, two-tone linen damask. Each towel has an "IL" monogram and displays a stylized floral pattern with curvaceous, elongated, and interlaced stems, interspersed with small, naturalistic flower-heads. *c.1900*

117cm (46in) long

£70–120 BMN

Printed cotton panel (one of a pair) attributed to the Wiener Werkstätte. The repeat wave pattern, in light-to-dark shades of red and grey, is divided by abstract and irregular vertical lines in graduated shades of red. *c.1900*

284cm (111¾in) long

£1,700–1,900 (the pair) Wrob

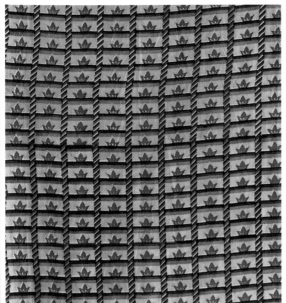

Woven silk panel by Dagobert Peche for the Wiener Werkstätte, with a geometric "Liszt" pattern comprising rows of stylized red flower-heads divided vertically by red-and-black rope borders. *1911–13*

101.5cm (40in) long

£800–1,000   **Wrob**

Woven cotton panel with a repeat pattern of highly stylized plant-form motifs bordered with rows of geometric forms in pale yellow-green on a dark green ground. Probably Austrian. *1900–10*

146cm (57½in) long

£400–600   **Wrob**

Printed silk panel by Arthur Berger for the Wiener Werkstätte in "Mekka" pattern comprising stylized blooms, buds, and scrolling stems in brown, pink, blue, and green. *1911–13*

95cm (37½in) long

£700–900   **Wrob**

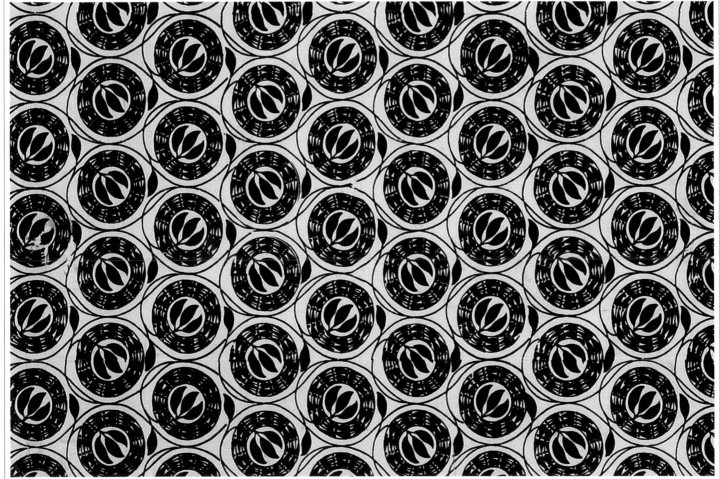

Printed cotton panel designed by Josef Hoffmann, joint founder of the Vienna Secession and Wiener Werkstätte. The "Luchs" (or Lynx) pattern comprises wreath-like plant-form motifs with triple-leaf or petal centres, joined by interlaced delicate scrolling stems. The plant forms are in shades of brown, grey, and black, and are set against a parchment-coloured ground. *1910–12*

94cm (37in) long

£1,700–1,900   **Wrob**

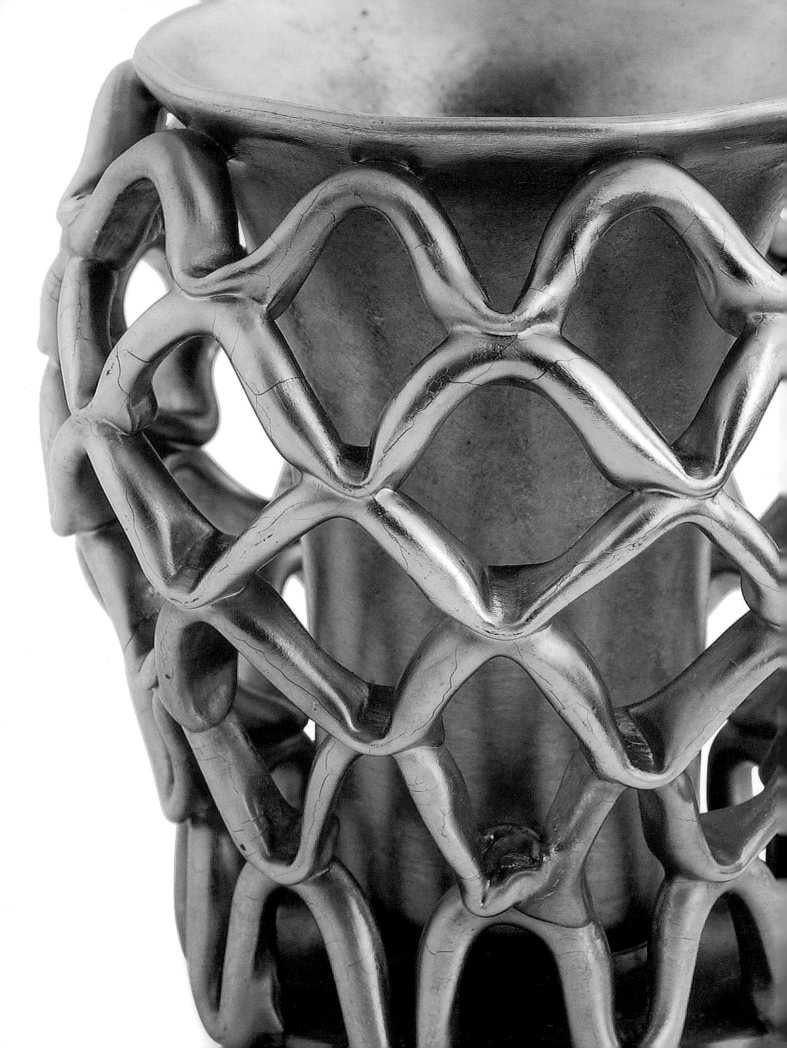

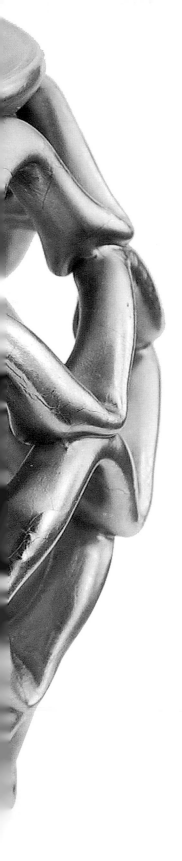

Glass

Glass played a pivotal role in the development of Art Nouveau style. Its malleable, fluid nature and potential for creating multi-layered, richly dramatic works of art lent itself perfectly to the swirling, organic style that lay at the heart of Art Nouveau. The glass industry, which had long been stagnating, underwent an astonishing explosion of creativity and technical mastery.

By the 1890s, glassmakers had delved into historic techniques and styles, such as *pâte-de-verre*, the delicate medieval Islamic art of enamelling, antique Venetian glass, and the swirling, asymmetrical Rococo style of the mid 18th century, reviving and reinterpreting them in new and modern forms. Recent excavations of Roman glass, with its lustrous surfaces caused by centuries of decay, inspired dedicated glassmakers in various countries to try to recreate the effect of iridescence in their own glass. All of these influences were decisive in shaping the development and form of Art Nouveau glass.

INDIVIDUAL MASTERPIECES
During the last decade of the 19th century, glassmakers turned their backs on the industrialized methods of production that had spawned the heavily decorated cut glass of earlier decades. Instead they began to create inventive studio and limited-edition pieces by hand, working with highly skilled designers and craftsmen. French glassmakers in particular created stylized pieces based on natural forms, experimenting with new techniques and exploring the sculptural possibilities of glass to create bold, multi-layered forms in rich, glowing colours. They did not, however, neglect the commercial possibilities of technological advances, and applied industrial techniques, such as acid-etching, to mass-produced glass to achieve similar effects.

Ultimately, Art Nouveau glass transcended the functional and utilitarian to enter the realm of the ornamental, celebrating the aesthetic qualities of both form and decoration.

Louis Comfort Tiffany "Diatreta" vase of waisted cylindrical form, enclosed within a web-like cage and exhibiting a golden iridescence shading through other vivid colours. Signed "L.C. Tiffany Favrile 5804 D".
10cm (4in) high **£15,000–18,000 MACK**

THE NEW STYLE

French glassmakers, particularly those based in and around Nancy in the province of Lorraine, were the first to develop the new style of glass. Nancy soon became internationally celebrated for glassmaking, a trail blazed by the influential and creative artist-glassmaker Emile Gallé. A keen botanist and skilled draughtsman, Gallé based his designs on local flowers and insects and experimented with new techniques, creating innovative pieces of unrivalled skill and beauty. Other French glassmakers also developed successful ranges of Art Nouveau glassware, including Daum Frères – who were particularly known for their lamps – Müller Frères, D'Argental, and the designer Auguste Legras.

The influence of these French glassmakers soon spread far and wide. Their bold craftsmanship captured the imagination of the glassmaking industry from Belgium to Bohemia and Scandinavia. Coloured, layered, etched, and engraved glass that drew inspiration for both its form and decoration from nature were embraced as the blueprint of the new modern, sophisticated art.

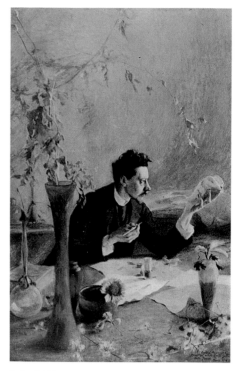

Emile Gallé, shown in his studio surrounded by botanical specimens and drawings, sensitively painted by his colleague and collaborator Victor Prouvé in 1909.

BOHEMIAN WARES

Bohemian glassmakers were especially receptive to the new style. Historically, Bohemian cut and engraved glass had relied on the patronage of wealthy princes with a taste for elaborately cut gemstones, but by the 19th century, glassmakers had to adapt to more modest circumstances. Distinctive regional characteristics soon emerged. One of the most successful Bohemian glass producers, the Loetz glassworks at Klastersky Mlyn, employed a number of avant-garde Viennese designers, such as Josef Hoffmann. Loetz produced art glass in rich colours

Loetz iridescent vase with dimpled sides and four pulled loop handles of sinuous outline. It exhibits random splashes of peacock blue and mauve iridescence against a pinkish ground.
29.5cm (11¾in) high **£9,000–13,500 MACK**

DEFINITIVE STYLES

Naturalistic forms and decoration are the basic tenets of Art Nouveau glass. In Nancy, Gallé created impressive sculptural vessels and cameo vases enamelled with naturalistic motifs such as dragonflies. Daum Frères created spectacular cameo and enamelled wares, while in Germany and Austria, vessels were either organic in form with iridescent surface decoration, or more geometrically shaped with pared down Secessionist-style silver appliqués.

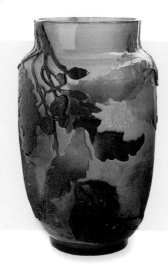

Gallé cameo vase of flattened shouldered oviform. The apple green translucent body is overlaid with reddish-brown glass, acid-etched with varying levels of relief decoration showing oak leaves and acorns. Signed "Gallé" in relief.
24.7cm (9¾in) high **£7,000–10,000 MACK**

Thomas Webb & Sons cameo scent bottle in pale amber with a milky opalescent overlay carved with a flowering shrub. It has a silver hinged cover embossed with leaves and ferns, and stamped "Tiffany & Co New York". *c.1900*
12.7cm (5in) high **£1,200–1,800 Qu**

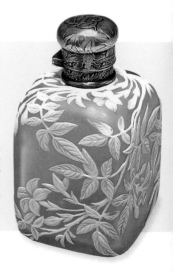

reminiscent of precious hardstones, and pieces inspired by excavated Roman glass, as well as layered, acid-etched, and iridescent glass with a metallic lustre.

RESTRAINED STYLE

In Britain, the Art Nouveau style was taken up by only a handful of glass designers and makers. The Stourbridge firm of Webb & Sons, who had long been producing high-quality cameo glass, successfully turned their hand to creating gilded opalescent art glass in the new style. The Stevens and Williams glassworks produced engraved, intaglio, and cameo glass pieces often decorated with motifs inspired by nature, though in a more restrained style than their French contemporaries. Harry Powell at the Whitefriars glassworks broke with convention and created vases in sinuous, organic forms in the Art Nouveau style and decorated vessels with finely engraved plant and flower motifs, applied decoration, and embedded silver foil.

THE AMERICAN WAY

Across the Atlantic, the American glassmaker Louis Comfort Tiffany became known as a master craftsman of Art Nouveau glass. His extensive experiments in glassmaking enabled him to create

a new style of glass characterized by a vivid, luminous iridescence and glowing colours, made to emulate the aged appearance of excavated Roman glass, which had taken on a natural sheen after years of being buried in the sand. Tiffany's art glass designs were inspired not only by nature, but were also influenced by the art of China, Japan, and the Middle East. Following in his wake, other glassworks in the United States such as the Pairpoint Corporation, Handel Company, Steuben Glass Works, and Quezal all produced fine-quality Art Nouveau glass in jewel-like colours, often enriched with swirls of iridescence.

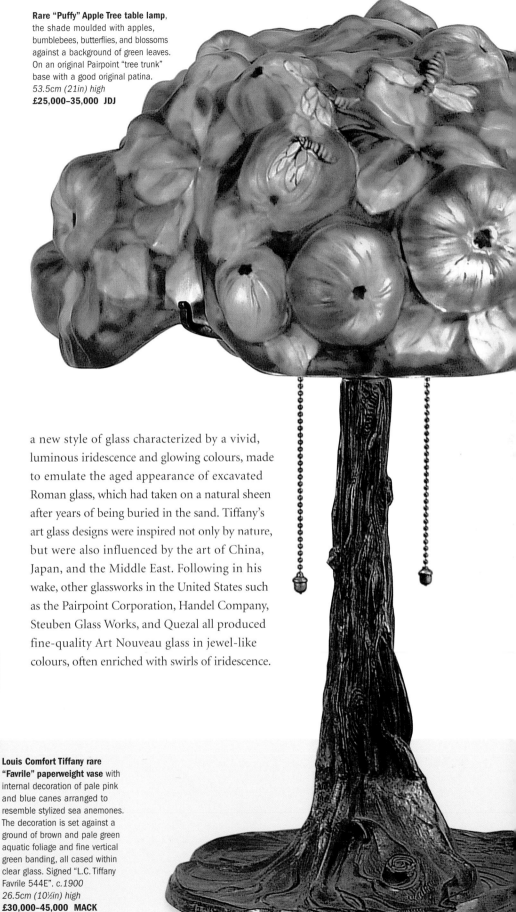

Rare "Puffy" Apple Tree table lamp, the shade moulded with apples, bumblebees, butterflies, and blossoms against a background of green leaves. On an original Pairpoint "tree trunk" base with a good original patina. *53.5cm (21in) high* **£25,000–35,000 JDJ**

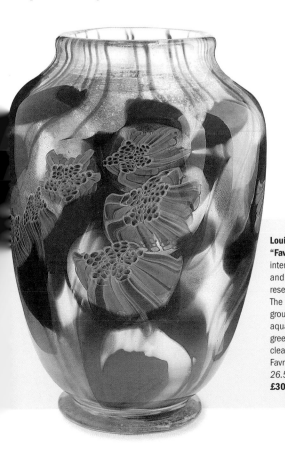

Louis Comfort Tiffany rare "Favrile" paperweight vase with internal decoration of pale pink and blue canes arranged to resemble stylized sea anemones. The decoration is set against a ground of brown and pale green aquatic foliage and fine vertical green banding, all cased within clear glass. Signed "L.C. Tiffany Favrile 544E". *c.1900 26.5cm (10½in) high* **£30,000–45,000 MACK**

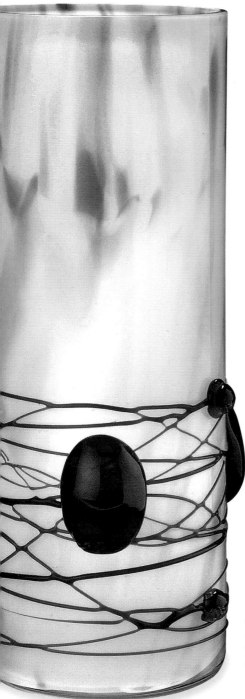

NATURAL V. LINEAR

The principal characteristic of most Art Nouveau glass is its fluid line and form. Inheriting the Rococo penchant for swirling arabesques and asymmetry, Art Nouveau glass is often organic in form, adopting light, delicate shapes inspired by nature. The natural world – plants and flowers, insects, birds, animals, marine life, and even the human figure – provided the glassmaker with a rich vocabulary of forms, often imbued with symbolic meaning. Inspiration did not just extend to decoration, but often dictated the form of the piece itself, as in the case of Daum's magnolia- and mushroom-shaped lamps, Tiffany's flower-shaped glass vases, or Karl Koepping's exquisitely fragile tulip-shaped glass goblets.

Leading craftsmen, such as Gallé, were initially influenced by the naturalistic work of Japanese artists, with their reverence for all forms of nature, and their flowing use of line. Other French glassmakers used oriental motifs in their work, or created pieces with shapes based on traditional Japanese forms, even imitating lacquerware by encasing vases in opaque, rich red glass.

In contrast to the naturalistic, flowing lines of the work produced by French and Belgian glassmakers, however, the designers of the Wiener Werkstätte, who produced work for many of the Bohemian manufacturers, created vessels that were linear and geometric in form. Pieces were often made of single coloured glass and decorated with simple, stylized floral or geometric motifs. Some designers followed the traditional Bohemian technique of casing clear glass in another colour and then cutting through to the clear glass beneath it.

THE ART OF EXPERIMENTATION

Experimentation was key to the development of the Art Nouveau style. While Victorian glass depended upon a team of artisans working to a pattern laid down by a designer, the Art Nouveau craftsman started with a design, which would then be brought to life by working closely with a glassblower and perhaps a highly-skilled cutter.

Art Nouveau artists experimented with a variety of glassmaking techniques in an effort to capture the delicate shades of colour found in the natural world. Among the techniques they used to achieve this were cameo carving, cold-working methods – such as wheel engraving and etching with acids – opaque and

Von Poschinger milky glass vase, designed by Georg Carl von Reichenbach, streaked with pink and yellow. It is decorated with fine green glass webbing and applied with amethyst glass prunts. *c.1905. 25.3cm (10in) high* **£600–800 VZ**

FORM AND DECORATION

The fluid nature of glass gave designers the opportunity to create simple, geometric shapes or flowing, organic forms, such as the Tiffany "Favrile" glass vase (see right). Some glassmakers, however, chose instead to embellish plain-shaped vessels with elaborate painted, carved, or applied decoration, often featuring nature-inspired floral and foliate motifs, such as the Amédée de Caranza vase (see opposite).

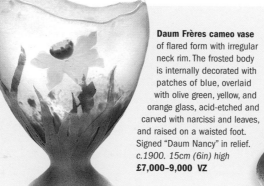

Daum Frères cameo vase of flared form with irregular neck rim. The frosted body is internally decorated with patches of blue, overlaid with olive green, yellow, and orange glass, acid-etched and carved with narcissi and leaves, and raised on a waisted foot. Signed "Daum Nancy" in relief. *c.1900. 15cm (6in) high* **£7,000–9,000 VZ**

Louis Comfort Tiffany "Favrile" iridescent glass vase, of pentagonal flower form. The flared "petals" have onion-skin texturing, supported on a slender knopped stem above a domed spreading circular foot and exhibiting an overall rich golden sheen. Signed "LCT 2936B". *26.5cm (10½in) high* **£4,500–7,000 MACK**

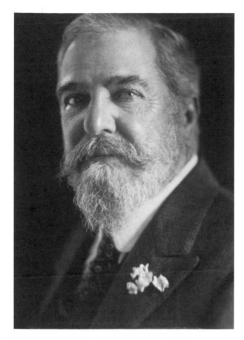

Louis Comfort Tiffany (1848–1933) founded his own decorating company, producing the world famous Tiffany lamps and "Favrile" glass.

glassmakers. By the end of the 19th century, these glassmakers were coating coloured glass with metallic oxides in an attempt to recreate the iridescent sheen and prismatic effect of light falling on glass vessels that had been buried for centuries.

EASTERN INFLUENCE

The ancient technique of enamelling was enthusiastically adopted in France in the later years of the 19th century by glassmakers trying to emulate Japanese and Islamic designs. In Austria and Bohemia, enamelling was used in a different form to enhance the geometric versions of the Art Nouveau style championed by the Wiener Werkstätte.

Forms were also borrowed from older Persian glass designs. The slender, gooseneck vessels created in the 1880s (*see p.13*), had a strong influence on the European Art Nouveau designers who emulated and built upon their sinuous, organic shapes.

In glass, more than any other field of the decorative arts, master craftsman working in the Art Nouveau period combined new technical expertise with fresh, imaginative design to create true works of art with a lasting appeal.

internally crackled effects, enamelling, free-form blowing, and iridescent decoration.

The success of Emile Gallé's cameo carved glass – where the outer layer was cut away to reveal a relief pattern silhouetted against the frosted or clear body – was widely imitated throughout Europe and in the United States. By 1900, glassmakers had started using hydrofluoric acid to cut back the overlay, thus revolutionizing a technique that had previously demanded highly skilled levels of craftsmanship.

Iridescent glass, with its subtle nuances of colour and swirling patterns, was developed in response to excavations of Roman glass, and was pivotal in the vocabulary of many Art Nouveau

MARQUETRIE-SUR-VERRE

Similar to the marquetry technique used in furniture making, *marquetrie-sur-verre* in glassmaking is the process of applying pieces of coloured glass to the surface of a vessel in order to enhance its beauty. It was devised and patented by Emile Gallé in 1898. Working to a design, it involves the application of shaped pieces of hot glass onto the surface of a gather of glass that has been heated in the kiln on a blow pipe. It is vital that the heat of each surface is the same, otherwise the glass may crack. The required shape of the vessel can then be blown, and the *marqueterie* areas can be carved to give finer detail. The whole vessel can then be cased in a clear glass.

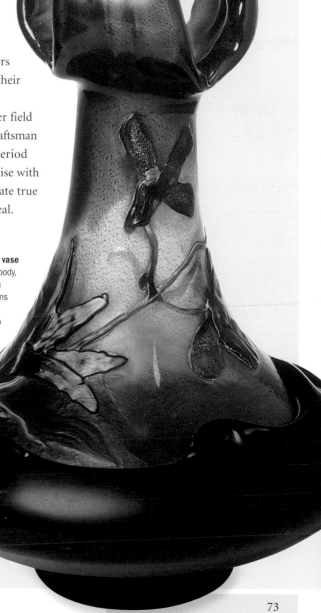

Right: Emile Gallé *marqueterie-sur-verre* vase entitled "La Girofleé de Muraille". The amber body, suffused with fine bubbles, is applied with carved coloured stems and wallflower blooms with foil inclusions. Signed "Gallé". *c.1900* *20.5cm (8in) high* **£40,000–60,000 BonLo**

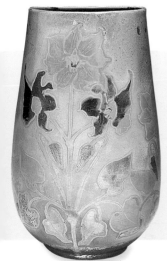

Amédée de Caranza painted lustre vase, of flattened oviform, decorated with a formalized flowering plant with scrolling foliage. The motif is painted in golden and violet lustres shading through other colours, against a pale peacock blue ground. Designed in collaboration with the maker Jeanne Duc, Paris, Signed "DUC-A. de CARANZA". *c.1902. 19.7cm (7¾in) high* **£2,500–3,000 Qu**

Emile Gallé

Designer and glassmaker Emile Gallé was a leading light and pioneer of the Art Nouveau style in France. His studies in botany, art history, and drawing influenced his imaginative glass designs and creations.

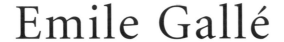

Born in 1846 in Nancy in eastern France, Gallé forged his career with the family business manufacturing decorative faience and traditional French glass. In addition to the scientific and technical training that was essential for his destined career as head of the family firm, Gallé received an education that embraced the rich traditions of literature, history of art, Symbolist poetry, and botany. These disciplines were to influence his art to great effect throughout his career.

Gallé's visits to London and Paris in the late 1860s and early 1870s opened his eyes to innovative methods of glass production, such as cameo glass and enamelling, which he saw in the collections of the Louvre and the British Museum. Following the precedent set by the gifted glass artist François Eugène Rousseau, Gallé had, by the time he took over his father's factory in 1874, introduced Japanese styles to the faience works. He also established his own art glass workshop, where he put these new ideas into practice.

NEW ART

Gallé's glass was refreshing and different and he pushed the boundaries of glass as a medium of artistic expression to the farthest limits. He combined cameo with other ancient glassmaking techniques, including enamelling, mould casting, and marquetry inlay. The results were totally in keeping with the French spirit of the "New Art",

Above: Cameo glass vase with a milky white and pale amber body overlaid with acid-etched ruby red anemones and brown foliage. Signed "Gallé" in cameo. *12.7cm (5in) high* **£1,500–2,500 JDJ**

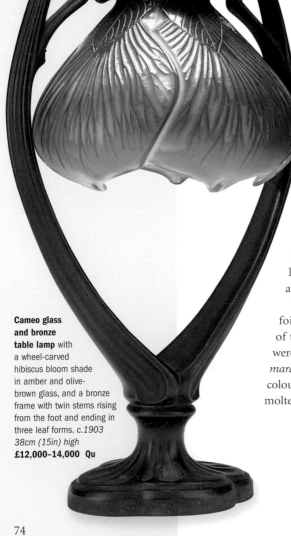

Cameo glass and bronze table lamp with a wheel-carved hibiscus bloom shade in amber and olive-brown glass, and a bronze frame with twin stems rising from the foot and ending in three leaf forms. *c.1903* *38cm (15in) high* **£12,000–14,000 Qu**

CAMEO GLASS

Gallé's cameo glass is made from up to five layers of different-coloured sheets of glass. The outer layers have been cut or carved away by hand or wheel, or acid-etched, to leave the design standing out in relief against a different-coloured background.

Cameo glass often incorporates metallic foil between the layers to highlight some of the more decorative details. Some pieces were also made using a unique process called *marqueterie-sur-verre*, in which slabs of hot coloured glass were pressed and rolled into the molten body of a piece, then carved once cool.

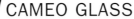

At Emile Gallé's glassworks in Nancy in 1913, a glass decorator puts the finishing touches to a large Art Nouveau cameo glass vase.

ENAMELLED DESIGNS

In enamelling, colours in the form of metallic oxides are mixed with glass and suspended in oil. These colours are then painted onto glass in various decorative designs and fired at high temperatures. In Gallé's hands enamelling was treated differently from the way that other Art Nouveau glassworkers made use of the technique. He achieved the spectacular effect of delicately painted and gilded flower blooms hanging mysteriously and melting into the underlying acid-etched textured background. Gallé's love of nature is apparent in his enamelled designs, such as this jardinière decorated with blossoms and fern leaves (*see left*), and this vase covered with delicate dragonfly motifs (*see right*).

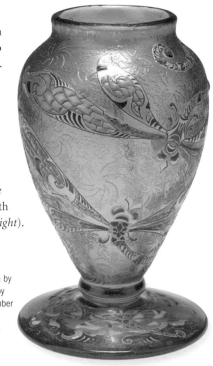

"Aux libelulles" vase made by Emile Gallé and designed by Eugène Kremer. The pale amber glass is etched, enamelled, and gilded with dragonflies. *13cm (5in) high*
£1,500-3,000   Qu

Moss-green glass jardinière with acid-etched surface; relief-enamelled with wild forest flowers and fern leaves. Signed "Emile Gallé déposé". *c.1892 8.25cm (3¼in) high* **£1,000-1,200   FIS**

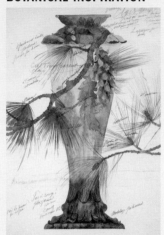

INFLUENCES

As a passionate botanist, philosopher, and poet, Gallé drew inspiration from the plant world for his unique glass creations. His genius soon became apparent, as every object he produced married technical virtuosity with breathtaking beauty.

BOTANICAL INSPIRATION

Early on in his career, Gallé studied botany, art history, and illustration. This training is expressed in his Art Nouveau designs and glasswork and is in keeping with the French spirit of "New Art", which drew heavily on the inspiration of flowers and plants. This sketch of a vase, drawn by Gallé in about 1902 (*see above*), is decorated with pine cones and flowing branches.

where nature played an important role, and which borrowed heavily from the art of Japan.

In Gallé's ambitious hands glass became a versatile art form. It was brought to life and transformed into a medium of simulated motion and blended colours, layered with internal patterns and surface textures. His imaginative practice of embellishing vessels with poetic verses – known as *verreries parlantes* – was among the trademarks that made Gallé's compendium of techniques the most comprehensive in the history of glassmaking.

Eager to broaden his palette and to fuse colour and decoration within the body of glass itself, Gallé searched for the formulae that would bring to his glass the rich lustres of semi-precious stones. He achieved astonishing effects by trapping chemical inclusions of coloured glass or metal foils within thick walls of glass.

DESIGNS OF NATURE

At the heart of Gallé's art was nature, which furnished him with a never-ending source of creative inspiration for forms and decoration. He rendered in glass all species of flowers and insects such as dragonflies, butterflies, moths, ants, and beetles. Driven by a Symbolist philosophy, Gallé turned to nature, with its inexhaustible vocabulary of motifs, to create a richly symbolic art with the power to leave its mark on the human soul.

Gallé exhibited his sculptural glass pieces at the Paris Expositions of 1878 and 1884, and also those held in 1889 and 1900. His influence spread far and wide. Having built his firm into the largest manufacturer of luxury glassware in Europe, Gallé helped establish the Ecole de Nancy in 1901, which would rival Paris as a centre of Art Nouveau production.

By 1900, the Gallé factory was producing "standard Gallé" vases, table lamps, and tableware using industrial techniques in order to meet the high demand for decorative glassware bearing his name. Gallé also continued to indulge his fancy for creating works of art in glass, including the dazzling and very costly individual masterpieces of glassmaking.

Emile Gallé's untimely death in 1904 saw his factory continue to operate under the direction of his widow and Victor Prouvé. A star beside Gallé's engraved signature indicates work produced after his death, representing the loss of one of the shining stars of France.

THISTLE MOTIFS

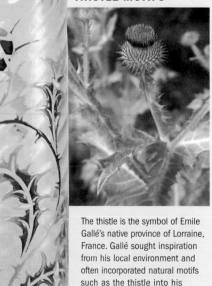

The thistle is the symbol of Emile Gallé's native province of Lorraine, France. Gallé sought inspiration from his local environment and often incorporated natural motifs such as the thistle into his designs. This Art Nouveau tube vase (*see left*) features thistles enamelled in burgundy and mauve on a swirled clear and amber glass ground. It is signed "E. GALLE Déposé" on the base of the vase. *19cm (7½in) high* **£700-800   JDJ**

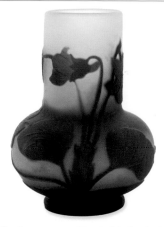

Small cameo vase with a greyish glass body overlaid with darker and lighter tones of ruby red glass, acid-etched with violets and foliage, and signed "Gallé" in cameo.

10cm (4in) high

£400–600   **MW**

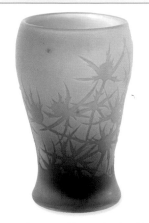

Cameo glass vase with an amber-tinted body overlaid with pale green glass acid-etched with thistles – emblematic of the Lorraine region of France. Signed "Gallé" in cameo.

14cm (5½in) high

£700–1,000   **AL**

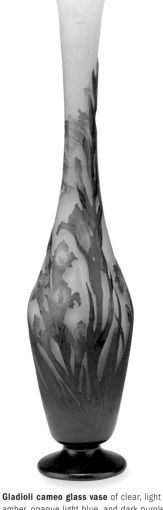

Gladioli cameo glass vase of clear, light amber, opaque light blue, and dark purple glass with etched gladioli, on a matte etched ground. Signed "Gallé". *1900–04*

73cm (28¾in) high

£3,500–4,500   **Qu**

CORNERSTONE PIECE

"Araignée et feuilles" cameo glass carafe with an elaborate silver gilt mounting by Ludwig Rühle of Vienna. The clear glass body is overlaid with acid-etched and wheel-carved ruby glass maple leaves, and a cabochon-centred spider resting on an engraved cobweb. Signed "Gallé". This is an excellent, early studio piece marking the transitional period between the enamelled and cameo styles. *c.1895*

33cm (13in) high

£10,000–12,000 Qu

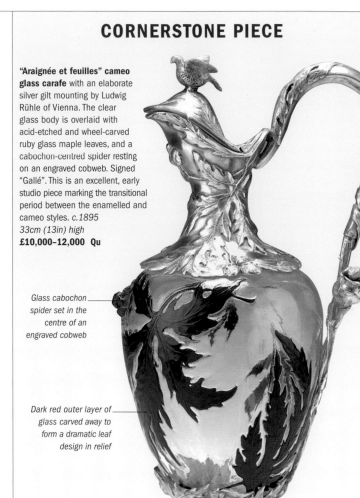

Glass cabochon spider set in the centre of an engraved cobweb

Dark red outer layer of glass carved away to form a dramatic leaf design in relief

Elaborate gilt silver mounting reiterates the autumn leaf motif featured in the glass

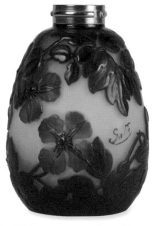

Mould-blown cameo lamp base with wheel-carved and acid-etched blue-purple clematis flowers over a yellow ground. Signed "Gallé". *1900–04*

16.5cm (6½in) high

£2,200–2,800   **JDJ**

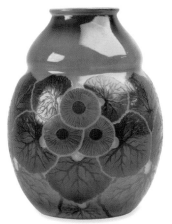

Rare fire-polished cameo glass vase decorated with amethyst and blue leaves and blossoming flower-heads. Signed "Gallé" on the side.

28cm (11in) high

£4,500–5,500   **JDJ**

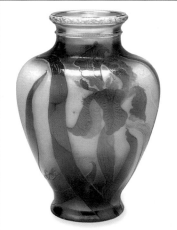

Baluster-shaped cameo glass vase with Louis XVI-style gilded bronze mounting. The clear, milky white, and purple glass is etched with irises. Signed "Gallé". *c.1902*

28cm (11in) high

£1,400–1,600   **Qu**

Cameo glass landscape vase in amethyst and blue over a clear and amber ground. The view over Lake Como shows trees and a peacock in the foreground.

35cm (13¼in) high

£18,500–20,000   **JDJ**

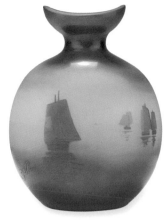

Cameo glass vase with sailing boats of opaline white, clear, purple, and blue glass, and etched decoration. With original label, "Gallé Nancy Paris". c.1910

14cm (5½in) high

£1,200–1,800   **Qu**

MARKS AND DATES

During the course of Gallé glass production there were various signatures in use. These were not actual signatures by Emile Gallé but facsimiles. On early enamelled glass, a signature such as "E. Gallé à Nancy", often accompanied by a patriotic cross of Lorraine, was painted in black, red, or gilt. Look carefully – marked in such tiny script it could easily be missed.

By marked contrast, the signature on many standard cameo glass pieces is bold and obvious (*see right*). It had a star added to it from 1904 – following Gallé's death – until 1914. Surprisingly, important pieces that involved hours of handiwork often have a fine, understated signature. Pieces that have an oriental feel to them usually have a mark resembling Chinese characters. Another unusual mark is the signature incorporated on a leaf, acid-etched on the base of a piece.

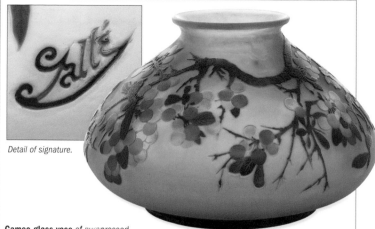

Detail of signature.

Cameo glass vase of compressed form. The amber-tinted body is acid-etched with pale blue and amethyst blueberries on thorny branches. The yellow colour beneath the berries is removed from the interior, accentuating the blue colour. Signed "Gallé" in relief. c.1900

17.5cm (6¾in) high

£7,000–8,000   **MW**

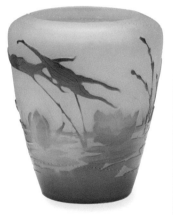

Pond landscape cameo vase with waterlilies and marsh Marigolds etched in purple and brown over yellow and clear glass. Signed "Gallé". c.1910

19cm (7in) high

£900–1,000   **Qu**

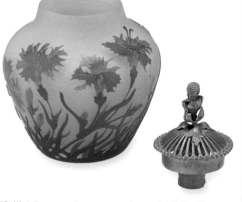

"Oeillets" cameo glass vase used as a nightlight with a detachable brass mount with a floral finial. The body is decorated with pink and red cornflowers etched over a yellow ground. Signed "Gallé". 1906–10

9cm (3½in) high

£1,100–1,300   **Qu**

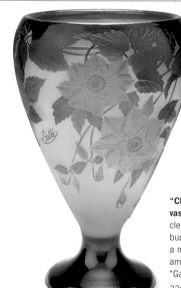

"Clematis" cameo glass vase decorated with etched clematis leaves, tendrils, buds, and flower-heads over a matte-etched yellow and amber ground. Signed "Gallé". 1920s

32cm (12¼in) high

£4,700–5,000   **Qu**

Fuchsia vase of clear, light amber and ruby red cameo glass etched with drooping fuchsia branches, blossoms, and buds.

15.5cm (6in) high

£900–1,100   **Qu**

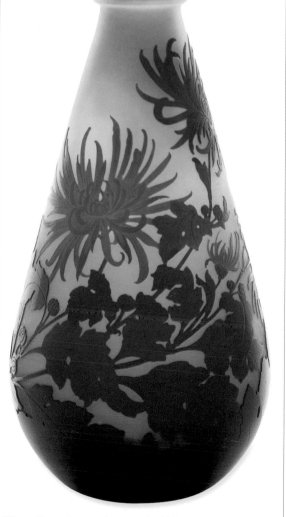

"Chrysanthemum" cameo glass vase of ovoid form tapering to a narrow rimmed neck. The chrysanthemum blossoms, buds, and branches are etched in dark and ruby red glass over a yellow and amber ground. Signed "Gallé". c.1900

31.5cm (12½in) high

£7,000–8,000   **MW**

The Daum family name is signed on their glassware along with the cross of Lorraine that claimed pride in their local heritage.

Direct representation of nature was the emphasis behind the designs of Daum Frères's pieces.

Cameo glass items were series produced with acid-etched or enamelled decoration.

Miniature vases embellished with colourful blossoms were among Daum's innovative glassware.

Table lamps and ceiling lamps were particularly successful for the Daum brothers, especially after the invention of the light bulb.

Daum Frères

The Daum brothers brought to the Art Nouveau movement in France their own unique and individual vision of what art glass could be, and succeeded in creating a thriving *industrie d'art*.

The brothers Jean-Louis Auguste (1853–1909) and Jean-Antonin (1864–1930) Daum assumed control of their father's glass factory in Nancy – the Verriere de Nancy – which specialized in the production of decorative table and domestic glassware. After visiting an exhibition of Emile Gallé's work in Paris in the early 1890s, the Daum brothers decided to devote their attention and considerable skill to producing art glass. In this venture they made rapid artistic and technical progress.

The fruits of their endeavours – especially in the realm of cameo glass – were similar to the glassware conceived by Emile Gallé (*see pp.74–77*). Looking to nature and the countryside as a source of inspiration, along with images taken from the East, the workshops of Daum Frères explored a variety of complex decorative techniques.

Assembling a team of artists, including the talented painter and sculptor Henri Bergé, Amalric Walter, and Charles Schneider, the Daum brothers developed their own variants on the *marqueterie-sur-verre* process, producing a number of designs for a series of vases centred on the archetypical Nancy themes of dragonflies and lily ponds. They also experimented with textures, such as the *martelé*, or hammered, technique. Many of their most successful pieces were created from cased glass skilfully cut in the cameo technique.

Among the innovative glassware created by Daum Frères was a wide variety of decorative lamps with glass shades and elegant bronze or iron mounts, which were created in collaboration with Louis Majorelle, the leading Nancy furniture maker and metalworker (*see pp.28–29*).

Above: "Pavots" cameo glass bowl with scalloped rim, enamelled with red poppies and green foliage over a gold-dusted yellow and brown ground. Signed "Daum Nancy" with the cross of Lorraine. *1898. 6.35cm (2½in) high* **£1,400–1,700 Qu**

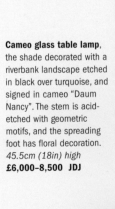

Cameo glass table lamp, the shade decorated with a riverbank landscape etched in black over turquoise, and signed in cameo "Daum Nancy". The stem is acid-etched with geometric motifs, and the spreading foot has floral decoration. *45.5cm (18in) high* **£6,000–8,500 JDJ**

ELECTRIC LAMP DESIGNS

The advent of electricity and its use in domestic lighting revolutionized lamp design. Previously, lighting had involved a naked flame from a candle, an oil lamp, or from a glowing gas mantle and meant that a hole or chimney in the shade was needed for the heat and fumes to escape. Electricity allowed clean, safe, and instant light, and with it came stunning new lamp designs. Glass lamps could remain functional yet highly decorative with the illumination enhancing the decorative motifs on the shade. The Daum brothers embraced this new area of glass design and created elegant cameo shades in floral forms, and decorative hollow glass stems that could also be lit to enhance the effect even further.

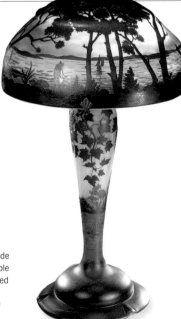

Cameo glass table lamp with an acid-etched shade with trees and a river landscape in brown and purple over yellow and clear glass. The landscape is echoed on the base and augmented with green foliage. Signed "Daum" with the cross of Lorraine. *c.1910 82cm (32¼in) high* **£4,000–4,500 FIS**

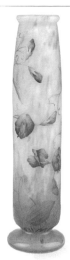

"Pois de senteur" tubular vase with enamelled sweet pea decoration. Signed "Daum Nancy" with the cross of Lorraine, and the painter's monogram "W. H". *1910*

47.5cm (18¾in) high

£1,400–1,800   **Qu**

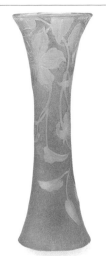

Cameo glass vase with a clematis design etched in pale amber and pink over a textured, white frosted ground. Signed "Daum Nancy" with the cross of Lorraine. *c.1900*

33cm (13in) high

£3,700–4,500   **Qu**

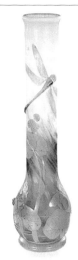

Slim glass vase with dragonflies and marsh plants etched in pale green and yellow over a pale blue glass ground. Signed "Daum Nancy" with the cross of Lorraine. *c.1904*

30.5cm (12in) high

£10,500–11,500   **FIS**

"Coeurs de Jeanette" vase of slim baluster shape in cameo glass, with pink and green inclusions and etched blossoms enamelled in green and rust red.

60cm (22¾in) high

£4,000–5,000   **Qu**

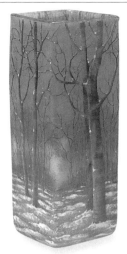

"Arbres sous la neige" glass vase with an etched forest landscape heightened with coloured enamels. Signed "Daum Nancy" with the cross of Lorraine. *1903*

19cm (7½in) high

£1,800–2,000   **Qu**

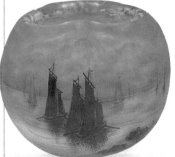

Oval cameo glass vase with black glass over a mottled orange-yellow body, acid-etched with sailing ships. Signed "Daum Nancy" with the cross of Lorraine. *1910*

7.5cm (3in) high

£1,100–1,300   **Qu**

CORNERSTONE PIECE

Barrel-shaped cameo glass vase with pond-life decoration, including bog flowers and dragonflies – quintessential Art Nouveau motifs – etched and enamelled in wonderfully subtle shades of deep purple, green, yellow, and blue. *1904–09*

24cm (9½in) high   £22,000–24,000   **Qu**

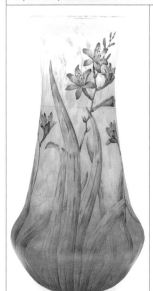

Cameo glass vase with bulbous base tapering into a trumpet-shaped mouth. It has an etched "Montbretias" rose pattern and is enlivened with enamelling. *1910*

33.75cm (13½in) high

£3,500–4,000   **Qu**

Cameo glass vase of footed, elongated baluster-shape. A "Marguerite" (daisy) pattern, is carved and etched over a mottled blue and yellow ground. *1905–08*

40.5cm (16in) high

£12,000–13,000   **HERR**

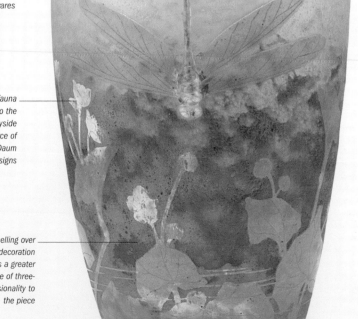

Internal mottling, shown here in shades of sky-blue, was often employed on Daum Frères cameo glass wares

Flora and fauna indigenous to the French countryside was a source of inspiration for Daum Frères's designs

Enamelling over etched decoration adds a greater sense of three-dimensionality to the piece

KEY FEATURES

Wheel-carving, fire polishing, and acid-etching were techniques favoured by the Müller family for the decoration of their art glass.

The *fluogravure* technique was developed by the brothers and was used to decorate glass with autumnal or twilight themes.

Imaginative and adventurous designs became characteristic of Müller glass.

Specialized in cameo glass with natural motifs.

Müller Frères

Beyond Nancy, inspired followers of Emile Gallé included the Müller Frères, a large group of siblings who operated glassworks at Luneville, in Lorraine, and the neighbouring town of Croismare.

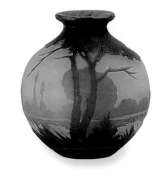

The Müllers were forced to flee their home in Alsace-Lorraine by the Franco-Prussian war. Five Müller brothers went on to learn glass engraving and carving at the Gallé factory in Nancy. One of them, Henri, set up a decorating studio in Lunéville in 1895 and was soon joined by his four brothers. A further three brothers and their sister joined the operation later. Henri Müller went on to found a glassworks in Croismare in 1900, and the pieces decorated at the Lunéville studio were made to their specifications at the Croismare glassworks. By 1910, Henri Müller had set up a second glasshouse in Lunéville with his brother Désiré.

Both factories specialized in the production of art glass using a variety of techniques. Impressive large cameo pieces and objects with an overlay of two or three colours, especially dark brown and yellow, were among their specialities. The decoration included flowers, birds, and landscapes, occasionally with Symbolist allusions, and was usually wheel-carved and acid-etched.

Much of the glassware created by the Müller brothers exhibited a taste for dusky autumnal or twilight themes and hues that were achieved by their own original technique, which they termed *fluogravure*. By this method, hydrofluoric acid was used to etch the body of the glass vessel as well as the areas of applied enamel decoration, creating a rich, glowing colour.

Above: Small cameo globular vase, its amber-tinted body overlaid with ruby glass. Acid-etched with a landscape of trees and a lake. Signed "Müller Fres./Lunéville". *11cm (4¼in) high* **£500–700 JDJ**

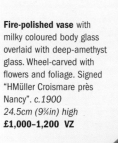

Fire-polished vase with milky coloured body glass overlaid with deep-amethyst glass. Wheel-carved with flowers and foliage. Signed "HMüller Croismare près Nancy". *c.1900* *24.5cm (9¾in) high* **£1,000–1,200 VZ**

FIRE POLISHING

The technique of fire polishing is used to give a degree of added sparkle and shine to the surface of a piece. It is a highly skilled exercise achieved by returning the vessel to the factory's "glory hole" (kiln), which carefully and subtly melts the surface of the glass. Since this is commonly used on cameo-decorated pieces, it can smooth out any irregularities that may have been caused during the acid-etching stage. Further improvements may be made by polishing on the wheel. Many art-glass studios utilized this technique besides the Müllers, including Gallé and Daum. Fire polishing has the effect of adding value to the piece, is appreciated by collectors, and is therefore considered worthy of mention in exhibition or auction catalogues.

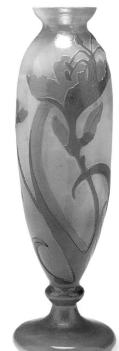

Fire-polished cameo vase with an opalescent baluster body overlaid with amber and green coloured glass. Acid-etched with lilies. Signed "HMüller Croismare près Nancy". Foot slightly trimmed. *c.1900* *27.5cm (10¾in) high* **£1,200–1,800 Qu**

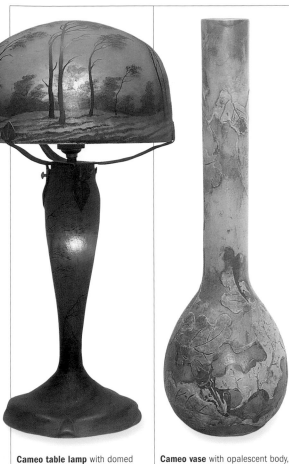

Cameo table lamp with domed shade and baluster stem. The reddish-tinted body is overlaid with black glass acid-etched with a sparse winter landscape. *c.1900*

42.5cm (16¾in) high

£2,800–3,200   **HERR**

Cameo vase with opalescent body, covered with a multicoloured-glass patination. Acid-etched with oak leaves, acorns, and stag beetles. Signed "Müller Croismare". *c.1900*

23.5cm (9¼in) high

£2,000–2,500   **HERR**

Cameo vase of round form. The amber-tinted body is overlaid with amethyst and pale blue glass, acid-etched with passion flowers and leafy branches. Signed "Müller Fres./Lunéville".

18cm (7in) high

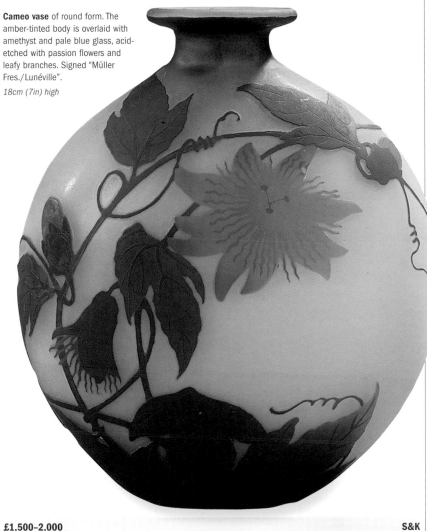

£1,500–2,000   **S&K**

Val-Saint-Lambert

In the early 1900s, the Belgian glassworks Val-Saint-Lambert contracted Désiré and Henri Müller to design cameo glass using the unique *fluogravure* technique pioneered by their family. The glassworks was first established in 1825 near Liège, when it employed English craftsmen to produce English-style crystal glassware. By the middle of the 19th century, it had achieved considerable renown for its colourful *millefiori* paperweights, as well as tableware and ornamental glass. In the late 1890s, the company had come under the influence of the Art Nouveau movement and began specializing in cased-glass vessels with deep-cut, abstract decoration developed by Henry van de Velde. One of the principal in-house designers was Léon Ledru, who worked for the company from 1888 to 1926, and was responsible for a number of beautifully designed Art Nouveau cameo vases. Today the factory is a leading maker of cut and engraved glass.

Val-Saint-Lambert cameo tapering vase designed by Léon Ledru for the glassworks. The clear body is overlaid with white, grey, and black glass, acid-etched with magnolias. *1906–08*

38cm (15in) high

£2,000–2,500   **Qu**

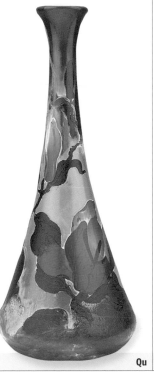

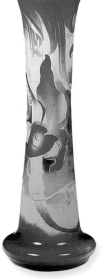

Val-Saint-Lambert cameo vase acid-etched with a stylized iris and foliage. Monogrammed "VSL". *c.1906*

37cm (14½in) high

£1,000–1,500   **FIS**

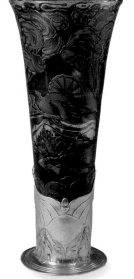

Val-Saint-Lambert cameo vase, with coloured overlay, acid-etched with a village scene. With a gilded pewter mount signed "Orivit". *c.1905*

35.5cm (14in) high

£2,800–3,200   **FIS**

Auguste Legras

The two glassworks established in 1900 by Auguste J.F. Legras in the Paris suburbs of Saint-Denis and Pantin earned a formidable reputation as the makers of decorative ware in the popular Art Nouveau taste.

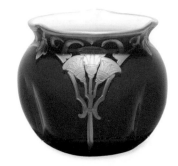

Most of the glass manufactured at the Legras & Cie glassworks near Paris had few artistic pretensions. Looking to appeal to a wide audience with aspirations for fashionable taste, the Legras firm followed the path forged by the leading pioneer of Art Nouveau glass Emile Gallé, by venturing into the manufacture of naturalistic cameo glass.

Legras produced a number of versions of glassware made in this highly popular technique, the most distinctive being those objects that imitated the semi-precious carnelian stone. These fine pieces were carved in a variety of sumptuous floral, landscape, or fruit-inspired patterns. These pieces were always signed.

Legras also introduced a number of pieces in opaque glass. These were made up of layered shades of rich colours, ranging from golden beige to rosy pink, which were then acid-cut to create sumptuous, voluptuous patterns – bouquets of flowers, bunches of ripe fruit, or even seaweed. As a final touch, the glass was enamelled in shades of red or brown with leaves in rich shades of green.

Above: "Egyptianesque" glass vase with dimpled sides and flared neck. It has a white body overlaid in semi-translucent red glass and is decorated with gilded, stylized papyrus fronds, C-scrolls, and foliate motifs. *10cm (4in) high* **£120–170 DN**

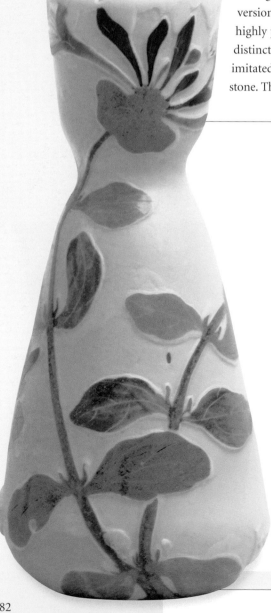

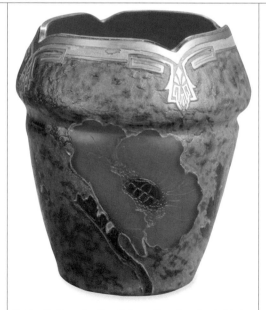

"Indiana" glass vase of ovoid form with scalloped and gilded rim. The interior is enamelled red and the exterior is acid-etched with poppies and foliage on a mottled green ground.
15.5cm (6in) high

£600–700	**L&T**

Cameo glass vase with a cylindrical body flaring from a round base and tapering to a cupped neck. The decoration comprises etched floral blossoms and leaves over an opaque, cream-coloured ground. Signed "Legras" in script on the side.
18.5cm (7¼in) high

£100–200	**JDJ**

Tall cameo vase with cupped neck and slim, gently tapering cylindrical body. Acid-etched with poppies and leaves against a pale brown ground. Signed "Legras" on the base.
35.5cm (14in) high

£1,500–2,200	**JDJ**

D'Argental

On the site of a glassworks originally founded in 1586, the St Louis factory was established at Munzthal, Lorraine, in 1767. The "D'Argental" mark originates from the French name for Munzthal.

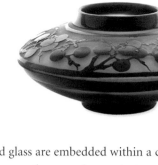

The reputation of the St Louis factory was cemented with the production of glass vessels in the Bohemian style, as well as with crystal glass that looked to Britain's celebrated lead glass for new and inspired ideas.

By the mid 19th century, the St Louis glassworks had become the most important producer of fine table-glass in France. It was also successfully experimenting with a variety of innovative and fashionable glassmaking techniques, including wheel-engraving and acid-etching. Opaline glass, *millefiori* paperweights, and vessels made by the complex Venetian method known as *latticinio* – where canes of

coloured glass are embedded within a clear-glass body – were other popular products.

By the 1890s, the St Louis factory had begun to create simple, modern shapes fashioned of cameo glass in the Art Nouveau style, which were typically decorated with lavish floral bouquets and flower blossoms, stylized leaves, stems, and fruit, or lush landscapes in rich, vibrant colours. The St Louis glassworks remains one of the most important in France today.

Above: Cameo glass vase of squat, bowl-like form, which tapers at either end. Decorated with acid-etched thorny branches and berries. Signed "D'Argental". *19.5cm (7¾in) wide*
£1,200–1,500 CR

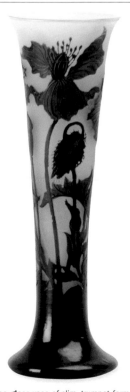

Cameo glass vase of slim, trumpet form with a splayed foot. It is acid-etched with stylized poppies and leaves in shades of blue. It is signed "D'Argental" on the side.
15cm (6in) high
£500–650 JDJ

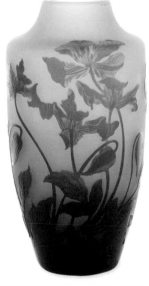

Cameo glass vase of shouldered, ovoid form. Decorated with acid-etched lilies, stems, and leaves in smoky brown over a caramel yellow coloured ground. Signed "D'Argental".
15cm (6in) high
£350–550 CR

Cameo glass bottle of shouldered, ovoid form and short neck. Decorated with carved, stylized flowers, trailing stems, and leaves in deep red over a red and yellow coloured ground. Signed "D'Argental".
20cm (8in) high
£1,300–1,700 CR

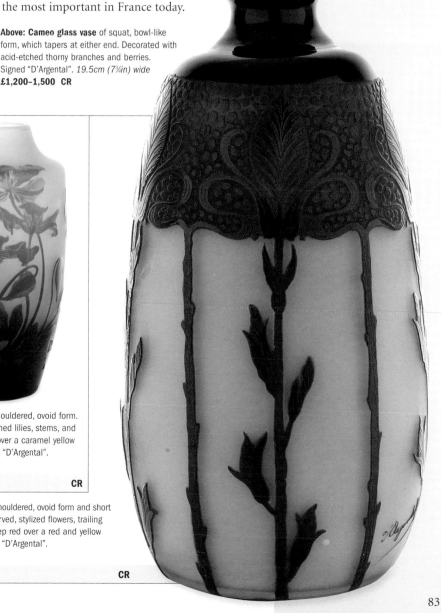

French and Belgian Glass

By the late 19th century, the taste for Art Nouveau had taken hold at glass-making factories throughout France and Belgium. In France, Eugene Rousseau's glassmaking techniques had already helped pave the way for designers such as Emile Gallé and René Lalique to experiment in Art Nouveau glass styles to much commercial success. While in Belgium, the Val-Saint-Lambert glassworks near Liege had become so successful that its large workforce was producing glass with deep-cut, abstract decoration in the style developed by the architect Henry van de Velde. In both countries, lesser-known glass designers and factories were experimenting with new ways of colouring glass as well as reviving ancient glassmaking techniques.

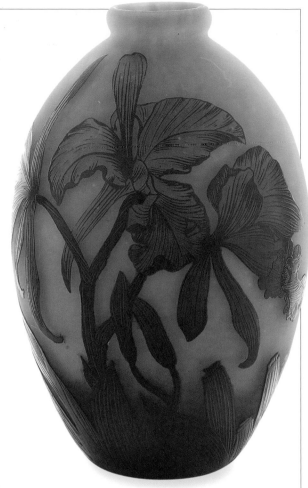

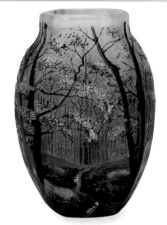

Lamartine "Landscape" vase of flattened oviform shape, with acid-etched decoration enamelled in autumnal colours. Internally streaked and signed "Lamartine". *c.1890*

10.5cm (4¼in) high

£450–550　　　　　　　　　　**DN**

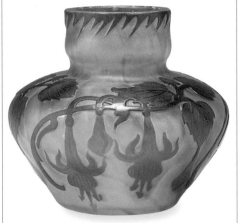

Stumpf, Touvier, Viollet & Cie cameo vase with opalescent body overlaid with pinkish-red and grey. Acid-etched with branches of fuchsias and foliage, and signed "Cristallerie de Pantin STV & C". *1901*

7.6cm (3in) high

£350–450　　　　　　　　　　**Qu**

DeLatte cameo vase of oviform shape with a short neck. The pink-tinted body is overlaid with amethyst and green glass, and acid-etched with full bloomed orchids on foliate stems. Marked "A DeLatte/Nancy".

20cm (8in) high

£1,200–1,500　　　　　　　　　**CR**

Vallerysthal

Among the many glassworks that thrived in the Alsace-Lorraine region of France with stylistic connections to Emile Gallé and the Daum Brothers was Vallerysthal & Portieux. Their speciality was vessels decorated with flowers and insects rendered in powdered colours, as well as layered, applied, and cut glass. In 1898, the factory commissioned designs from talented French artists who were celebrated for their work in the Art Nouveau style. These included free-form vessels decorated with pulled threads, internal bubbles, and opaque colours forming irregular patterns in the translucent glass

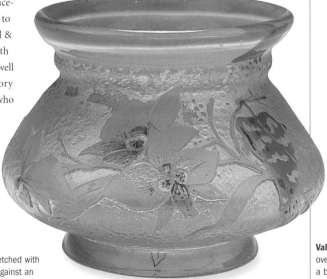

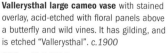

Vallerysthal cameo vase with a two-tone pink overlay acid-etched with orchid blooms, which have yellowish further detail, in relief against an acid frosted background. Partially gilded. Signed "Vallerysthal". *c.1900*

9cm (3½in) high

£700–1,000　　　　　　　　　　**Qu**

Vallerysthal large cameo vase with stained overlay, acid-etched with floral panels above a butterfly and wild vines. It has gilding, and is etched "Vallerysthal". *c.1900*

35.5cm (14in) high

£3,000–4,000　　　　　　　　　**FIS**

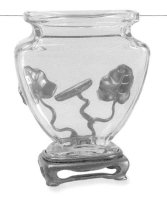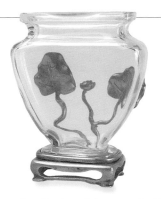

Pair of Baccarat crystal vases of flattened baluster form. They have gilt bronze stands with leaves on sinuous stems that extend onto the body. Marked "E. Enot Paris" (possible retailer).

18.5cm (7¼in) high

£1,800–2,200   JDJ

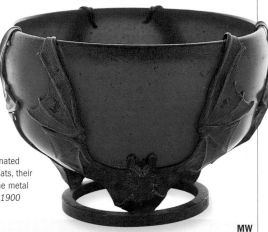

Val glass bowl with a shaded orange surface, held within a bronze-patinated metal mount formed of bats, their wings gripping the rim. The metal base is stamped "Val". *c.1900*

4in (10cm) high

£2,500–3,500   MW

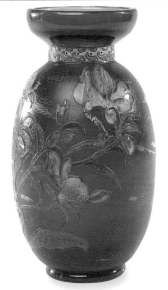

Jacques Gruber rare cameo glass panel of milky glass with purple overlay, and acid-etched landscape. In leaded surround, within a mahogany firescreen carved with leaves.

111.7cm (44in) high

£5,000–7,000   CR

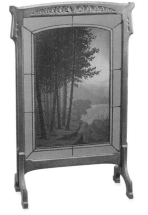

Burgun, Schverer & Co. rare olive green vase with acid-etched butterfly and plants. It has an enamelled band around the neck and internal decoration. *1889–95*

17.8cm (7in) high

£15,000–18,000   VS

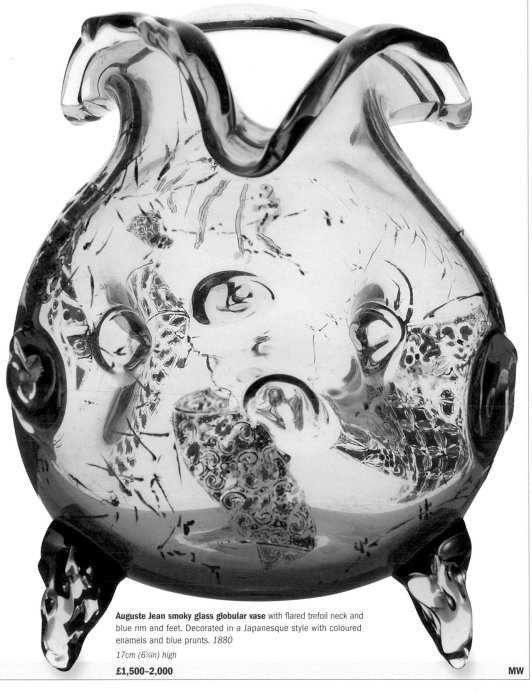

Auguste Jean smoky glass globular vase with flared trefoil neck and blue rim and feet. Decorated in a Japanesque style with coloured enamels and blue prunts. *1880*

17cm (6¾in) high

£1,500–2,000   MW

KEY FEATURES

Vivid, iridescent colours inspired by natural sources such as peacock feathers are typical of Loetz pieces.

Many vases are organic in shape, with undulating neck rims or slender, attenuated necks.

Rippled surfaces and limpet-like applied decoration show the importance of water imagery.

Twin-handled mounts, some with sinuous outlines and others more rectilinear, are frequently used.

Loetz

The Bohemian glassworks acquired by Johann Loetz in 1840, grew to be one of the most successful manufacturers of Art Nouveau glass, and its pieces were widely imitated by regional competitors.

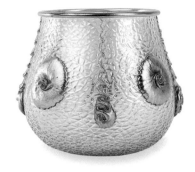

In the early 1890s, the Loetz glassworks specialized in artistic glass that looked like semi-precious stones, such as agate and aventurine, but it then moved into producing iridescent glass. Max Ritter von Spaun, Johann Loetz's nephew, did many experiments with lustred glass, resulting in a wide range of decorative effects, including iridescent spots, ribbons, and streaks, which were sometimes embellished with an openwork overlay of silver.

The shimmering glass vessels, often blue-green in colour, varied in form from simple, twisted, onion-gourd- and mallet-shaped vases to more complex shapes with ruffled rims, extended goose-necks, exotic handles, indentations, and applied trailing pads.

Much of Loetz's Art Nouveau iridescent glass was exported to the United States. It bore such a close resemblance to the favrile glass produced by Louis Comfort Tiffany that litigation was initiated in 1901, preventing unsigned Loetz pieces from being imported into North America. Many pieces made for export after 1891 are signed "Loetz Austria", while those destined for domestic sale bear the engraved signature of "Loetz Klostermühle", with crossed arrows set within a circle.

As well as designing glass himself, von Spaun commissioned designs for Loetz from many celebrated Wiener Werkstätte artists and architects, such as Koloman Moser, Josef Hoffmann, Otto Prutscher, and Maria Kirschner.

Above: "Nautilus" vase in textured, iridescent silver glass decorated with marine motifs in iridescent silver, amber, and yellow glass. The rim is of iridescent gold glass. *c.1903 20cm (8in) high* **£3,300–3,700 TEL**

IRIDESCENT GLASS

The initial inspiration behind iridescent glassware was the excavation at archaeological sites of ancient Roman glass. The chemicals in the soil had reacted with the surface of the glass, corroding it and giving it an unearthly, lustrous sheen. Glassmakers, including Loetz, subsequently experimented with chemical compounds and gases to try to recreate the iridescent effect that nature had taken centuries to achieve. These experiments became increasingly selective and sophisticated, bearing results of exquisite beauty.

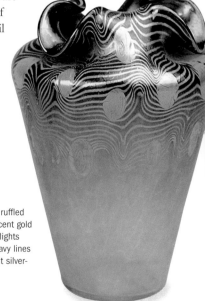

Rare iridescent lamp with a bronze base in the shape of a peacock holding the art glass lampshade in its beak. The "eyes" of the tail feathers are set with iridescent green and blue glass cabochons, echoing the feather motifs in the greenish-tinged amber shade. *49.5cm (19½in) high* **£1,000–1,200 JDJ**

Art glass vase with a ruffled rim, made from iridescent gold glass with purple highlights and decorated with wavy lines and spots in iridescent silver-blue. Unsigned. *18cm (7in) high* **£2,000–2,200 JDJ**

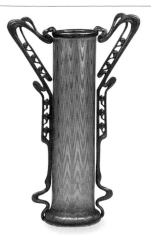

Cylindrical glass vase with pewter handles and a brass base and lip. The glass is streaked with columns of raindrops in shades of iridescent peacock blue. Unsigned. *c.1900*

23.5cm (9¼in) high

£1,100–1,300   **BMN**

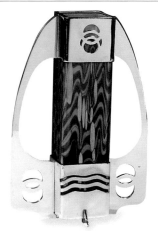

Rectangular glass vase with a twin-handled, chromed-brass mount with cut-out circles and a wave motif. The glass has a wave pattern in cobalt blue and yellow. *c.1904*

21.5cm (8½in) high

£4,200–6,400   **FIS**

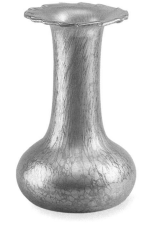

"Creta Papillon" vase in iridescent green and silver-yellow glass, with a bulb-shaped base, a long cylindrical neck, and an undulating rim. Unsigned. *c.1900*

31.5cm (12¼in) high

£1,000–1,200   **HERR**

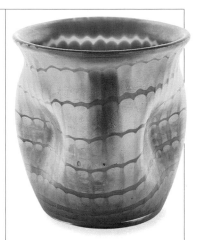

Iridescent glass vase with dimpled sides. The pinkish-red horizontal bands of feathering echo the predominant colour inside the rim of the vase. *c.1900*

11.5cm (4½in) high

£1,500–2,000   **MW**

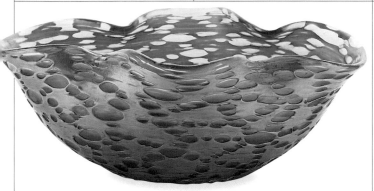

Large "Crater" glass vase with a splayed and undulating rim, made from clear glass decorated with a random bubble pattern in vibrant orange-red. *c.1900*

27cm (10½in) wide

£2,000–3,000   **MW**

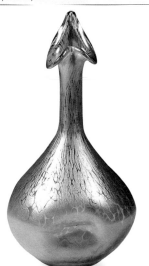

"Papillon" (butterfly) vase in iridescent silver and yellow glass with a bulb-shaped body and goose-neck inspired by a traditional Turkish rosewater sprinkler. *c.1898*

25cm (10in) high

£500–700   **FIS**

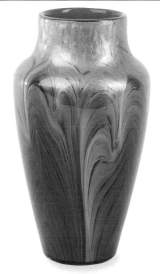

Baluster-shaped "Titania" vase with a sinuous, stylized floral pattern in shades of leaf green and orange-red, cased in clear glass.

20.25cm (8in) high

£4,500–5,000   **TEL**

CORNERSTONE PIECE

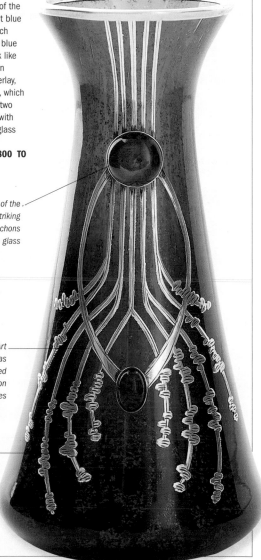

Tall sea-green glass vase with a silver overlay. The base of the vase is made of iridescent blue and blue-black glass, which graduates into green and blue glass up the neck, to look like aquatic plants. The pattern is echoed in the silver overlay, shaped like stylized roots, which descend from the rim on two sides and are decorated with round and oval ruby red glass cabochons. *c.1905*

15cm (6in) high   **£600–800**   **TO**

The vibrant composition of the vase is enhanced by the striking contrast of the red cabochons set against the green glass

A silver overlay in classic Art Nouveau patterns, such as these elongated, stylized roots, was used by Loetz on many of its glass vases

Sinuous plant motifs are a recurring feature of European Art Nouveau glass design

87

Bohemian Glass

By the late 19th century, Bohemian glassmakers – who had for centuries relied on the patronage of wealthy princes – began to seek new ways to appeal to a wider market. To this end, the Art Nouveau style was taken up by a number of glassworks – the Loetz and Harrachov glassmakers among them – who employed avant-garde designers such as Josef Hoffmann and used new technologies to create a variety of sophisticated effects. A few Bohemian glasshouses successfully experimented with hydrofluoric acid to create cameo-carved, cased glass vessels. They also produced colourful art glass that mimicked precious hardstones, and incorporated historical designs that looked back to the iridescence of ancient Roman glass vessels.

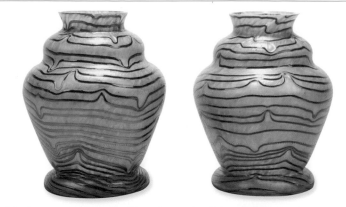

Pair of vases, probably by Palme-König, of stepped ovoid form with spreading bases. Decorated with splashes of golden iridescence and fine, wavy amethyst coloured banding.

20cm (8in) high

£350–450   DN

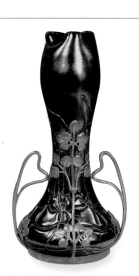

F. van Poschinger lustrous vase with applied webbing in a pewter mount. This German example exhibits the same characteristics of contemporary Bohemian pieces. *c.1900*

35cm (13¾in) high

£1,200–1,700   FIS

Art glass bowl with a pinched, square top tapering to a round base. The blue iridescent glass is decorated with flowers, leaves, and trailing stems in white, blue, and grey enamel.

9.5cm (3¾in) high

£350–400   JDJ

Art glass vase with a pinched rim, tapering round body, and spreading bulbous base, in shades of dark red and purple iridescent glass with an all-over crackle finish.

28cm (11in) high

£250–350   JDJ

Iridescent glass vase of slender baluster form with pinched sides and a ruffled rim. The iridescent green glass has purple and blue highlights and a rippled finish.

33cm (13in) high

£200–250   JDJ

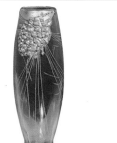
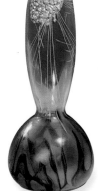

Harrach iridescent glass vase, internally silver-yellow, externally with plant form pattern in dark red, green, and blue, and a gold and yellow ochre pine cone under the rim. *c.1902*

25cm (10in) high

£550–700   FIS

"Secessionist" table lamp with an "oil-spot" glass shade, bronze rim and supports, and a blown-glass stem. The bronze and mahogany base is embellished with Glasgow-style roses.

68.5cm (27in) high

£5,500–7,000   DRA

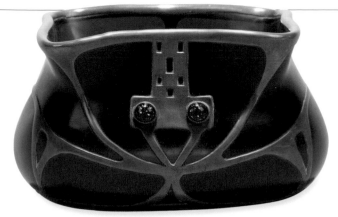

"Secessionist" bowl of bulging rectangular form. The glass body has an iridescent sheen and the applied copper mount is set on one side with two foil-backed, ruby red glass cabochons. *13.5cm (5¼in) wide*

£500–700 DN

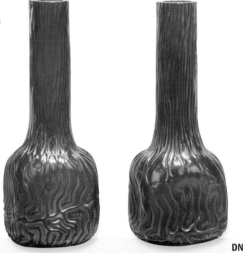

Unsigned pair of vases, of dimpled square section with long, cylindrical necks. The iridescent ruby red glass is mould-blown with stylized, trailing plant forms and exhibits a lustrous sheen. *18.5cm (7¼in) high*

£70–90 DN

Wilhelm Kralik Sohn

Like many Bohemian glasshouses with a tradition for high-quality glass, the firm of Wilhelm Kralik Sohn – which had factories in southern Bohemia – sought to emulate the success enjoyed by the well-established glassworks whose ventures in the Art Nouveau style had met with great acclaim. Founded in the 1880s, the Kralik glassworks imitated the widely admired iridescent glass produced by Loetz and L.C. Tiffany. A speciality of the Kralik factory were iridescent glass vessels in irregular shapes, with pewter mounts decorated with stylized flower and fruit patterns typical of the Art Nouveau style. Kralik also supplied glass to the successful J. & L. Lobmeyr glassworks for the Art Nouveau designs that had been commissioned from contemporary artists and architects.

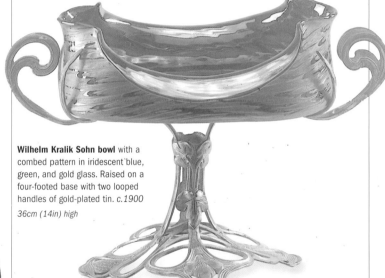

Wilhelm Kralik Sohn bowl with a combed pattern in iridescent blue, green, and gold glass. Raised on a four-footed base with two looped handles of gold-plated tin. *c.1900* *36cm (14in) high*

£850–1000 HERR

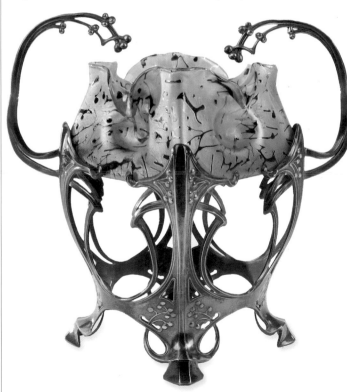

Wilhelm Kralik Sohn bowl of pale amber glass with shaded coloured iridescence and amethyst "peloton" decoration within a plant-form pewter mount. *1900–05* *10cm (4in) high*

£2,300–2,600 TEL

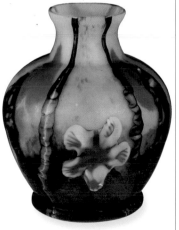

Wilhelm Kralik Sohn vase of squat ovoid form with gently flared neck. Flower-heads and bands of trailing leaves are set against a greyish-white ground. *c.1905* *23.5cm (9¼in) high*

£350–500 FIS

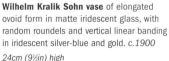

Wilhelm Kralik Sohn vase of elongated ovoid form in matte iridescent glass, with random roundels and vertical linear banding in iridescent silver-blue and gold. *c.1900* *24cm (9½in) high*

£500–600 FIS

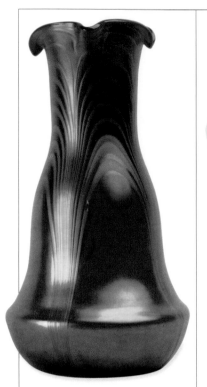

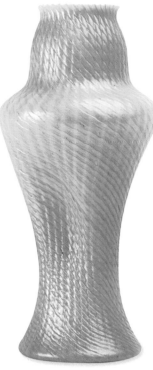

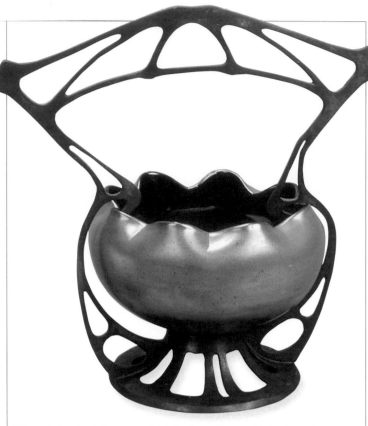

Unsigned art glass vase of stepped and tapering form with a pinched and splayed lip, in iridescent red glass decorated with a pink and blue pulled-feather pattern.

30.5cm (12in) high

£350–450 — **JDJ**

Unsigned art glass vase of baluster form with three dimples to the tapering body and a ground lip. The all-over swirling pattern is textured and in iridescent pink.

30.5cm (12in) high

£90–160 — **JDJ**

Iridescent glass bowl of compressed globular shape with an undulating rim and lustrous sheen. The bronze mount displays sinuous open-work handles linked to a circular foot. *c.1890*

33cm (13in) high

£200–250 — **DN**

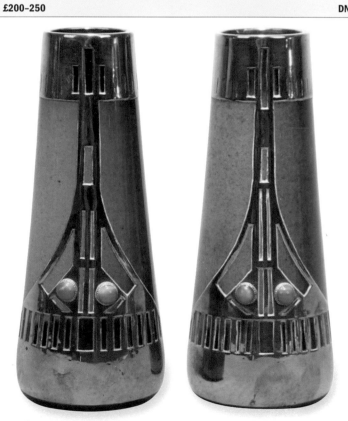

Centrepiece iridescent glass bowl, probably by Pallme König. The flat-bottomed bowl has an undulating rim, and sits in a pewter stand with foliate supports, stems, and base.

23.5cm (9¼in) high

£650–750 — **DN**

Pair of "Secessionist" vases of tapering, cylindrical form. Set within selectively pierced, geometric patterned copper mounts, each with two pairs of jade-green glass cabochons.

18.5cm (7¼in) high

£550–650 — **DN**

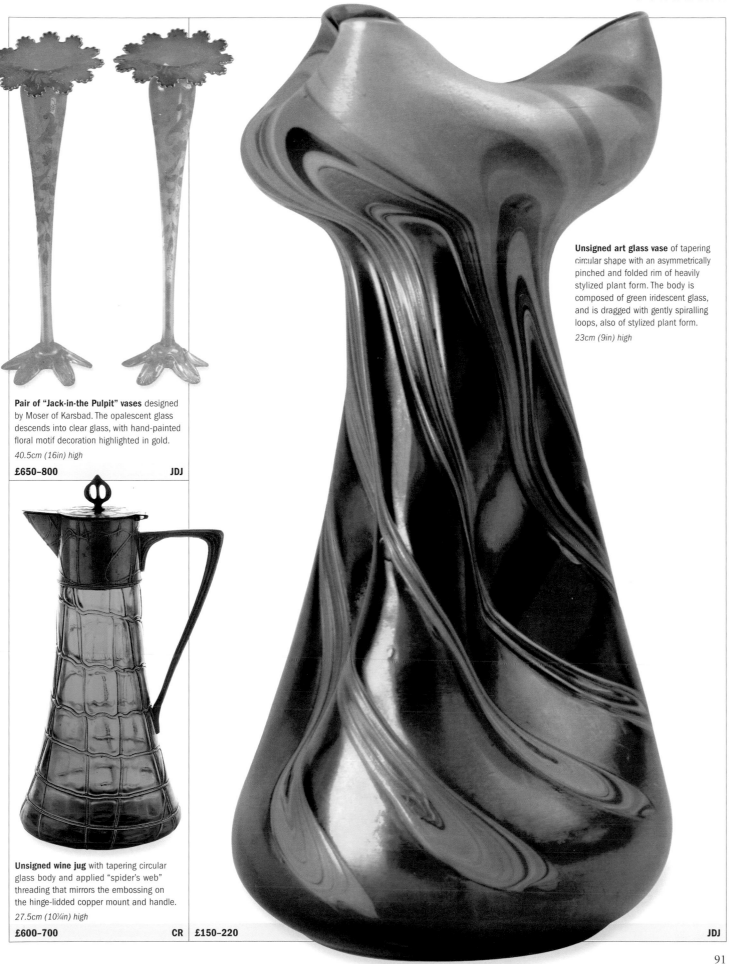

Pair of "Jack-in-the-Pulpit" vases designed by Moser of Karsbad. The opalescent glass descends into clear glass, with hand-painted floral motif decoration highlighted in gold.

40.5cm (16in) high

£650–800   **JDJ**

Unsigned wine jug with tapering circular glass body and applied "spider's web" threading that mirrors the embossing on the hinge-lidded copper mount and handle.

27.5cm (10¾in) high

£600–700   **CR**

Unsigned art glass vase of tapering circular shape with an asymmetrically pinched and folded rim of heavily stylized plant form. The body is composed of green iridescent glass, and is dragged with gently spiralling loops, also of stylized plant form.

23cm (9in) high

£150–220   **JDJ**

KEY FEATURES

A variety of glass vessels were produced by Webb & Sons, including vases, boxes, posy bowls, decanters, and jugs.

Sumptuous colours, ranging from pale translucent shades to deep opaque hues, were commonly used.

Stylized and naturalistic plants, flower blooms, and insects in the Art Nouveau style, decorated Webb & Sons vessels.

Painted enamels and gilding embellished some of their vases.

"Vaseline" glass in slick, opalescent shades of yellow, green, blue, and red was sometimes used.

Webb & Sons

In the late 19th century, the Stourbridge factory of Thomas Webb & Sons, established in 1837, produced decorative ornamental glassware in the popular Art Nouveau style.

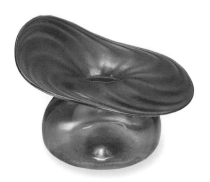

The British glassworks of Thomas Webb & Sons captured the spirit of art glass when it promoted its "Works of Art in Sculptured Glass" in 1889. Like many Stourbridge factories, Webb was well-known for the production of luxury tablewares and high-quality art glass, which was aimed at a wealthy clientele.

Influenced by the brightly coloured glass manufactured by glassworks in Bohemia, Webb & Sons excelled in the production of glassware in a variety of rainbow hues that were created by adding metallic oxides to the glass mix. Webb's most celebrated coloured ware, known as "Queen's Burmese", boasted an opal glass body of shaded tones ranging from pale lemon yellow to salmon pink, and often enamelled or gilded with stylized or naturalistic flower patterns.

Webb's other successes in glassmaking include "vaseline" glass, "peach" glass – a type of cased glass that shaded from pink to deep red – and delicately carved cameo glass creations.

Above: Iridescent glass vase of "Jack-in-the-Pulpit" form, with a pinched, globular base below a broad collar that swells into the shape of an orchid-like bloom. Printed maker's mark on the base. *10.5cm (4in) high* **£100–200 BonE**

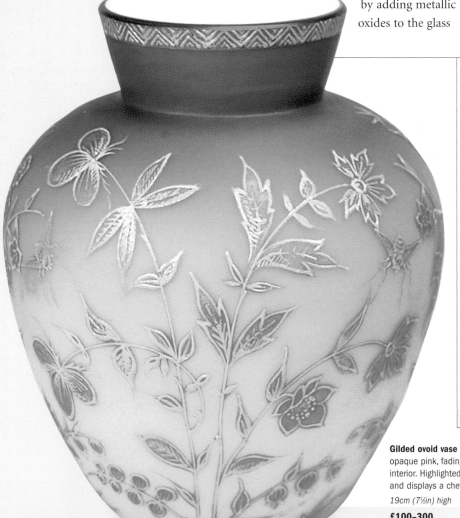

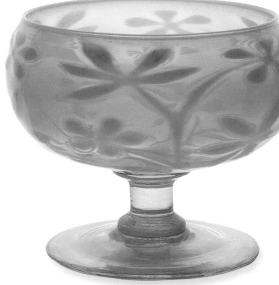

Opalescent "vaseline" glass fruit dish with an ovoid bowl decorated with stylized leaves and flowers, a short stem, and a wide, circular foot. The glass is in shades of yellow and green.
14cm (5½in) high

£300–500 **MW**

Gilded ovoid vase with a short, flared, circular neck. The blown glass body is in a rich, opaque pink, fading to lighter, more translucent tones of pink, and has a creamy white interior. Highlighted with gilding, the body is decorated with flowers, leaves, and butterflies, and displays a chevron pattern border around the rim.
19cm (7½in) high

£100–300 **JDJ**

Stevens & Williams

One of the most innovative of the Stourbridge glassworks in England was Stevens & Williams, which developed an inspiring and inventive range of decorative art glass in the late 19th and early 20th centuries.

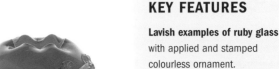

Established in 1847 at Stourbridge, Stevens & Williams is most celebrated for the work of John Northwood. From 1882 onwards, Northwood produced several distinctive lines of art glass.

Combining craftsmanship with inventiveness, his "Matsu-no-ke" glass had colourless stems swirling over a coloured body, and flower forms stamped with a patent-stamping device. The "Silveria" line, introduced by his son John in the late 1890s, had silver foil embedded between layers of clear and coloured glass to create a silvery effect, which was then covered with trailing glass threads.

As well as intaglio – fine, engraved glass – and cameo glass, Stevens & Williams manufactured decorative glass known as "Alexandrite", named after the rare gemstone that appears to change colour depending on the light.

From 1900, art director Frederick Carder – who later founded the Steuben Glassworks in New York (see p.98) – steered the firm towards more advanced taste, as demonstrated by the Japanese-inspired naturalistic decoration of their rock crystal pieces.

Above: "Matsu-no-ke" glass vase with a hombe-shaped body and a crimped rim, and a turquoise case over an opaline ground. The vase has three clear glass feet shaped like scrolling leaves and branches. *c.1885*
18cm (7in) high **£500–800 AL**

KEY FEATURES

Lavish examples of ruby glass with applied and stamped colourless ornament.

Fine engraved glass known as intaglio and Art Nouveau-style cameo glass were produced.

Silvery effects were created by embedding silver foil between different layers of glass.

Multicoloured glass that changes hue from pale amber and blue to deep, vibrant tones was typical of Stevens & Williams vessels.

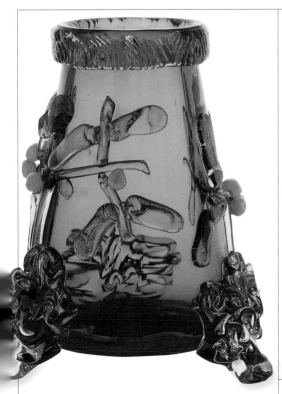

Pale cranberry glass vase of tapering, circular form on three applied, clear glass feet. The vase is decorated with applied and carved mistletoe motifs, and has impressed plant-like motifs on the rim around the neck. *c.1887*
20.25cm (8in) high
£500–800 **AL**

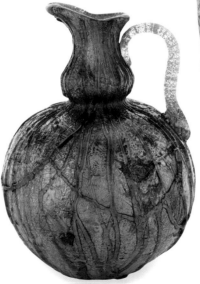

"Silveria" glass ewer with a gourd-like body of opaque, metallic-speckled glass, a rare light blue in colour, and applied glass threads. *c.1901*
17cm (7⅛in) high
£300–500 **AL**

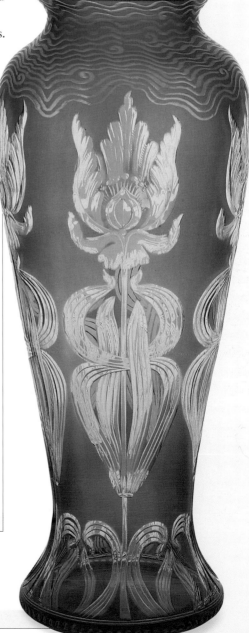

Double-cased red glass vase possibly by Joshua Hodgetts. Baluster-shaped and intaglio cut, it has stylized tulip flower decorations in the restrained English Art Nouveau style. *c.1900*
31cm (12¼in) high
£1,500–2,500 **AL**

KEY FEATURES

Subtle colouring is usual in Powell glassware – often of pale olive-green tint and occasionally featuring pale aquamarine or honey-yellow hues.

Simple but elegantly shaped glass vessels favoured functional designs over a taste for decorative ornament.

Art Nouveau glass by Powell & Whitefriars boasts sinuous organic shapes embellished with finely engraved plant and flower motifs.

The influence of Venetian glass forms is present in much Powell glass, as are decorative techniques such as pincering, moulded fluting, ribbing, filigree, and festooning.

Powell & Whitefriars

Founded in London in the 17th century, the Whitefriars Glassworks made little impact before being acquired in 1834 by James Powell. His innovative son, Harry, became the guiding light of the Art Nouveau period.

With a repertoire of glass forms inspired by ancient Roman glass vessels as well as Venetian, medieval, and simple versions of 18th-century glass, James Powell & Sons came into its own with the production of simple but elegant glassware made from 1859 for the home of William Morris.

The glassworks responded enthusiastically to the criticism levelled at heavy Victorian cut-glass designs by such visionaries as William Morris and John Ruskin, who demanded that the process of working glass material not undermine its qualities.

To this end, Powell embraced the revolutionary fashions in glass, taking up many of the traditional devices found in Venetian glass making, such as pincering, moulded fluting, filigree, festooning, and ribbing.

The company's move to Art Nouveau was guided by Harry Powell, art director and chief designer from 1875. During the 1880s and 90s, Powell glass tended to be decorated with finely engraved plant and flower motifs, and by the end of the century was influenced by the sinuous, organic shapes typical of the Art Nouveau style.

Both the Guild of Handicraft, founded by Charles Robert Ashbee, and the London firm of Liberty & Co. called upon Powell & Whitefriars to produce Art Nouveau designs made from its popular opalescent glass (*see below*), and also glass liners, decanters and crewets.

Above: Opalescent glass fruit bowl by James Powell & Sons. Its bulbous body has a ruffled rim and floral motifs. On a short, knopped stem above a spreading, circular foot. *c.1904* *14cm (5½in) high* **£300–400 MW**

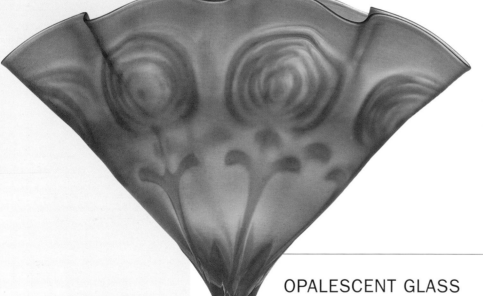

Opalescent glass vase by James Powell & Sons. The fan-like body has a pinched and ruffled rim. It is decorated with stylized flower-heads and plant forms, in shades of pale red and turquoise, and tapering to a slender stem rising from a bell-domed, circular foot. *c.1900* *15.5cm (6in) high* **£500–600 L&T**

OPALESCENT GLASS

Opalescent glass is a heat-sensitive material with a milky-white colouring and, as the name suggests, resembles the gemstone opal. It exhibits a different characteristic when viewed by either reflected or transmitted light, usually showing a yellowish-amber colour when viewed by the latter. Powell's produced three types of opalescent glass: a Venetian type produced in the 1860s that is sometimes streaky with added turquoise threaded decoration; a more yellowish version called "straw opal"; and finally a blue-tinted version called "blue opal". These latter "opals" were developed by Harry Powell between 1877 and 1879.

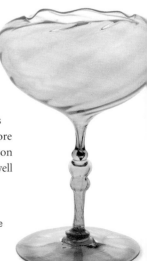

Opalescent glass fruit bowl by the Whitefriars Glassworks. The ruffled-rim bowl, the elongated cup-and-ball knopped stem, and the spreading, circular foot are in "straw opal". *c.1890* *23cm (9in) high* **£1,200–1,500 AL**

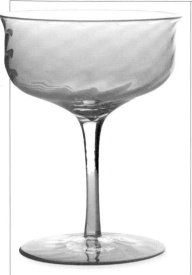

Opalescent wine glass (one from a set of six) made by James Powell & Sons, with a wide bowl tapering to a slender stem on a slightly domed circular foot. *c.1900*

11.5cm (4½in) high

£800–1,200 (the set)   MW

Bell-bowled wine glass by James Powell & Sons. The bottom of the clear glass bowl and tapering stem have stylized floral motifs with trailing stems in green glass. *c.1900*

14.5cm (5¾in) high

£500–700   AL

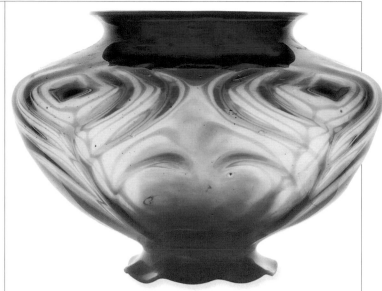

English glass light shade tapering to a circular short neck and rim and a ruffled base. With stylized floral motifs in shades of cranberry. *c.1900*

18.5cm (7¼in) high

£1,000–2,000   MW

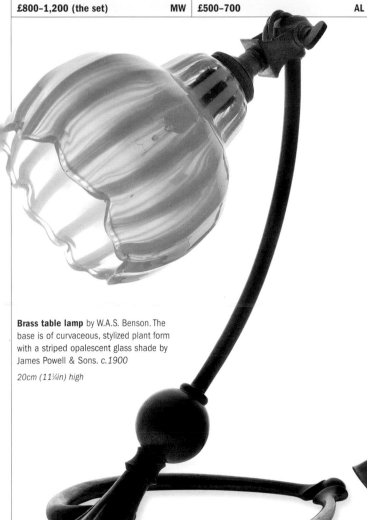

Brass table lamp by W.A.S. Benson. The base is of curvaceous, stylized plant form with a striped opalescent glass shade by James Powell & Sons. *c.1900*

20cm (11¼in) high

£800–1,000   MW

VASELINE GLASS

The late 1870s saw a type of opalescent glass developed in Britain at the Whitefriars Glassworks of James Powell & Sons. Called vaseline glass because of its slick, greasy appearance resembling vaseline, it was initially designed in an attempt to emulate the Venetian glass of the 15th and 16th centuries. The yellowish-green colour of vaseline glass was produced by adding very small quantities of uranium to the batch – a process that has antecedents in Germany in a type of fluorescent glass known as Annagrun or Annagelb glass, which was developed by Josef Riedel in the late 1830s. When this concoction was combined with other metal oxides, vibrant shades of yellow, green, blue, and, more rarely, red were produced. Many household items were made of vaseline glass.

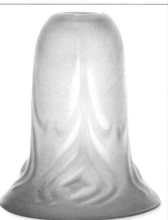

English glass light shade of bell-like form with highly stylized plant-form decoration in pale and dark shades of vaseline glass. *c.1900*

17cm (6¾in) high

£100–150   MW

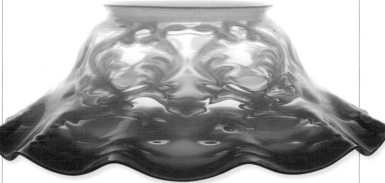

English glass light shade with ruffled rim and stylized plant-form decoration in shades of vaseline-graduating-into-cranberry coloured glass. *c.1900*

34cm (13¼in) diam

£1,400–1,800   MW

Tiffany Studios

Louis Comfort Tiffany, son of jewellery maker Charles, was the most important exponent of Art Nouveau design in America. He is best remembered for his unique glass designs, and in particular, his exquisite lamps.

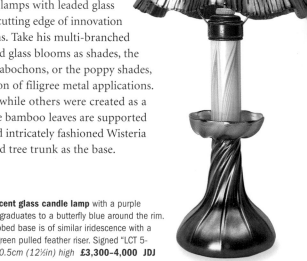

Louis Comfort Tiffany (1848–1933) initially trained as a painter, but later studied glass under Andrea Baldini, a Venetian glass blower. In 1878, he formed Louis Comfort Tiffany and Associated Artists. Tiffany experimented with different glass-making techniques, and in 1880 patented his own type of iridescent glass, known as "Favrile" (meaning handcrafted).

A true perfectionist, Tiffany's earliest examples of freeblown glass finally went on sale in 1892, a line he was to continue until 1928.

It is difficult to categorize these pieces because they were produced in hundreds of forms and thousands of colour combinations. The majority of important pieces were vases, ranging from flower forms, goose-necks, miniatures, and even floor vases. Pieces could be of a single hue, such as gold or blue, or a mixture of colours. Red is the most rare and most valuable colour. The best pieces are decorated with blown-in floral decoration.

Tiffany is best remembered for his leaded lamps (*see below*), which were also his most commercially successful area of production. Designs could be as simple as a geometric pattern in a single colour to a domed Laburnum lamp with dripping blossoms under a confetti ground.

Tiffany also introduced a broad range of table pieces, including plates, goblets, and bowls. These were usually in a single colour, most often gold.

Above: Wisteria blossom Favrile glass chandelier with a domed-drapery shade and a bronze mount. This piece is exceptionally rare and there are only two other known examples in existence. *61cm (24in) wide* **£200,000–250,000 SI**

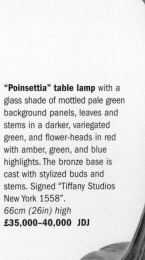
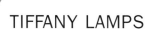

"Poinsettia" table lamp with a glass shade of mottled pale green background panels, leaves and stems in a darker, variegated green, and flower-heads in red with amber, green, and blue highlights. The bronze base is cast with stylized buds and stems. Signed "Tiffany Studios New York 1558". *66cm (26in) high* **£35,000–40,000 JDJ**

TIFFANY LAMPS

The name of Tiffany to many people is either synonymous with breakfast or, more importantly, stunning lamps with leaded glass shades. Louis Comfort Tiffany was at the cutting edge of innovation when it came to these wonderful creations. Take his multi-branched Lily lamps with their dangling bell-shaped glass blooms as shades, the dragonfly lamps applied with jewel-like cabochons, or the poppy shades, their blooms emphasized with the addition of filigree metal applications. Some lamps came with separate stands, while others were created as a whole. For instance, shades fashioned like bamboo leaves are supported on a bronze stem simulating bamboo, and intricately fashioned Wisteria lamps, in various colours, have a gnarled tree trunk as the base.

Blue iridescent glass candle lamp with a purple shade that graduates to a butterfly blue around the rim. The swirl-ribbed base is of similar iridescence with a white and green pulled feather riser. Signed "LCT 5-66639". *30.5cm (12½in) high* **£3,300–4,000 JDJ**

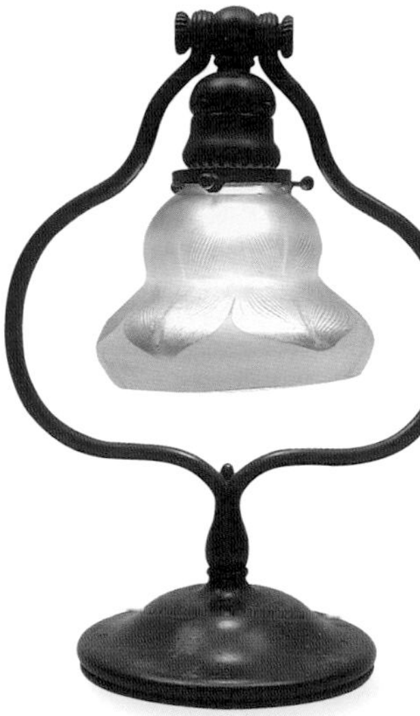

Harp desk lamp with bronze base and pulled-feather glass shade. The shade is signed "LCT" and the base is signed "Tiffany Studios New York 419. 5-66640".

34.5cm (13½in) high

£1,200–1,800 **JDJ**

CORNERSTONE PIECE

Rare "Nasturtium trellis" pattern hanging lamp of outstanding quality. The glass shade features nasturtium flowers executed in red, amber, and lavender, and mottled green leaves and stems all set against a blue-grey background. The composition also incorporates numerous pieces of confetti glass. The lower rim of the shade is trimmed with bronze beads. All of the glass panels are tight and intact.

71cm (28in) wide **£60,000–70,000 JDJ**

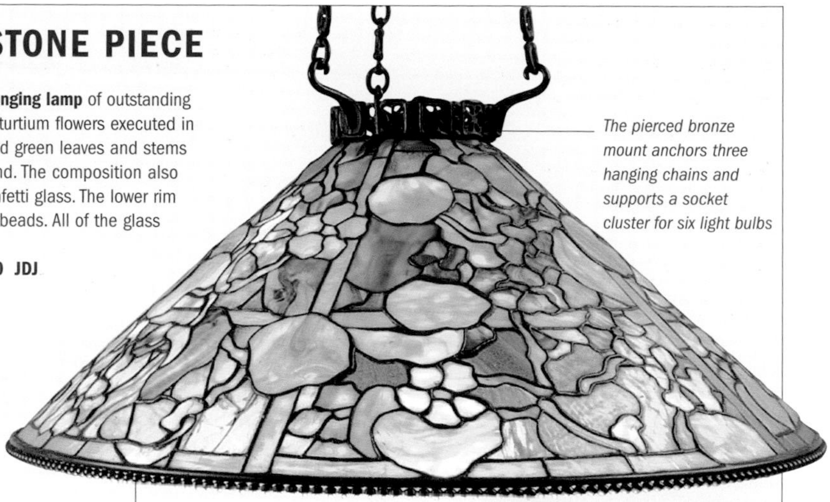

The pierced bronze mount anchors three hanging chains and supports a socket cluster for six light bulbs

The lower rim of the shade is trimmed with bronze beading that echoes the bronze mount and chains of the upper rim. Over time the beading has developed an aesthetically pleasing, rich, dark reddish-brown patination

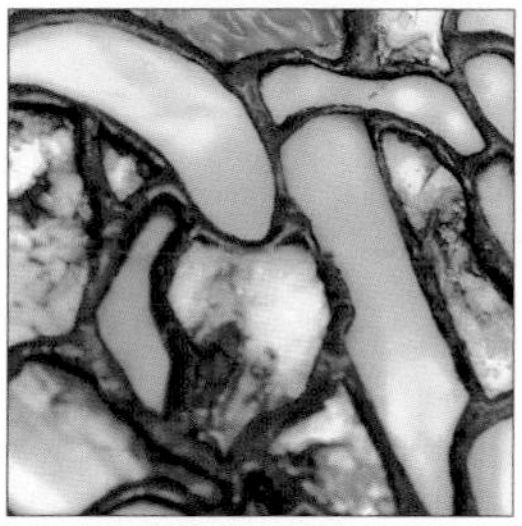

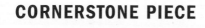

An intricate composition of subtle colouration in which nasturtiums, leaves, and stems are set against a mottled blue-grey ground.

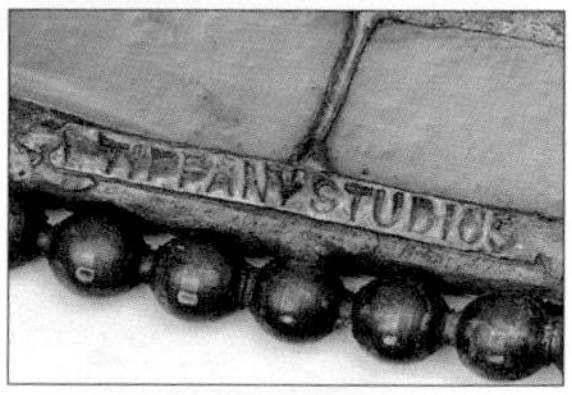

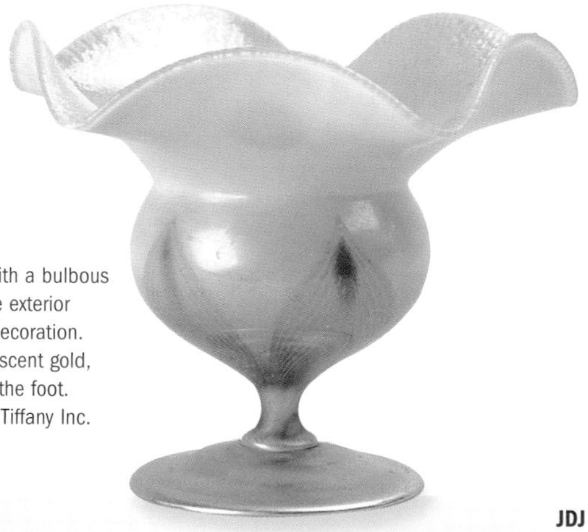

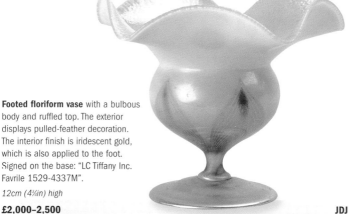

Footed floriform vase with a bulbous body and ruffled top. The exterior displays pulled-feather decoration. The interior finish is iridescent gold, which is also applied to the foot. Signed on the base: "LC Tiffany Inc. Favrile 1529-4337M".

12cm (4¾in) high

£2,000–2,500 **JDJ**

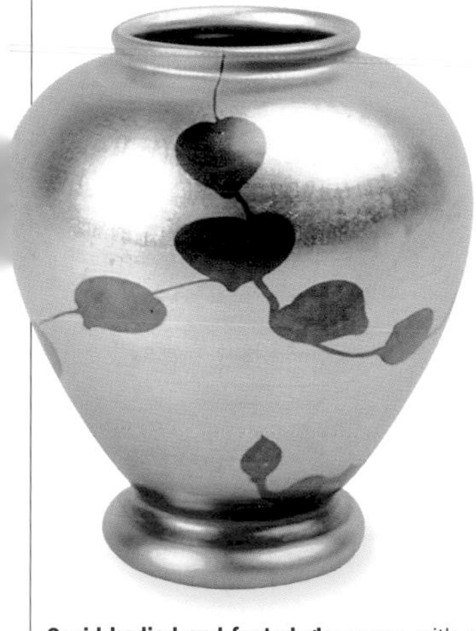

Ovoid-bodied and footed glass vase with an iridescent blue finish and vine-leaf motifs in shades of green. The underside of the base is signed "LC Tiffany Favrile. 244G".

17.5cm (7in) high

£2,200–2,700 **JDJ**

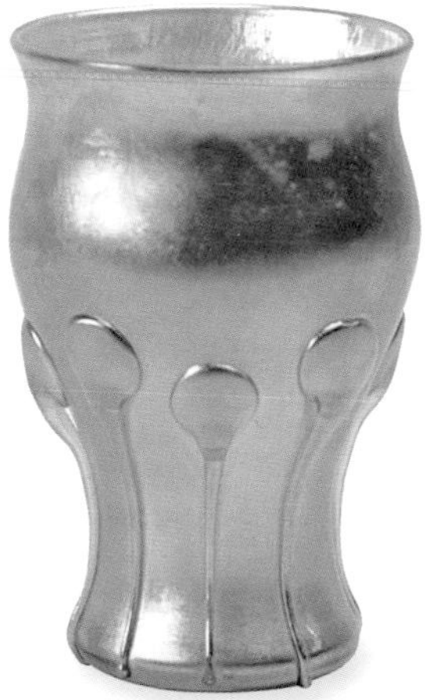

Small iridescent gold vase with blue and amethyst highlights and eight stylized flower-heads with elongated stems. Signed on the base "LCT M5649".

10cm (4in) high

£400–500 **JDJ**

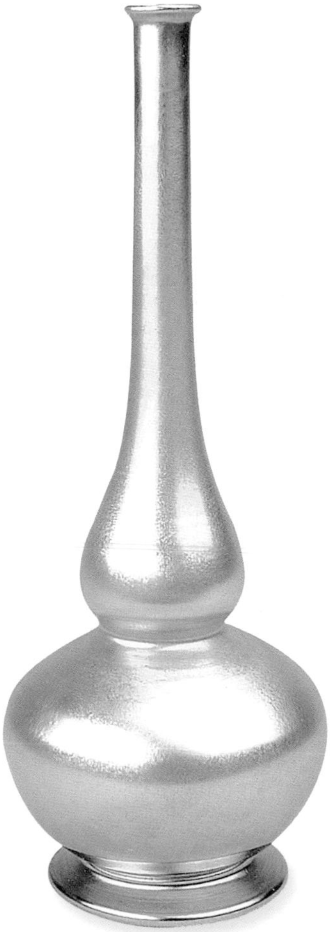

Bulbous stick vase of double-gourd shape with an elongated neck and iridescent finish. In good-to-excellent condition and signed on the base "LC Tiffany-Favrile 9000G".

30cm (11¾in) high

£2,000–2,400 **JDJ**

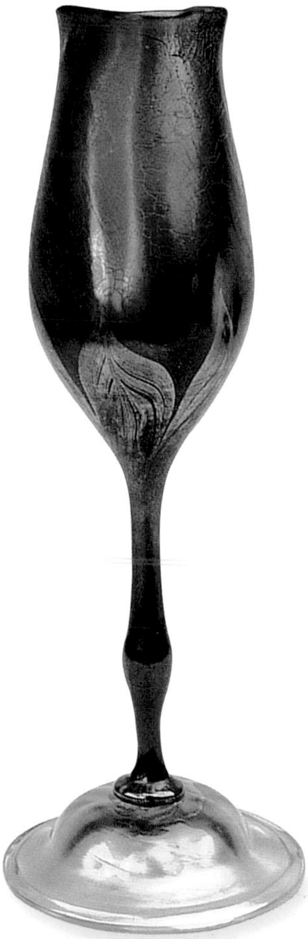

Tulip-shaped vase of exceptional quality. The gold iridescent foot has five leaves and the stem and bowl have a pulled flower and leaf design. Signed "LCT M3446".

44.5cm (17½in) high

£25,000–30,000 **JDJ**

Steuben Glass Works

Named in 1903 after the US county in which it was based, the Steuben Glass Works grew during the Art Nouveau period to become one of the finest glass-making enterprises in the United States, producing a large variety of shapes and finishes.

The story of Steuben is the story of Frederick Carder (1863–1963), a talented English glass designer who moved to Corning in New York's Steuben county, to manage the newly expanded T.G. Hawkes & Co. glass studio, which was later renamed the Steuben Glass Works.

Carder is accredited with over 6,000 glass shapes in over 100 finishes in his 30 years at Steuben. The most popular ware, named "Aurene" after the Latin for gold, was a series of plain or decorated gold and blue lustred glass, produced from 1904 to 1930. Bowls, vases, glasses, and decanters were all produced using Aurene glass. Another important line was *verre-de-soie*, a lightly iridescent glass that was much favoured during the Art Nouveau period. Carder's broad range of techniques included blown glass, engraved crystal, acid-cut, *pâte-de-verre*, and pressed glass.

Carder continued to design after the Art Nouveau style declined, but was less comfortable with designing simpler, modern forms.

Above: "Tyrian" glass vase of baluster shape decorated with heart and vine motifs. The body has blue and purple shading with solid purple around the base. The underside of the base is signed "Tyrian". *18.5cm (7¼in) high* **£6,500–£7,500 JDJ**

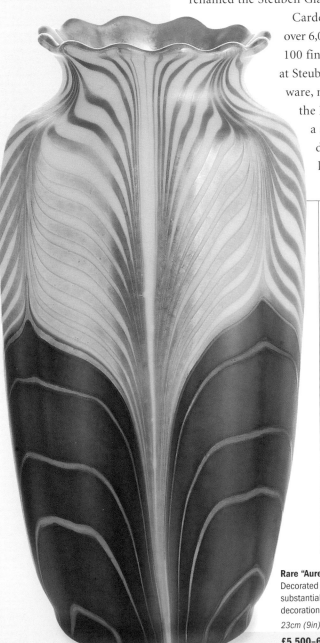

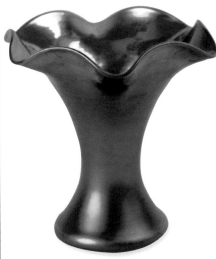

"Aurene" glass vase in iridescent dark blue. Its concave body flares down to a round foot and up to a wider ruffled rim. Signed on the base "Aurene 723".
15cm (6in) high
£300–450 JDJ

Rare "Aurene" vase of baluster shape with a flared and ruffled rim. Decorated Aurene pieces are more desirable and command substantially higher prices than their plain equivalents. This vase's decoration comprises iridescent pulled feather motifs. *c.1915*
23cm (9in) high
£5,500–6,000 TDC

Verre-de-Soie crystal glass in the Venetian style. It has a stepped round foot, slender stem, and tulip-shaped bowl with ruffled iridescent rim. *c.1912*
21cm (8¼in) high
£300–400 TDC

Quezal

The Quezal Art Glass and Decorating Company operated throughout the later part of the Art Nouveau period, and produced vibrant, highly collectable ornamental glass, using old and contemporary styles.

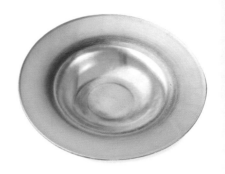

Two Tiffany glassworks employees, Martin Bach and Thomas Johnson, founded the Quezal Art Glass and Decorating Company in 1901 in Brooklyn, New York, for the production of fine art glass pieces. The company name comes from the quetzal, a Central American trogon bird with emerald, ruby, and gold plumage.

The vases, glasses, lampshades, and tableware follow the classical, organic shapes, rich lustrous colours, and decorating techniques (applied shells and silver overlay) that were used at Tiffany. Their unmarked pieces made before 1902 can be mistakenly attributed to Tiffany or Steuben, among others. An outraged Louis Comfort Tiffany purportedly wished to stop

Quezal producing the copied lustred pieces, and his firm eventually developed new colours to differentiate their products.

Perhaps it was the difficulty inherent in producing this labour-intensive glass, but the company finally closed in 1924, three years after Martin Bach's death.

Above: Footed glass comport with flat rim in iridescent green graduating to iridescent blue at the inner rim. The bowl section and the foot are in bright iridescent gold. Unsigned.
24cm (9½in) wide **£550–750 JDJ**

KEY FEATURES

Glass is mostly freeblown, usually symmetrical in form, and decorated with pulled designs.

Applied handles, pedestals, or bases are found on some pieces.

A variety of marks was used by the company, but many pieces, especially flower forms, remain unmarked.

High standards of workmanship make Quezal glass valuable, especially flower forms.

Strong colour, bright lustre, and decoration on both sides, as well as any unusual features, increase the value of a piece.

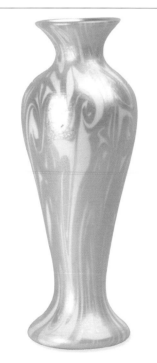

"King Tut" glass vase of elongated baluster shape with iridescent gold pattern in a swirling stylized plant-form. The interior also has an iridescent gold finish. Signed "Quezal" on the base.
21.5cm (8½in) high
£1,500–1,800 **JDJ**

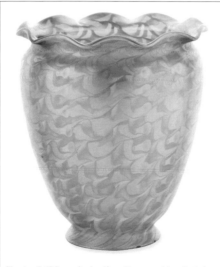

"Lustre Art" lampshade shaped to resemble a footed vase with a ruffled rim. It is decorated with a diagonal wave-like pattern sponged in white against a bright gold iridescent background, and is engraved "Lustre Art".
12cm (4¾in) high
£140–200 **CR**

Floriform gold lustre glass vase with ruffle-rimmed and flared body above a bulbous stem that tapers to a splayed round foot. The yellow-gold lustre of the body graduates to a foot of green and pinkish-red. The base is etched "Quezal".
16cm (6¼in) high
£450–550 **CR**

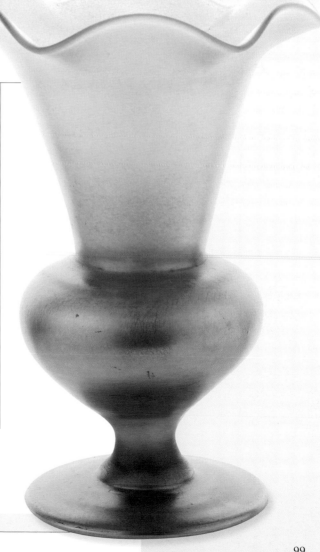

Handel Co.

The Connecticut-based Handel Company, most famous for its glass lampshades, produced a range of decorative glass items from 1893. A unique, frosted, ice finish and reverse-painted method was used to decorate many pieces.

Philip Julius Handel grew up in one of the most important glass-making centres of the United States – Meriden, Connecticut – and in 1885, with his colleague Adolph Eydam, he set up the Eydam and Handel Company. This early incarnation decorated mostly opal glassware such as shades and vases, for which it purchased blanks. The partnership with Eydam ended in 1892 and the firm then became Handel Co., before being incorporated in 1903.

The rapid spread of domestic electricity in the United States brought much success to the company, and, before long, Handel was producing a wide array of finely crafted table, floor, and hanging lamps. Most lamps were leaded or reverse-painted and commonly decorated with floral patterns or landscapes, or, more unusually, Venetian or tropical scenes.

Handel also successfully produced reverse-painted lampshades in a type of enamel-decorated, frosted, textured glass called "Teroma", as well as a range of art glass known as Handel Ware.

Above: Leaded glass table lamp with a mottled blue shade with pink and red blossoms and green leaves around the rim. The bronze base is embossed with floral motifs.
52cm (20½in) high **£2,000–2,500 BMN**

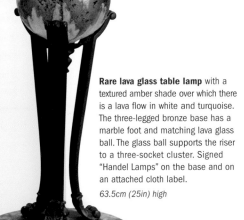

Rare lava glass table lamp with a textured amber shade over which there is a lava flow in white and turquoise. The three-legged bronze base has a marble foot and matching lava glass ball. The glass ball supports the riser to a three-socket cluster. Signed "Handel Lamps" on the base and on an attached cloth label.
63.5cm (25in) high

£8,000–9,500 **JDJ**

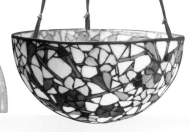

Hanging light shade of inverted dome form. The leaded glass is executed in an all-over floral design in mauve, yellow, blue, white, and green. The inner rim bears the factory monogram.
30.5cm (12in) wide

£400–600 **L&T**

"Teroma" reverse-painted table lamp decorated with oak leaves and acorns. The base has a three-socket cluster and acorn pulls. Signed "Handel Pat'd No. 979664".
57cm (22½in) high

£2,400–2,800 **JDJ**

Leaded glass table lamp with drop-apron domed shade with an apple blossom and foliage pattern. The patinated bronze base rises to a three-light cluster.
65.5cm (25½in) high

£3,200–3,800 **SI**

Pairpoint Corp.

By combining mass-production and artisanal techniques, the Pairpoint Corporation produced a successful range of artistic glass and metal products as well as popular reverse-painted moulded lampshades.

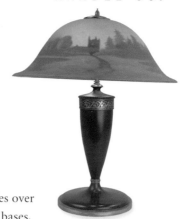

The Pairpoint Manufacturing Company was established in 1880 to supply the Mount Washington Glass Company with the Britannia metal, or white-metal alloy stands and holders needed for its glass items. It was erected right next door to Mount Washington, and took on the name of its first superintendent, Englishman Thomas J. Pairpoint. The two companies merged in 1900 to become the Pairpoint Corporation.

The new company produced cut, etched, moulded, and blown glass, along with a selection of quadruple-plated metal items. Pairpoint is best known today for its Puffy lamps (*see p.71*) and its table lamps with reverse-painted, acid-etched blown glass shades over patinated spelter bases, which came on the market in around 1904.

Like many other luxury goods companies, Pairpoint suffered greatly during the Great Depression of the 1930s, and their glass and silver departments were sold in 1938. However, the company was ultimately re-organized, and operates today a thriving business in Cape Cod, Massachusetts.

Above: Reverse-painted table lamp decorated with a rural landscape and bearing the artist's signature, "A Fox". The turned wooden base has a brass-trimmed foot and filigree brass-banded shoulder. Marked "5-66844". *61cm (24in) high* **£1,800–2,600 JDJ**

KEY FEATURES

The Pairpoint mark is a "P" within a diamond, and is used on some pieces.

Art glass by Pairpoint is generally more affordable and easier to come by than the valuable and sought-after Pairpoint lamps.

Three types of lampshade were produced by Pairpoint: the Puffy lamp with a blown-out shade, often with reverse-painted, floral designs; "ribbed", reverse-painted lampshades; and "scenic" lamps, occasionally signed by the artist.

Typical characteristics include frosted lampshades and lamp bases made of bronze, copper, brass, silver, or wood.

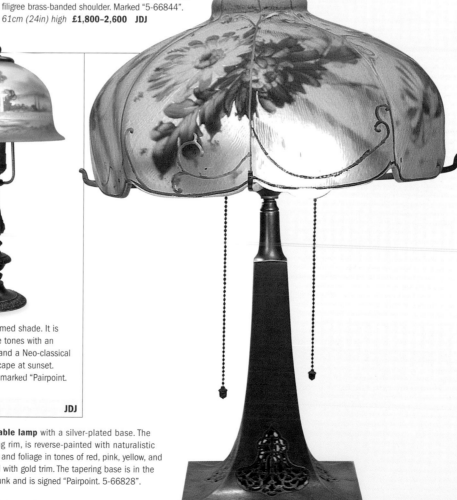

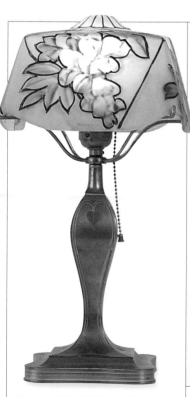

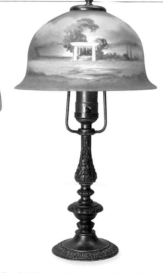

Boudoir lamp with a domed shade. It is reverse-painted in subtle tones with an exterior stone staircase and a Neo-classical folly set in a park landscape at sunset. The brass-finish base is marked "Pairpoint. 5-66723".

£1,400–2,200 **JDJ**

"Portsmouth" boudoir lamp with a shade reverse-painted with pink, white, and mauve flowers, and green stems and leaves outlined in black. The wooden base is painted with leaves. Signed "Pairpoint Corp".

20.25cm (8in) high

£2,300–3,000 **JDJ**

"Florenceian" shade table lamp with a silver-plated base. The shade has an undulating rim, is reverse-painted with naturalistic chrysanthemum blooms and foliage in tones of red, pink, yellow, and green, and is highlighted with gold trim. The tapering base is in the form of a stylized tree trunk and is signed "Pairpoint. 5-66828".

53.5cm (21in) high

£5,000–6,000 **JDJ**

American Glass

The art of glassmaking underwent a renaissance in the United States after the seminal 1876 Centennial Exposition in Philadelphia, and styles developed at a rapid pace under the influence of the Arts and Crafts movement and the Art Nouveau designs coming out of Europe. The florid style that was popular at the main northeastern factories, such as Tiffany, Mount Washington, and Handel during the 1890s, fell out of favour by the end of the century and the companies adopted a simpler, bolder aesthetic, producing striking pieces resplendent with peacock feathers and plumes on lustred surfaces, or setting strong geometric patterns in leaded glass. These later pieces are still very popular with collectors today.

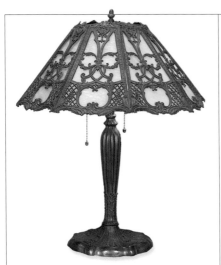

Unsigned table lamp with octagonal, patinated bronze base and shade. The shade has cast floral and foliate motifs, pierced latticework, and pearl-grey slag glass.

57.75cm (22½in) high

£250–400   SI

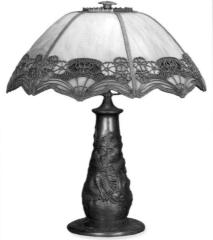

Charles Parker table lamp with patinated bronze base with relief dragon imagery. The bronze shade has pearl-grey slag glass and a floral polychrome glass border.

57cm (22½in) high

£900–1,100   SI

Unsigned table lamp with a patinated bronze, urn-shaped base. The domed, drop-apron, leaded glass shade has rows of mottled mint and apple green tiles, above an irregular-shaped floral and foliate border.

55.75cm (21¾in) high

£2,000–2,500   SI

Kew Blas

Kew Blas art glass was manufactured by the Union Glass Company from the late 1890s to 1924. Many of the company's designs were heavily influenced by Tiffany, Quezal, and other Art Nouveau manufacturers, but the Kew Blas range featured two distinctive types of art glass of its own. The first was opaque glass, often white, decorated with iridescent green and gold feathering on the exterior and gold iridescence on the interior. The second type was amber glass in a freeblown, single-layer style. Most Kew Blas pieces were well designed and executed, but the quality was variable. Flaws, discolouration, and poor workmanship lower a piece's value. Signed pieces, as ever, command a premium.

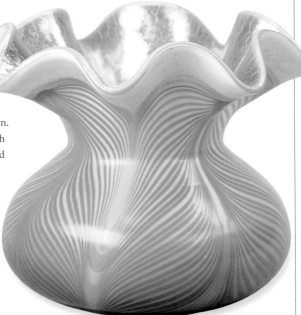

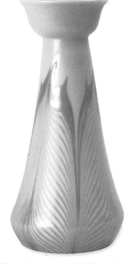

Kew Blas glass vase with iridescent green and gold pulled-feather decoration on a creamy white ground, beneath an iridescent gold rim. The interior is finished in iridescent blue.

13.5cm (6½in) high

£1,500–1,800   JDJ

Kew Blas glass vase with iridescent green and gold pulled-feather decoration on a creamy white ground. The inside is iridescent gold. Signed "Kew Blas" on the base.

23cm (9in) high

£650–850   JDJ

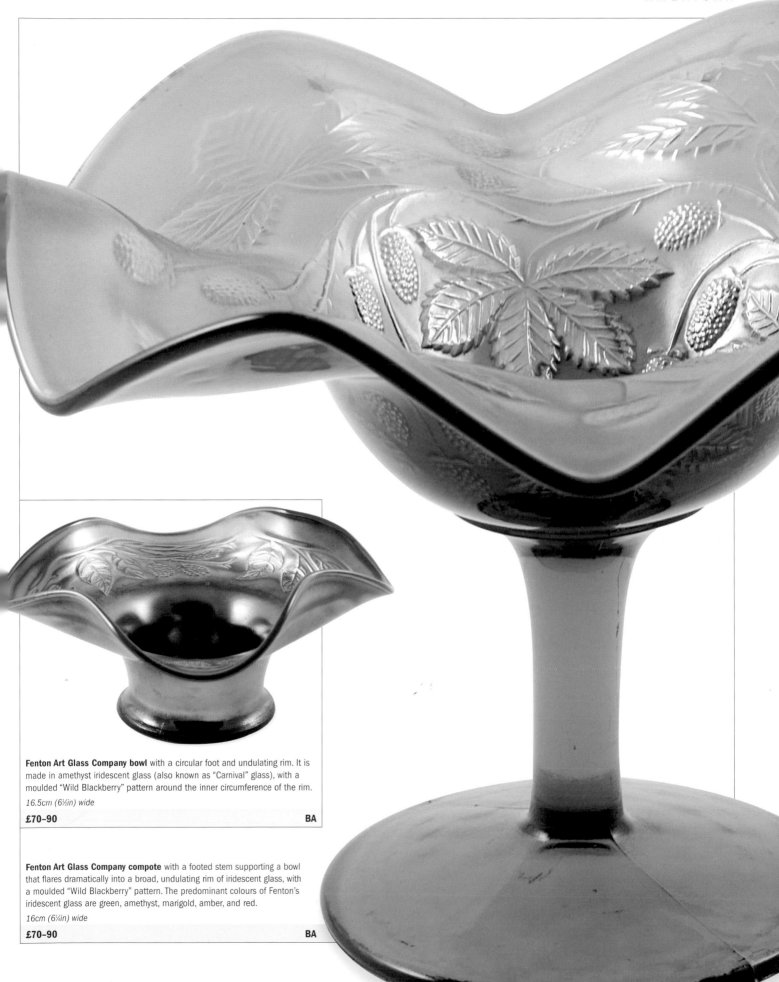

Fenton Art Glass Company bowl with a circular foot and undulating rim. It is made in amethyst iridescent glass (also known as "Carnival" glass), with a moulded "Wild Blackberry" pattern around the inner circumference of the rim.

16.5cm (6½in) wide

£70–90   **BA**

Fenton Art Glass Company compote with a footed stem supporting a bowl that flares dramatically into a broad, undulating rim of iridescent glass, with a moulded "Wild Blackberry" pattern. The predominant colours of Fenton's iridescent glass are green, amethyst, marigold, amber, and red.

16cm (6¼in) wide

£70–90   **BA**

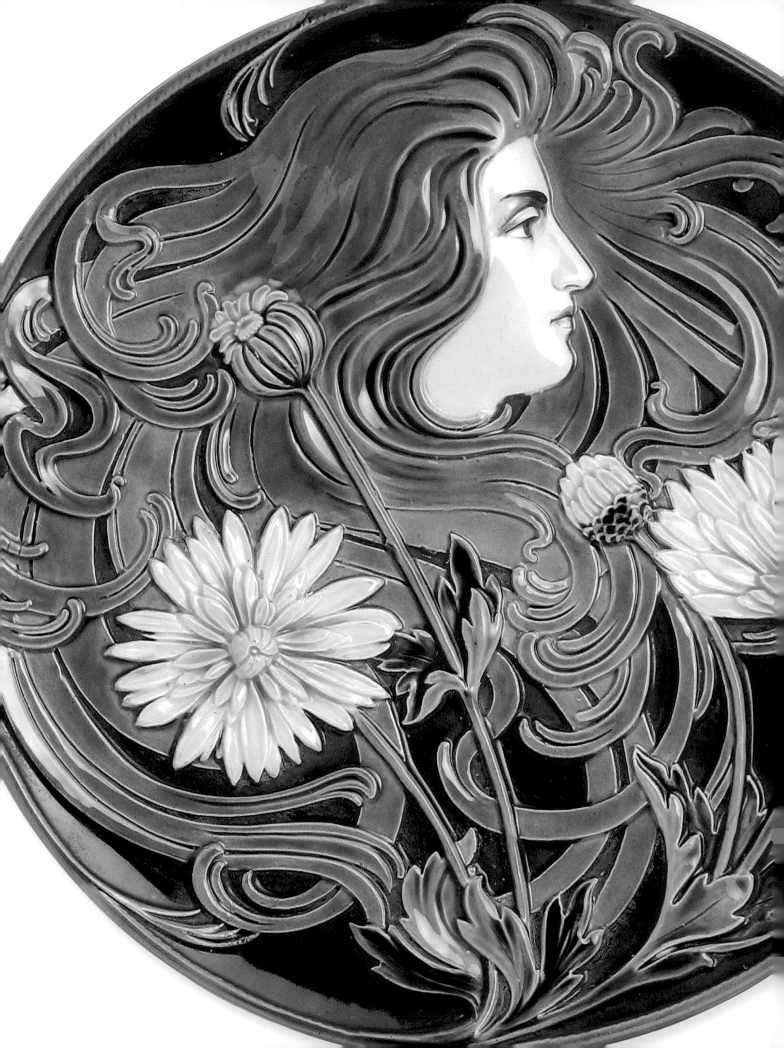

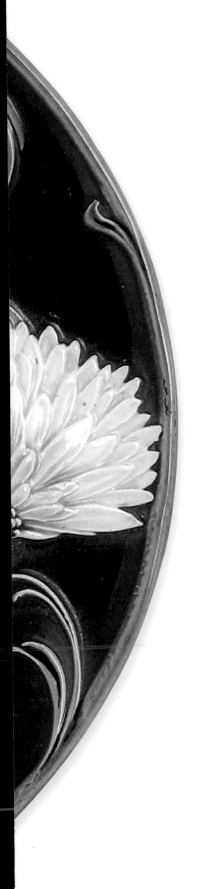

Ceramics

The changes brought about by the development of the Art Nouveau style in the late 19th century were less conspicuous in ceramics than in other areas of the decorative arts, such as furniture, glass, or jewellery. This was due in part to the very nature of the material, which, being opaque, lacks the dramatic radiance of a glass vessel or a sparkling gemstone.

Of all the ceramicists who embraced the "New Art", no single figure emerges as its champion, as did Lalique in jewellery or Tiffany and Gallé in glass. Ceramics was nonetheless a medium well suited to the Art Nouveau style, as the malleable nature of clay meant that it could easily be moulded into organic, curving forms.

Decorative motifs were painted in a broad range of shades and frequently took their inspiration from the natural world: long, slender-stemmed flowers and grasses in soft hues were as common as swirling leaves and branches picked out in bold, contrasting colours. Potters also explored a variety of manufacturing and sculptural techniques, such as hand-painting, slip trailing, and transfer-printing, and employed them to great effect to create distinctive organic shapes embellished with sinuous, trailing designs.

A NEW DIRECTION

Reacting against mass-produced, flamboyantly decorated ceramics that relied on historical styles for inspiration, a small but forward-looking band of potters across Europe – especially in France – forged a new direction. They created highly influential designs, rejecting the constraints of traditional forms in favour of individually crafted, high-quality ceramic wares. These artist-potters were so successful in their mission that industrial ceramics manufacturers were inspired to invest in art-potteries.

Across the Atlantic, ceramics cast off its image as a wholly utilitarian medium and also embraced a decorative role. Potters took their cue from Europe and experimented with new and unusual shapes, lustrous glazes, and naturalistic, decorative motifs.

Circular earthenware plaque, probably German, naturalistically coloured and moulded in relief with a profile of a girl with sinuous hair surrounded by chrysanthemums.
31.5cm (12½in) wide **£400–500 DN**

EXPERIMENTAL GLAZES

As with other disciplines in the decorative arts, France led the way for change in ceramics, with artist-potter Joseph-Théodore Deck (1823–91) rejecting conventional decorative imagery in favour of the bold designs found on ancient Turkish, Persian, and Far Eastern pottery, on which the glaze rather than imagery took centre stage.

For Deck and his disciples throughout France – including Félix Bracquemond, Ernest Chaplet, Clément Massier, Pierre-Adrien Dalpayrat, and Taxile Doat – it was Japan that exercised the most influence. For many of these artist-craftsmen, the form of the pot was merely a vehicle for a wide variety of experimental glazes. As a statement, a pot that was an organic, naturalistic shape often mattered less than the coloured glazes that were used to cover it.

VARIATIONS ON A THEME

Beyond France, Art Nouveau ceramics tended to show both national and regional characteristics, but with obvious influences from other countries. The new styles that emerged were particularly successful in Germany and Scandinavia, where they were adopted for serial production in around 1900 by the large factories.

Sèvres porcelain crystalline glaze vase of merging reddish-grey tones, with a gilt-bronze raspberry-and-leaf modelled stand. The bronze cover is modelled to match. Displays a stamped code. *1906*
16.5cm (6½in) high **£7,000-11,000 MACK**

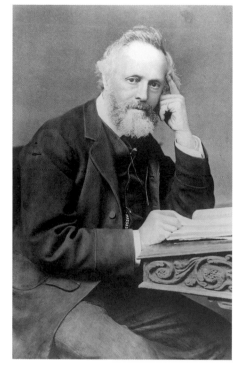

Sir Henry Doulton established the art-pottery department at his family pottery, utilizing the talents of young men and, importantly, women from the Lambeth School of Art.

In Berlin, the tradition-bound Königliche Porzellan Manufaktur (K.P.M.) ventured tentatively into Jugendstil following the arrival of Theodor Schmuz-Baudiss in 1902, decorating its vases and tableware with curving lines and flower patterns. The Staatliche Porzellan Manufaktur at Meissen also commissioned outside designers, including Henry van de Velde and Peter Behrens, to create innovative modern styles.

The art pottery that took centre stage in the Netherlands from the 1880s onwards fell into two distinct categories. Some designers embraced the fluid, curvaceous style and the asymmetrical

DEFINITIVE STYLES

Stylized motifs from nature influenced Art Nouveau ceramics designs, with established factories taking a commercial view, adapting their wares to accommodate. Many took the organic and naturalistic route, in tandem with those of more innovative and abstracted form, but few slavishly copied nature. The lichen-covered appearance of the Sèvres vase (above) contrasts with the formalized treatments of the lustrous Zsolnay flask or the mossy-green glaze of the Grueby vase (both opposite).

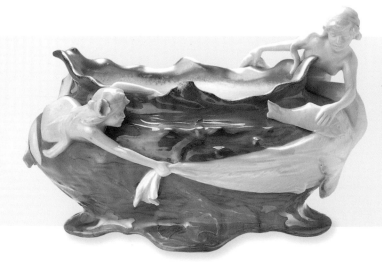

Rosenthal "Kronach" porcelain jardinière of an oval shape with an undulating rim. The body is of marbled grey tone and is applied in relief with white, slightly lustrous figures of two mermaids, one removing a fish from the net they are both holding. With gilded detailing. *c.1900*
23cm (9in) high **£700-900 VZ**

naturalistic decoration promoted by the School of Nancy, while others preferred a more formalized geometric approach. As both strands of the Art Nouveau style increased in popularity, however, many designers and factories shrewdly accommodated the taste for both. At the Rozenburg works, the chemist M.N. Engelden introduced a wafer-thin "eggshell porcelain", which was used to create a delightful line of Art Nouveau-inspired wares vividly decorated in a style more evocative of Java in the Dutch East Indies than of Japan.

CERAMICS FOR THE MASSES

With the exception of the Viennese workshops that employed designers such as Josef Hoffmann, Michael Powolny, and Otto Prutscher, ceramic production in central Europe tended to cater mainly to popular taste. The family firm of Zsolnay at Pecs in Hungary produced a range of vividly coloured lustreware, while the Amphora factory at Teplitz and the Royal Dux works near Prague turned out ceramics embellished with coloured cabochons, and accented with gilding, and sculpture in the style of languid bronze *femmes-fleur* seen at Paris Salons.

The late-Victorian ceramics industry in Britain charted its own path, too caught up in the revival of various eclectic historical styles to pay much attention to developments in Europe. However, a small group sought inspiration in the Arts and Crafts designs of William Morris, and were influenced by the elegant, Japanese-style decoration favoured by the Aesthetic movement. This led them to create new ceramic forms and invent a breathtaking range of glazes.

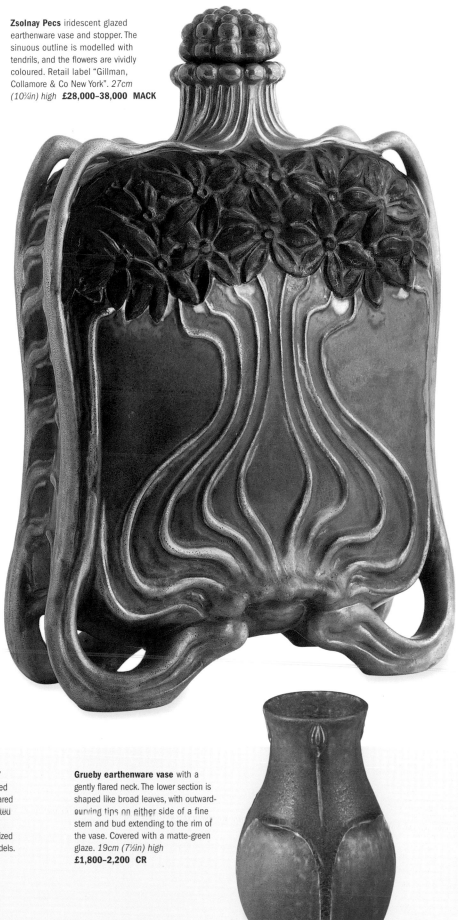

Zsolnay Pecs iridescent glazed earthenware vase and stopper. The sinuous outline is modelled with tendrils, and the flowers are vividly coloured. Retail label "Gillman, Collamore & Co New York". *27cm (10¾in) high* **£28,000–38,000 MACK**

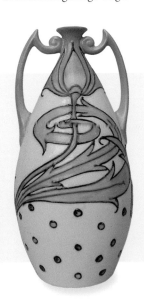

Minton earthenware "Secessionist" twin-handled vase, probably designed by John Wadsworth. It has a short, flared neck and sinuous loop handles painted in pale blue. Further tube lining is decorated in colours with highly stylized leaves and flowers above small roundels. *22cm (8½in) high* **£400–600 PC**

Grueby earthenware vase with a gently flared neck. The lower section is shaped like broad leaves, with outward-curving tips on either side of a fine stem and bud extending to the rim of the vase. Covered with a matte-green glaze. *19cm (7½in) high* **£1,800–2,200 CR**

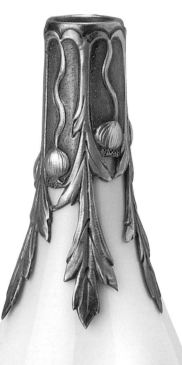

BOLD DESIGNS

Among the most innovative of British ceramics designers was William Moorcroft at Burslem, whose Florian ware was decorated with arrangements of flowers and peacock feathers. At Doulton, Eliza Simmance, Frank Butler, Mark V. Marshall and Margaret E. Thompson, were the chief exponents of the Art Nouveau style and produced stunning pieces. Meanwhile, the Minton factory created its own version of Austrian ceramics with the Secessionist-inspired wares designed by Louis Solon and John Wadsworth. But without question the most unusual and amusing designs to emerge were the grotesque animals, birds, and mythological beasts created in salt-glazed stoneware by the Martin brothers in London.

Developments in the United States often mirrored those in Europe. Tiffany was successful with boldly sculpted, nature-inspired pieces with earth-toned glazes. Meanwhile natural themes received a different treatment with the delicate palette of the Rookwood Pottery. The truly American "New Art" was also being established in this medium by remarkable figures such as George Ohr, who seemed to completely abandon traditional ideas for new and experimental designs.

NEW TECHNIQUES

Broadly speaking, Art Nouveau ceramicists – from individual artist-potters and small studios to large commercial factories – fall into three distinct categories depending on their technical specialities. In many cases, craftsmen used two or all three of these techniques together to stunning effect.

Heading this list are the craftsmen or factories that created breathtaking new decorative glazes. Across Europe and in the United States, much time and energy was spent experimenting with glazes in an effort to produce dramatic visual and textural effects to rival those of Japanese ceramics. The Fulper and Grueby potteries in the United States were particularly innovative with new, rich glazing techniques, which became the signature of their Art Nouveau work. At Fulper, glazes were even scientifically researched to produce recreations of ancient and rare art glazes.

The success of the glaze hinged on the creation of the perfect recipe. A combination of skilfully blended ingredients would ultimately achieve a desirable colour, lack of transparency, and surface textures when fired at a specific temperature. The erratic nature of the kiln could be depended upon to produce unpredictable and decorative results – such as veining, blistering, or unevenness of colour – that created beautiful, highly individual ceramics.

Among the many types of sumptuous glazes developed during the Art Nouveau period and practised in France were those boasting two-colour "marbleized" and crystalline effects, the distinctive rich red *sang-de-boeuf*, high-fired flambé matte glazes, and shimmering metallic lustreware in vivid violets, oranges, lemon yellows, and blues.

Bing & Grondahl porcelain vase, delicately painted in soft colours with clover leaves, and further embellished with elaborate poppy seed-pod silver mounts. c.1902. 17cm (6¾in) high **£550–650 VZ**

FORM AND DECORATION

Artists experimented with different forms, decoration, and coloured glazes to create ceramics in the Art Nouveau style. Pieces were commonly decorated with naturalistic motifs – flower-heads, trailing stems and leaves, birds, and animals – as well as the figural motif of the femme-fleur, which met with a particularly eager public. Sculptural elements such as figural handles or floral blooms forming the rim of a vase, were further incorporated to beneficial effect.

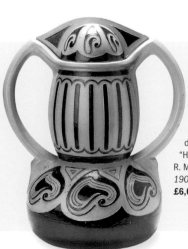

Henry van de Velde grey stoneware vase with twin handles, moulded with stylized sinuous leaves with a deep-blue glaze. It has a drop-in domed cover. Embossed "H.v.d. Velde"; produced by R. Merkelbach, Grenzhausen. 1902. 17cm (13½in) high **£6,000–7,000 VZ**

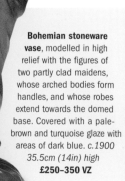

Bohemian stoneware vase, modelled in high relief with the figures of two partly clad maidens, whose arched bodies form handles, and whose robes extend towards the domed base. Covered with a pale-brown and turquoise glaze with areas of dark blue. c.1900 35.5cm (14in) high **£250–350 VZ**

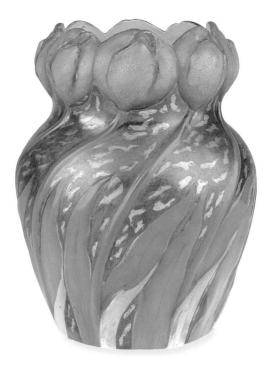

Utzschneider & Cie, Sarreguemines stoneware vase, the neck relief-moulded with pink tulip blooms, and the pale blue stems and leaves set against a partially lustrous ground. *1900* *22.5cm (8¾in) high* **£400-600 Qu**

SCULPTURAL FORMS

The second technical speciality embraced by studio potters and commercial factories alike was modelling, or sculpting. Jean Carriès was influenced by Japanese forms and made many simple pots with fine glazes. He was perhaps best known, however, for creating a wide range of sculptural stoneware busts in the form of portraits, vegetables, fruits, grotesque masks, amphibians, and monsters. Several of his students followed his lead, including Alexandre Bigot, who produced architectural and sculptural designs in glazed faience.

At his workshop near Paris, Emile Müller turned out garden statuary and ornaments in the naturalistic Art Nouveau style, while the multi-talented Taxile Doat designed vessels sculpted to look like fruits and vegetables, plaques, masks, paperweights, and portrait medallions. Three-dimensional effects were also achieved by modelling damp and pliable clay to produce relief ornament featuring organic motifs such as bands of flower buds or plant stalks.

SURFACE DECORATION

Unlike the Art Nouveau studio potter, many large commercial factories in Europe, as well as in the United States, took a third, more conservative approach, choosing to decorate their mass-produced wares with painted flowers and plants rather than random glaze experiments. Artist-decorators were employed to paint pottery and porcelain vessels with their own interpretations of simple, elegant Japanese floral designs. Other popular methods of ceramic decoration were impasto and the barbotine technique *(see right)*.

CERAMICS INNOVATORS

The great success of Art Nouveau ceramics was largely due to the imagination and skill of many talented designers, artists, and potters working to raise the status of the humble clay material.

COLOURED SLIP

Slip is liquid clay that can be coloured with pigments and used to decorate pots in various different ways. A technique called tube lining has been used to paint the flowers on the vase below, in the same way that icing is piped on to a cake. Mintons used this technique to decorate tiles, while Moorcroft used thin lines of trailed slip to prevent two colours next to each other from merging. In the barbotine and impasto techniques, used by Doulton and some French factories, coloured slips are applied thickly like oil paints, with colours overlapping.

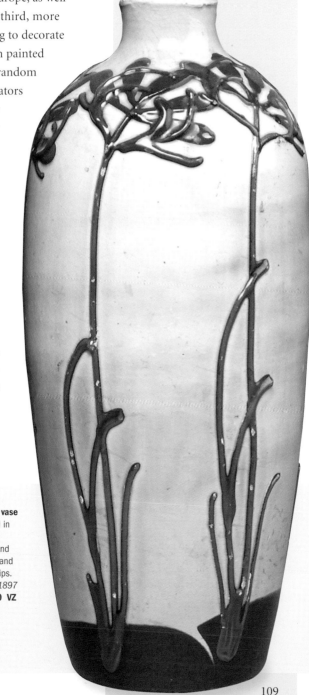

Rookwood pottery baluster vase designed by William Hentschel. It is modelled in relief around the shoulders with tassel-like flower-heads, and coated with an indigo and caramel glaze. The neck of the vase is deep blue. Marked with "XIV/856B/WEH", and with the original paper price tag. *1914* *42cm (16½in) high* **£4,000-5,000 CR**

Max Laeuger tall earthenware vase of slender oval form. It is glazed in pale green and decorated with freesias with red flower-heads and long, slender dark green stems and leaves, painted with coloured slips. Produced by Tonwerke Kandern. *1897* *19.5cm (7¾in) high* **£600-800 VZ**

KEY FEATURES

The organic, naturalistic strain of Art Nouveau was favoured for the porcelain vases and tableware produced by Sèvres.

Sculptural forms display Chinese influence, while the spare, elegant-painted decoration looks to Japanese art for inspiration.

Porcelain wares are typically hand-painted in subtle shades with gilded highlights.

Gilt-bronze plinths or mounts were frequently used to embellish vases.

Sèvres

As it had championed the Rococo style in the 18th century, so the celebrated porcelain factory at Sèvres was once again a vanguard of fashion a century later as the leading commercial producer of luxury French Art Nouveau ceramics.

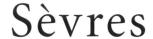

Established in 1756 under the patronage of King Louis XV, the Sèvres Factory produced high-quality porcelain in the fashionable taste into the 19th century. Under sculptor Albert-Ernest Carrier-Belleuse, the firm manufactured elaborate vases richly embellished with sculptural ornament. The popular enthusiasm for Japanese art found its way into tableware and other decorative objects elegantly painted by Albert-Louis Dammouse and the multi-talented painter Felix Bracquemond.

In 1887, the artist-potter Joseph-Théodore Deck – who was among those who led the way in developing the new glazes that played a pivotal role in Art Nouveau ceramics – assumed the directorship. By this time, the trend towards pieces decorated in the organic, naturalistic Art Nouveau style had begun to take hold in France. Sèvres pioneered a number of technical advances and the factory's porcelain vases on display at the 1900 Universal Exposition in Paris received massive acclaim.

Table settings featuring lyrical female figures and vases boasting Chinese-inspired sculptural shapes were made of high-quality slip-cast porcelain, although the factory later also produced earthenware pieces. The naturalistic plants, flowers, birds, and insects in the Art Nouveau taste were typically painted in subdued shades – soft greens, yellows, and mauves – highlighted with gilding. Sèvres pieces were also frequently embellished with mounts or plinths of gilt bronze (*see below*).

Above: Porcelain vase of waisted form. The bulbous neck has thistle motifs, their stems extending to the base and painted in greens and browns and highlighted with gilding. With a black date stamp and paper label. *1904. 22.5cm (9in) high* **£3,000–4,500 MACK**

DECORATIVE MOUNTS

The application of mounts to vases elevates their stature, both artistically and physically, and should ideally be in sympathy with the original decoration of the piece. For example, a vase with painted chrysanthemum blooms might have silver mounts with similarly fashioned florets in relief. The vase shown here is decorated with crystalline glaze in soft colours, which resembles Monet's lily pond. The gilt bronze mounts – embellished with frogs, waterlilies, and a floral finial – also reflect this theme. If, unlike this example, the mounts look awkward and out of place with a vase, it may be that they have been added at a later date, possibly to hide some damage.

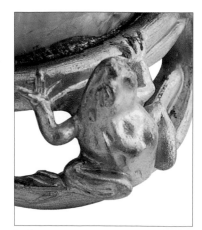

Porcelain vase with a high-fired crystalline glaze of shaded pale blue, purple, and green. It has a gilt-bronze base and floral finial. With a stamped date code. *1897. 17cm (6¾in) high* **£7,500–11,000 MACK**

The frog motif used here is sympathetic with the pond-like effect of the glazed colours.

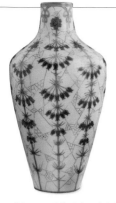

Porcelain vase delicately painted with vertical bands of stylized harebells and gilt spider webs. Blue factory stamp. *1900*

17.5cm (7in) high

£1,800–2,600   **MACK**

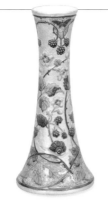

Earthenware vase attributed to Paul Jean Milet. Tube-lined with branches of brambles, fruit, blossoms, and snails. Marked "MP" and "Sèvres".

24cm (9½in) high

£300–400   **DN**

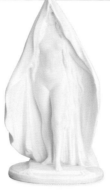

Théodore Rivière porcelain figure of a naked woman revealed from beneath a cloak. Signed "Théodore Rivière" and "Sèvres".

16.5cm (6½in) high

£500–700   **DN**

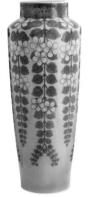

Porcelain vase by L. Mimard, enamelled in naturalistic colours with stylized trailing shrubs on a blue ground. Date stamp; signed. *1897*

40.5cm (16in) high

£5,500–7,500   **MACK**

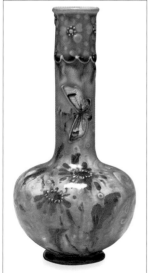

Paul Jean Milet earthenware vase with relief decoration of a butterfly and amber and turquoise glazes with gold-leaf inclusions. *c.1905*

18cm (7in) high

£150–250   **Qu**

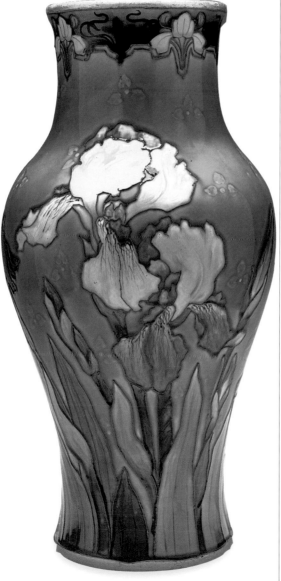

Paul Jean Milet earthenware vase depicting naturalistic irises; with gilded rims. Signed "V. Yung" (as designer), "MILET Sèvres". *c.1900*

40.5cm (16in) high

£1,000–1,500   **Qu**

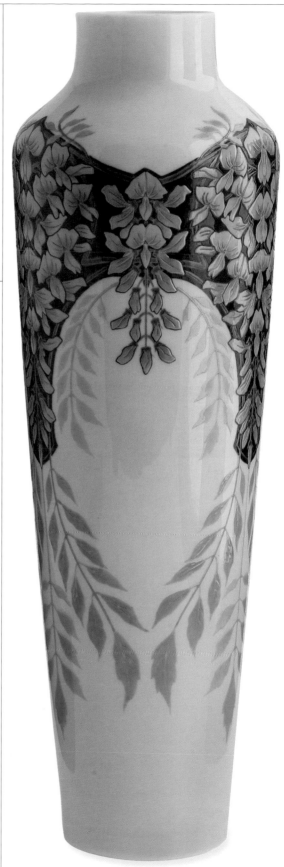

Porcelain vase painted with yellow laburnum against dark blue cartouches and green foliage against pale blue. Stamped with a date code. *1905*

43.5cm (17in) high

£6,000–9,000   **MACK**

Earthenware is highlighted with lustrous, iridescent glazes, many in unusual, sombre tones.

Art-studio ceramics with painted decoration in the Art Nouveau style by Symbolist painter Lucien Levy-Dhurmer were unique to Massier.

Decorative schemes looked to nature for inspiration, as well as featuring figural designs with sensuous female figures moulded in low relief.

Massier

The lustrous, iridescent glazes successfully developed by artists and commercial manufacturers alike, were a key feature of Art Nouveau ceramics, and found a champion in French potter Clément Massier (1845–1917).

By the 1880s, the family company of Massier, near Nice in southern France, was under the direction of Clément Massier, who – like many artist-potters at the time – had turned his attention to the development of iridescent and lustre glazes. By 1883, the company was producing a range of earthenware pieces, which served as a fitting canvas for these very subtle but nonetheless stunning lustrous and iridescent effects.

Of particular note was the collaboration between the Massier ceramics factory and the Symbolist painter Lucien Levy-Dhurmer – the ultimate objective being the creation of a collection of art-studio ceramics that boasted painted decoration in the Art Nouveau style. These designs included figural scenes – such as moulded low-relief images featuring the American dancer Loïe Fuller, or slender female nudes forming the handles of an equally slender, tapering vase – as well as the familiar themes and rich, glowing colours found in the natural world. Vessel shapes echo natural forms, and decoration celebrates the luscious bounty of nature: pink and red flower blooms; green sea grass, bamboo plants, and trees; the rich turquoise of the sea; lively frogs; and birds and insects hovering over a pond filled with waterlilies.

Clément's brother Delphin (1836–1907) followed the family tradition at his own pottery in Vallauris, producing distinctive and different work with naturalistic decoration. Also at Vallauris, their second cousin Jean Baptiste (1850–1916), who was the son of Jerome Massier, introduced a sculptural aspect to his work (*see below*).

Above: Bulbous porcelain vase with twin loop handles, by Delphin Massier. Painted with a sparse autumnal scene of birch trees lining the banks of a stream. Vellum finish. Artist-signed "JN/JH" and "Delphin Massier/Vallauris". *13.5cm (5¼in) high* **£350–450 DRA**

SCULPTURAL DETAIL

The application of sculptural detail to ceramics was used successfully by the Massier factories, the work of Jean Baptiste Massier being evident in the pieces shown here. The ewer is extremely plain despite the neck being very organic in shape (*see right*). The use of a slender maiden emerging from the surface, rising to grip the neck rim and, in the process, forming a handle is very poetic, as is the vase that is shown (*left*). The natural form with a rim that resembles a poppy-seed pod, emblematic of the night or possibly drug-induced sleep, and an owl that rests on one edge beneath dark, nocturnal, and lustrous glazes warrants the name it has been given – "La Nuit". In marked contrast is the naturalistic and amusing approach to the Delphin Massier earthenware vase with frogs emerging from a pool and clambering over the neck rim (*see opposite*).

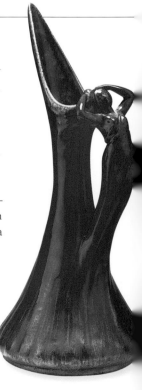

"La Nuit" pottery vase by Jean Baptiste Massier, applied with an owl in relief beneath an overall iridescent glaze. Signed "Jerome Massier Fils, Vallauris, ANL". *26cm (10¼in) high* **£4,000–4,500 MACK**

Jean Baptiste Massier earthenware ewer with a slender female figure forming the handle, beneath predominantly shaded red glaze. Signed "Jerome Massier Fils, Vallauris (AM)". *c.1900. 47cm (18.5in) high* **£750–850 Qu**

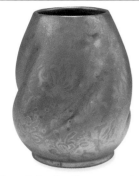

Iridescent glazed earthenware vase by Clément Massier. It is decorated with honeysuckle blooms and tendrils. Signed "Clement Massier Golfe Juan A-M". *c.1900*

19.5cm (7¾in) high

£700–800   **Qu**

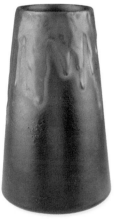

Earthenware tapering vase by Clément Massier. Purple, metallic glaze beneath olive green flowing from the neck. Signed "MCM Golfe-Juan (AM)". *1900*

19cm (7½in) high

£250–350   **Qu**

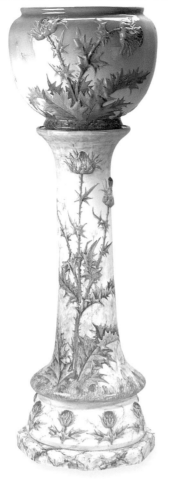

Delphin Massier jardinière, decorated in relief with thistles against a pink background and supported on a slender stand. Marked "Delphin Massier Vallauris (A. M.)". *1900*

140cm (53in) high

£1,500–1,800   **Qu**

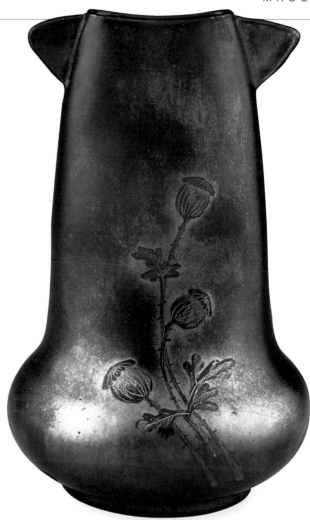

Iridescent glazed earthenware vase by Clément Massier, with a bulbous base and twin lug handles. Decorated with poppy-seed pods and foliage. *1900*

22cm (8¾in) high

£220–280   **Qu**

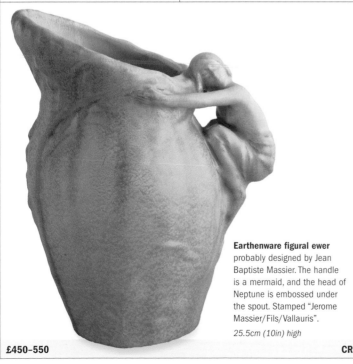

Earthenware figural ewer probably designed by Jean Baptiste Massier. The handle is a mermaid, and the head of Neptune is embossed under the spout. Stamped "Jerome Massier/Fils/Vallauris".

25.5cm (10in) high

£450–550   **CR**

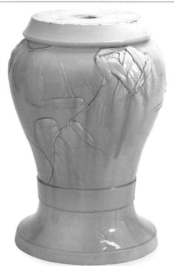

Earthenware jardinière stand by Clément Massier. Of baluster form, decorated in relief with bamboo and leaves beneath a pale green glaze. Signed "CM 1888".

67.5cm (26½in) high

£450–550   **Qu**

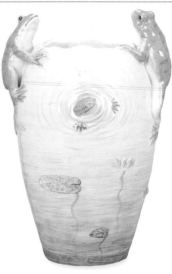

Delphin Massier earthenware vase modelled with naturalistic frogs emerging from a waterlily-filled pond. Painted "Delphin Massier, Vallauris (A.M.)".

29.5cm (11½in) high

£900–1,200   **DN**

Earthenware and porcelain
Rozenburg pieces generally favour
bold abstract designs inspired
by Japanese art and the Art
Nouveau style.

Eggshell porcelain boasts a very
thin, translucent ceramic body in
elongated shapes.

Angular vessels with attenuated
forms are often painted in bright,
vivid colours with decoration from
the Art Nouveau repertoire, such
as peacocks, flaccid lilac bouquets,
and overblown poppies.

Rozenburg

The Netherlands embraced the Art Nouveau style with
enthusiasm, fostering a ceramics industry led by the
Rozenburg Factory, which celebrated exotic, voluptuous
forms enhanced with delicate decoration.

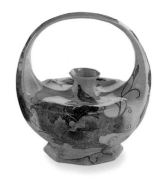

In 1883, the Dutch Rozenburg Factory was
established at the Hague by Wilhelm Wolff von
Gudenberg with the paramount objective being
the production of Delft-style blue-and-white
ceramic ware. By the late 1880s and early 1890s,
the company – under the directorship of
Theodoor C.A. Colenbrander – was producing a
range of exciting, innovative earthenware and
porcelain designs. The pieces were embellished
with bold abstract decoration that was
influenced by both Japanese art and the
curvaceous nature-inspired Art Nouveau
style that was sweeping across Europe.
The Rozenburg Factory's most
celebrated contribution to Art
Nouveau ceramics was its
range of "eggshell porcelain",
which was developed by
Jurriaan Kok in 1899
(*see below*).

At the 1900 Universal Exposition in Paris,
Rozenburg's eggshell porcelain vessels met
with great acclaim. They were created by
slip-casting the clay into elegant and highly
innovative shapes that tended to be razor-thin,
elongated in design, and slightly concave away
from the rim.

No two pieces of Rozenburg ceramic ware
were alike, which remains one of the tantalizing
and attractive hallmarks of this highly creative
range. The curving and elongated forms of
the vessels were embellished with delicate
naturalistic decoration – usually depicting
flowers, insects, and birds – typically hand-
painted by artists such as Samuel Schellink
and R. Sterken.

Above: Eggshell porcelain vase of compressed globular shape,
with a short neck and overhead loop handle. It is finely painted
with stylized flowers and foliage on a white ground. Marked with
the factory stamp. *15.5cm (6in) high* **£4,500–7,500 MACK**

EGGSHELL PORCELAIN

The very fine and delicate pieces from the Rozenburg Factory
in the Hague are often referred to as "eggshell porcelain". While the
eggshell aspect of the product cannot be denied, with its incredibly
light weight and extreme thinness, the "porcelain" part is a misnomer.
It is, in fact, earthenware, but so thin as to be effectively "a breath of
ceramic" held between two membranes of glaze. The beautiful and
delicate painting appears simply to float across its white surface.
It seems almost miraculous that these pieces have survived, and
many understandably carry small damages. By marked contrast,
the more robust and thickly potted vessels are as distant cousins
but still have their own quality with earthy, muted colours and
hand-painted floral and organic images, often based on batik
decoration from the Dutch colonies in Southeast Asia.

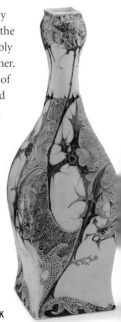

Tall eggshell porcelain vase of slightly
swollen and square-sectioned baluster
shape with a short, flared neck. Finely
painted by Samuel Schellink in
naturalistic colours with lilies against
white. Slightly flawed. *1901–02
21.5cm (8½in) high* **£1,700–2,000 Qu**

Eggshell porcelain vase of slender,
double-gourd form on a square base.
Possibly painted by Sterken, with all-
over thistle decoration in vivid colours
against white. Marked "Rozenburg den
Haag" with a date code for 1902.
27cm (10¾in) high **£6,000–9,000 MACK**

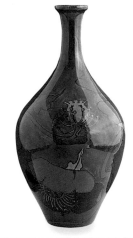

Earthenware vase with slender neck. Painted with an overall design of a raven amid stylized pomegranates on a swirling deep-blue ground. Signed "Rozenburg den Haag".

30.5cm (12in) high

£2,500–4,000   **MACK**

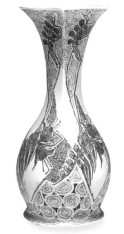

Small eggshell porcelain vase with flared square neck, finely painted by J.L. Verhoog with herbaceous flowers and leaves in vivid colours. Signed and dated. *1900*

16.5cm (6½in) high

£1,800–2,200   **Qu**

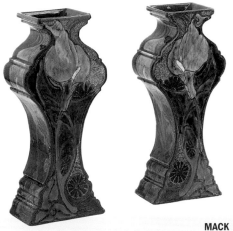

Pair of earthenware vases of squared baluster shape, each painted with a dense pattern of lilies and small red flower-heads against a yellow and green ground. Each signed "Rozenburg den Haag". *c.1899*

25cm (10in) high

£3,000–4,500   **MACK**

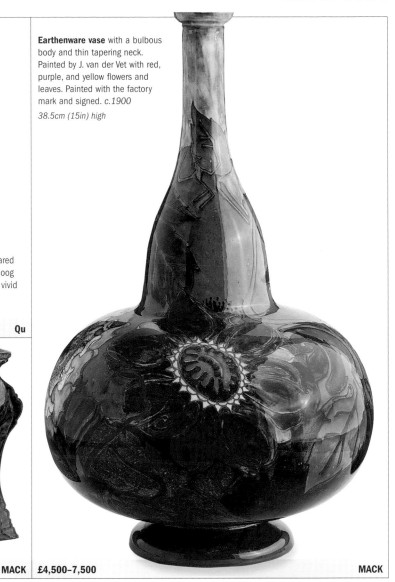

Earthenware vase with a bulbous body and thin tapering neck. Painted by J. van der Vet with red, purple, and yellow flowers and leaves. Painted with the factory mark and signed. *c.1900*

38.5cm (15in) high

£4,500–7,500   **MACK**

Gouda

Founded in 1898, the Gouda Ceramic Factory became one of the leading potteries in the Netherlands until its closure in 1965. The influential Dutch architect Theodoor Colenbrander, who was also a talented textile designer, worked as a designer for Gouda between 1912 and 1913. Colenbrander had turned to pottery in the 1880s, and from 1884 until 1889 he worked for the Dutch firm of Rozenburg, evolving a new decorative style well suited to the Art Nouveau taste for naturalism that was sweeping across Europe. His signature designs include abstract plant-like forms painted in bold, bright colours that took inspiration from Javanese batik ware. Later pottery produced at the Gouda factory shows the influence of the De Stijl group, and geometrical decoration became the order of the day.

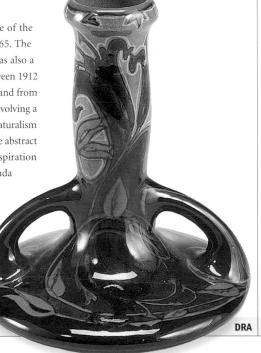

Gouda twin-handled earthenware vase with squat base and tall neck. Painted with pink and purple flowers with green leaves against a beige and indigo ground. Painted with the factory mark and "Zuid Holland".

24cm (9½in) high

£350–450   **DRA**

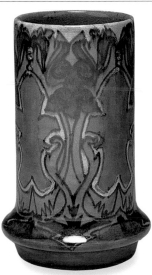

Gouda earthenware vase of cylindrical shape swelling at the base. Painted olive green and purple with stylized flowers and tendrils. Marked "LMB Zuid Holland Gouda". *1899*

15cm (6in) high

£250–350   **Qu**

European Ceramics

Across Europe, artist-potters enthusiastically embraced the sensuous, organic Art Nouveau style. Ceramics proved to be the ideal medium for the new taste, since the form and decoration adapted easily to the asymmetrical, curving shapes and trailing, naturalistic, Japanese-style designs. Plant, flower, and insect motifs – florid in France, but more stylized and restrained in Germany and Austria – were typically applied by hand-painting, transfer printing, or slip trailing.

Eager to break free from traditional constraints, pottery artists from Paris to Copenhagen experimented with new kinds of glazes to dazzling effect. Commercial ceramics manufacturers – including the Sèvres Porcelain Factory; Meissen, near Dresden; and the Staffordshire potteries in Britain – were quick to accommodate the production of Art Nouveau ware.

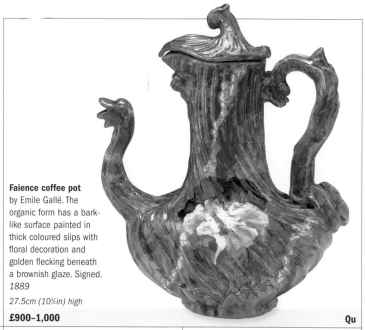

Faience coffee pot by Emile Gallé. The organic form has a bark-like surface painted in thick coloured slips with floral decoration and golden flecking beneath a brownish glaze. Signed. *1889*

27.5cm (10¾in) high

£900–1,000　　　　Qu

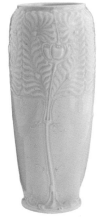

Rare Limoges porcelain vase by Edward Colonna, designed for Siegfried Bing. The relief decoration is of trailing peacock feathers. Colonna stamp; marked "Leuconoe".

31.5cm (12½in) high

£7,500–11,000　　MACK

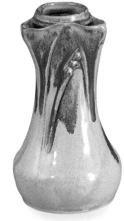

Porcelain vase (one of a pair) by Denbac. The embossed body has stylized flowers and is microcrystalline glazed. The neck opens into three smaller apertures.

20cm (8in) high

£350–450 (the pair)　　DRA

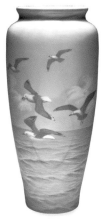

Royal Copenhagen porcelain "Seagulls" vase by Arnold Krog. Painted in naturalistic colours, with seagulls flying above waves. Signed. *1896*

45cm (17¾in) high

£350–450　　　　Qu

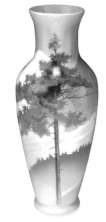

Royal Copenhagen porcelain baluster vase by Arnold Krog and Anna Smidth. Painted in pastel colours with trees in a mountain landscape. Signed "A. Smidth". *1900*

42cm (16½in) high

£1,300–1,600　　Qu

LA MAISON MODERNE

La Maison Moderne opened in 1898 in Paris with showrooms designed by Henry van de Velde. It was established by Julius Meier-Graefe, a German art critic who had been editor of the avant-garde journal *Pan*. The new gallery was a primary source for the marketing of Art Nouveau, as was Siegfried Bing's L'Art Nouveau, also in Paris, which had opened in 1895. Both shops were important centres for the promotion of the new style, created by vibrant and groundbreaking young artists working in all mediums.

The porcelain tea service shown on the right was designed around 1900 by one such French artist, Maurice Dufrène (1876-1955), then a young designer at the forefront of the new style. The set was made to form part of the stock at La Maison Moderne.

Three-piece porcelain tea set by Maurice Dufrène. The set comprises teapot, sucrier, and milk jug, each of sinuous outline with arched scrolling handles. Painted decoration shows stylized leaves and flower-heads in deep red and dark green. Signed.

Teapot 13.5cm (5½in) high

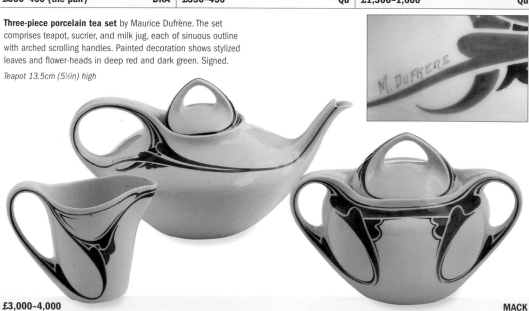

£3,000–4,000　　　　　　　　　　　MACK

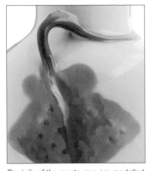

The tails of the manta rays are modelled in high relief to form twin handles.

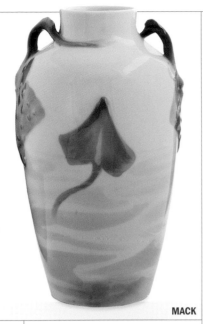

Rorstrand porcelain vase In the manner of Alf Wallander. Painted in soft colours with manta rays and swirling currents as decoration. Stamped with the factory mark on the base.

23cm (9in) high

£2,250–4,000   **MACK**

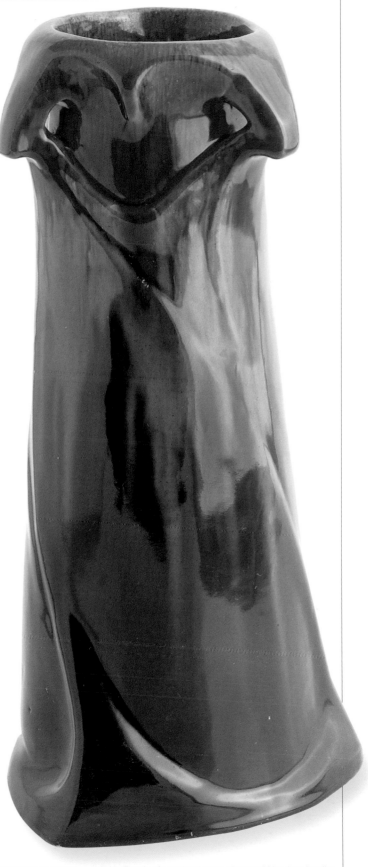

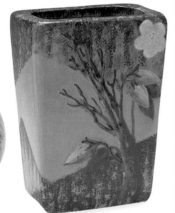

Stoneware and pewter mounted inkwell by Alexander Bigot, designed by Gaillard. Applied with a pierced pewter cover and panels. Muted glazes. Inscribed "Grès De Bigot, Paris, D162".

15cm (6in) wide

£2,250–3,750   **MACK**

Faience flared rectangular vase by Emile Gallé. Painted in thick coloured slips with flowering plants and leaves against brownish panels. Signed. *1880*

18.5cm (7¼in) high

£1,200–1,500   **Qu**

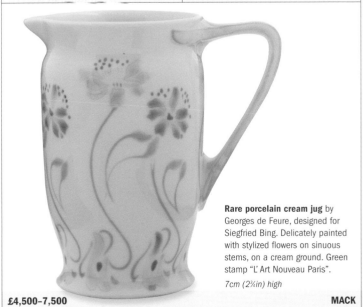

Rare porcelain cream jug by Georges de Feure, designed for Siegfried Bing. Delicately painted with stylized flowers on sinuous stems, on a cream ground. Green stamp "L' Art Nouveau Paris".

7cm (2¾in) high

£4,500–7,500   **MACK**

Pottery vase by Henry van de Velde. Tapering form with sinuous, abstract ribbing, loop handles at the neck, and honey-coloured glaze, shading to green. Unmarked. *c.1900*

28.5cm (11¼in) high

£4,000–5,000   **MACK**

KEY FEATURES

High-quality porcelain was typical, where the quality of the vessel took preference over decoration.

Vases decorated with underglaze enamels boast matte, semi-matte, and crystalline glazes.

Art Nouveau objects include small sculptures and figurines, candlesticks, and table services.

Meissen

The celebrated porcelain factory at Meissen, near Dresden, rejected the florid examples of the Art Nouveau style that had been set by France, Belgium, and the Netherlands in favour of a more conservative and stylized interpretation.

From its founding in the early 18th century, Meissen was keen to emphasize the quality of its porcelain over decoration. Nearly two centuries later, this highly respected enterprise held on to its illustrious past, retaining traditional shapes that flaunted the superiority of the porcelain and paying homage to the Art Nouveau style with restrained naturalistic motifs and a variety of glazes.

One of the most successful designers at Meissen during this period was Julius Konrad Hentschel. He created many of the factory's early ventures into Art Nouveau – primarily ornamental vases frequently rendered in *pâte-sur-pâte*, where layers of paste are built up to create ornamental designs in relief. Working alongside his brother Johannes Rudolf, Hentschel produced a wide range of decorative objects including vases and sculptures.

From the 1890s, Meissen also produced Art Nouveau ware in new shapes and patterns created by celebrated designers from other parts of Europe, including Peter Behrens, Henry van de Velde, and Richard Riemerschmid. Figural groups were produced for the factory by Paul Scheurich.

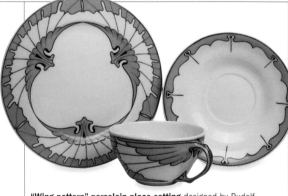

Above: Miniature porcelain vase of baluster shape with flared cylindrical neck. Decorated with leaves, possibly horse chestnut, in white reserved against an olive green ground. Blue crossed-swords mark and stamped numbers. *11cm (4¼in) high* **£450–550 FRE**

Covered vase of compressed globular shape. It has a domed lid with lobed finial and is covered with streaked glazes of muted mauve, pale brown, and green tones. With a blue swords stamp. *c.1900*

13cm (5¼in) high

£800–1,200   **BMN**

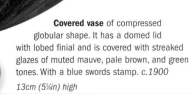

"Wing pattern" porcelain place setting designed by Rudolf Hentschel, comprising a cup, saucer, and plate. Painted underglaze in grey and fine blue lines, showing highly stylized foliate stems resembling wings. Has a blue swords stamp. *c.1900*

£800–1,200   **BMN**

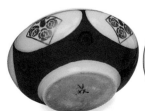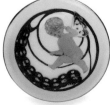

Porcelain lidded box decorated and signed by William Baring. The lid shows a cherub sitting amid stylized branches; the sides feature highly stylized rose panels. With a blue swords mark. *c.1910*

7.5cm (3in) wide

£1,000–1,500   **BMN**

K.P.M.

The prestigious Königliche Porzellan Manufaktur (Royal Porcelain Factory) in Berlin, which, from the late 18th century, had reflected the power and status of the Prussian throne, came gradually to the new fashion for Art Nouveau.

Originally established in 1751, K.P.M. was celebrated in the late 19th century for its range of finely painted large porcelain vases and plaques and richly painted cabinet ware. At the end of the century, the factory began to employ outside designers to breathe new life into what had become a tradition-bound repertoire of time-honoured vessel shapes and decoration. Charged with creating porcelain ware in a wholly modern style, these designers were not constrained by convention, and they led the factory's charge into the 20th century.

Among the designers lured to Berlin was the talented sculptor and modeller Paul Scheurich, who produced a series of asymmetrical, Rococo-inspired figures wearing contemporary dress. The porcelain works tentatively explored Jugendstil-inspired designs following the arrival in 1902 of designer Theodor Schmuz-Baudiss. Under his direction, a range of porcelain vases and tableware was created that featured Art Nouveau decoration – such as curvilinear and flower patterns – reflecting the new fashion and proving widely popular.

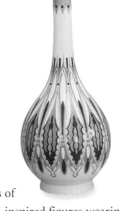

KEY FEATURES

Porcelain ware produced by the Königliche Porzellan Manufaktur in Berlin were marked in underglaze blue with an orb underlined by the initials K.P.M. since 1832.

A popular range of porcelain vases and tableware decorated with curvilinear and floral Art Nouveau patterns was designed by Theodor Schmuz-Baudiss.

Large porcelain vases and plaques were produced by K.P.M., featuring finely painted landscapes and copies of well-known paintings.

Above: Porcelain pear-shaped vase decorated by Heinrich Lang with elliptical panels of highly stylized plant forms in olive green, mint green, and black outline. With blue sceptre and red orb marks. *18.5cm (7¼in) high* **£250–350 HERR**

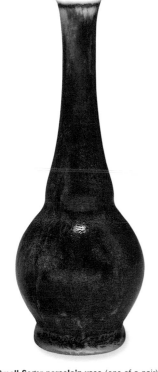

Small Seger-porcelain vase (one of a pair) with slender tapering neck. Covered overall with a rich and slightly streaked high-fired ox-blood glaze. With a blue underglaze and Seger mark. *c.1899*

14.5cm (5¾in) high

£600–800 (the pair) **Qu**

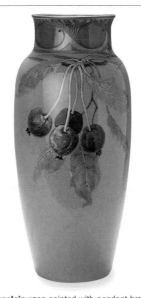

Porcelain vase painted with pendant branches of cherries and leaves, heightened with gilding, as is the frieze on the short cylindrical neck. Reserved against a mauve ground. Sceptre and orb marks; "putti" date mark. *1900*

25.5cm (10in) high

£2,000–3,000 **VZ**

Porcelain double-gourd vase decorated by Willy Stanke, with a broad frieze of highly stylized floral blooms in vivid colours. Further floral decoration on the neck and base. Factory marks. *1914*

18cm (7in) high

£2,500–3,500 **HERR**

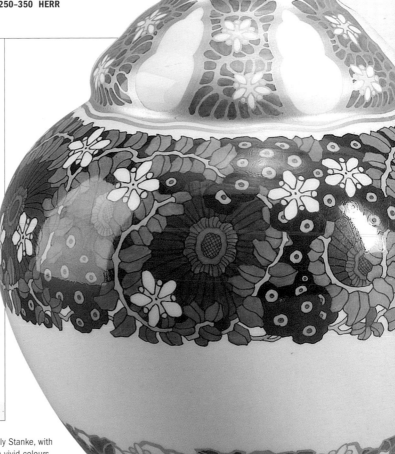

A strong sculptural quality is evident in most pieces.

Monotone colours, often greyish and heightened with gilding, were intended to resemble bronze.

Classical subjects and willowy female figures were popular.

Often marked with the sculptor's facsimile signature.

Goldscheider

The popular enthusiasm for decorative objects made in the Art Nouveau style was addressed in Vienna by the award-winning Goldscheider Earthenware and Porcelain factory, which specialized in porcelain figurines.

Founded by Friedrich Goldscheider in Vienna in 1884, the Goldscheider factory initially produced figurative subjects in the Victorian taste, such as mythological and historical personalities. The wide variety of decorative models were supplied by a pool of talented young artists and then carefully reproduced. With the expansion of the Art Nouveau movement, however, the company turned to a more experienced and sophisticated group of artists – including some from the Wiener Werkstätte – whose work eloquently captured the flowing forms of the French style along with the more linear shapes favoured by the Jugendstil and Secessionist movements.

Production at the Goldscheider factory focused primarily on figures and figurines made of terracotta, alabaster, and bronze. This figurative tradition continued into the 1920s and 30s with an array of lamps, wall masks, and dancers, some designed by Joseph Lorenzl.

Above: Cylindrical ceramic vase with a violet-brown glaze. Flanked by four partially yellow-enamelled loin-clothed youths, standing on blue-enamelled pedestals and between similarly decorated oval plaques. *c.1902. 33cm (12¾in) high* **£1,500–1,800 HERR**

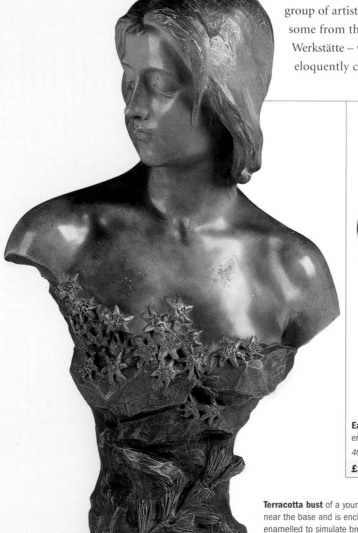

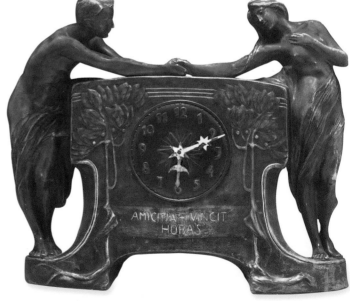

Earthenware mantel clock flanked by a young couple holding hands. It has bronze patination enamelling and is inscribed "Amicitia vincit horas" (Friendship overcomes the hours). *c.1902 40.5cm (16in) wide*

£1,100–1,400   **Qu**

Terracotta bust of a young girl emerging from a rock-like torso. The torso has a floral motif near the base and is encircled at the top with a garland of flowers. The piece is surface-enamelled to simulate bronze patination, a finish often employed by Goldscheider.

60cm (23½in) high

£850–1,250   **L&T**

Royal Dux

Among the celebrated champions in Bohemia of ceramics in the Art Nouveau style was the Royal Dux factory, which became renowned for producing high-quality, beautifully crafted ornamental pieces.

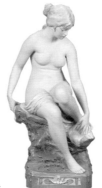

One of the earliest ceramics factories in Bohemia was established in 1853 in Dux (Duchov), north of Prague, where initially it manufactured utilitarian ceramic wares. The factory was purchased by the talented artist Eduard Eichler, and under the moniker E. Eichler Thonwaren-Fabrik, the company prospered, producing majolica, terracotta, and faience pieces in the tradition of Worcester, Sèvres, and Copenhagen porcelain.

By 1898, the company had moved from Dux to Berlin, where, in addition to traditional products, it began producing high-quality porcelain and became known as Duxer Porzellan-Manufaktur.

Typical products included ornamental household objects, statuettes, and tableware, with decorative motifs ranging from voluptuous maidens to Japanese-inspired stylized flowers and plants rendered in soft, muted colours.

During the Art Nouveau period, the enterprise gained enormous success under the direction of the modeller and designer Alois Hampel. Still in existence today, the company now goes by the name of Porcelain Manufactory Royal Dux Bohemia.

Above: "The Seated Bather" modelled in porcelain and naturalistically coloured. It is marked with the artist's signature, "P. Aichele". *48cm (19in) high* **£600–700 DN**

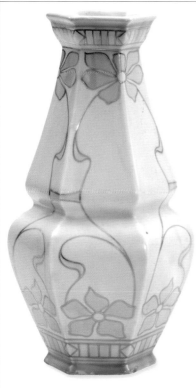

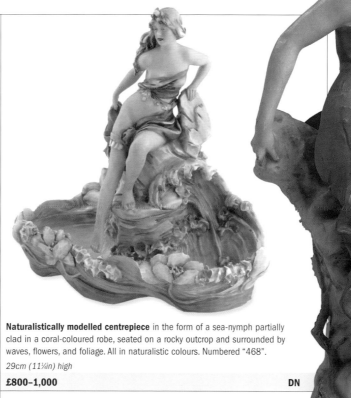

Naturalistically modelled centrepiece in the form of a sea-nymph partially clad in a coral-coloured robe, seated on a rocky outcrop and surrounded by waves, flowers, and foliage. All in naturalistic colours. Numbered "468".
29cm (11¼in) high

£800–1,000   **DN**

Waisted hexagonal vase with bulbous body, tapering neck, and flared foot and rim. Painted with delicate, stylized flowers, stems, and leaves in muted pink and green on a cream-coloured ground.
28cm (11in) high

£150–200   **FRE**

Figure of a young woman modelled on a rocky base. Her skin tone is naturalistic and her classically inspired off-the-shoulder tunic is subtly enlivened with gilded highlights. Marked with a salmon-pink triangular pad impressed with the mark "Royal Dux".
42cm (16½in) high

£650–800   **BONE**

KEY FEATURES

Innovative exotic shapes, often organic in form, are typical of R.S.K. pieces.

Dramatic relief-moulded plants and flowers are used to decorate many of the vases.

Portraits of mystical women with long hair feature on many pieces.

Subtle shades of pale green, ochre, and blue are often highlighted with gilding.

Amphora Ware

The most desirable range of Bohemian Art Nouveau ceramics was Amphora Ware produced by the porcelain manufacturer Reissner, Stellmacher & Kessel (R.S.K.), which was established in Turn-Teplitz in 1892.

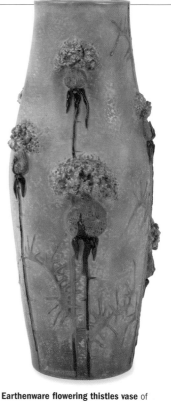

R.S.K. produced a range of ambitious vases under the name of "Amphora". These innovative pieces soon became their most popular product. Organic or exotic in shape, with designs inspired by Art Nouveau and Jugendstil, they often had incised and relief-moulded decoration, usually of stylized flowers with brightly coloured centres, or carefully moulded berries, leaves, and stems applied on top of a layer of thick on-glaze enamel.

R.S.K.'s Amphora vases had many Art Nouveau characteristics, such as whiplash or branch-shaped handles that terminated in curvaceous ornamental tendrils.

Other typical Art Nouveau motifs used by R.S.K. include portraits of dreamy, pale-faced women with long, flowing hair – their heads often surrounded by a halo – and lavish gilding used to highlight muted shades of green, ochre, and blue.

The Amphora range was so successful that R.S.K. adopted the name for all of their products, including wall masks, figural sculpture, and earthenware vases with applied glass cabochons.

Above: Earthenware "squeeze-bag" vase with finely painted polychrome enamels and gilding. A regal, Mucha-style maiden's head is surrounded by Glasgow-style roses.
14.5cm (5¾in) high **£1,200–1,500 DRA**

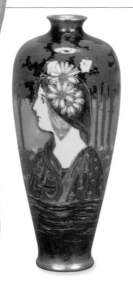

Porcelain oviform vase with gilded highlights. The design is of a young maiden in a deep stream, against a frieze of trees.
33cm (13in) high

£1,400–1,600   **DN**

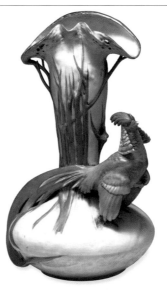

Earthenware vase with an applied and gilded pheasant on a squat, bulbous base. It has an elongated, plant-form neck and rim, with branches (some applied). *c.1905*
51cm (20in) high

£900–1,200   **Qu**

Earthenware vase of slender ovoid form. It has a ribbed brown base and cream-coloured ground, and is painted and moulded in relief with thistle flowers and foliage in naturalistic colours, enlivened with gilding. The stem decoration extends into curvaceous, branch-form handles linked to the rim of the neck.
43cm (16¾in) high

£150–200   **DN**

Earthenware flowering thistles vase of slender ovoid form, with painted and applied design in pink, brown, yellow, and green against a mottled, pale blue ground. *c.1905*
44cm (17¼in) high

£1,600–1,800   **TEL**

Zsolnay

Art Nouveau found powerful expression in Hungary, where designers, craftsmen, and scientists worked together to create bold, innovative ceramics in the spirit of the new style.

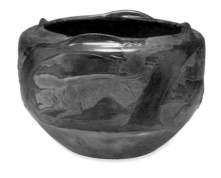

The renowned Hungarian ceramics factory of Zsolnay in Pécs was an important centre for Art Nouveau design. The visionary Vilmos Zsolnay purchased his brother's artisan pottery in 1865, and immediately set about competing with rivals in the Czech and Austrian ceramics industry by assembling highly skilled foreign craftsmen to oversee the company's production. Scientists started working on new techniques and recipes for lustres and iridized glazes, and designers were commissioned to create a totally new look.

Up until the 1890s, the company produced ornate pieces inspired by Islamic pierced wares. After 1893, however, when the chemist Vincse Wartha became artistic director, Zsolnay began to specialize in painted decoration using lustred glazes. It produced Art Nouveau-inspired ceramics with simple, naturalistic shapes, relief-moulded decoration, and a wide range of marbled, shaded, and crystalline glazes, the most successful of which was an iridescent glaze called eosin. These ceramics met with great success at the Budapest Exhibition of 1896 and the Vienna Exhibition of 1900.

Above: Iridescent jardinière decorated in low-relief with five gun-dogs chasing a rabbit through bushes, in eosin yellow, brown, green, and blue glazes and selective gilding. Impress-moulded with the five towers of Pécs medallion seal. *c.1900*
20.25cm (8in) wide **£5,000–6,000 Qu**

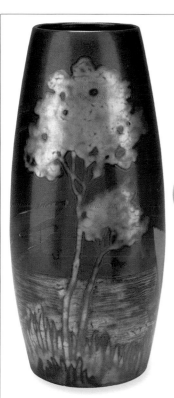

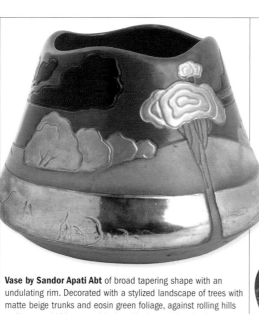

Vase by Sandor Apati Abt of broad tapering shape with an undulating rim. Decorated with a stylized landscape of trees with matte beige trunks and eosin green foliage, against rolling hills and a muted iridescent pink sky with deep violet clouds.
17cm (6½in) high
£1,600–2,200 DN

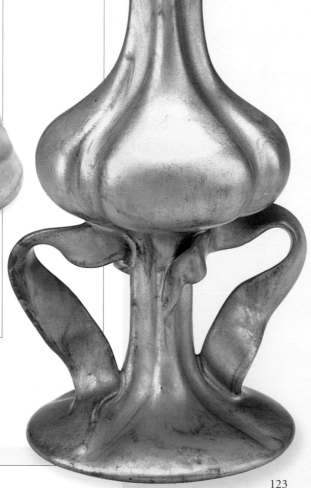

Slender ovoid vase decorated with a night-time river landscape with trees, a sailing boat, and a swan, in eosin red, purple, and green-gold glazes. *c.1900*
34.25cm (13½in) high
£8,000–10,000 Qu

Stylized plant form vase with waisted sides and a flaring, pinched rim, above an indented stem and round foot and flanked by sinuously curved stem handles. It is decorated in a mottled green and gold eosin iridescent glaze. *c.1899*
24cm (9½in) high
£2,200–2,600 Qu

German and Austrian Ceramics

In Germany, the reaction to the Art Nouveau style produced ceramic ware that was more restrained and conservative than that manufactured in France and The Netherlands. Nevertheless, nature remained the most important source of inspiration, and ceramics featured much naturalistic ornament characteristic of the Jugendstil movement. In Austria, a similar restrained decorative approach to ceramic ware helped pave the way for the abstract, geometric, and stylized designs of the Wiener Werkstätte artists, with Michael Powolny being especially known for his stylized figures *(see box below)*.

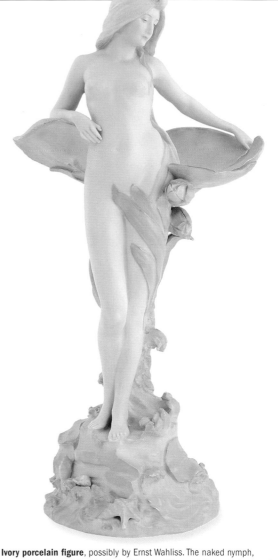

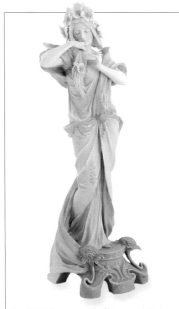

Ernst Wahliss porcelain ewer modelled as a trumpet–shaped flower with leafy handle, mounted with a maiden in diaphanous robes on a flower bed.
62.5cm (24½in) high

Ernst Wahliss porcelain figure modelled as a Mucha-style maiden, with flower-dressed hair, loosely wrapped robes, and jewelled belt, on a scrolled base with chrysanthemums.
44cm (17¼in) high

£950–1,000	DN	

£1,400–1,700	L&T	

Ivory porcelain figure, possibly by Ernst Wahliss. The naked nymph, naturalistically modelled, is flanked by waterlilies and flowers in bud, and stands on a shell-studded base lapped by waves. With gilt detailing.
41cm (16in) high

£1,100–1,200	DN

Michael Powolny

The Austrian ceramicist and sculptor Michael Powolny co-founded the Vienna Ceramics Factory with Bertold Loffler in 1905, which beca e the United Vienna and Gmund Ceramics Factory in 1913. The company produced a series of figural sculptures designed by Powolny. The small figures, made of white earthenware with details rendered in black, generally feature cherubic boys – although a few female pieces were made – holding flowers and standing on a base decorated with black chevron-style designs. Both as a teacher and craftsman, Powolny influenced ceramic design in Austria, Britain, and the United States.

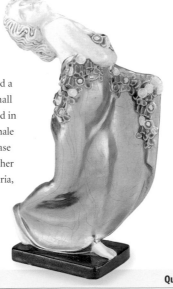

Michael Powolny dancer in white-glazed earthenware with a gilt-edged diaphanous robe embellished with stylized flowers, on a rectangular black base. *1907*
22.75cm (9in) high

£3,500–4,200	Qu

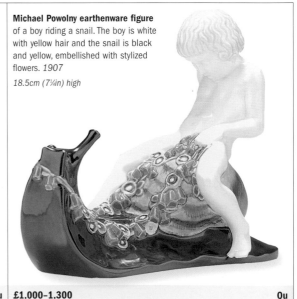

Michael Powolny earthenware figure of a boy riding a snail. The boy is white with yellow hair and the snail is black and yellow, embellished with stylized flowers. *1907*
18.5cm (7¼in) high

£1,000–1,300	Qu

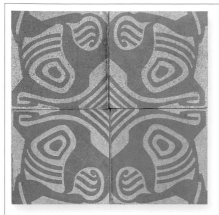

Stoneware tile picture by Henry van de Velde with stylized organic motifs in an overall geometric pattern. Signed "Mosaikfabrik Ransbach" on reverse. *c.1905*

28.5cm (11¼in) wide

£1,000–1,500   **Qu**

Ceramic rectangular plaque, designed by C.S. Luber, moulded in simulation of tube-lining, and hand-painted. A maiden plays a pipe in front of a rural landscape, partly overlaid with sinuous, stylized tendrils.

44.5cm (17¼in) wide

£750–850   **DN**

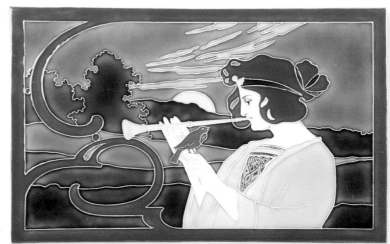

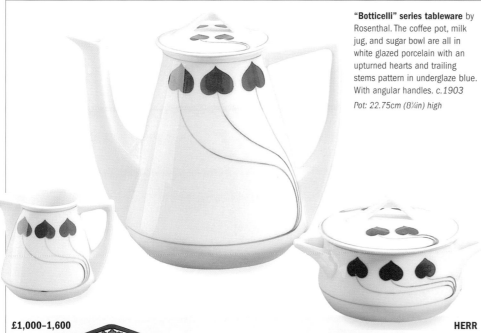

"Botticelli" series tableware by Rosenthal. The coffee pot, milk jug, and sugar bowl are all in white glazed porcelain with an upturned hearts and trailing stems pattern in underglaze blue. With angular handles. *c.1903*

Pot: 22.75cm (8¾in) high

£1,000–1,600   **HERR**

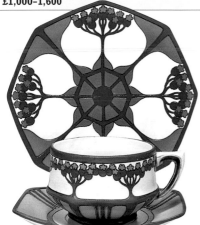

Cup, plate, and saucer from Villeroy & Boch's "Mettlach" range. Octagonal, and mechanically incised and enamelled with a rosehip pattern. *1902–15*

Plate: 19cm (7½in) wide

£160–220   **Qu**

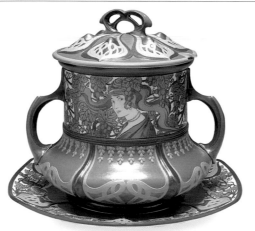

Punch bowl and coaster by Hans Christiansen for Villeroy & Boch's "Mettlach" range. It has applied foliate mouldings, and incised and polychrome enamelled girls' heads, flowers, and foliage. *1902*

33cm (13in) high

£1,400–1,800   **Qu**

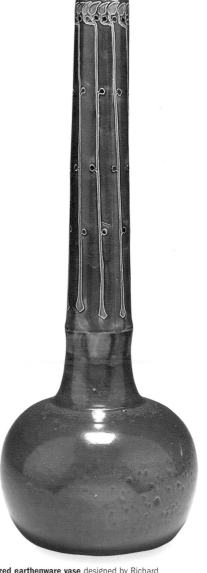

Glazed earthenware vase designed by Richard Riemerschmid. Its globular body and neck are red, with stylized, trailing plant motifs in black and blue. *c.1903*

42cm (16½in) high

£1,300–1,700   **Qu**

KEY FEATURES

Inspired by ancient Persian, Etruscan, classical Roman, and Far Eastern ceramic shapes.

Floral patterns and landscapes rendered in rich, vibrant colours are typical.

Aurelian Ware is decorated with transfer-printed designs, enamelled in red and blue, and highlighted with gilding.

Florian range features exuberant Art Nouveau patterns hand-painted in bright colours.

Tube lining was a favoured technique for Moorcroft ceramics.

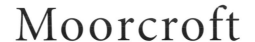

Moorcroft

The English ceramicist William Moorcroft (1872–1945) brought to his art pottery inventive floral designs that had their roots in the Art Nouveau style already so popular in continental Europe.

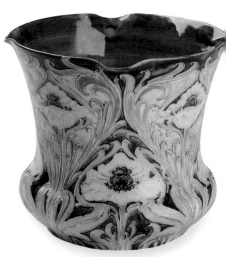

William Moorcroft started out as a designer, before becoming director of the art-pottery department at the factory of James Macintyre & Co. at Burslem, Staffordshire, in 1898. Here, he produced designs for useful tea and tableware, as well as art-pottery vases, jugs, loving cups, jardinières, and biscuit barrels. Inspired by ancient pottery shapes found in Persian, Etruscan, classical Roman, and Far Eastern ceramics, Moorcroft embellished his designs with floral patterns and landscapes in rich, vibrant hues. His distinctive style soon established him as a ceramicist of international acclaim.

Moorcroft's early ceramics work shared more with William Morris and other Arts and Crafts designers than with the continental interpretation of Art Nouveau. From his early designs in distinctive stylized patterns that were transfer-printed, enamelled in red and blue, and embellished with gilding – known as Aurelian domestic ware – Moorcroft moved on to produce his celebrated range of Florian ceramics.

Decorated with colourful formal arrangements of flowers and peacock feathers, the handmade Florian Ware was the most exotic version of Art Nouveau adopted by a British manufacturer, and the visual splendour of Moorcroft art pottery remains unsurpassed.

Moorcroft left Macintyre & Co. to establish his own ceramics works in 1913. The pottery remains active today, creating exotic designs based on natural shapes decorated with rich, vibrant colours.

Above: Florian Ware vase with everted rim and twin handles painted blue. Decorated with forget-me-nots and green feathery foliage on a white ground. With printed marks and signed in green. *12.5cm (5in) high* **£1,000–1,200 L&T**

TUBE-LINED DECORATION

The decorative technique known as tube lining was used extensively by William Moorcroft to create flowing Art Nouveau patterns in relief. By this highly distinctive technique, thin raised trails of slip – potter's clay that has been mixed with water to a semi-liquid, creamy state – are applied to the body of a vessel to form an ornamental pattern comprised of lines or dots. These outlines for broad areas – leaves, flower blossoms, and peacock feathers, for example – give the vessel texture and a tactile quality that is enhanced when filled with brightly coloured glazes.

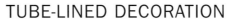

Florian Ware "Peacock" pattern vase of round, tapering shape with incurving neck rim. Tube-line decorated with stylized peacock-feather panels against a pale blue ground. *c.1900* *36cm (14¼in) high* **£3,000–3,500 Rum**

Florian Ware jardinière of broad, flared form. Tube-line decorated with repeated patterns of yellow poppies, flanked by feathery green foliage against an inky-blue ground. With printed marks "326471"; signed in green. *20cm (7¾in) high* **£1,000–1,200 L&T**

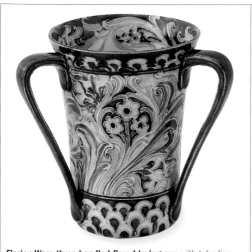

Florian Ware three-handled flared loving cup with tube-line decoration externally and on the inner neck rim. *c.1900*

15.3cm (6in) high

£3,000–3,500   **Rum**

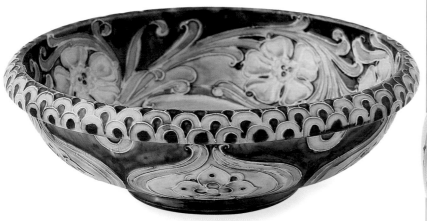

Florian Ware comport with tube-line decoration on the interior and exterior, with stylized poppies and sinuous foliage in dark and pale blue.

20.5cm (8in) high

£220–280   **GorB**

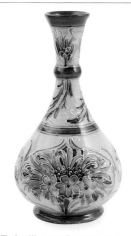

Florian Ware small pear-shaped vase with dark blue cornflowers against a pale blue ground.

12.5cm (5in) high

£550–650   **GorL**

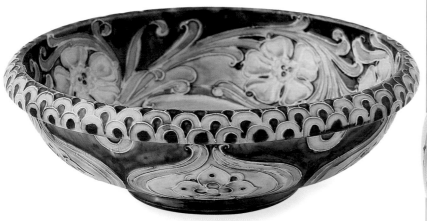

Florian Ware "Freesia" pattern bowl with an interior frieze of tube-lined yellow flowers and foliage. The exterior is decorated with floral panels. *c.1900*

17.5cm (6¾in) wide

£1,600–1,800   **Rum**

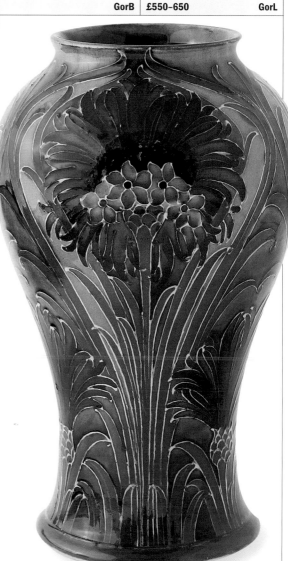

Florian Ware goblet with tube-line decoration in a "Dahlia" variant pattern. Further decoration on the inner neck rim. *c.1904*

23cm (9in) high

£2,500–3,000   **Rum**

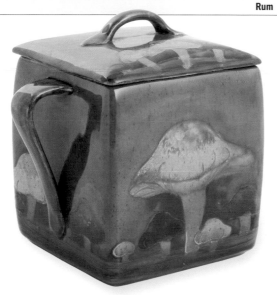

"Claremont" twin-handled biscuit box and cover with mushroom decoration in naturalistic colours, against a streaked, olive green ground.

16.5cm (6½in) high

£2,300–2,500   **DN**

"Brown Cornflower" pattern baluster vase tube lined and painted in autumnal colours, with a repeat pattern of cornflowers and foliage.

24cm (9½in) high

£3,000–3,500   **Rum**

Minton & Co.

One of Britain's best-known ceramics factories, Minton was established in 1783. Almost one hundred years later the Minton Art Pottery Studio – set up to produce hand-decorated pieces – opened in London.

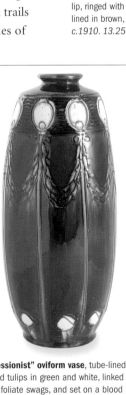

In 1871, the Minton Art Pottery Studio was established under the direction of William Stephen Coleman in London. It gave painters the chance to decorate wares such as tiles and plaques with animals, flowers, and genre scenes. The blank pottery wares were supplied by the factory founded by Thomas Minton at Stoke-on-Trent in 1783.

The pioneering designer Christopher Dresser supplied designs to the factory in the 1870s. This legacy of "design" concept at Minton & Co. can be seen in its range of Art Nouveau earthenware decorated with distinctive, organic designs using tube-lining – where thin trails of slip outline coloured areas. A series of

"Secessionist" pieces was designed by Leon Solon, who was artistic director of the company from 1900 to 1909, in collaboration with John Wadsworth. Vases in tubular or ovoid forms were decorated with stylized plant forms and geometric patterns. These details, and the choice of vibrant colours – purple, red, leaf green, ochre, white, and turquoise – reflect the influence of the Viennese artistic groups known as the Secessionists.

Above: "Secessionist" ware vase with tapering body and rounded lip, ringed with stylized tree motifs rooted in the base. It is tube-lined in brown, green, white, and black against a turquoise ground. *c.1910. 13.25cm (5¼in) high* **£150–180 ADE**

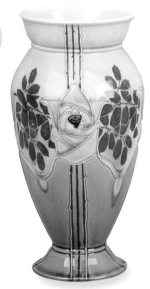

Baluster-shaped "Secessionist" vase – one of a pair – with tube-lined roses in mustard and mauve, stylized stems, and transfer-printed leaves on a green ground. *1908*
27cm (10½in) high

£600–700 (the pair)   **DN**

"Secessionist" oviform vase, tube-lined with stylized tulips in green and white, linked by green foliate swags, and set on a blood red and streaky black ground.
32cm (12⅝in) high

£250–300   **DN**

"Secessionist" ware tubular vase of elongated form with angular handles. It is tube-lined with stylized tulips in white and green, linked by green and yellow foliate swags, and set on blood red and green grounds. Printed mark "Minton Ltd. No 1" on the base.
31cm (12in) high

£450–500   **BonS**

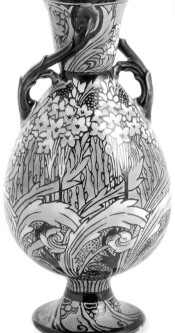

"Secessionist" ware vase of oval section with flared neck, spreading circular foot, and twig handles. It is transfer-printed with stylized flowers and foliage.
26.5cm (10½in) high

£250–300   **DN**

Doulton

Doulton was founded in the early 19th century to produce salt-glazed ware. Henry Doulton later set up a studio in London to concentrate on ornamental pieces, and the firm became Royal Doulton in 1901.

Doulton & Co., founded in 1815 by John Doulton (1793–1873), has a long and successful history of producing ceramics. In 1871, John's son Henry set up a studio in Lambeth, south London, specifically to produce handcrafted, decorated pieces. It was out of this studio that Doulton produced a range of Art Nouveau pieces – especially popular with the overseas market.

Central to the success of Doulton's Art Nouveau line was the relationship the studio formed with the nearby Lambeth School of Art. This association provided the firm with many talented designers including Frank Butler, Arthur, Florence, and Hannah Barlow, George Tinworth, and Emily

Edwards. The artists were given the freedom to choose the shape and decoration of each vessel. Vases were often simple in form, and were used as a vehicle for designs that were embellished with animal motifs or abstract leaf patterns.

In 1877, the former works of Pinder, Bourne & Co. in Burslem were taken over by Doulton and produced successful artistic ware of a totally different nature to those made at Lambeth.

Above: Doulton Burslem ewer and basin set transfer-printed and hand-painted with a stylized "Kelmscott" plant form pattern. *26cm (10¼in) high*
£320–380 L&T

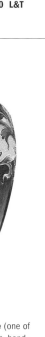

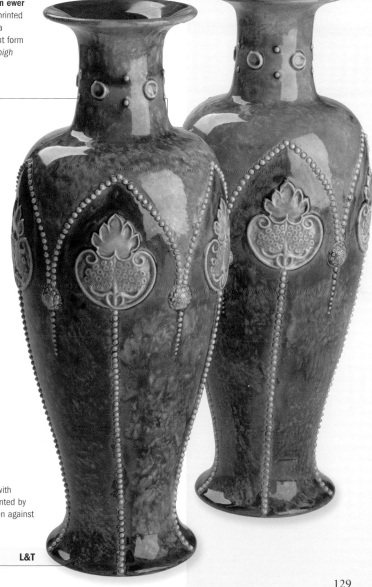

Royal Doulton stoneware vase by Francis C. Pope, of broad oviform shape tapering to a flared neck. It is incise-decorated with panels of flowers flanked by scrolls of stems and foliage against a pale olive and blue ground.
30.5cm (12in) high
£300–400　　　　　　　　　**DN**

Doulton Lambeth stoneware vase (one of a pair) of shouldered baluster form, hand-painted by Eliza Simmance with a band of scrolling foliage against a mottled ground.
30.5cm (12in) high
£350–450 (the pair)　　　　**L&T**

Pair of Royal Doulton vases of baluster shape with applied floral, foliate, and beadwork designs painted by Ethel Beard in brown, faun, white, blue, and green against mottled brown and blue-grey grounds.
33cm (12¾in) high
£350–450　　　　　　　　　**L&T**

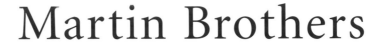

Martin Brothers

The most curious and amusing designs to emerge during the Art Nouveau period were those created in England by the four Martin brothers, headed up by Robert Wallace Martin, who trained at the Lambeth School of Art.

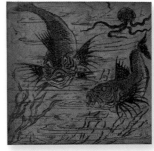

The career of Robert Wallace Martin (1843–1923) began at the Doulton Pottery where he worked on a freelance basis. He also studied stone carving and sculpture, and his work at the Houses of Parliament strengthened his taste for the Neo-Gothic style, as well as for the grotesque.

Robert Wallace established his pottery in Fulham, London, in 1873, although by 1877 he had moved to larger premises at Southall, Middlesex. There, he and his brothers produced an extraordinary range of salt-glazed stoneware.

Every aspect of the family business was covered by one of the Martin brothers: Walter Frazer was charged with the throwing of pottery shapes, developing coloured glazes, and creating some of the incised decoration. Edwin was chief decorator, with aquatic subjects his speciality. Charles administered business affairs on a part-time basis.

The Martins' highly original objects often featured grimacing, grotesque, quizzical birds; grinning human faces; whimsical creatures such as fish, owls, frogs, armadillos, and salamanders; and menacing goblins. This widely celebrated menagerie of quirky, mythical beasts was superbly modelled or beautifully drawn and incised. Glazes were typically mottled in muted tones. From the 1890s, the Martin ceramics works decorated its stoneware shapes with painted flowers and birds that were influenced by the Art Nouveau style. The factory closed in 1914.

Above: Stoneware tile incised with two grotesque fish and a jellyfish in shades of green, blue, and ochre. In a wooden frame added later. The tile is unmarked. *14cm (5½in) wide* **£600–700 WW**

GROTESQUE IMAGERY

The delight in fanciful decoration featuring unusual combinations of men, beasts, flowers, fish, and birds that appeared in Martin Brothers ceramic ware originated in Roman antiquity and emerged during the Renaissance with the discovery of ancient buildings such as the Golden House of Nero in Rome. Taking the name from the subterranean ruins, or *grotte*, where the decorations had been buried, grotesque motifs were appropriated by early Renaissance artists until Raphael revived them for decorative schemes in 1516, and by 1519 for the Vatican Logge. The 19th-century fashion for Gothic decoration saw exotic, whimsical beasts applied to furniture, ceramics, and metalwork in imaginative combinations.

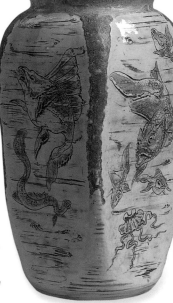

Stoneware vase incised with a frieze of four comical long-billed birds. In muted colours against a biscuit-brown ground. Marked "5-1894 Martin Bros. London & Southall". *22cm (8¾in) high* **£5,000–6,000 WW**

Earthenware vase with everted rim, incised with panels of exotic fish and other sea creatures in soft colours. Marked "Martin Bros. London & Southall, 2-1903". *24cm (9½in) high* **£2,800–3,200 L&T**

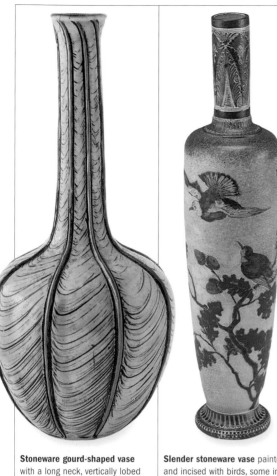

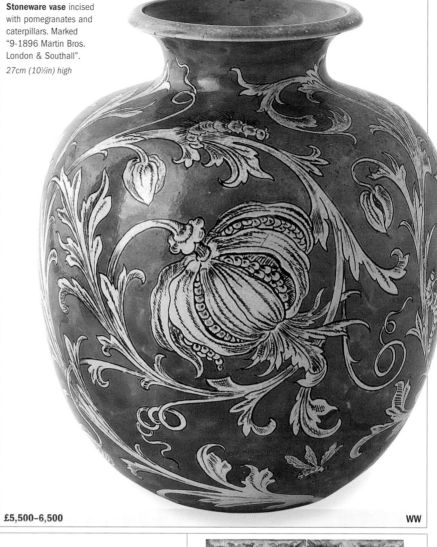

Stoneware vase incised with pomegranates and caterpillars. Marked "9-1896 Martin Bros. London & Southall".
27cm (10½in) high

Stoneware gourd-shaped vase with a long neck, vertically lobed in blue. Each panel is scalloped in black against a blue-grey ground. *1903*

18.5cm (7¼in) high

£650–750   **DN**

Slender stoneware vase painted and incised with birds, some in flight and some perched on oak branches. In soft naturalistic colours. *1883*

51cm (20in) high

£3,000–3,500   **DRA**

£5,500–6,500   **WW**

William de Morgan

A leading English pottery designer who trained at the Royal Academy schools, William de Morgan (1839–1917) joined the influential and trailblazing circle established by William Morris, Edward Burne-Jones, and Dante Gabriel Rossetti in the early 1860s. After a period producing tiles and pottery in London, he moved in 1882 to Morris's celebrated Merton Abbey, but by 1888 had established his own factory in London. De Morgan looked for inspiration to Persian, Iznik, Hispano-Moresque, and ancient Greek pottery, producing earthenware tiles, plates, and vases painted in the lustre technique or Persian style. His stylized patterns featuring animals, fish, birds, foliage, and even Greek ships accommodated the vessel shapes and produced an effect of opulence and luxury.

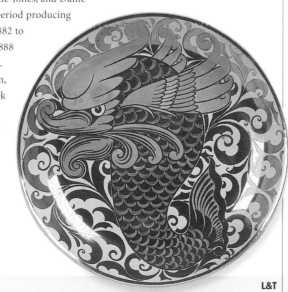

William de Morgan circular ruby lustre charger painted with a fantastical fish on a foliate ground. The underside has concentric and leafy bands.

36.5cm (14¼in) wide

£2,000–2,500   **L&T**

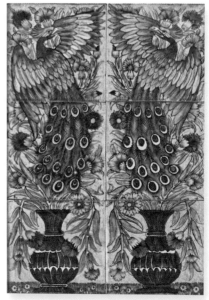

William de Morgan "Persian" tile panel composed of a pair of three-tile vertical friezes depicting peacocks above vases of flowers. In a wooden frame added later.

61cm (24in) high

£9,500–10,500   **WW**

British Ceramics

In Britain a small but influential band of potters rejected the organic sensuality of French Art Nouveau ceramics in favour of the simple and functional wares promoted by Arts and Crafts designers such as William Morris, and the elegant Japanese-style decoration championed by the Aesthetic Movement. Inspired by the individuality and quality of these designs, and recognizing that ceramics were ideal for mass production, several British manufacturers opened art pottery studios, where designers could experiment with flowing, organic forms, new methods of glazing, and naturalistic forms of decoration.

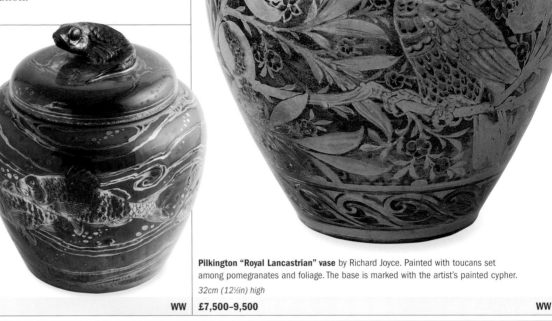

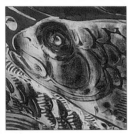

Pilkington's designs often feature exotic lustre and iridescent glazes.

Pilkington "Royal Lancastrian" vase by Richard Joyce. Ovoid body with relief moulding, decorated with silver and iridescent lustre carp swimming among waves. The lid is decorated with a carp-shaped knob. *1913*

23cm (9in) high

£3,000–4,000 WW

Pilkington "Royal Lancastrian" vase by Richard Joyce. Painted with toucans set among pomegranates and foliage. The base is marked with the artist's painted cypher.

32cm (12½in) high

£7,500–9,500 WW

Charles H. Brannam

In the late 18th century, the Brannam family established a pottery in Barnstaple in North Devon. Thomas Brannam subsequently exhibited his ceramics at the Great Exhibition of 1851. When Charles Hubert Brannam, who had studied art, took over his father's pottery in 1879, he carried on producing traditional sgraffito and slip-decorated pottery, but also introduced more fashionable designs under the name of Barum Ware. This art pottery, which was usually made of terracotta decorated with a lustrous, shiny blue and green glaze, was sold through the leading retailers of the day, including Liberty & Company and Heal & Sons. Brannam's sons carried on with the family business and it is still in operation today, although under different ownership.

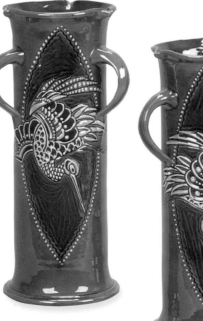

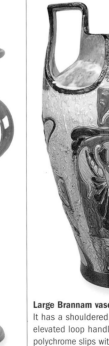

Pair of Brannam earthenware vases of cylindrical shape with triple loop handles. Decorated in sgraffito and painted slips with a stork in flight. Impressed with the mark "Royal Barum" Ware.

30cm (11¾in) high

£250–300 DN

Large Brannam vase by Frederick Braddon. It has a shouldered, tapering ovoid form, elevated loop handles, and sgraffito and polychrome slips with birds and plants. *1904*

50cm (20in) high

£800–1,000 PC

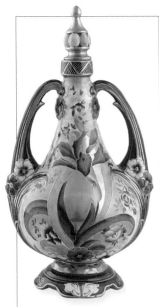

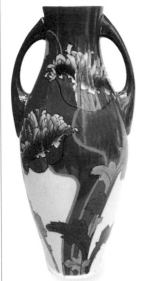

Foley "Intarsio" vase of Persian-inspired, twin-handled, tapering form. Transferred and enamelled with flowers and foliage.

30cm (11¾in) high

£200–250   Clv

Foley "Intarsio" vase by Frederick Alfred Rhead. The twin-handled, tapering baluster form is transferred and enamelled.

27.5cm (11in) high

£350–400   PC

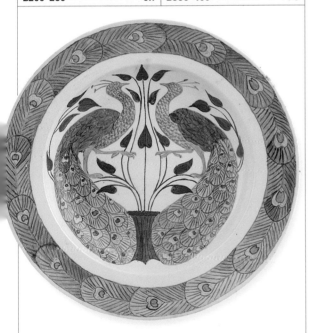

Wedgwood earthenware bowl of shallow, circular form featuring a pair of peacocks around a highly stylized vase of flowers and foliage. The peacock feather rim is painted in naturalistic colours.

26cm (10¼in) wide

£50–100   Clv

Pilkington "Royal Lancastrian" vase by Gordon M. Forsyth. The body is of shouldered ovoid form and is painted with bell flowers and foliage. The patches of iridescence, particularly in evidence around the neck, emerge unpredictably during a third, low-temperature firing, and are a much-prized decorative detail. Marked with the artist's painted cypher. *1912*

34.5cm (13½in) high

£3,200–4,200   WW

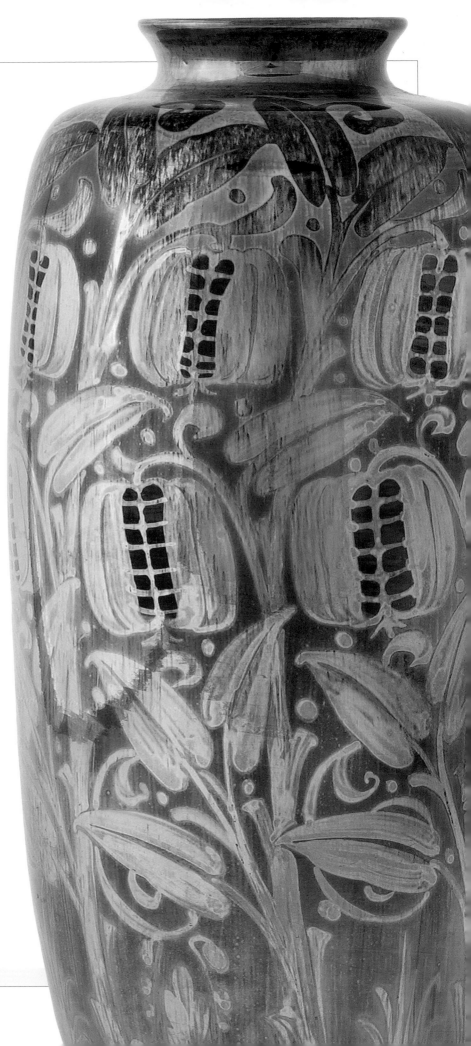

KEY FEATURES

Pieces are marked profusely, including the die-stamped company flame mark, a Roman numeral date, shape number, clay composition, and, when applicable, the artist's signature.

"Iris Glaze" was used on some of the most successful Art Nouveau pieces. They are typically decorated with painted flowers and plants. Land- and seascapes are very rare.

"Vellum Glaze" pieces often have a blurred decoration and date from before 1915.

Arts and Crafts pieces are coated in a rich matte glaze and are either hand-carved or matte-painted in strong colours.

Rookwood

Rookwood is considered to be the most well-known and influential American art pottery manufacturer, combining the best ceramic artists with factory production processes to produce high-quality pieces.

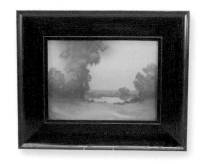

Founded in 1880, Rookwood Pottery is probably the most famous and highly regarded of America's art pottery companies. During its reign, it created pots, vases, jugs, and plaques in a huge array of styles, including Art Nouveau. The antithesis of the smaller Arts and Crafts studios, where the fewer hands on a piece the better, Rookwood was a large, production-oriented factory with a strict division of labour: artists were not even responsible for glazing the pieces they decorated.

Rookwood's first achievement was the development of air-brushed backgrounds for their floral designs. This technique was developed and patented by the famous artist Laura Fry. Having hired the best artists and technicians, Rookwood continued to create new glazes and explore new decorative techniques.

Rookwood produced decorated ware throughout its tenure as the most important pottery company in the United States. However, after about 1905, it introduced a "production" line, where decoration was embossed in the mould and not hand applied. Such pieces proved to be the foundation of Rookwood's financial success, although a testament to how quality in American decorative arts would devolve in the years to come.

Above: Large "Vellum" matte glazed plaque painted by Lenore Ashbury with a landscape of trees by a pond at dusk. Mounted in a new oak frame. Signed "L.A." on the front, and with a flame mark and "XV" on the back. *32cm (12½in) wide* **£6,000–7,000 DRA**

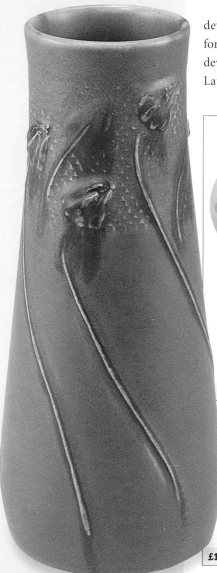

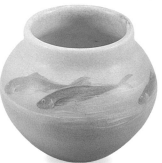

"Vellum" matte glazed vase of ovoid form painted by Edith Noonan, with trout in shades of silver-grey swimming around the upper body against a shaded pink, ivory, and teal ground. Impressed with a flame mark and "VIII/911/V/EN". *1908*
12.5cm (5in) wide

£1,000–1,300   **DRA**

Large tubular vase by William Hentschel. The gently tapering body has flower pods carved around the upper section, with elongated, spiralling stems trailing below. The pods are set against a partially "hammered" background and highlighted with a blue glaze against a matte green glazed ground. *1910*
26.5cm (10½in) high

£1,300–1,600   **DRA**

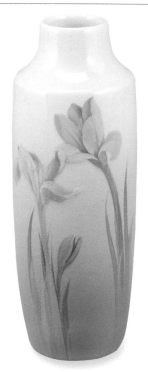

"Standard" glazed vase of elongated, tapering cylindrical form, painted by Frederick Rothenbusch, with blue crocuses on a pale, muted grey "Iris" ground. *1904*
24cm (9½in) high

£1,000–1,500   **CR**

Tall "Standard" glaze pitcher painted by Sallie Toohey, with orange tiger lilies on a blended, two-tone, light-to-dark umber ground. *1899*
25.5cm (10in) high

£700–1,000   **DRA**

Newcomb College

Along with George Ohr and Grueby, Newcomb College art pottery – which from 1895 onwards was produced primarily by women – ranks among the most important made in the United States during the Art Nouveau period.

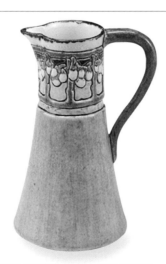

An adjunct of Tulane University in New Orleans, the Sophie Newcomb Memorial College was intended to assist the women of the deep South develop work skills that would ultimately bring them into the labour force. The enterprise began in 1895 and continued until 1941.

The decorating staff consisted primarily of women students at the college, although it was augmented by a handful of important instructors and designers such as Sadie Irvine, Henrietta Bailey, Harriet Joor, and Anna Frances Simpson. The students were allowed to sell their better work in the gallery shop to help fund their tuition. Their work dating from about 1898 until about 1910 is the most daring and desirable. These

unique pieces, hand-thrown, and individually designed and decorated, usually have floral or scenic designs hand-painted or modelled onto the surface, and are covered with a clear high glaze.

Most pieces have survived in good condition, as the biscuit used was fairly dense, but some minor damage is acceptable to collectors. Pieces with stronger, brighter colours will fetch higher prices.

Above: "Transitional" ovoid-form vase by A.F. Simpson, with oak trees covered in Spanish moss, in shades of blue and green over buff with a semi-matte finish. Marked "NC/AFS, FZ79/ 184/JM/B".
20.5cm (8in) high
£5,500–7,500 DRA

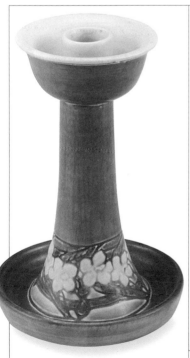

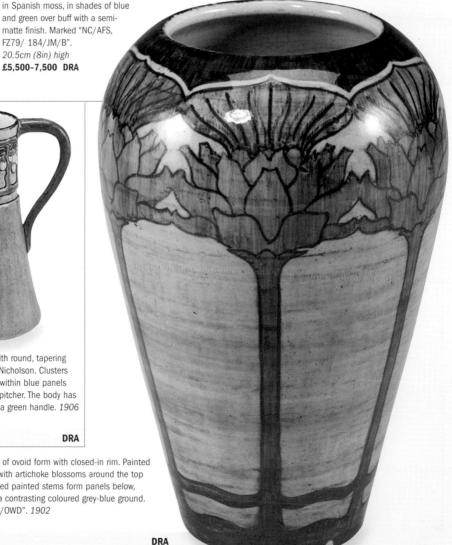

"High glaze" pitcher with round, tapering body, incised by Leona Nicholson. Clusters of white flowers are set within blue panels around the neck of the pitcher. The body has a blue-grey ground with a green handle. *1906*
19cm (7½in) high
£4,500–6,500 DRA

"Transitional" candlestick by Leona Nicholson, incised with blossoms and leaves around the base of the stem. The exterior has a blue-green ground and the candle-holder and surrounding cup are in ivory-white. *1912*
16cm (6¼in) high
£1,300–1,800 DRA

Rare "high glaze" vase of ovoid form with closed-in rim. Painted by Olive Webster Dodd with artichoke blossoms around the top of the body. The elongated painted stems form panels below, which are filled in with a contrasting coloured grey-blue ground. Marked "NC/P99/JM/Q/OWD". *1902*
24cm (9¼in) high
£11,000–13,000 DRA

KEY FEATURES

Wafer thin of body, with a folded rim, an in-body twist, and a pucker or a pinch, typical pieces of Ohr are about 10cm (4in) tall and wide.

Large pots – those over 22cm (7in) tall – are rarer and bring disproportionately more money.

The more manipulated the pot, the more elegant the result, and the more valuable the piece.

Pieces are usually marked, with a few exceptions. Most pieces bear a die-stamped "G.E.O. Biloxi" mark. Later pieces have "GEOhr" incised by Ohr into their base.

George Ohr

A potter from Biloxi, Mississippi, George Ohr worked from about 1883 until 1907 creating paper-thin vessels, which he manipulated with turns, ripples, and twists, and treated with colourful glazing.

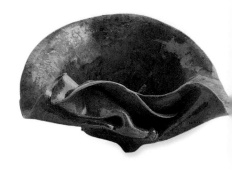

George Ohr is best remembered for the prescient modernity of his works, which were inconceivably out of place in the turn-of-the-century American South, or just about any place else for that matter. He dug his own clays, mixed his own glazes, and even built his own kiln and pottery. He made nearly every piece himself by hand, from start to finish, and created about 10,000 pots, or "mud babies", during his career.

Ohr's glazing is perhaps the most remarkable part of his craft. With sleight of hand, he would cover a vessel with a bright red glaze sponged with traces of gun metal, deep blue, and soft white. Occasionally, he might use two entirely different glazes on opposite sides of the pot.

After 1900, Ohr became less interested in glazing and primarily concerned with the simplicity and honesty of his work. "God put no colour in souls so I'll put no colour on my pots", he once said. Ohr left his work in its bisque-fired simplicity, showing crisply the hand of the artist and the completeness of what flew off the wheel.

Above: Sculptural earthenware vase of clam-like form with abstract, possibly sexual, imagery beneath the lower lip. The mottled glaze is in shades of brown, pink, red, metallic blue, and black. *c.1900. 20.25cm (8in) wide* **£2,700–3,000 LGA**

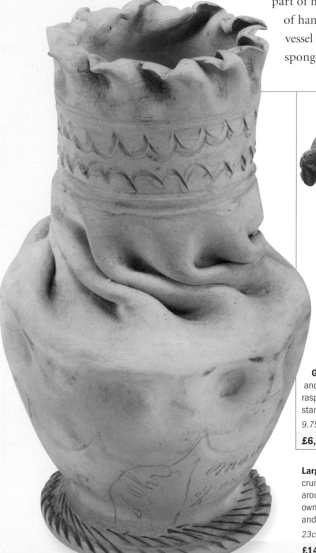

Glazed earthenware vase with pinched and ruffled rim, and bulbous knopped stem. On the outside it has a speckled raspberry and black glaze with green colouring at the rim. It is stamped "BILOXI, MISS/GEO. E. OHR".
9.75cm (3¾in) high

£6,000–10,000 DRA

Large unglazed earthenware vase with a folded rim, deep crumpled twist, and notched wave and geometric patterns around the foot and neck. Incised: "Made in the presence of owner John Power/By his friend/G E Ohr/Biloxi 1-24-1903", and "Mary had a little Lamb & Ohr has a little Pottery". *1903*
23cm (9in) high

£14,500–17,000 DRA

Red earthenware vase of bulbous, waisted form finished with an unusual and vibrant volcanic-like glaze in raspberry and white, applied over a high-gloss, dark blue ground.
15cm (6in) high

£10,000–11,000 CR

Clifton

Although only in operation for three years (1905–08), Clifton founder William Long drew on his considerable experience to produce highly collectable pottery, including the "Crystal Patina" range with its distinctive micro-crystalline glaze.

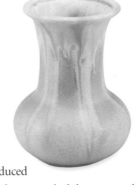

The Clifton pottery was formed in 1905 in Newark, New Jersey, by William A. Long, who had been involved in several other ceramic ventures including the Lonhuda Pottery of Steubenville, Ohio. Despite its small size, the company produced a wide selection of designs and experimented with a variety of decoration techniques. Clifton was renowned mainly for its four types of decorative ware: Crystal Patina, Robin's egg blue, Tirrube, and Indian.

Crystal Patina ware, the most Art Nouveau of its offerings, was typified by striking micro-crystalline glazes of amber, cream, green and/or brown flowing unevenly over a porcelain body.

A few pieces were produced using flambé glazes of orange, dark brown, and occasionally, gold. The vessels, moulded from hard, white Jersey clay, were occasionally embossed with decorative elements such as raised fish or blossoms. The majority, however, were moulded smooth.

Although highly collectable, damage, such as chipping, can reduce the value of Crystal Patina pottery by up to half.

Above: Crystal Patina vase with an elongated neck rising from a squat, bulbous body. Decorated with a pale amber glaze over a celadon micro-crystalline ground. Incised "Clifton/CAP/1906/141". *16.5cm (6½in) high*
£300–450 DRA

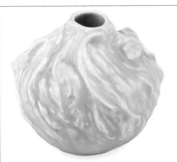

Small cabinet vase of ovoid shape with narrow, circular rim. Moulded in relief with fish swimming through waves. Incised "Clifton/CAP/1906/108".
9cm (3½in) wide
£800–900   **DRA**

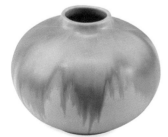

Crystal Patina vase of smooth, spherical shape, decorated with a sunburst-effect pattern in matte green and yellow over a celadon ground. Incised "Clifton/CAP/1906".
18cm (7in) wide
£650–750   **DRA**

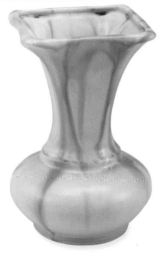

Crystal Patina vase with a squat, bulbous body and a round, elongated neck with a four-sided rim. The streaky pattern, in a crystalline flambé glaze, is of stylized, trailing plant forms. Incised "Clifton/1907".
18.5cm (7¼in) high
£275–400   **DRA**

Rare silver overlay vase with bulbous body and long, wide neck. The highly stylized poppy pattern is silver-plated (like the rim) and the flower-heads are "sponged" in matte grey-blue. Incised "Clifton/CAP/1906/141" and stamped "Electrotytic/Trenton NJ".
17cm (6¾in) high
£600–700   **DRA**

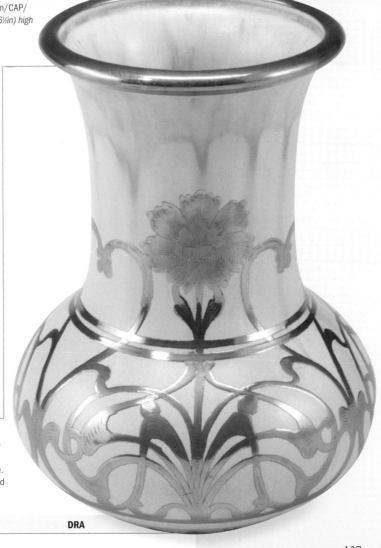

Grueby Faience Co.

William Grueby (1867–1925), who opened his pottery in 1894 in Boston, Massachusetts, is commended for his pursuit of "organic naturalism", and the company's pieces rank among the best ceramic work of the Art Nouveau period.

Though Grueby initially produced some glossy finished pieces, the bulk of its production centred on vegetal matte glazed ware. It was, in fact, the finest such glaze in the United States, influencing no fewer than 50 other American companies, from Rookwood to Arequipa.

While some of Grueby's pots are undecorated, displaying only the simple thrown form, it is better known for pots bearing organic designs. The most common of these are simple broad leaves, occasionally alternating with applied buds. The pots are almost alive, looking more picked from a garden than cut from a potter's wheel. They are often covered with the richest matte finishes, which flow over deep body cuts and rows of folded leaves. Grueby pots have a quiet power that distinguishes them as objects of mood rather than mere decorative ware.

Grueby also produced some of the best tiles of the period, employing the same glazing they used on their vases. These, however, are often decorated with scenes and flowers, usually in many colours.

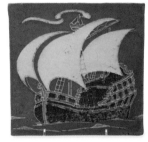

Above: Rare large earthenware tile design by Addison LeBoutiller in cuenca (relief) depicting an oak tree in dark green oatmeal glaze over green grass, ivory clouds, and a slate blue sky. *31cm (12¼in) square* **£27,000–30,000 DRA**

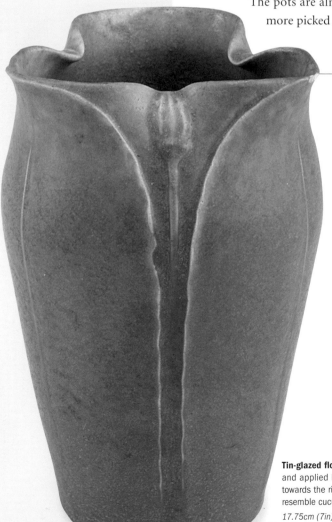

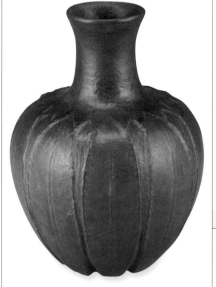

Rare tin-glazed vase by Marie Seaman, the bulbous body of gourd-like shape with tooled and applied leaf motifs, finished in a textured matte green glaze. Stamped "Grueby Faience" and incized "MS/152." *31.5cm (12½in) high*

£8,000–10,000	CR

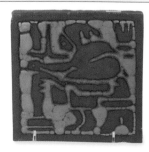

Tin-glazed tile of fine quality, decorated in cuenca with an indigo and ochre coloured galleon with billowing sails against a dark teal blue sea and sky. Signed "GM". *20.25cm (8in) square*

£1,000–1,500	DRA

Tin-glazed floriform vase decorated by Gertrude Priest with tooled and applied broad leaves alternated with small buds and stems towards the rim. The rich moss green glaze is textured and pitted to resemble cucumber skin. Marked with the artist's initials on the base. *17.75cm (7in) high*

£1,250–1,500	DRA

Red clay floor tile with stylized decoration comprising a seated monk reading a manuscript in a matte brown glaze against a matte ochre ground. Unsigned. *15cm (6in) square*

£300–400	DRA

Van Briggle

Artus and Anna Van Briggle founded the Van Briggle Pottery at the turn of the 20th century. Their slip-cast, embossed vases combine Art Nouveau style and Native American design with organic floral decoration in natural colours.

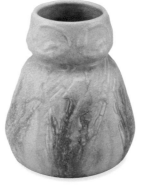

Artus and Anna Van Briggle moved to Colorado Springs in 1899 for the mountain climate because Artus was suffering from tuberculosis. Here, the Van Briggles continued the work they had developed while working at the Rookwood Pottery (*see p.134*) in Cincinatti, Ohio, emphasizing the modelling of organic and figural designs under rich matte glazes.

The company, which remains in business today, produced a quality of work ranging from high-end studio ware to fairly commercial products. Earlier pieces are almost always better, and the period prior to Artus's death in 1904 saw the production of the Van Briggle's best work.

Pieces were nearly always moulded, usually with embossed floral and/or leaf patterns. Less common are vases with moulded figures of people or animals.

From 1905 until Anna's departure in about 1912, the company continued to produce quality art ware, employing the same rich matte finishes pioneered during the early period. While greens, blues, and deep reds were the most common, ochre, white, pink, black, and other earthy hues were also used.

Above: Gourd-shaped vase embossed with poppies under a frothy matte turquoise and purple glaze, with sections of buff clay showing through. Incized "AA/Van Briggle/1903/III/137". *1903*
22cm (8¾in) high **£1,800–2,600 DRA**

KEY FEATURES

Floral and leaf patterns usually decorate Van Briggle pottery, but moulded figures of people and animals are occasionally found.

Earlier pieces are considered superior, especially those produced by Artus between 1902 and 1904.

Pieces are well marked, bearing at least the founders' famous conjoined "AA" cipher incised into the bottom of each item.

A four-digit date is almost always incised below the company's mark on pieces made prior to 1908.

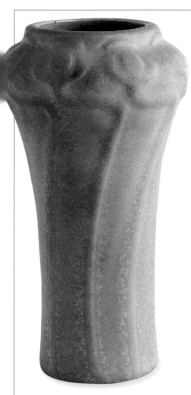

Slender corseted vase embossed with stylized poppy pods and stems under a turquoise glaze, with sections of the underlying buff clay body showing through. *1908–11*
17.75cm (7in) high

£750–900   **CR**

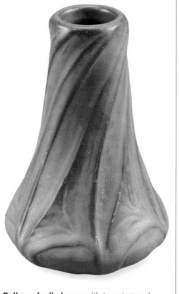

Bulbous-bodied vase with tapering neck embossed with stylized leaf forms under a feathered, matte green glaze with sections of brown clay showing through. *1904*
14cm (5½in) high

£750–1,000   **DRA**

Earthenware vase with elongated, tapering body and a short cup or bowl neck. It is embossed with stylized daffodils under a matte pale green glaze, with sections of the underlying buff clay body showing through. The subtle texture and delicately subdued colour of this glaze is highly characteristic of Van Briggle's work. *1907–12*
26.5cm (10½in) high

£450–550   **DRA**

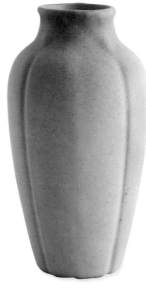

Baluster-shaped vase with lightly embossed, stylized daisy heads and stems under a graduated blue-green glaze. *1903–12*
19cm (7½in) high

£300–400   **CR**

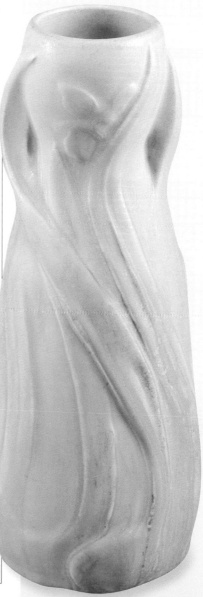

American Ceramics

Early American art pottery was simple and imitative. By 1900, however, American potters had developed their own style and were busily researching new glaze and modelling techniques. Soon there were over 200 companies across the nation producing decorative ware. These ranged from the large kilns at Rookwood to small studio ventures, such as the Jervis Pottery in Oyster Bay, New York, and the Rhead Pottery in Santa Barbara, California. Although the production of art pottery was in decline by the 1920s, it paved the way for the studio movement that flourished later.

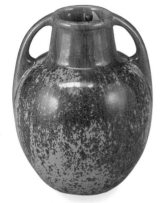

Fulper Pottery earthenware vase of gourd-like shape with two curved handles. Covered in a characteristic crystalline glaze and incised with a "racetrack" mark on the base.

19cm (7½in) high

£350–450   **CR**

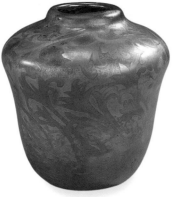

Weller Pottery vase by Jacques Sicard, of shouldered ovoid form. Decorated with a foliage pattern on an iridescent ground. Signed "Weller Sicard" in script. *c.1905*

11.5cm (4½in) high

£250–350   **SI**

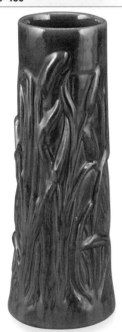

Fulper Pottery "Cat's-tail" vase of tubular form, embossed with bulrushes and finished in a glossy blue-grey and moss green flambé glaze. The base has a rectangular ink mark.

33cm (13in) high

£2,800–3,200   **CR**

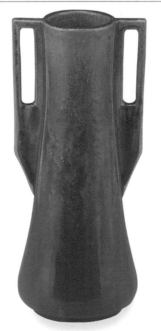

Early Fulper Pottery vase of tapering tubular form with two angular buttressed handles. Finished in a fine "moss-to-rose" flambé glaze. Underside has its original paper label.

28.5cm (11¼in) high

£220–300   **CR**

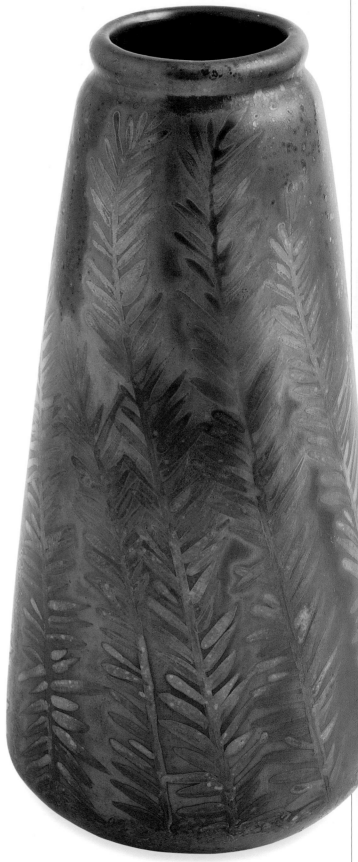

Weller Pottery vase designed and made by Jacques Sicard, of tapering circular shape and decorated with leaf and branch forms against an iridescent copper-gold ground. *c.1905*

22.5cm (9in) high

£850–1,200   **LGA**

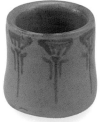

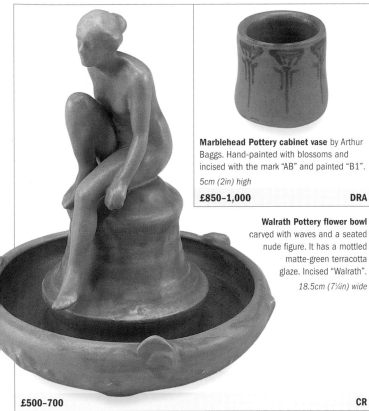

Marblehead Pottery cabinet vase by Arthur Baggs. Hand-painted with blossoms and incised with the mark "AB" and painted "B1".

5cm (2in) high

£850–1,000 DRA

Walrath Pottery flower bowl carved with waves and a seated nude figure. It has a mottled matte-green terracotta glaze. Incised "Walrath".

18.5cm (7¼in) wide

£500–700 CR

Marblehead Pottery bowl of tapered cylindrical form, with an incised, floral pattern, and impressed ship mark "MT".

9.5cm (3¾in) high

£2,800–4,500 CR

Marblehead Pottery bowl of flaring, circular form. Hand-painted with a band of stylized trees, and with an impressed ship mark.

11.5cm (4½in) high

£600–700 CR

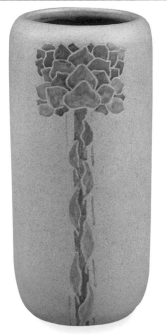

Marblehead Pottery tall cylindrical vase decorated by Hannah Tutt with tree forms, and with an impressed ship mark.

21cm (8¼in) high

£5,500–7,500 CR

Teco Pottery

The Teco line of art pottery was introduced in 1902 by William Day Gates at the Gates Potteries in Illinois. Influenced by the Prairie School, most Teco stoneware was thickly walled and architectural in shape. The pieces were completely moulded, but some designs had additional handcrafted decorative features. Up until 1910, the only glaze used by the company was a high-quality, fine green micro-crystalline glaze with a matte effect, but charcoal highlighting was sometimes added. Teco's organic Art Nouveau pieces feature curved handles and whiplash buttresses, as well as some embossed floral designs. It is rare to find a piece that does not have minor damage, such as chips or hairline cracks.

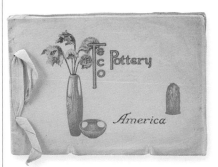

Teco Pottery America catalogue, 1906.

Teco Pottery four-sided vase with impressed, rectangular panels and four curved and pierced handles at the base. Its matte green glaze is "charcoaled" by a metallic black overglaze. The base is stamped "Teco 258".

34cm (13½in) high

£7,000–8,000 CR

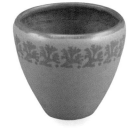

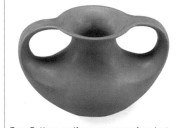

Teco Pottery earthenware vase of ancient and stylized organic form with twin handles looped to the neck. Finished in a smooth, matte glaze. The base is stamped "Teco".

21.5cm (8½in) high

£1,200–1,600 CR

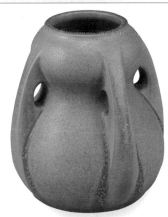

Teco Pottery double-gourd-shaped vase with buttressed handles, covered in a matte glaze and "charcoaled" with metallic black overglaze. By W.B. Mundie and stamped "Teco".

17cm (6¾in) high

£2,800–3,200 CR

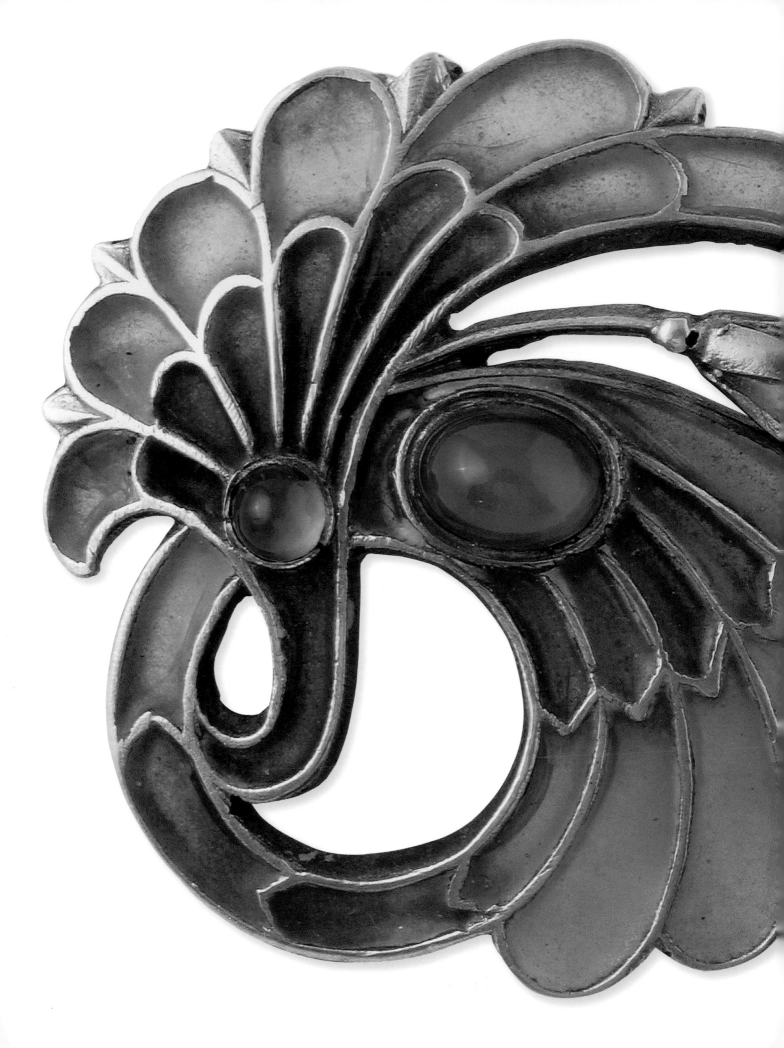

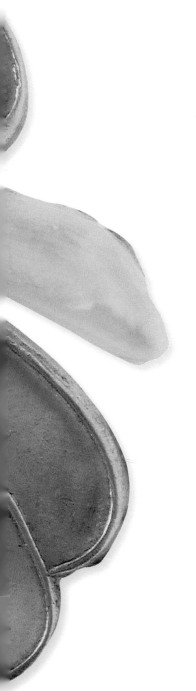

Jewellery

The late 19th century witnessed a fervent reaction against the deteriorating quality of mass-produced jewellery and the flamboyant and indiscriminate use of expensive materials such as diamonds. Throughout Europe and in the United States, jewellers sought to re-establish the age-old traditions of fine craftsmanship and create a dynamic new style.

During the Art Nouveau period, jewellery finally came into its own as an art form, rather than being considered primarily as the showpiece of ostentatious wealth. The cost of the precious stones and metals used to make a piece of jewellery became less important than innovative design and high quality of workmanship.

JOAILLERIE AND BIJOUTERIE
Distinctive for its use of semi-precious stones and unusual, inexpensive materials, Art Nouveau jewellery celebrates the imagination and fine craftsmanship of individual designers. In their search for innovation, these designers sought inspiration in previously neglected materials, such as opals, silver, rich enamelling, moonstones, turquoise, ivory, horn, bone, mother-of-pearl,

and frosted glass. In France, *joaillerie*, which placed emphasis on the intrinsic value of the materials used and was created for a wealthy clientele, vied with *bijouterie*, where the value of a piece of jewellery depended on artistic interpretation, and which used inexpensive materials to establish the modern style.

The imaginative and technically brilliant jewellery designs of René Lalique paved the way for the Art Nouveau aesthetic in a medium that was suffocating under the weight of historicism. In the hands of Lalique and other leading designers, jewellery emerged as one of the finest expressions of Art Nouveau. As in other fields of the decorative arts, nature provided the main source of inspiration, along with the graceful figures of young girls.

Silver and *plique-à-jour* brooch of fan-shaped flower form. The extraordinary petals are embellished with shaded coloured enamels and set with green-stained chalcedony cabochons and a freshwater pearl. Unmarked; probably German. *c.1900. 3cm (1¼in) wide* **£700–1,000 VDB**

FORGING THE WAY

The supremacy of French jewellers at the vanguard of Art Nouveau was assured at the 1900 Universal Exposition in Paris, where pride of place went to the exquisite jewellery of René Lalique. Rejecting the prevailing taste for diamonds, his innovative pieces featured naturalistic motifs realised with inexpensive materials and the ancient enamelling technique of *plique-à-jour*.

Several skilled craftsmen, such as Georges Fouquet, Lucien Gaillard, and Henri Vever, produced work using similar motifs and materials. Designers working for Siegfried Bing's L'Art Nouveau and Julius Meier-Graefe's La Maison Moderne, such as Paul Follot and Edward Colonna, created pieces that also drew on nature for inspiration, but were stylized and organic in appearance.

BELGIAN STAR

Across Europe, jewellers initially embraced the style set by the Parisian avant-garde. The Belgian jeweller and *orfévrier* (goldsmith) Philippe Wolfers posed the greatest challenge to Lalique, creating an astonishing collection of jewellery and precious objets d'art. He usually worked in gold or silver, and used ivory, *plique-à-jour* enamelling, baroque pearls,

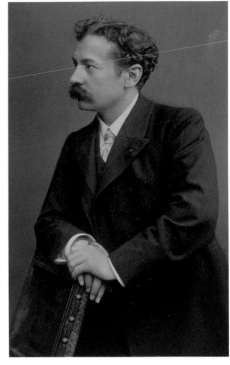

René Lalique, the most prominent Art Nouveau jewellery designer, utilized glass alongside non-precious materials, leading ultimately to his famous Art Deco glass creations.

and both precious and semi-precious stones to create fantastic jewellery featuring birds, insects, and flowers.

Although Scandinavian jewellery makers were barely influenced by Art Nouveau, the Danish silversmith Georg Jensen interpreted the style with imagination, creating jewellery with curved, fluid shapes and streamlined, lyrical simplicity, that incorporated semi-precious materials such as coral, amber, and moonstone. Jensen's mentors Mogens Ballin and Thorvald Bindesboll also created jewellery in the Art Nouveau style.

Henri and Paul Vever "Sylvia" gold pendant in the form of a highly stylized nymph, with *plique-à-jour* and diamond wings. The carved agate body has two large rubies and yellow enamel robes. *1900.* **NPA BRI**

DEFINITIVE STYLES

The top end of French Art Nouveau jewellery represented all the flamboyance and verve of the period, with its designs incorporating wild symbolism and poetic natural imagery, and the ubiquitous female form emerging from floral sprays or languid pools. The German and Austrian approach to jewellery design was generally a more formalized take on nature. The Danish silversmith Georg Jensen's early work was simple, taking a lead from Charles Robert Ashbee's designs, as was much of Liberty's output, albeit with strong Celtic influences. Tiffany incorporated colour through precious stones and enamelling.

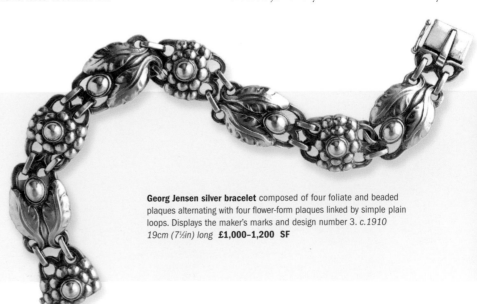

Georg Jensen silver bracelet composed of four foliate and beaded plaques alternating with four flower-form plaques linked by simple plain loops. Displays the maker's marks and design number 3. *c.1910* *19cm (7½in) long* **£1,000–1,200 SF**

JUGENDSTIL DESIGNS

By 1900, the floral style favoured for German Jugendstil jewellery in the late 1890s had given way to a more abstract, linear style. The hub of the German jewellery industry was Pforzheim, where workshops produced commercial wares based on plant and animal motifs. Jewellery designers at the artist's colony at Darmstadt, including Peter Behrens and Hans Christiansen, created simple, geometric designs that paid tribute to the Vienna Secessionist movement. Architect Joseph Maria Olbrich created pendants and brooches that echoed the strong simple forms and restrained use of ornamentation typical of his architecture.

GEOMETRIC JEWELS

In Austria, Josef Hoffmann and Koloman Moser were the dominant figures in jewellery design. Jewellery created at the Wiener Werkstätte in Vienna was made in collaboration with a team of craftsmen, and tended to have the same spare, linear characteristics as their designs for household accessories. Hoffmann's symmetrical open-work designs of squares, straight lines, and stylized plant motifs in silver were set with richly coloured semi-precious stones, mother-of-pearl and coral.

AMERICAN EXCELLENCE

While British jewellery makers, led by Liberty & Co., were less influenced by Art Nouveau than by the Arts and Crafts movement, American jewellers embraced the Art Nouveau style. By 1900, firms such as Unger Brothers and the Gorham Corporation were producing inexpensive silver jewellery that commonly featured the archetypal Belle Epoque maiden.

By contrast, Julia Shearman created handmade jewellery decorated with enamel and semi-precious stones at Tiffany & Co., made to the designs of Louis Comfort Tiffany. Paying tribute to the French master Lalique, Tiffany's designs celebrated exquisite craftsmanship as well as the natural world, using motifs such as richly coloured fruit, wild flowers, and berries.

Philippe Wolfers gold hair ornament in the form of an orchid, the petals picked out with fine gold veins and mauve *plique-à-jour* enamels. Two of the petals are further enhanced with pavé-set rubies. With a diamond set centre. 1902. **NPA V&A**

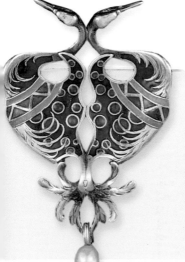

Lalique silver and enamel brooch, formed as a pair of swans in conjoined flight, and linked at the neck and tail feathers. The plumage of the swans is embellished with blue enamel, circular roundels, and grey enamelled banding. With a baroque pearl drop. *c.1900* **NPA Soth**

Rare Tiffany & Co. gold, enamel, and diamond brooch fashioned as a plant resembling a buddleia. Picked out with naturalistically coloured enamelled foliage and red berries, and interspersed with butterflies with diamond-set wings. The plain gold stem is flanked by leaves picked out with further diamonds. *c.1890* **NPA Soth**

A NEW PALETTE

By 1900, the historic revivalism of the *joaillerie* industry in France had begun to give way to the new fashion for naturalistic designs. Yet it still held fast to the traditional taste for precious stones and formality that rendered Art Nouveau motifs, such as butterflies, insects, and garlands of flowers, dull and lifeless. However, the new generation of jewellery makers preferred the design-driven *bijouterie* style, choosing decorative, semi-precious stones such as opals, moonstones, topazes, jades, agates, and amethysts, to replace the diamonds and rubies used traditionally. The Renaissance art of enamelling was revived, and unconventional materials such as horn and ivory were favoured for carved or sculpted detail.

GLOWING ENAMELS

Widely popular at the turn of the 20th century, enamelling was ideally suited to the Art Nouveau style. In the hands of designers such as Georges Fouquet and René Lalique, enamels were used to create a wide variety of dazzling effects. Not only could they be used to imitate the vibrant colours of precious gems, they could also be shaded to create life-like portraits, and add depth, translucence, and radiance to a piece. Other enchanting effects could be achieved by applying

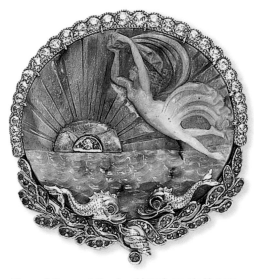

Marcus & Co. rare gold and opal brooch carved with a sea nymph against the diamond set sun. Edged with diamonds and demantoid garnets foliage, and applied with stylized dolphins. Signed. *c.1890.* **£25,000–30,000 CHR**

complex enamelling techniques favoured by contemporary Japanese craftsmen, including *plique-à-jour*, *champlevé*, and *cloisonné*.

SOURCES OF INSPIRATION

Like other Art Nouveau craftsmen, the *bijoutier* sought motifs for his jewellery designs in nature, and the countryside furnished him with a rich source of imagery. Common flowers such as irises, marguerites, thistles, forget-me-nots, and wisteria, were thoughtfully portrayed both in their entirety and in detailed close-up studies. Humble grains, including wheat, barley, and corn were used as motifs for brooches and pendants. Naturalistic birds and insects, especially dragonflies and butterflies, were also popular motifs. Another theme that found favour with Art Nouveau jewellery designers was the figure of a nude or partly-clad woman. These languid

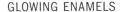

W. Rothenhöfer ornamental comb of silver, *plique-à-jour*, and tortoiseshell. The central clover frond is picked out with bright, translucent coloured enamels and is set within a silver framework embellished with grapes and vines. Displays German standard marks and "WR". *c.1902. 11cm (4½in) long* **£1,200–1,800 VZ**

FORM AND DECORATION

Jewellery generally took a naturalistic form, resembling the true nature of a flower or seashell, for example, or was embellished with a female figure that implied the fruitful and constant regenerating qualities of nature. Pieces were often fashioned in precious materials, but not always – the preciousness being achieved through the quality of design rather than by the materials used. Natural stones such as carved opal, simple agate cabochons, or plaques of mother-of-pearl provided subtle hints of colour.

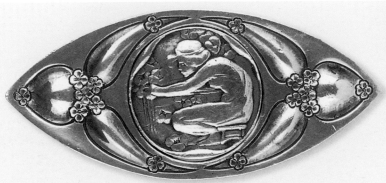

William Hutton & Sons silver two-piece belt buckle, designed by Kate Harris, elliptical in shape with lobed panels. It is enhanced with tiny florets, and centred with a circular panel showing, in relief, a figure of a naked girl crouching and gathering flowers. Maker's marks for London 1900. *8.5cm (3½in) wide* **£320–380 VZ**

maidens with long, flowing hair were portrayed on jewellery as modern interpretations of femmes fatales with biblical or classical origins, such as Salome or Leda. The representation of the female form was also often combined with nature, as in images of winged females blossoming forth from a flower. Real-life celebrities, such as the American dancer Loïe Fuller, were also popular motifs for jewellery, just as they were in sculpture and ceramics.

PAINTERS' JEWELS

In Paris, the vagaries of fashion played a pivotal role in jewellery design. Changing fashions were naturally reflected in the shape, size, and purpose of the jewellery created to enhance them. In response to the prevailing fashion for *bijouterie*, established jewellery houses, such as Boucheron, Caumet, and Cartier, looked for new ways to appeal to their customers by using precious gems in the modern idiom.

Among the hybrid styles for jewellery that emerged were *bijoux de peintres* (painters' jewels), in which a painting of a languid nymph on a central medallion of ivory or other material was encircled with precious materials, as in the bold examples designed by Alphonse Mucha for Georges Fouquet. Brooches were another example – known as medal jewellery, they were made of silver or gold, cast in bas-relief, and often depicted Art Nouveau maidens.

INTERLACING LINES

Outside France, the flowing lines of the nature-inspired Art Nouveau mode of expression were repeated in jewellery designs across Europe, albeit in a variety of interpretations. British jewellery makers were less inspired by the pure Art Nouveau style, and created their own unique jewellery that was more influenced by the Arts and Crafts movement.

Designers working for London's Liberty & Company, most notably Archibald Knox and Jessie M. King, produced striking pieces in matte, hand-hammered metal. Many of these pieces were decorated with interlacing and knotted lines, flattened leaves, and whiplash motifs based on those in ancient Celtic art. Like other Art Nouveau jewellery makers, however, they used semi-precious cabochon stones, such as garnets, turquoises, baroque pearls, and bright blue green enamels to embellish their pieces.

PRECIOUS JEWELLERY

The notion of the "preciousness" of a piece could be thought to depend on its rare and valuable component parts – the amount of gold, diamonds, emeralds, or rubies, and how big they are – but this is not necessarily the case. A well-designed lacquered-copper necklace or a stylish piece of costume jewellery with little intrinsic value but created by a highly sought-after designer can cost more than an ill-conceived diamond-set gold brooch that is worth little more than its "break value". Lalique jewellery, for example, does not always have "precious" gemstones, but it is nonetheless exquisite and valuable.

Liberty & Co. necklace designed by Archibald Knox. The suspended plaque of opal within a mount of interwoven entrelacs is set with demantoid garnets, with two baroque pearl drops. The necklace is suspended on chains with triangular spacers, and is set with opal and mother-of-pearl plaques. 1900–04.
Pendant: 4.75cm (1¾in) long
£20,000–25,000 Soth

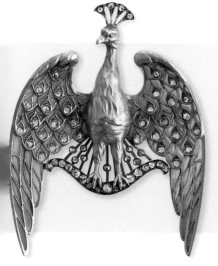

French gold brooch with *plique-à-jour*, enamel, and rose-cut diamonds, fashioned as a peacock. The central golden body is chased to subtly imply plumage, with the diamond-set crest and outspread wings picked out in translucent green enamels. The bird's wings have blue enamelled "eyes", punctuated with diamonds. 5cm (2in) wide
£18,000–26,000 MACK

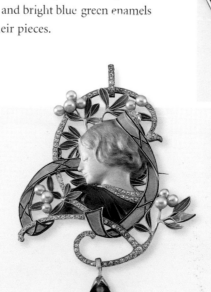

Henri and Paul Vever gold pendant, with the profile head and shoulders of a Breton woman at its centre. Clad in a blue dress with diamond collar, she is flanked by a blue enamel ribbon and is further enclosed within fine, sinuous diamond-set bands from which sprout green *plique-à-jour* enamel leaves punctuated with pearls. With an amethyst drop. c.1900. 9cm (3½in) high
£60,000–80,000 Soth

KEY FEATURES

Innovative jewellery featuring sculptural figurative or nature-inspired motifs, rendered in gold and embellished with subtle enamel colours are Lalique trademarks.

***Plique-à-jour* technique**, in which coloured enamels are cradled within an unbacked metal framework, is incorporated into many Lalique designs.

Enamels and glass are often combined with precious or semi-precious stones, or celebrate the translucent beauty of inexpensive materials such as horn.

Popular motifs include naked females, flowers, butterflies, and snakes.

René Lalique

Breathing life into a dying craft, the leading light of Art Nouveau jewellery design was René Lalique, who overturned traditions to create a new language and elevated jewellery to the realm of fine art.

Moving from conventional, diamond-set designs to jewellery in the Art Nouveau style propelled René Lalique (1860–1945) onto the international stage, especially after his creations were displayed at the 1900 Universal Exposition in Paris. This was jewellery as it had never been imagined or seen before, and Lalique's designs became widely influential. In his hands, semi-precious stones and inexpensive materials such as horn were first used to dramatic effect, and he was largely responsible for the renaissance of outmoded techniques such as *plique-à-jour* enamelling, applied as detail to the wings of his delicate and celebrated dragonfly brooches (*see p.9*).

Lalique's extensive range of fantasy jewellery was interpreted in a variety of decorative subjects, including languorous young women with flowing tresses, stylized plants, snakes, and insects. Many of these were rendered in imaginative combinations of fine materials. Lalique's jewellery has been widely copied, but it is rare to find an imitation that reaches his level of craftsmanship.

Above: Symbolist gold pendant-brooch with the profile faces of two maidens, their flowing tresses picked out in translucent blue enamel, resembling clouds through which blue swallows fly. With a baroque pearl drop. *1898–1900. 7cm (2¾in) high* **NPA Soth**

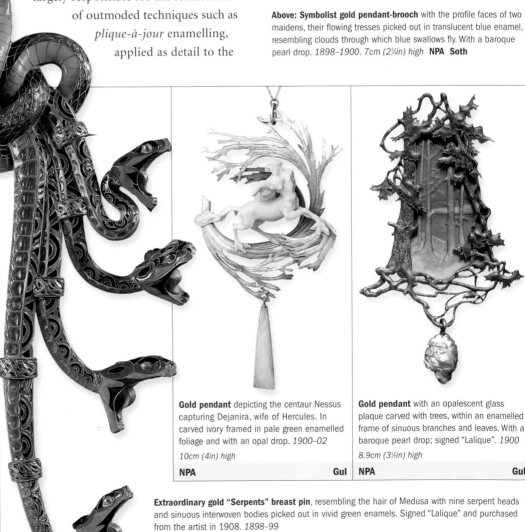

Gold pendant depicting the centaur Nessus capturing Dejanira, wife of Hercules. In carved ivory framed in pale green enamelled foliage and with an opal drop. *1900–02*
10cm (4in) high
NPA   **Gul**

Gold pendant with an opalescent glass plaque carved with trees, within an enamelled frame of sinuous branches and leaves. With a baroque pearl drop; signed "Lalique". *1900*
8.9cm (3½in) high
NPA   **Gul**

Extraordinary gold "Serpents" breast pin, resembling the hair of Medusa with nine serpent heads and sinuous interwoven bodies picked out in vivid green enamels. Signed "Lalique" and purchased from the artist in 1908. *1898–99*

NPA   **Gul**

Georges Fouquet

Three generations left their mark on the Paris jewellery firm of Fouquet, a pioneer of innovative jewellery design in the Art Nouveau taste, which was founded in 1860 by Alphonse Fouquet, Georges's father.

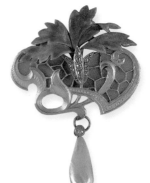

Alphonse Fouquet originally specialized in fashionable Neo-Renaissance jewels made of heavily chiselled gold, and embellished with painted enamels. In 1895, his son Georges (1862–1957) took over the company, and this led to a commitment to jewellery in the Art Nouveau style and a collaboration with the celebrated French designer Charles Desrosiers.

Largely due to the organic designs of Desrosiers, Fouquet was soon established as a leading Art Nouveau jeweller. The firm's foray into *plique-à-jour*, for example, produced celebrated, beautiful designs by Desrosiers. Fouquet also collaborated with the talented Czech designer Alphonse Mucha, leading to a fertile period of design between 1899 and 1901. Inspired by his earlier designs for Sarah Bernhardt, Mucha created for Fouquet a variety of extravagant jewels in sumptuous materials.

Despite their technical expertise, however, the designs produced by Fouquet lacked the originality and, ultimately, the beauty found in the work of René Lalique.

Above: Gold and enamelled brooch with a central carnation bloom in red enamels, set with a cut diamond, against a honeycomb panel of *plique-à-jour* enamel. With a freshwater pearl drop. Engraved "G. Fouquet". *c.1900*
6.3cm (2½in) long **£3,000–3,500 DOR**

KEY FEATURES

Wild flowers, mistletoe, leaves, sycamore seeds, peacocks, and exotic orchids were the inspirations for Fouquet's jewellery embellishments.

Plique-à-jour and other techniques were used to realize imaginative jewellery designs that combined a variety of precious and semi-precious materials.

Stylized designs were called upon to decorate theatrical jewels after designs by Mucha for Sarah Bernhardt.

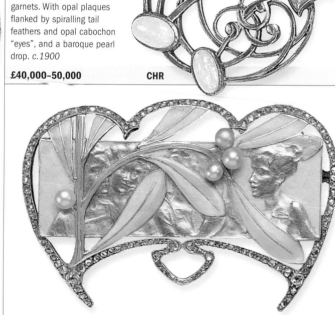

Elaborate enamelled gold brooch of two highly stylized peacocks, their tails and necks entwined, set with demantoid garnets. With opal plaques flanked by spiralling tail feathers and opal cabochon "eyes", and a baroque pearl drop. *c.1900*

£40,000–50,000 **CHR**

Gold brooch with a central rectangular plaque embellished with the head and shoulders of young women in shallow relief against a soft enamel ground, partially obscured by enamel foliage and pearl berries. The plaque is enclosed within a diamond-set band of sinuous outline.

V&A

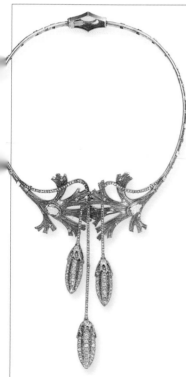

Gold necklace with the central portion composed of *plique-à-jour* fronds of seaweed punctuated with diamonds, and set with two aquamarines. It has three buds banded with hessonite garnets and diamonds suspended on diamond-set threads.

£160,000–180,000 **CHR** **NPA**

French Jewellery

Some of the most dramatic and stylish Art Nouveau jewellery was created in France. Resisting the mainstream of traditional French jewellery making – with its taste for precious stones and metals – the new generation of innovative Art Nouveau craftsmen believed that quality of design and artistic interpretation determined the value of a piece of jewellery. Led by the celebrated virtuoso René Lalique, jewellery makers such as Georges Fouquet and Eugene Feuillatre introduced a palette of semi-precious stones – amethysts, opals, and jades – and unconventional materials, including horn and ivory, to their nature-inspired designs, as well as reviving the Renaissance art of enamelling. The result was a breathtaking array of flowing, lyrical jewels unlike any that had gone before.

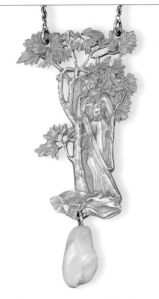

Gold and baroque pearl pendant by René Lalique, of a woman leaning against a tree decorated with green translucent enamel, with a large baroque pearl drop, on a gold loop-linking neckchain. *c.1900*

NPA   **Soth**

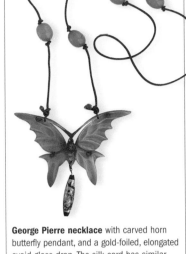

George Pierre necklace with carved horn butterfly pendant, and a gold-foiled, elongated ovoid glass drop. The silk cord has similar glass beads and four amber beads. *c.1900*

Pendant: 8cm (3in) high

£250–350   **RG**

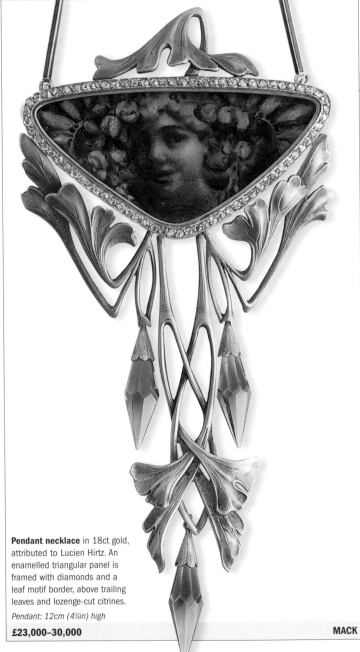

Pendant necklace in 18ct gold, attributed to Lucien Hirtz. An enamelled triangular panel is framed with diamonds and a leaf motif border, above trailing leaves and lozenge-cut citrines.

Pendant: 12cm (4¾in) high

£23,000–30,000   **MACK**

Eugene Feuillatre brooch of a female bust in profile, her flowing hair entwined with pink and green matte enamelled flowers against a dark blue *plique-à-jour* background. With maker's mark "EF".

£7,000–8,000   **Soth**

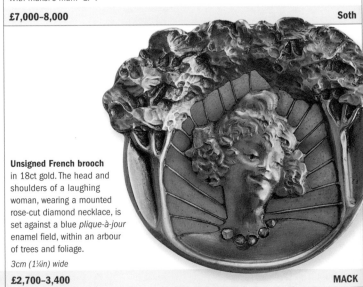

Unsigned French brooch in 18ct gold. The head and shoulders of a laughing woman, wearing a mounted rose-cut diamond necklace, is set against a blue *plique-à-jour* enamel field, within an arbour of trees and foliage.

3cm (1¼in) wide

£2,700–3,400   **MACK**

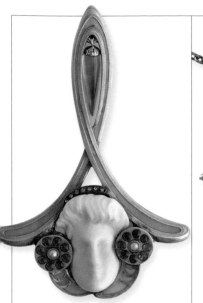

Leo Laporte-Blairsy pendant with ivory head below looped leaves and a teardrop amethyst. Set within flower-heads of 18ct gold and enamel, with diamonds and seed pearls.

7.5cm (3in) high

£15,000–23,000 MACK

Edmond-Henri Becker gold pendant, depicting a young girl with flowers, on a small pearl-and-gold chain with a pearl drop. *c.1900*

Chain: 14in (38cm) long

£300–400 VDB

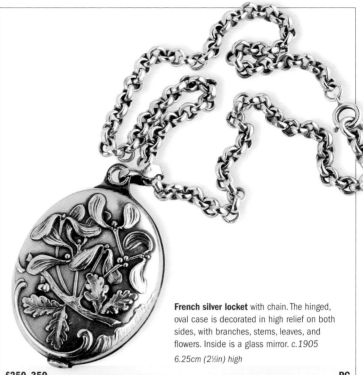

French silver locket with chain. The hinged, oval case is decorated in high relief on both sides, with branches, stems, leaves, and flowers. Inside is a glass mirror. *c.1905*

6.25cm (2½in) high

£250–350 PC

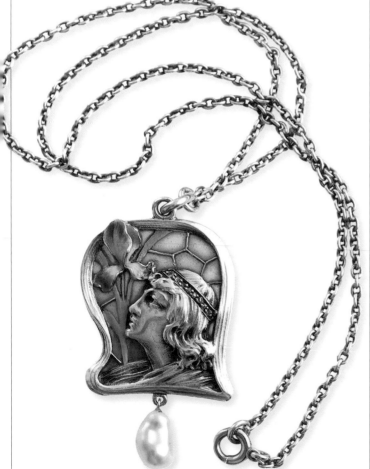

Eugene Feuillatre enamelled gold brooch, showing the head and shoulders of a *femme-fleur* encircled by white enamelled petals, golden leaves, and green enamel buds, with a pearl drop.

NPA Soth

French heart-shaped silver locket with a pierced frame, displaying interlinked C-scroll and scrolling foliage motifs, encasing an amber-coloured glass centre.

5cm (2in) high

£100–150 PC

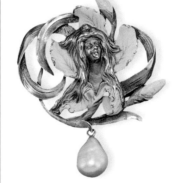

Piel Frères belt buckle with a woman's head, in the style of Alphonse Mucha. The face is carved ivory and the whiplash hair is polished brass, set against coloured enamels. *c.1898*

7.5cm (3in) wide

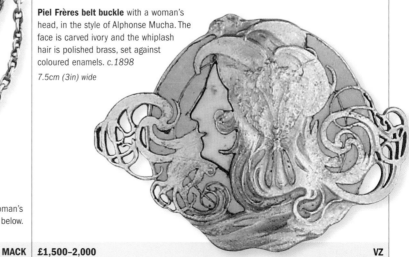

French pendant necklace in 18ct gold. The pendant has an asymmetrically framed woman's head and a *plique-à-jour* enamel floral spray on a green ground, with a seed pearl drop below.

4cm (1½in) high

£2,700–3,400 MACK

£1,500–2,000 VZ

Rounded and sculptural shapes are typical of Jensen jewellery.

Precisely rendered motifs found in nature have a plump, curvaceous softness.

Jewellery is nearly always marked with Jensen's name or initials, with a design number, and sometimes also with the initials of the designer.

Georg Jensen

Danish jewellery design is synonymous with the name of Georg Jensen (1866–1935), whose work in the Art Nouveau idiom manages to retain a distinctive Scandinavian flavour.

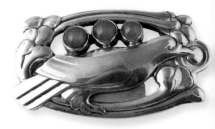

In Denmark, jewellery design achieved celebrity in the early 20th century with an Art Nouveau style that reflected and adapted international trends, while having very little to do with shaping and developing it.

The new designs coming out of France and Britain had been enthusiastically received in Copenhagen in 1899, with an exhibition of the work of Charles Robert Ashbee, and again in 1900, when the newly established Danish Museum of Decorative Art displayed the recently acquired work of René Lalique among other Art Nouveau jewellery designers.

The innovative Danish style pioneered by a relatively small collection of architects, artists, and craftsmen was known as skonvirke or "aesthetic work". The most famous of Danish jewellers, Georg Jensen

trained as a sculptor and goldsmith before moving to the workshop of the talented *skonvirke* artist and metalworker Mogens Ballin.

Jensen established his own workshop in 1904, and he created a small range of silver jewellery that was exhibited in the Danish Museum of Decorative Art. Although intended for an artistically enlightened middle class, Jensen's jewellery received widespread international acclaim.

While Jensen designed many pieces himself, he also employed skilled draughtsmen and artists to work in a similar style, whose contributions were always recognized by the firm.

Above: Silver brooch incorporating an openwork relief design of a bird enclosed within a stylized foliate framework, with three green-stained chalcedony cabochons. Design number 187. *c.1915* *4cm (1½in) wide* **£450–550 SF**

SCULPTURAL SILVERWORK

Silver – typically worked in high relief, with a surface patterning of hammer marks – was the favoured material for Danish jewellery, which had a distinctive look characterized by fluid, organic, abstract forms. Enamels were rarely used, with semi-precious stones – lapis lazuli, amethyst, amber, and agate, for example – preferred to add colour. Influenced by the aesthetic of the Arts and Crafts movement, Jensen's sculptural jewellery designs looked to nature for inspiration, with flowers, animals, and fruit rendered in a literal and stylized manner that highlighted and showed to best advantage the qualities of the materials. His plump, curvy, silver jewellery occasionally incorporated coral or semi-precious stones such as moonstone, opal, and amber.

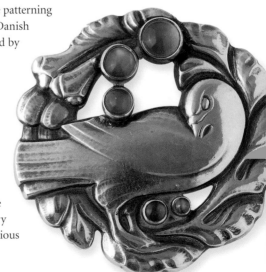

Silver oval openwork pendant designed by Georg Jensen. The pendant is formed by the foliage of two flowers, each centred with an oval, green-stained chalcedony cabochon. Design number 15. *c.1910.* *5.5cm (2in) long* **£2,500–3,000 SF**

Silver brooch featuring a dove enclosed within a circular foliate framework and punctuated with five moonstone cabochons graduating in size. Design number 123. *c.1915.* *4.5cm (1¾in) long* **£150–250 SF**

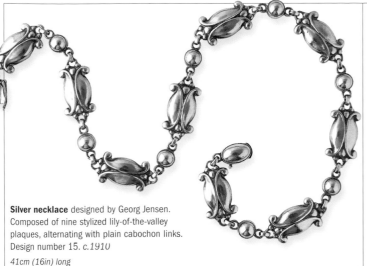

Silver necklace designed by Georg Jensen. Composed of nine stylized lily-of-the-valley plaques, alternating with plain cabochon links. Design number 15. *c.1910*

41cm (16in) long

£800–1,200   SF

Silver brooch designed by Georg Jensen. A circular wreath formation featuring highly stylized overlapping foliage. The two florets have amber cabochon centres. Design number 42. *c.1910*

5cm (2in) wide

£300–400   SF

Silver, circular, openwork brooch depicting a crested water bird – possibly a lapwing – foraging amid stylized marsh grasses. Design number 297. *c.1910*

4cm (1½in) long

£350–450   SF

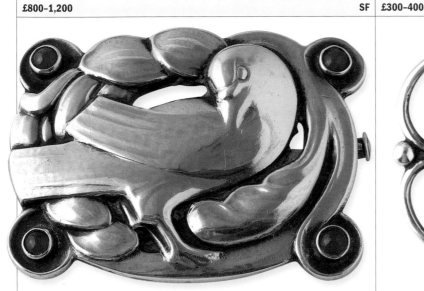

Silver rounded rectangular brooch depicting, in relief, a dove enclosed within stylized foliage. The four corners are set with garnet cabochons. Design number 204. *c.1910*

4cm (1½in) long

£600–700   SF

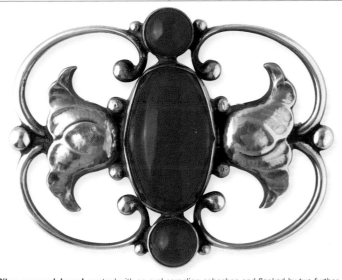

Silver openwork brooch centred with an oval carnelian cabochon and flanked by two further carnelians. The whole is held within a looped foliate mount. Design number 236 B. *c.1910*

4cm (1½in) long

£600–700   SF

DANISH DESIGNS

Although Scandinavian jewellery remained largely unaffected by the "New Art", a few pioneering designers in Denmark worked in an innovative, modern style known as *skonvirke*. One of the most talented of these, Mogens Ballin, created jewellery – combs, buckles, and clasps in silver or bronze – featuring simple, rounded shapes and abstract patterns. At the turn of the 20th century, Ballin began working with Georg Jensen, whose designs typically combined natural motifs with cabochons of amber, moonstones, coral, or other inexpensive coloured gems to create silver jewels with an almost lyrical purity. Other Danish jewellers who worked in the Art Nouveau idiom were Harald Slott-Moller, whose work was frequently produced by the Danish Court Jeweller Michelsen, Bernard Hertz, Kay Bojesen, and Ferdinand Svinth.

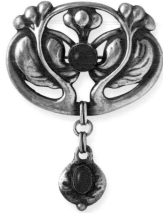

Skonvirke silver openwork brooch by Bernard Hertz. Created in a stylized foliate form and centred with a cornelian cabochon. The foliate drop has a further cornelian.

7.5cm (3in) long

£400–600   VDB

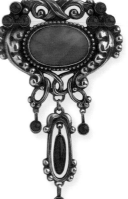

Skonvirke silver brooch by Kay Bojesen. The elaborate foliate framework is set with garnet cabochons and has an amber-plaque centre. With several carnelian-set drops below. *1910*

10cm (4in) long

£1,500–2,500   VDB

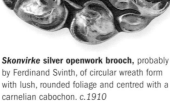

Skonvirke silver openwork brooch, probably by Ferdinand Svinth, of circular wreath form with lush, rounded foliage and centred with a carnelian cabochon. *c.1910*

5cm (2in) wide

£300–400   VDB

KEY FEATURES

The maiden with long, flowing hair is the most popular motif used by Kerr & Co.

The European influence is obvious in the motifs used in their Art Nouveau designs.

Pieces were stamped out of sheet metal instead of being cast.

Highly collectable, the once cheap pieces can now fetch high prices.

Kerr & Co.

The firm of William B. Kerr took a democratic approach to silver and gold manufacture by producing less expensive jewellery and other small decorative items for the lower-income consumers.

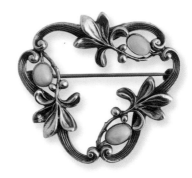

Established in New York City in 1891, William Kerr changed partners and moved his business to Newark, New Jersey, in 1903. Until about 1910, the firm concentrated on Art Nouveau designs, which it mostly borrowed from European catalogues. Kerr & Co. became known for its depictions of maidens with flowing hair, little angels, and stylized plant forms, which appeared in ladies' and men's jewellery and the customary assortment of necessities of the day: buttons; buckles for belts, shoes, and braces; girdles; châtelaines; card and vanity cases; purses; powder boxes; hatpins; and even sidesaddle spurs.

One of the cost-saving production methods used by Kerr & Co. was the stamping of embossed designs out of silver or gold sheets, to create the appearance of heavier and more important pieces of jewellery.

Kerr was purchased by Gorham in 1906, but continued operating in Newark under the same name, participating in the 1916 Newark Industrial Exposition. The company moved to Providence, Rhode Island, in 1927, and continued producing a variety of small items, but no longer any jewellery.

Above: Heart-shaped brooch with a framework of C-scrolls and floral motifs in gold-washed sterling silver with three oval, faux moonstone cabochons. *c.1903. 6.25cm (2½in) wide* **£250–300 CGPC**

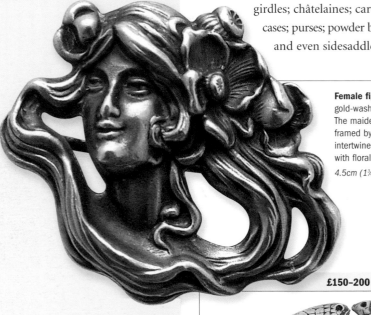

Female figural brooch in gold-washed sterling silver. The maiden's face is framed by sinuous, intertwined, flowing locks with floral motifs. *c.1900 4.5cm (1¾in) wide*

£150–200   PC

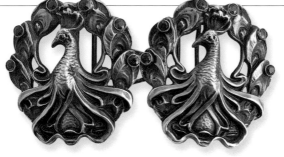

Gold-washed silver belt buckle comprising a pair of stylized peacocks set in flowers and foliage with bud-like, glass cabochon highlights. *c.1903 9cm (3½in) wide*

£300–370   CGPC

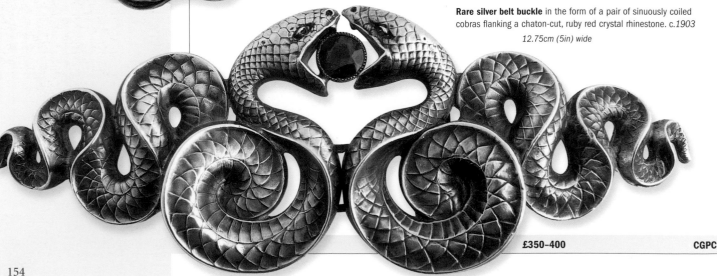

Rare silver belt buckle in the form of a pair of sinuously coiled cobras flanking a chaton-cut, ruby red crystal rhinestone. *c.1903 12.75cm (5in) wide*

£350–400   CGPC

Unger Bros.

The Unger Brothers were an important Newark jewellery manufacturer that rivalled the William B. Kerr company in making decorative and mass-produced stamped sterling silver Art Nouveau jewellery and small items.

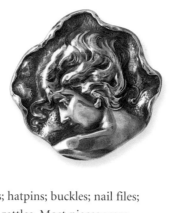

Started in 1878 as H. Unger & Co. by Herman, Eugene, and Frederick Unger, the jewellery firm became Unger Bros. in 1879. It was led by designer Philemon Dickinson, and the company took out several design patents in 1903. Like silvermakers Kerr, Unger Bros. specialized in jewellery depicting "Floradora" and "Gibson Girl" maidens with long, flowing hair and made into brooches, link bracelets, pendants, earrings, and necklaces.

Other popular designs included Rococo flowers and leaves, colonial revival, faux-ancient coins, and simple Arts and Crafts patterns featured on everyday items of the Victorian era: girdles; vest chains and châtelaines with sewing equipment;

glove buttoners; hatpins; buckles; nail files; and even baby rattles. Most pieces were made in sterling silver, sometimes in gold, with enamelling or semi-precious stones.

Unger Bros. continued in Art Nouveau design until 1910. The original dies have since been used to reproduce their jewellery, but, unlike the original pieces with their silver backs, most have soldered pins directly affixed to the backs.

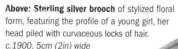

Above: Sterling silver brooch of stylized floral form, featuring the profile of a young girl, her head piled with curvaceous locks of hair. *c.1900. 5cm (2in) wide*
£350–550 VDB

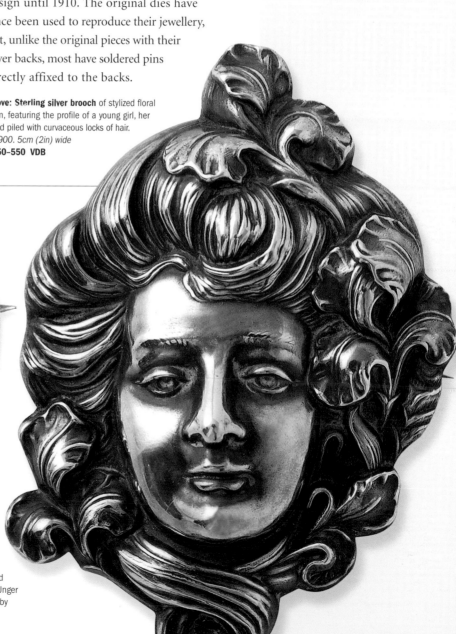

Medallion-like brooch with the head and shoulders of a young girl with whiplash hair, in sterling silver with matte finish gold plating. *1904–05*
4.5cm (1¾in) wide
£400–500   **CGPC**

Sterling silver brooch in the form of a young female's head with upswept and flowing hair interwoven with curvaceous flower and leaf motifs. Like much of Unger Bros.'s sterling silver Art Nouveau jewellery, this piece was probably designed by Emma L. Dickinson. *c.1900*
7.5cm (3in) high
£400–600   **VDB**

American Jewellery

The United States emulated European jewellery fashions throughout the 19th century. By the 1880s, Japanese taste was also influencing jewellery made of silver, gold, or a combination of metals, using techniques such as damascening and inlay. Tiffany and Co. produced exquisite jewels made in the Japanese style, using coloured gold to imitate mixed metalwork techniques. By the end of the 19th century, American jewellery was embracing the fashionable French Art Nouveau style, with two main centres of mass production – Newark, New Jersey, and Providence, Rhode Island – creating pieces for the new fashion-conscious middle classes.

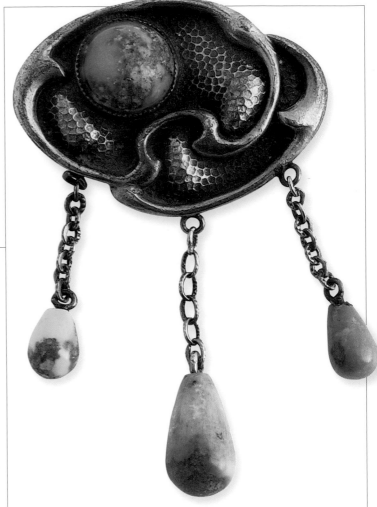

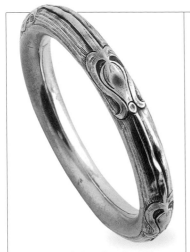

La Pierre bangle in sterling silver with a stylized, sinuously curvaceous flower-head and elongated stem motifs moulded and chased in relief around its perimeter. c.1902

7.5cm (3in) wide

£120–150   **CGPC**

Sterling silver bangle by Blackinton. Bands of scrolling leaf and floral motifs are chased in relief around its perimeter, with amethyst-coloured glass cabochons. *1895–1900*

7.5cm (3in) wide

£250–300   **CGPC**

Brooch of stylized organic shape in hammered gilt metal with a mottled turquoise and gilt ceramic cabochon, and three turquoise drops suspended from gilt metal chains. *c.1910*

3cm (1¼in) wide

£100–120   **CGPC**

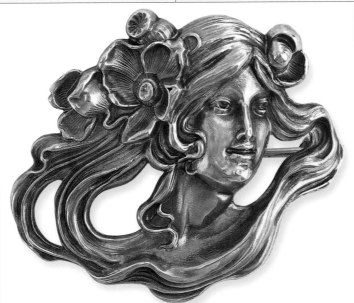

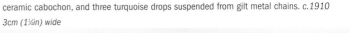

Sterling silver brooch by Averbeck & Averbeck. In the form of a woman's head with flowing hair, known as "Floradora" after the 19th-century musical comedy. *1902*

6.5cm (2½in) wide

£200–350   **RG**

Sterling silver belt buckle by the Pryor Novelty Company. Moulded in relief in the form of a bust of a young woman with long, sinuously flowing hair dressed with flower-heads. *1903*

6.25cm (2½in) wide

£300–350   **CGPC**

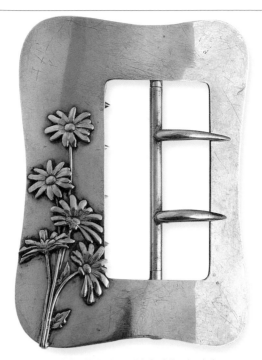

Sterling silver belt buckle by Howard & Co. It has two belt prongs and is of concaved rectangular outline with a naturalistic sprig of flowers to one side, moulded in relief. *1885–1900*

8.25cm (3¼in) high

£120–140   CGPC

Open cuff bangle by George W. Shiebler & Co. of New York. Of sterling silver with highly naturalistic floral and foliate decoration applied in deep relief around the perimeter. *1900–05*

6.25cm (2½in) internal width

£1,300–1,500   CGPC

Sterling silver brooch by Gorham & Co. In the form of two heavily scaled fish, with a goldwash finish and green enamel highlights. Their open mouths surround a central, amethyst coloured glass cabochon. *1900–05*

5.75cm (2¼in) wide

£550–650   CGPC

Louis Comfort Tiffany

With the death of his father in 1902, Louis Comfort Tiffany became design director of Tiffany & Co. and, in 1904, began designing jewellery. He created the most stunning examples of American Art Nouveau jewellery and his life-long passion for colour permeated all his designs. Even with the company's huge wealth of gemstones at his disposal, Tiffany rarely used diamonds, and when he did he chose them for their colour, favouring a rich yellow. His naturalistic designs often combined less-precious stones set in fine wirework or golden mounts and were highlighted with shaded, coloured enamelling.

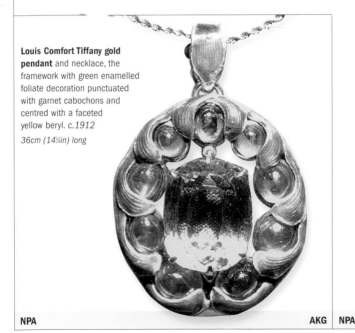

Louis Comfort Tiffany gold pendant and necklace, the framework with green enamelled foliate decoration punctuated with garnet cabochons and centred with a faceted yellow beryl. *c.1912*

36cm (14¼in) long

NPA   AKG

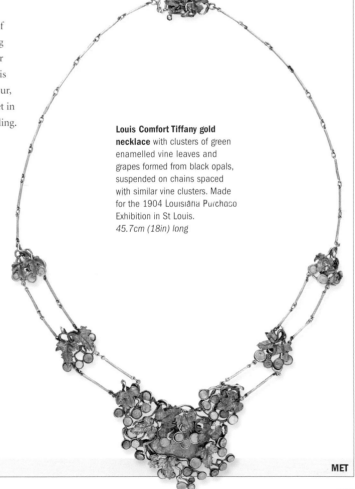

Louis Comfort Tiffany gold necklace with clusters of green enamelled vine leaves and grapes formed from black opals, suspended on chains spaced with similar vine clusters. Made for the 1904 Louisiana Purchase Exhibition in St Louis.

45.7cm (18in) long

NPA   MET

Lavish handmade pieces in gold, with the more common mass-produced silver cleverly disguised by incorporating mock hammer marks into the stamping dies.

Curving, silver openwork in stylized floral motifs, is often decorated with enamels.

Turquoise, opals, moonstones, and blister pearls, which usually had to be set by hand, are often set behind a hole in the silver rather than within a separate collet.

Liberty & Co.

Since it was founded in 1875, Liberty & Co. has remained at the forefront of advanced taste and innovative design – and its Art Nouveau jewellery designs are no exception.

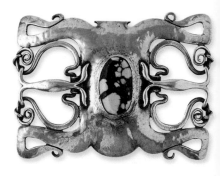

By 1900, the graceful designs of Art Nouveau had become influential throughout Europe. In Britain, the London department store Liberty & Co. on Regent Street was the most important firm working in this innovative new style. Liberty employed leading British Arts and Crafts designers – including Archibald Knox (1864–1933), Jessie M. King (1876–1949), and Oliver Baker (1856–1939) – to create jewellery, silver, and pewter for industrial production.

Although the company insisted that its designers remain anonymous and that no pieces bear signatures, the styles of Knox and King remain particularly distinctive. The subtle and elegant Celtic interlacing, flowing lines, whiplash motifs, and complex knots in silver, decorated with turquoise, mother-of-pearl, and blue and green enamels characterize the highly popular Cymric range of

jewellery created by Archibald Knox, whose ability to adapt his complex patterns to machine production demonstrated impressive technical skill. Jessie M. King – whose training at the Glasgow School of Art saw him influenced by the celebrated architect and designer Charles Rennie Mackintosh – is best known for a range of belt buckles rendered in hammered silver in curled and interlacing designs, which frequently boast settings of cabochon hardstones.

Liberty's greatest achievement lay in its ability to bring art jewels to the general public by uniting artistic innovations with commercial considerations. The firm helped shape British and continental tastes for Art Nouveau by producing decorative ornaments that were aesthetic, well made, widely appealing, and affordable.

Above: Rectangular silver openwork buckle to a design attributed to Oliver Baker. Centred with a plaque of turquoise matrix, flanked by pierced-and-wire scroll work. Birmingham. *1900. 7cm (2¾in) wide* **£850–1,200 VDB**

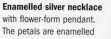

ENAMELLING

The ancient technique of enamelling has enabled craftsmen throughout the centuries to add colour to silver vessels and jewellery. The coloured area of enamel on a piece of jewellery is a fine layer of coloured glass, fused to the surface of the metal by heating a powder compound containing coloured oxides at high temperatures. Enamelling beautifully enhances many Liberty jewels, as well as those of its contemporaries. Various colours exist but we see predominantly blues and greens, sometimes with mother-of-pearl or cabochons of similar colour adding extra verve to a piece. Some pieces incorporate detailed miniature landscape plaques, or else they have simple spots of enamelled colour decorating flower and leaf motifs.

Enamelled silver necklace with flower-form pendant. The petals are enamelled in blue, green, and white, with mother-of-pearl studs, and suspended on chains with enamelled spacers. *c.1905 Pendant: 4cm (1½in) wide* **£800–900 RG**

***Plique-à-jour** and gilt-metal necklace* composed of ten pale blue translucent enamelled floret plaques, alternating with pairs of apple green translucent enamelled plaques. *1900–05 38cm (14¾in) long* **£3,000–3,500 NBlm**

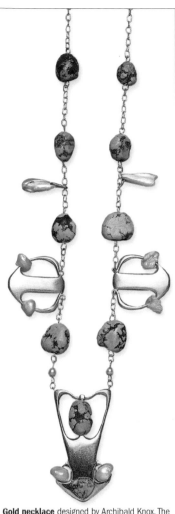

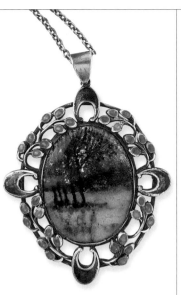

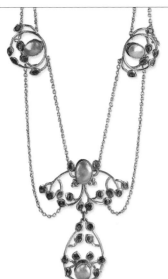

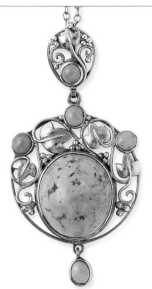

Enamelled silver oval pendant centred with a winter landscape plaque by Charles Fleetwood Varley, within an enamelled foliate mount designed by Jessie M. King. *c.1910*

46cm (18in) long

£1,000–2,000   **VDB**

Gold enamelled moonstone necklace designed by Jessie M. King, with openwork panels and a pendant of enamelled leaves and moonstone cabochons. *c.1900*

Pendant: 5cm (2in) long

£4,000–6,000   **VDB**

Gold and turquoise pendant of circular form, centred with a turquoise cabochon flanked by lush leaves and tiny berries. It has a smaller, similar plaque above. *c.1900*

Pendant: 6cm (2¼in) long

£1,300–1,500   **VDB**

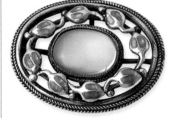

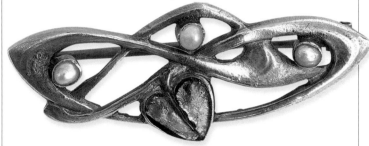

Gold necklace designed by Archibald Knox. The pendant is set with turquoise matrix and two freshwater pearls. The chain has two pearl-set plaques and turquoise matrix pebbles. *c.1900*

49cm (19¼in) long

£3,000–5,000   **VDB**

Silver, gold, and enamel oval brooch centred with a moonstone cabochon, encircled by Jessie M. King-style enamelled leaves. The outer edge has rope-work banding. *c.1900*

2.5cm (1in) long

£300–400   **VDB**

Gold and enamelled brooch designed by Archibald Knox. Set with three tiny half-pearls and a green enamelled heart-shaped leaf. With maker's mark "W.H. Haseler". *1905*

3.5cm (1⅛in) long

£650–750   **RG**

Charles Horner

In Halifax, Yorkshire, the family firm of Charles Horner paved the way for machine-made jewellery in the Art Nouveau style. From design to finished product, every stage of manufacture was carried out within the factory – the only company in Britain to do this at the time. Despite using industrial methods, Horner jewellery was well designed and of high quality, with typical patterns featuring silver twist, knot, or geometric triangle motifs. Many of the styles produced by Liberty were adapted and simplified by Horner, and decorated with peacock blue or a blend of yellow and green enamels. A favourite motif for hatpins, pendants, and brooches was a winged scarab enamelled in blue and green with purple highlights.

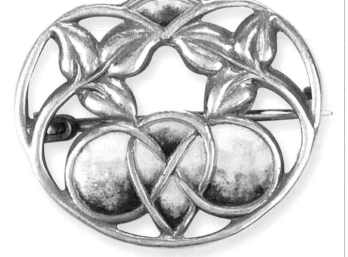

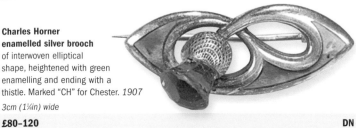

Charles Horner enamelled silver brooch of interwoven elliptical shape, heightened with green enamelling and ending with a thistle. Marked "CH" for Chester. *1907*

3cm (1¼in) wide

£80–120   **DN**

Charles Horner enamelled silver brooch composed of interwoven foliate stems heightened with blue-green enamelling. Marked "Sterling Silver" and with Charles Horner marks.

4.5cm (1¾in) wide

£80–120   **DN**

KEY FEATURES

Forms were either sinuous in outline and edged with tendrils, or geometric and rectilinear in shape.

Coloured enamels or cabochons, usually turquoises or opals, are used to punctuate many pieces.

Finely hammer-textured surfaces are often adorned with small bumps simulating rivets.

Murrle Bennett

With an eye for innovative designs that were both artistic and commercial, the London-based firm of Murrle, Bennett & Company was an important retailer of fine Art Nouveau jewellery in England.

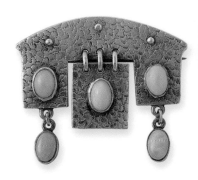

Murrle, Bennett & Co. was founded in 1884 by the German Ernst Murrle and an Englishman, about whom little is known, called Mr Bennett. The company specialized in inexpensive gold and silver pieces in a variety of styles, including the bold, geometric style characteristic of German Jugendstil and the Cymric range of silver sold by Liberty & Co.

Typical jewellery designs sold by Murrle, Bennett & Co. during the Art Nouveau period include pendants and necklaces in gold with a rich matte sheen, often inset with turquoises, amethysts, and mother-of-pearl. Gold or silver wires were frequently entwined around a pearl or a turquoise, sometimes forming a cage-like structure reminiscent of designs by the Austrian Wiener Werkstätte.

Much of the jewellery was linear but fluid in outline, often with Celtic-style interlacing. Some pendants and brooches, however, were rectilinear and geometric in shape, closely following the new German designs of the time (*see box on Theodor Fahrner, opposite*). Long necklaces decorated with stylized leaves and luminous blue-green enamels were especially popular. Distinctive continental silver designs boasted a finely hammered finish embellished by tiny pinhead bumps resembling rivets, a feature that was particularly characteristic of Murrle, Bennett & Co. jewellery.

Above: Geometric textured silver brooch set with three polished silver studs and five opal cabochons. *c.1900 3.5cm (1½in) wide* **£300–400 VDB**

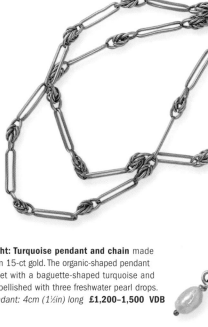

Right: Turquoise pendant and chain made from 15-ct gold. The organic-shaped pendant is set with a baguette-shaped turquoise and embellished with three freshwater pearl drops. *Pendant: 4cm (1½in) long* **£1,200–1,500 VDB**

Left: Celtic-style cast silver pendant with a raised centre lozenge of mottled and graduated blue and green enamel, and indented slivers of turquoise enamel. *4.5cm (1¾in) long* **£300–350 LynH**

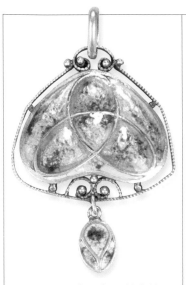

Silver and enamel pendant with Celtic-inspired motifs highlighted in yellow, orange, and green enamel, and an enamelled drop suspended from beaded wirework.

4.5cm (1¾in) long

£250–350　　　　　　　　　**DN**

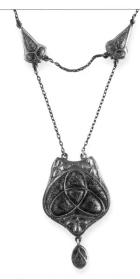

Cast silver pendant necklace of stylized floral form, with Celtic-style motifs in the centre highlighted with iridescent, mottled blue enamel.

Pendant: 4.5cm (1¾in) long

£650–750　　　　　　　　　**RG**

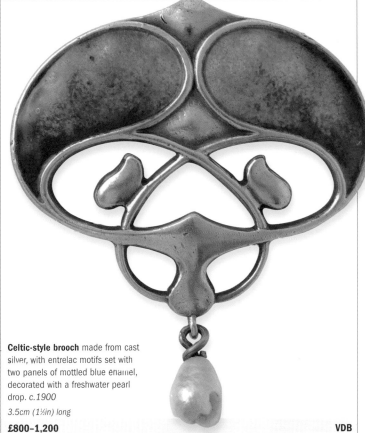

Celtic-style brooch made from cast silver, with entrelac motifs set with two panels of mottled blue enamel, decorated with a freshwater pearl drop. *c.1900*

3.5cm (1½in) long

£800–1,200　　　　　　　　**VDB**

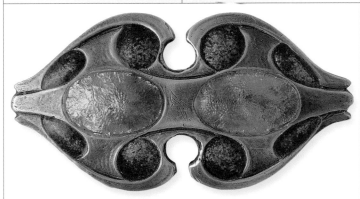

Twin-heart cast silver brooch set with panels of mottled blue and textured and mottled gold enamel. Designed in Germany and supplied to Liberty & Co. *c.1900*

4.5cm (1¾in) wide

£650–950　　　　　　　　　**VDB**

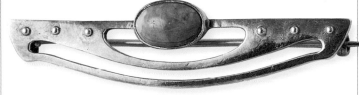

Gold-washed sterling silver brooch decorated with an oval cabochon of mottled yellow and green semi-precious stone flanked by six small studs.

4.5cm (1¾in) wide

£250–300　　　　　　　　　**LynH**

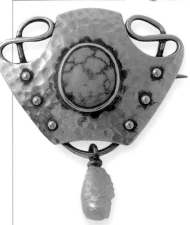

Shield-shaped brooch made from hammered silver with three studs set on each side of an an oval turquoise cabochon, and decorated with a freshwater pearl drop.

3cm (1¼in) wide

£500–800　　　　　　　　　**VDB**

Theodor Fahrner

Much of the jewellery sold by Murrle, Bennett & Co. was produced at a factory in Pforzheim, Germany, by Theodor Fahrner (1868–1928). Fahrner was a successful manufacturer of inexpensive but fashionable jewellery made from silver or low-carat gold set with semi-precious stones. Largely due to his connections with avant-garde designers at the artists' colony at nearby Darmstadt, Fahrner produced the abstract, modernistic jewellery that was popular in Germany and Austria at the time. This style, known as Jugendstil, made its way to Britain via Murrle, Bennett & Co., where it was integrated into British Art Nouveau jewellery design.

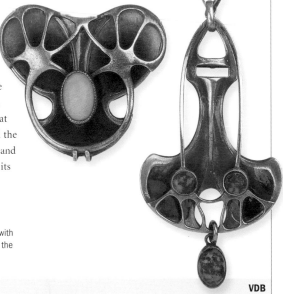

Theodor Fahrner brooch and pendant necklace of cast silver inset with panels of blue-green enamel. The brooch has an opal cabochon and the pendant has two turquoise matrix cabochons and a drop. *c.1900*

Brooch: 4cm (1½in) wide; Pendant: 5cm (2in) long

£1,500–2,000 each　　　　　　　　**VDB**

British, German, and Austrian Jewellery

British Art Nouveau jewellery was heavily influenced by the Arts and Crafts Movement, which used simple floral and figural patterns for decoration, along with interlacing motifs inspired by ancient Celtic art. British craftsmen chose affordable, semi-precious materials for their jewellery. Richly coloured cabochon stones, mother-of-pearl, and turquoise were combined with metal that was finely hammered to create a soft, matte appearance.

In workshops in Germany and Austria, designers and craftsmen worked together to create handcrafted, one-off pieces, as well as jewellery for mass production. They favoured symmetrical openwork designs of stylized leaf and geometric motifs set within finely wrought metal borders.

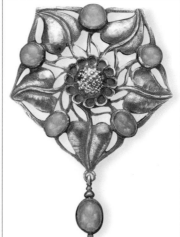

Guild of Handicraft brooch by C.R. Ashbee. A central flower-head is surrounded by stems and leaves in silver, five opal cabochons, and an opal cabochon drop. *c.1900*

5cm (2in) long

£4,000–6,000　　　　　　　　**VDB**

Harold Stabler brooch in the form of an oval wreath with enamelled green leaves and blue ribbon. It is punctuated with pearl and garnet berries on gold stems. With original case.

5cm (2in) long

£1,200–1,500　　　　　　　　**DN**

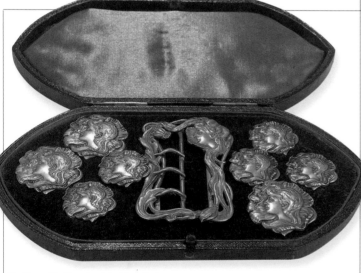

Buckle and buttons in original box. Each piece is cast in silver with the head of a maiden with flowing hair set on a poppy flower-head. Marked JMS (Chester). *c.1902*

Large buttons: 3cm (1¼in) wide.

£200–300　　　　　　　　**L&T**

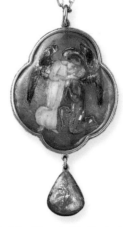

Quatrefoil gold pendant by Phoebe A. Traquair. It depicts an angel and kneeling figure in coloured enamels on a blue-green ground, above a blue enamelled drop. *c.1906*

4cm (1½in) long

£7,000–10,000　　　　　　　　**VDB**

Silver and enamel pendant by Omar Ramsden. It comprises a tasselled wreath of silver leaves and flower-heads around a ruby red enamelled centre.

4cm (1½in) long

£1,500–2,500　　　　　　　　**VDB**

BUCKLES

17th-century English gentlemen took to wearing buckles instead of shoelaces, and by the 18th century buckles made of silver, gold, Sheffield plate, or cut steel were commonly used to fasten shoes and knee breeches, as well as to hold neckbands and sashes in place. In the late 19th and early 20th centuries, buckles in a wide variety of shapes and sizes incorporated elaborate Art Nouveau decorative features, such as trailing scrolls, stylized flowers, birds, and leaves, and intricate, sinuous forms. They were often embellished with colourful enamelling. Many buckles of this period were threaded onto a fabric strap, and used to fasten the belts of ladies' dresses.

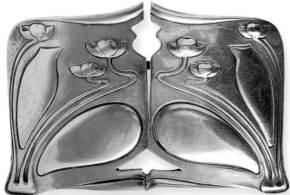

Two-piece silver belt buckle by W. Hutton & Sons. Each side has plain, teardrop lobes and stylized lilies with elongated and whiplash stems. It has a maker's mark for London. *c.1902*

8.5cm (3½in) wide

£170–220　　　　　　　　**DN**

Two-piece belt buckle by H. Matthews. Each side is cast in silver with an openwork design of two swallows in flight amid scrolling flowers and foliage. *c.1900*

7.5cm (3in) wide

£120–180　　　　　　　　**DN**

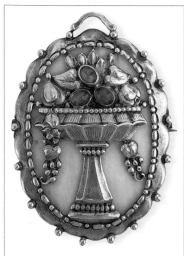

German Secessionist brooch cast in silver with a jardinière of fruits, flowers, and leaves, against an ivory ground and with three sapphire highlights. Unsigned. *c.1910*

5cm (2in) long

£350–400   **RG**

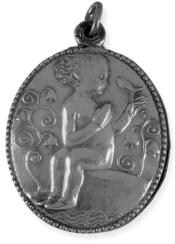

Oval silver medallion by Bertold Löffler for the Wiener Werkstätte. Embossed with a seated putto holding a small bird and flanked by stylized, scrolling bell-flower tendrils. *1904*

5cm (2in) long

£1,000–1,200   **DOR**

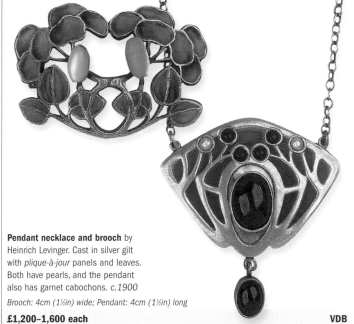

Pendant necklace and brooch by Heinrich Levinger. Cast in silver gilt with *plique-à-jour* panels and leaves. Both have pearls, and the pendant also has garnet cabochons. *c.1900*

Brooch: 4cm (1½in) wide; Pendant: 4cm (1½in) long

£1,200–1,600 each   **VDB**

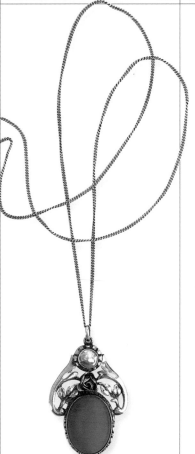

German pendant necklace cast with silver scrolling leaves and flowers. It has a mother-of-pearl cabochon, an oval chrysoprase, and a mother-of-pearl drop. *c.1905*

Pendant: 6cm (2¼in) long

£180–220   **RG**

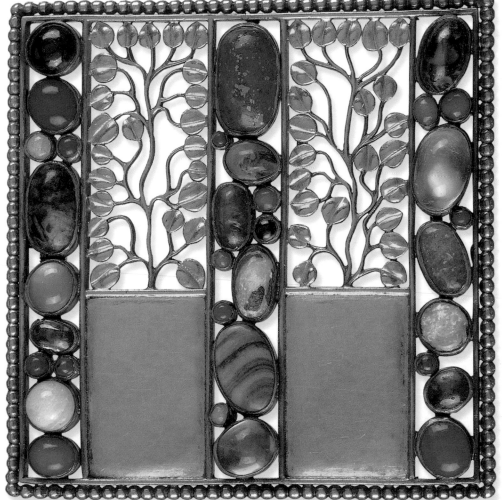

Rare Wiener Werkstätte brooch designed by Josef Hoffmann. The silver frame is of square form with a beaded perimeter, enclosing two vertical panels with stylized and gilded potted plants, and three panels of diverse, round, and oval semi-precious stone cabochons. *1910*

5cm (2in) wide

£35,000–50,000   **DOR**

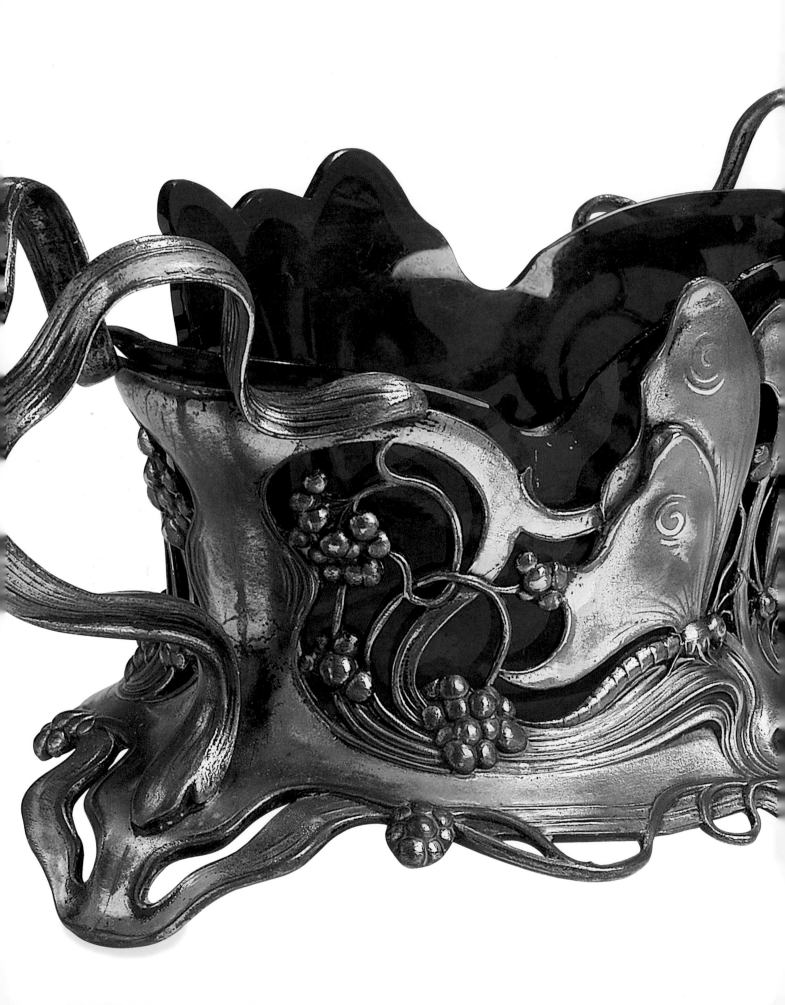

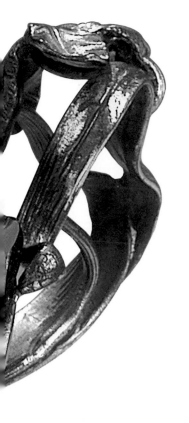

Silver and Metalware

By the 1890s, many silversmiths and metalworkers across Europe, Britain, and the United States longed for change. Rejecting mass production and the stranglehold of historicism that informed 19th-century design, and inspired by the recent influx of Japanese art, they branched out to create innovative new pieces in their interpretation of the Art Nouveau style.

Traditionally conservative, the 19th-century silver and metalware industry relied on catering for the needs of a wealthy upper class and tended to mass-produce versions of historical styles.

In the last decade of the century, however, silverware designers throughout Europe and the United States turned to the organic forms found in nature for inspiration. They interpreted nature in different ways, depending on their nationality, and did not attempt to imitate it slavishly, but used it as a basis for patterns featuring plants and animals. Many of them also sought inspiration in the art of ancient and exotic cultures – Celtic, Japanese, Byzantine, Gothic, and Indonesian among them – searching for decorative motifs they could adapt.

RETURN TO TRADITIONAL SKILLS
Innovative craftsmen also challenged the methods of mass production commonly used at the time, such as die-stamping and pressing, believing

them to have lowered aesthetic standards, and strove to revive the role of the artist-craftsman. Many believed that a silversmith could only achieve the status of a true artist when using traditional techniques such as planishing, raising, and chasing, to create works in the new, modern style.

MASS PRODUCTION
There were, however, some designers who opted for compromise. These craftsmen valued the possibilities offered by industrial methods and wanted their wares to reach as wide a market as possible. Encouraged by the popular appeal of Art Nouveau, manufacturers and retailers seized the opportunity to provide their customers with affordable silverware in the new style. Factories commissioned well-known designers and craftsmen to create special lines of domestic and decorative silverware that were mass produced, but hand-finished to a high standard of craftsmanship.

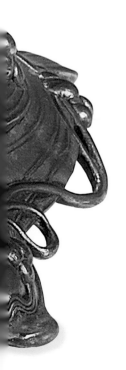

W.M.F. twin-handled jardinière with openwork side panels cast with butterflies flanked by sinuous tendrils and berries. It has a whiplash foliate handle and shaped base. With a blue glass liner and stamped marks. *29.5cm (11½in) wide* **£180–220 L&T**

CURVACEOUS FORMS

In Paris, a small band of designers and craftsmen, many of whom had already forged successful careers as jewellery designers, such as René Lalique, Eugène Feuillatre, and Lucien Gaillard, abandoned the traditional styles of silver and metalwork popular during the 19th century and started to create small *objets d'art* in silver, such as boxes, cups, bowls, and scent bottles, all in forms inspired by nature. Exquisitely decorated with semi-precious stones and unusual materials, these pieces met with great acclaim when they were exhibited at the Paris Salons.

Some of the more established silver manufacturers in France, such as Boucheron and Christofle, however, were resistant to change, and continued to produce traditional ranges of silverware. Their only compromise was to introduce small ranges of Art Nouveau alongside their main ranges.

Finely crafted domestic silverware based on abstract, curvilinear shapes, female nudes, and flowers, emerged from the workshops of Belgian designers such as Philippe Wolfers. Trained as a jeweller, Wolfers also excelled at the elaborate

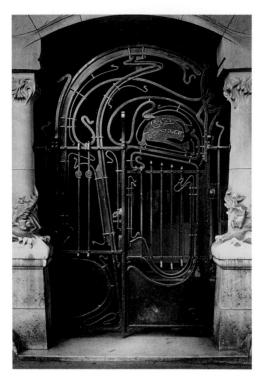

The entrance gates of Castel Beranger in Paris, designed by Hector Guimard as an organic, integral part of the family home, show tremendous virtuosity from both designer and blacksmith.

silver mounts for ceramic and glass vessels that were an important dimension of the silversmith's art. Georg Jensen, a Danish designer working in Copenhagen, created lyrical pieces with simple organic forms, with lids, handles, and finials modelled on fruit and flowers.

SIMPLE STYLE

In Britain, silver and metalware was one of the few crafts to adopt the Art Nouveau style, albeit more influenced by the Arts and Crafts movement than by the work being produced in France and Belgium. The new style was forged mainly by

W.M.F. silver-plated dressing-table mirror with a central figure of a classical maiden with arms raised, and flanked by extended stems that support the circular bevelled glass between them. *c.1905. 50.5cm (20in) high* **£1,500–1,800 TO**

DEFINITIVE STYLES

Although styles of Art Nouveau metalware varied from one country to another, they were merely variations on a theme. All were inspired by nature and represented a break from the traditional styles. The flowing, sinuous contours of W.M.F. metalware echo the themes found in French Art Nouveau, as do pieces by Tiffany & Co. British pieces are influenced by Celtic art, and also have flowing lines and simple decoration. Olbrich's wine jug (see right) demonstrates the more linear approach to Art Nouveau taken by many German and Austrian designers, yet still borrows its motif and form from nature.

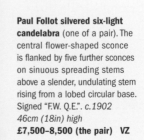

Paul Follot silvered six-light candelabra (one of a pair). The central flower-shaped sconce is flanked by five further sconces on sinuous spreading stems above a slender, undulating stem rising from a lobed circular base. Signed "F.W. Q.E.". *c.1902 46cm (18in) high* **£7,500–8,500 (the pair) VZ**

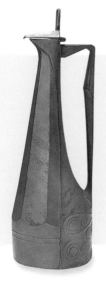

Joseph Maria Olbrich pewter wine jug made by Eduard Hueck. The shape resembles a highly stylized peacock. It has tapering facetted sides, a hinged cover, and an angular handle, and is decorated around the lower base with stylized peacock-feather motifs in relief. It has dark patination and is signed. *c.1901. 34cm (13½in) high* **£1,800–2,200 VZ**

Liberty & Co, whose elegant ranges of Cymric silver and Tudric pewter domestic ware were a great commercial success, especially the Celtic-inspired organic designs of Archibald Knox. Many gifted designers in Britain produced silverware in new, simpler, organic forms, including Omar Ramsden & Alwyn Carr, Charles Robert Ashbee, Gilbert Marks, and his contemporary Movio. The latter two produced similar high-quality work in heavy gauge silver richly embossed and chased with nature-inspired motifs.

LINEAR APPROACH

Art Nouveau adopted many different forms in Germany, as individual regions tended to develop their own styles. At the Darmstadt artists' colony, founded in 1899, designers such as Joseph Maria Olbrich produced work that was linear in style, with abstract decoration. Some German manufacturers rejected the ideal of hand-craftsmanship and aimed to produce high-quality metalware at affordable prices. W.M.F. (Württembergische Metallwaren Fabrik) mass produced Art Nouveau pieces in the fluid French style, but made them of electroplated brass or pewter rather than silver. In Austria, designers from the Vienna School of Arts and Crafts and the Wiener Werkstätte created finely crafted, linear, geometric forms with restrained decoration.

HAMMERED SURFACES

In the United States, Art Nouveau played a relatively minor role among silver and metalware manufacturers, with large factories and retailers continuing to produce traditional silver for a wealthy clientele. However, Tiffany & Co.

developed gourd-shaped pieces with finely hammered surfaces, and applied decoration in the Art Nouveau style. Unger Brothers also made silverware influenced by French Art Nouveau pieces. Other companies in the United States, such as Roycroft and Heintz, took influence from the American Arts and Crafts style, and created new, simple designs. The Gorham Corporation, in particular, created handmade pieces in the new style under the trade name of "Martelé", meaning "hand-hammered".

Rare Liberty Tudric pewter vase, designed by David Veazey, of compressed globular form with a slender neck flaring at the top. The plain polished surface is applied with sinuous handles embellished with interwoven knots and stylized seed pods. Displays the maker's marks. *34cm (13½in) high*
£1,000–1,500 WW

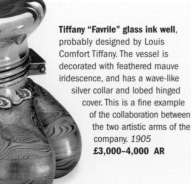

Tiffany "Favrile" glass ink well, probably designed by Louis Comfort Tiffany. The vessel is decorated with feathered mauve iridescence, and has a wave-like silver collar and lobed hinged cover. This is a fine example of the collaboration between the two artistic arms of the company. *1905*
£3,000–4,000 AR

JAPANESE INFLUENCE

Decorative motifs and metalworking techniques varied widely during the Art Nouveau period. Some interpretations borrowed heavily from nature, while others sought inspiration in the art of other cultures and eras. Japanese art was particularly influential. Simple and often architectural in form, Japanese vases, bowls, and other objects displayed unusual combinations of materials and used motifs drawn from nature. French silversmiths took their cue from these and adopted a wide range of materials to enhance their creations. Glowing enamels, mother-of-pearl, lacquer, and horn were combined with semi-precious stones to create innovative new effects. The naturalistic flowers, plants, fruit, birds, and insects seen in Japanese art became a favoured decorative theme for silverware produced in France, as well as in the workshops of Philippe Wolfers in Belgium and Georg Jensen in Denmark. Inspired by Japanese examples, designers like Lucien Gaillard also experimented with ways of patinating metal.

JEWEL-LIKE ENAMELS

The ancient art of enamelling was revived by many Art Nouveau designers, and silversmiths experimented with both old and new techniques. French designers, such as Feuillatre, made objects in which parts of the silver had been scooped out and filled with enamel to create delicate motifs, such as dragonflies and peacock feathers. *Plique-à-jour* enamelling was also popular, and some craftsmen set small flecks of silver and gold into enamelwork.

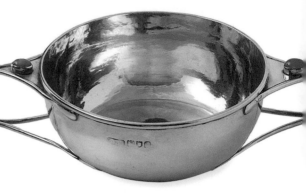

Charles Robert Ashbee silver bowl for The Guild of Handicraft, with twin wirework loop handles that, where they join at the neck rim, are set with green-stained chalcedony cabochons. Marked "G of H Ltd.", London. 1906. 10.5cm (4¼in) wide **£3,000–4,000 VDB**

CELTIC ART

British silversmiths, on the other hand, developed silver designs based on the simple forms and decoration found in ancient Celtic art. Much of the Tudric and Cymric ranges of silver and pewter domestic ware – bowls, muffin dishes, christening sets, and flatware – made by Liberty & Co. were embellished with Celtic-inspired interlacing patterns, stunning blue-green enamels, cabochons, and other sumptuous materials, such as turquoise, agate, mother-of-pearl, and lapis.

Guilds based on medieval models were established and operated as co-operatives where artists and craftsmen of various disciplines could work in

Lucien Gaillard "Scarabees" vase of brown patinated bronze. The base is cast in relief with four scarab beetles, whose bodies are patinated in red, while their exaggerated proboscises extend to form loop handles. Signed "Gaillard". 24cm (9½in) high **£15,000–25,000 MACK**

FORM AND DECORATION

The forms of Art Nouveau silver and metal-ware tend to fall into two groups: those that are rounded with sinuous decoration, and those that are elongated and geometric in form. Inspired by nature, motifs range from plants and winged insects to the typical femmes-fleur. Japanese influences are apparent in many pieces, such as the Gaillard vase (above) and the W.M.F. ewer (opposite). Celtic motifs are most evident in pieces designed for Liberty & Co.

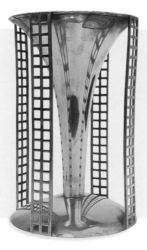

Left: Josef Hoffmann silver vase, made by the Wiener Werkstätte, with a central trumpet-shaped flute, its neck rim linked to the domed base by four vertical straps pierced with squares. c.1905. **NPA AKG**

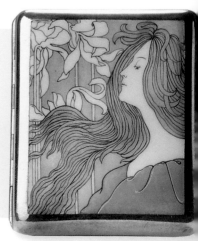

Right: G.A. Scheid enamelled silver cigarette case in the manner of Koloman Moser, depicting in naturalistic colours the head and shoulders of a young woman in profile, her flowing hair flanked by lilies. c.1901. 8cm (3¼in) long **£1,000–1,500 VZ**

tandem. Designer-craftsmen were often the
founder members and teachers. Guilds brought
their designs to fruition, but also taught
traditional skills such as raising, planishing,
repoussé, and chasing to a whole new generation.

SIMPLE GEOMETRY

Many German and Austrian designers created
elegant silverware in spare, streamlined shapes,
with little ornament other than finely
hammered surfaces and semi-precious
cabochons. This adherence to restrained
geometric forms – squares, rectangles,
ovals, and circles – for flatware and decorative
domestic ware was developed mainly by the
Wiener Werkstätte artists in Vienna, and found
its finest expression in the range of pierced silver
latticework vessels designed by Josef Hoffmann.
Based in Munich, designers such as Fritz von
Müller and Ernst Riegel combined traditional
forms and techniques with the influences of
Japanese art and the Arts and Crafts designs
prevalent in Britain.

MELANGE OF STYLES

In the United States, Arts and Crafts silver embraced
a variety of styles – floral, Art Nouveau, Gothic
Revival, and the rectilinear Glasgow style of Charles
Rennie Mackintosh, among others. Small, simple,
elegant metalware – boxes, flatware, and bowls,
for example – tended to be left bare without
ornament or, conversely, were decorated with
designs rendered in enamel or semi-precious
stones. The New Jersey-based Gorham Corporation
produced Japanese-style silverware in the 1870s
and 80s. These pieces incorporated common
oriental motifs including dragons, butterflies,
bamboo, and fans, as well as the birds and fish that
featured widely in the work of other manufacturers.

THE NEW ART

Although much of Art Nouveau silverware on both
sides of the Atlantic took its inspiration from
ancient Japanese art, the talents of European and
American silversmiths and metalworkers created
a distinctive and fresh new style of art.

REPOUSSÉ WORK

Taken from the French verb *repousser*,
"to push back", the result of repoussé
work (also called embossing), is relief
decoration, in which the image is
revealed standing away from its
background surface. The metal is
struck, from the back of the sheet
or from within a vessel, making the
decoration appear swollen and of
varying height. Tools of various sizes
are used, depending on the detail
required. When the basic form has
been achieved, it can then be sharpened
and the detail improved by chasing, or
engraving, the front surface.

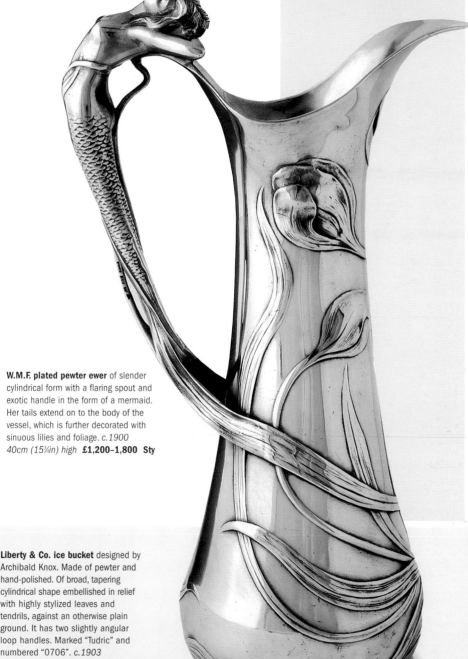

W.M.F. plated pewter ewer of slender
cylindrical form with a flaring spout and
exotic handle in the form of a mermaid.
Her tails extend on to the body of the
vessel, which is further decorated with
sinuous lilies and foliage. *c.1900*
40cm (15¾in) high **£1,200–1,800 Sty**

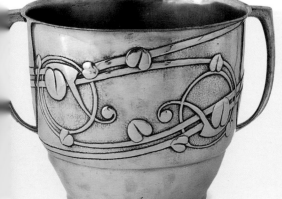

Liberty & Co. ice bucket designed by
Archibald Knox. Made of pewter and
hand-polished. Of broad, tapering
cylindrical shape embellished in relief
with highly stylized leaves and
tendrils, against an otherwise plain
ground. It has two slightly angular
loop handles. Marked "Tudric" and
numbered "0706". *c.1903*
19cm (7½in) high **£2,500–3,500 Sty**

W.M.F.

The German factory W.M.F. mass-produced some of the most elegant and evocative metalware in the Art Nouveau style from the beginning of the 20th century until the start of World War I.

KEY FEATURES

High-quality continental pewter and silver-plated tableware, kitchen utensils, and cutlery were produced. Sometimes the metals were combined with glass.

A maker's mark is impressed on all W.M.F. pieces, although it is often so small it must be read under a magnifying glass.

Exuberantly decorated household wares include punch bowls, wine coolers, fruit stands, cake baskets, candlesticks, mirrors, and clocks.

One of the most successful makers of commercial Art Nouveau metalware was the Wurttemberg Electroplate Company, originally founded in 1853 by Daniel Straub in Geislingen. It was renamed the Württembergische Metallwaren Fabrik – known as W.M.F. – in 1880 following an amalgamation of several firms. The company began with only 16 workers, but by 1914 the enterprise had grown to some 6,000 employees, with factories in Germany, Poland, and Austria, and showrooms in London, Paris, Hamburg, and Berlin.

The region of Wurttemberg, with a long history of manufacturing dating back to the 15th century, was home to a highly successful metalwork industry. A reservoir of skilled craftsmen – modellers, engravers, draughtsmen, chasers, turners, and brass founders –

facilitated the development of W.M.F. into one of the world's leading producers of high-quality tableware, kitchen utensils, and cutlery in silver plate and continental pewter – an electroplated metal alloy – from the late 19th century to the present day.

INTERNATIONAL WARES

W.M.F., which exhibited to great acclaim at the 1900 Universal Exposition in Paris, produced sales catalogues and supplements in three different languages on its own presses to publicize its wide array of metalware throughout Europe. Many of these catalogues boasted attractive cover decorations that were inspired by the fashionable Art Nouveau, or

Pewter syphon stand with undulating, four-pointed rim and a stepped round base. It has partly cut-out stylized flower-heads and stems on the body, and two whiplash foliate handles. *c.1906* *21.5cm (8½in) high* **£250–300 TO**

CURVACEOUS AND GEOMETRIC

One of the great achievements of the W.M.F. factory was its ability to serve the growing middle classes with commercially produced high-quality pieces rendered in a variety of popular styles. Favourite ornamental motifs were taken from the nature-inspired patterns championed by the French and Belgian Art Nouveau designers – the whiplash form, flower sprays, sinuous tendrils, fruits, leaves, and the sensuous, languid female. At the same time, the company catered for the demand for objects fashioned in the more restrained, geometric, and abstract taste promoted by the Austrian Secessionist and Wiener Werkstätte designers. As both strands of the Art Nouveau movement took hold across Europe in the early years of the 20th century, the W.M.F. enterprise shrewdly attended to the fashion for both.

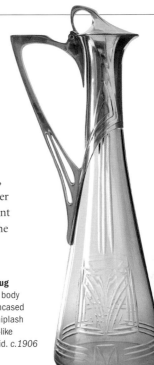

Large claret jug with a glass body encased in pewter. It has a foliate motif neck, a whiplash handle, a *femmes-fleur* base, and a fruit-and-berry motif stopper. *c.1900* *35cm (13¾in) high* **£1,300–1,800 Sty**

Geometrical claret jug with a tapering glass body with ribbing. Partly encased in pewter, it has a whiplash handle and a trumpet-like sleeve with a hinged lid. *c.1906* *43cm (17in) high* **£800–1,000 TO**

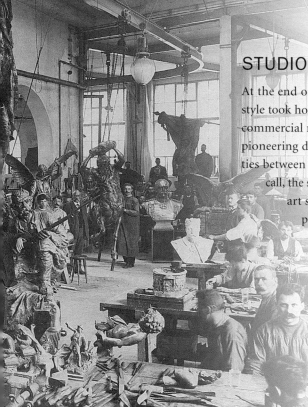

STUDIO DESIGNS

At the end of the 19th century, as the Jugendstil style took hold, the German government encouraged commercial manufacturers to employ progressive, pioneering designers in an effort to strengthen the ties between industry and culture. Answering this call, the sculptor Albert Mayer headed the W.M.F. art studio, where thousands of models and patterns for metalware – drawing on forms and ornaments created by leading artists working in contemporary decorative arts centres such as Darmstadt and Munich – were interpreted by modellers, sculptors, and art-metal craftsmen, and assembled in a broad variety of combinations.

INFLUENCES

Albert Mayer's penchant for incorporating into the design of everyday household objects the typical Art Nouveau female figures with billowing hair (femmes-fleur), succeeded in elevating to artistic status both the commercial and the commonplace.

FEMMES-FLEUR

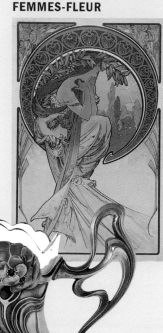

Jugendstil, taste, including the gently erotic designs of Alphonse Mucha and the Celtic interlace Tudric and Cymric metalware patterns of Liberty & Co. (*see pp.182–83*).

ART AND COMMERCE

W.M.F. formed a triple alliance between art, technical expertise, and commerce. Under the direction of Albert Mayer, the company produced a plethora of exuberantly decorated continental pewter and silver-plated household wares. Their pieces were rendered in both the French Art Nouveau style – embellished with female figures in flowing drapery and plant-form imagery – and also in the more geometric patterns of the German Jugendstil (*see box opposite*). Their prodigious output of domestic objects typically included cake baskets, bonbon dishes, biscuit barrels, toast racks, vases, lamps, candlesticks, visiting card and pin trays, mirrors, picture frames, and clocks. Other items – including punch bowls, cigar boxes, decanters, wine coolers, claret jugs, fruit stands, and coffee services – were also included in the firm's 1906 catalogue, which presented virtually the entire range to an enthusiastic buying public throughout Europe.

W.M.F. remains today one of the world's leading manufacturers of tableware, kitchen utensils, and cutlery. The factory's extensive output has included nearly every decorative style popular from the late 19th century – from historic styles such as the Rococo, Gothic, or Neoclassical, to the Secessionist, Modernist, and Art Deco. However, it is the naturalistic, curvaceous ornament of the French Art Nouveau and the more restrained, geometric patterns of its Jugendstil sister, which were particularly well-suited to the reflective qualities and malleability of metals and alloys.

The mark on W.M.F. silver-plate and pewter wares in the Art Nouveau style was initially an ostrich in profile above the initials "W.M.F." and the letter "G" – for Geislingen, where the first factory was founded in 1853 – all set within a diamond. In 1907, a stamp featuring only the initials "W.M.F." was introduced, and by 1930 this had become the company's official mark.

Pewter centrepiece vase, with original clear glass liner, from a three-piece garniture. The elongated, baluster-shaped body is embraced by a pair of *femmes-fleur* – the trains of their flowing robes forming the splayed foot. The glass liner is cupped at the rim on two sides by floral motifs, with sinuous stems extending down the neck, the latter is flanked by a pair of whiplash handles. *c.1900. 35cm (13½in) high* **£7,000–8,000 (the set) Sty**

CORNERSTONE PIECE

Pewter card tray of figural and plant form. The surface of the tray comprises undulating waterlily pads, with a large flower-head centrally positioned along one edge. The waterlily pads are supported on elongated, sinuously curvaceous stems, which flank a central figure and descend to a stepped, pool-like base. The figure is in the form of a young female, probably a water nymph, posing in a clinging halter-neck dress and holding a dove. The underside of the base is marked with the W.M.F. ostrich symbol set within a diamond-shaped surround. *c.1906. 29cm (11½in) wide* **£1,000–1,200 TO**

Stylized plant-form imagery is a recurring feature of W.M.F.'s designs. Although numerous floral species were employed, waterlilies, as used here, were particularly popular, as were poppies and sunflowers

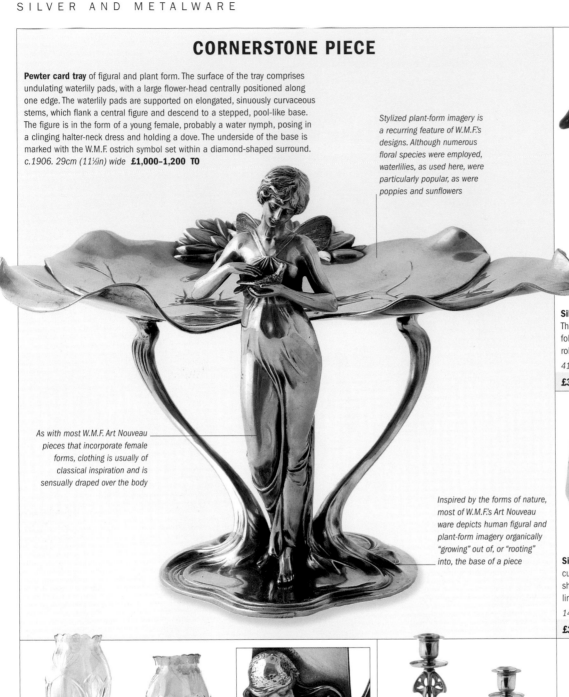

As with most W.M.F. Art Nouveau pieces that incorporate female forms, clothing is usually of classical inspiration and is sensually draped over the body

Inspired by the forms of nature, most of W.M.F.'s Art Nouveau ware depicts human figural and plant-form imagery organically "growing" out of, or "rooting" into, the base of a piece

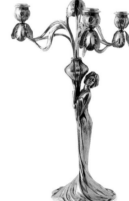

Silver-plated table lamp with a glass shade. The shade is suspended from a whiplash foliate form descending to a maiden whose robe trails into a tripod base. *c.1900*
41cm (16in) high
£3,800–4,500   **Sty**

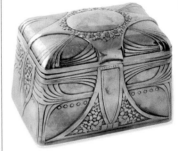

Silver-plated tea caddy of gently tapering, cube-like form. The hinged lid and sides have shield-like panels with flower-heads, and are linked by stylized foliate stems. *c.1905*
14cm (5½in) high
£200–250   **TO**

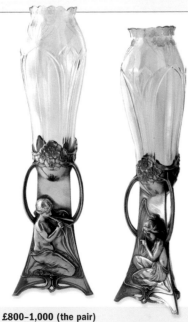

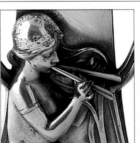

By not electroplating the pipes of one of the maidens, a subtle copper-pewter colour contrast is created.

Pair of vases, each with a glass vessel cut with plant-form decoration held in loop-handled pewter mounts embellished with female musicians and flowers. *c.1906*
33.5cm (13¾in) high

£800–1,000 (the pair)   **TO**

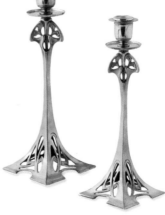

Pewter candlesticks with flared, Eiffel Tower-like bases, pierced with stylized tendrils and foliate motifs. They have circular drip-pans and single sconces.
27.5cm (10¾in) high

£900–1,200   **DN**

Silver-plated candelabra (one of a pair) with four bud-and-leaf form sconces. Tendrils rise from a figural base of a young woman with a robe pooling to a round foot. *c.1900*
49cm (19in) high

£10,000–15,000 (the pair)   **Sty**

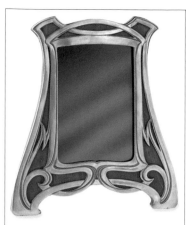

Pewter picture frame of curvaceous, waisted form. It has sinuous and interlaced stylized plant-form motifs, and a mahogany back on an easel support. *c.1905*

24cm (9½in) high

£400–500   **TO**

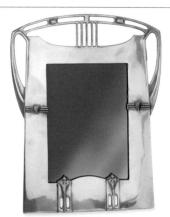

Silver plated picture frame of "Secessionist" style with a shield-like shape, pierced overhanging top, oval studs, and two rectilinear *fleur-de-lys* motifs. *c.1906*

19.5cm (7¾in) high

£400–500   **TO**

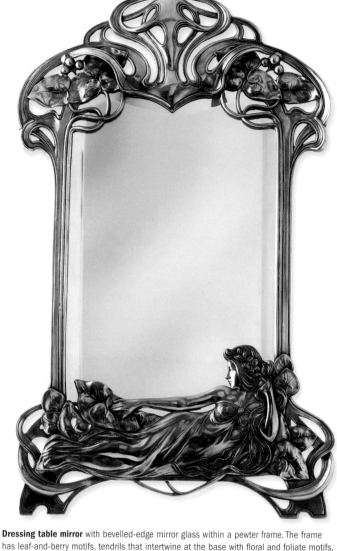

Dressing table mirror with bevelled-edge mirror glass within a pewter frame. The frame has leaf-and-berry motifs, tendrils that intertwine at the base with floral and foliate motifs, and a reclining, garlanded maiden in a flowing robe. *c.1905*

52cm (20¼in) high

£1,500–2,000   **TO**

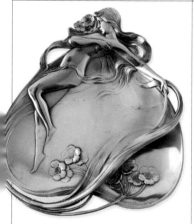

Pewter bottle stand of cut-out *femme-fleur* form. The dream maiden's hair descends sinuously to the base and is embellished with floral motifs. *c.1906*

11cm (4¼in) high

£200–250   **TO**

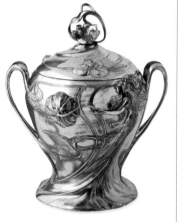

Silver-plated punch bowl of tapering ovoid form with a splayed foot, elongated loop handles, and lid with finial. Decorated with berries, poppies, and *femmes-fleur*. *c.1900*

34cm (13¼in) high

£2,500–3,500   **Sty**

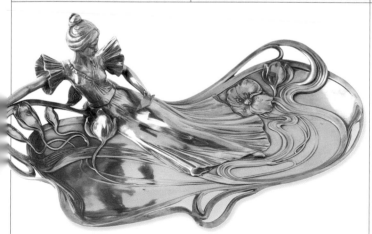

Pewter figural card tray in the form of a reclining maiden with flower-like sleeves, lying among stylized buds and flowers. The stems and tendrils curve sinuously and extend in a whiplash form around the hem of her long, pleated skirt. *c.1906*

34.5cm (13½in) wide

£1,000–2,000   **TO**

W.M.F. FAKES

As with any area of collecting, when pieces reach a certain value and demand outstrips supply, fakes appear on the market. The production of dubious "W.M.F." wares is an example of this. The two genuine W.M.F. dishes (*see left and right*) are popular designs and have recently been "reproduced". These reproductions, however, are often mistaken for genuine W.M.F. pieces. The fakes are generally crude in appearance with a poor finish and are much heavier than an original piece. The mark often seen is an angel motif that appears slightly worn and old. Strictly speaking these cannot be considered as "fakes" unless they intentionally copy the W.M.F. marks. Without replica marks they are purely "reproductions" that may confuse collectors who assume that they are buying a genuine W.M.F. piece at a bargain price.

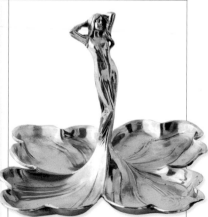

Pewter hors d'ouevres dish, in the form of a scantily clad, languidly posing *femme-fleur* emerging, Venus-like, from the centre of four leaf-form moulded dishes. *c.1906*

11.25cm (4½in) wide

£800–1,000   **TO**

Vertical, architectural forms are decorated with elaborate ornament in geometric shapes.

Crisp, rectilinear vessels in silver or painted metal are often pierced to create latticework designs.

Hammer marks formed during production are frequently left on the surface of the metal for decorative effect.

Josef Hoffmann

Founder and leading member of the Wiener Werkstätte, Josef Hoffmann (1870–1956) produced a wide range of Art Nouveau-style silver and metalware that was distinctive for its use of pure lines and geometric forms.

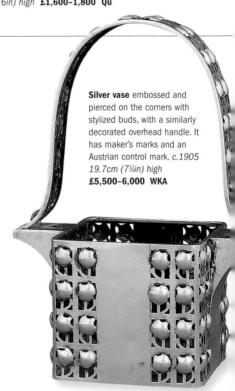

In the embryonic stages, Josef Hoffmann's designs were often simply drawn. However, when his designs were brought to three-dimensional life by a master craftsman working closely with him, the results were works of stunning originality.

Hoffmann's early designs exhibit a rectilinear purity of form often with simple hammer-textured surfaces. The starkness of a piece was sometimes softened by the considered application of one or more coloured hardstone cabochons, and strong architectural forms were often pierced with rows of square holes.

The influence of Charles Rennie Mackintosh on Hoffmann and his colleagues cannot be overestimated. In 1900, Mackintosh and his wife, Margaret Macdonald, exhibited at the Secessionist Exhibition in Vienna, where Hoffmann was greatly impressed by their work. Mackintosh had also designed a music salon for Fritz Warndorfer, another founder member of the Wiener Werkstätte.

Hoffmann and Koloman Moser (*see opposite*), while having their own particular artistic vision for designing silverware, were also influenced by graphic artist Franz Otto Czeschka. When Czeschka joined the Wiener Werkstätte in 1905, the emphasis on surface decoration was revived. Hoffmann continued to produce bold shapes, but he began to decorate the plain, polished surfaces with embossed plant-forms, scrolling tendrils, or geometric motifs.

Other silver manufacturers such as W.M.F. (*see pp.170–73*) took an interest in Hoffmann and Moser's work and created their own, often cheaply produced, versions to cater for a burgeoning market eager for fashionable silverware at a more affordable price.

Above: Silver-plated brass basket-shaped vase with a looped overhead handle and sides pierced with square apertures. The vase contains a clear glass liner. *1904* *15.3cm (6in) high* **£1,600–1,800 Qu**

GEOMETRIC BASKET DESIGNS

Among the most evocative examples of the pure lines and abstract, geometric forms that informed the work of Josef Hoffmann were the distinctive "basket" designs he created for the Wiener Werkstätte in the first decade of the 20th century. A range of wares in silver, white lacquered metal, and painted metal – vases, table clocks, candlesticks, and desk-stands – was made in basket shapes that were embellished with decoration comprising dazzling chequerboard patterns of pierced fretwork. Stark, elongated shapes that initially favoured smooth, shiny surfaces were ultimately transformed with the new taste for planished, faceted textures that reflected the prevailing Art Nouveau appetite for handcrafted decorative objects.

Silver vase embossed and pierced on the corners with stylized buds, with a similarly decorated overhead handle. It has maker's marks and an Austrian control mark. *c.1905* *19.7cm (7¾in) high* **£5,500–6,000 WKA**

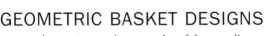

Silver trumpet vase, designed by Hoffmann and made by the Wiener Werkstätte. The neck rim and base are linked by vertical straps pierced with stylized florets, two of which extend to form a loop handle. *32cm (12¾in) high* **NPA Soth**

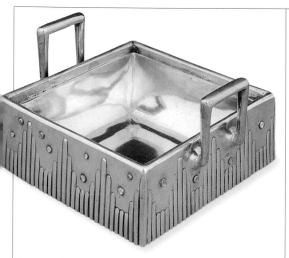

Square section silver bowl with plain square looped handles. Its sides are decorated in relief with vertical linear banding of graduated lengths, randomly punctuated on the remaining plain surfaces with 23 moonstone cabochons. Marked with the designer's monogram. *1905*
16.6cm (6¾in) wide

£15,000–20,000 WKA

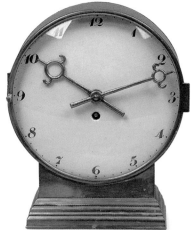

Circular brass table clock on a stepped base with a white enamelled dial and hammer-textured hands. Stamped with the designer's monogram, "Wiener Werkstätte" and "Made in Austria".
25.4cm (10in) high

£7,500–10,000 DOR

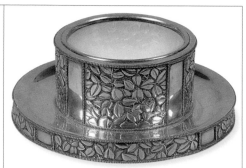

Circular silver caviar bowl with embossed foliate panels alternating with plain panels and a broader circular base similarly decorated. It has an opalescent glass liner. *1910*
19.7cm (7¾in) wide

£16,000–18,000 DOR

Koloman Moser

Having studied painting at the Vienna Akademie, the Austrian Art Nouveau designer Koloman Moser (1868–1918) continued his training in design at the Viennese School of Applied Arts where he became a faculty member in 1899. Celebrated as a painter and book illustrator, Moser also designed jewellery, metalwork, glass, textiles, and furniture, usually in a decorative, rectilinear style. He was a pioneer of the Vienna Secession movement, organizing the Secession section in the Austrian pavilion at the 1900 Universal Exposition in Paris. In collaboration with Josef Hoffmann, Moser established the groundbreaking Wiener Werkstätte in 1903, whose aim was to marry Austrian art with industry. Similar in style to Hoffmann's creations, Moser's metalware designs favoured small, decorative items, such as silver vases in simple, geometric shapes, often boasting planished outer skins that were pierced and embossed.

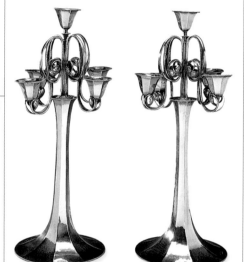

Pair of silver five-light candelabra designed by Hoffmann and made by Adolf Erbrich for the Wiener Werkstätte. With flower-form sconces on scrolling stems supported on circular bases.
48.5cm (19in) high

£22,000–26,000 Soth

Koloman Moser silver cylindrical beaker embossed and pierced with four rows of stylized florets. It has the designer's monogram, maker's trademarks, and Austrian control mark. *c.1905*
19.8cm (4½in) high

£2,500–3,500 WKA

Koloman Moser silver "skyscraper" vase made by the Wiener Werkstätte. The vase is formed as a narrow cylinder, with evenly spaced vertical bands of square apertures, and supported on a plain and domed circular base. The outer rim is embossed with a band of dots.

NPA

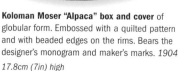

V&A

Koloman Moser "Alpaca" box and cover of globular form. Embossed with a quilted pattern and with beaded edges on the rims. Bears the designer's monogram and maker's marks. *1904*
17.8cm (7in) high

£5,000–6,000 DOR

German and Austrian Silver and Metalware

In Germany, the Art Nouveau Jugendstil style became widely popular at the end of the 19th century, with Darmstadt and Munich the pioneering centres for silver and metalwork. Darmstadt's avant-garde colony of artists rejected the flowing French style, preferring to bring a formal, abstract representation of the natural world to decorative wares. In Austria, the Wiener Werkstätte employed professional silversmiths who collaborated with talented designers, producing a wide range of distinctive metalwork with pure lines and geometric forms. Some designs were handmade to order, but most relied upon mechanized processes.

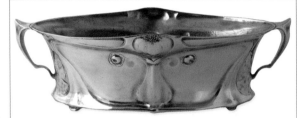

Orivit dressing table mirror with bevelled-edge glass set in a pewter frame. Decorated with a female head, the hair flowing into scrolled feet, and up through curvaceous, waisted sides to a serpentine top. *c.1905*

34.5cm (13½in) high

| £1,200–1,500 | TO |

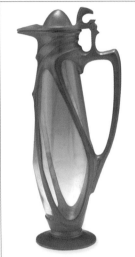

German glass and pewter decanter by Friedrich Adler, made in Munich. The spindle-shaped, glass body is set in a footed pewter mount with a beak-like spout. *1904*

22.75cm (9in) high

| £600–700 | Qu |

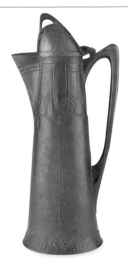

German pewter decanter by Albin Müller for Metallwaren Fabrik Eduard Hueck. The body is of tapering conical form with peacock feather decoration. *1903–04*

35.5cm (14in) high

| £600–700 | Qu |

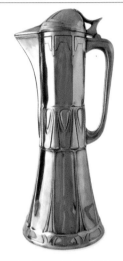

German pewter decanter by Albin Müller. The tapering, waisted form has an angular handle, hinged lid, bird-like spout, and stylized plant form motifs. *c.1902*

40cm (15¾in) high

| £1,000–1,2000 | TO |

Kayserzinn (Kayser pewter) jardinère by Hugo Leven for J.P. Kayser & Sohn, with angular, whiplash handles and cast with highly stylized plant-form decoration. The polished Kayserzinn body is not electroplated, and the solid pewter alloy exhibits a silvery sheen.

27cm (10½in) high

| £800–1,200 | Sty |

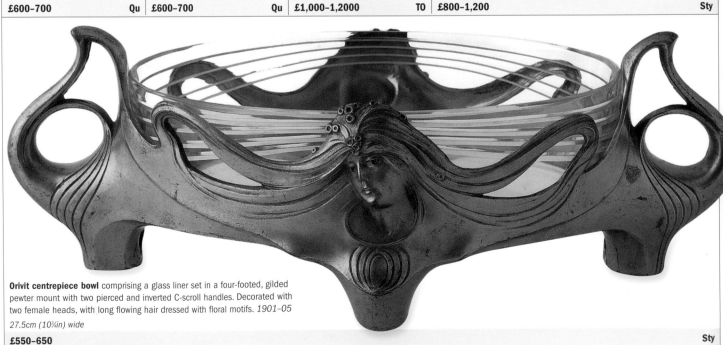

Orivit centrepiece bowl comprising a glass liner set in a four-footed, gilded pewter mount with two pierced and inverted C-scroll handles. Decorated with two female heads, with long flowing hair dressed with floral motifs. *1901–05*

27.5cm (10¾in) wide

| £550–650 | |

| | Sty |

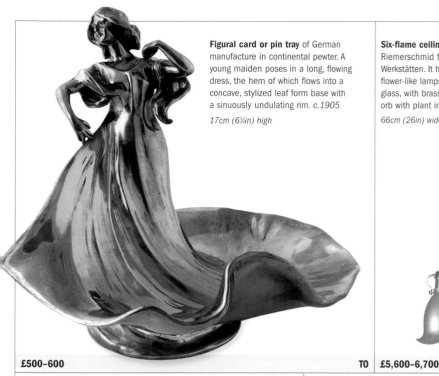

Figural card or pin tray of German manufacture in continental pewter. A young maiden poses in a long, flowing dress, the hem of which flows into a concave, stylized leaf form base with a sinuously undulating rim. *c.1905*

17cm (6¾in) high

£500–600   TO

Six-flame ceiling lamp by Richard Riemerschmid for Deutsche Werkstätten. It has six inverted bell-flower-like lamps of matte etched glass, with brass sockets, disc, and orb with plant imagery. *c.1911*

66cm (26in) wide

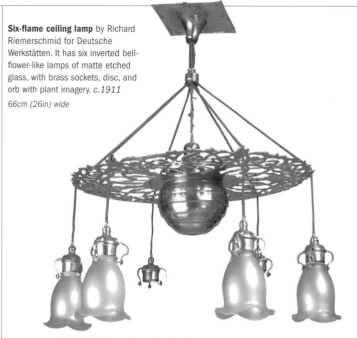

£5,600–6,700   Qu

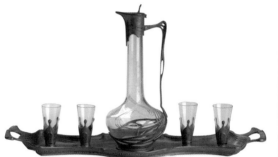

Orivit liquor set comprising a glass decanter in a pewter mount cut with sinuous tendril forms, pewter-mounted glasses of tapering form, and a serpentine-edged, twin-handled pewter tray. Stamped "Orivit". *1901–05*

Decanter: 22cm (8½in) high

£250–350   L&T

Preserve pot and tray by Joseph Maria Olbrich. The glass bowl is in a four-footed pewter frame with embossed rose motifs (also on the tray), and peacock feather motifs on the handles. *1903*

11.5cm (4½in) high

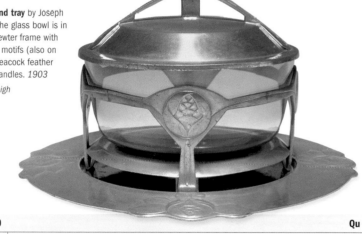

£2,000–2,500   Qu

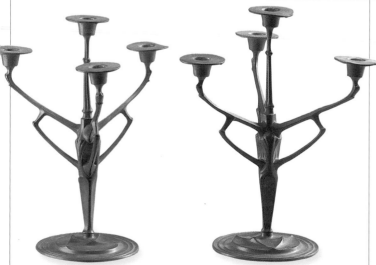

Pair of pewter candelabra by Friedrich Adler for Urania. Each has four candle holders of stylized flower-head form, supported on branch-like arms and a trunk-like shaft. *c.1904*

36cm (14in) high

£2,000–2,500   HERR

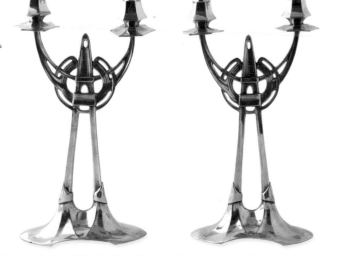

Pair of pewter candelabra by Albert Reinneman. They each have stylized plant form feet, split angular stems, and curving interlaced arms, with stylized flower-head candle holders. *c.1902*

39.5cm (15½in) high

£1,200–1,500   TO

Georg Jensen

The name Georg Jensen reaches far beyond his native Denmark and is synonymous with simple, elegant, and distinctive silver designs in a unique adaptation of the Art Nouveau style.

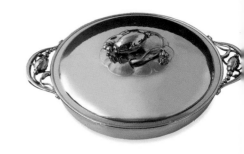

Following travels through France and Italy, and having trained as a goldsmith with ambitions to become a sculptor, the pre-eminent Danish silversmith and jewellery designer Georg Jensen apprenticed in the Copenhagen workshop of accomplished metalworker Mogens Ballin (1871–1914) before establishing his own studio in 1904. Initially producing only jewellery (*see pp.152–53*), Jensen ventured, two years later, into holloware and flatware with striking results.

During his brief Art Nouveau period, Jensen developed a highly original style that combined simple, elegant forms with ornamentation often inspired by nature. Along with other artists of his generation, he emulated the late 19th-century silver designs created by the architect Thorvald Bindesboll for the established Copenhagen silversmiths A. Michelsen (*see box opposite*).

Many of Jensen's timeless silverware designs for teapots, coffee pots, flatware, and other decorative ware – with pure, geometric outlines, a sense of harmony and balance, and a satin-like patina – were created by a team of designers, including painter Johan Rohde and Harald Nielsen. These artists helped establish Jensen's international reputation, and his modest workshop grew into a widely celebrated manufacturing and retail empire that remains in business today.

Above: "Blossom" silver tureen and cover designed by Georg Jensen, of circular form applied with openwork twin handles enclosing bud motifs. The drop-in cover has a bud finial. Design number 2. *c.1904*. 32cm (12½in) wide **£6,000–7,000 SF**

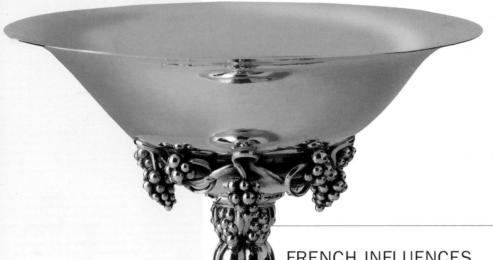

"Grape" silver tazza designed by Georg Jensen. The underside of the shallow, flared bowl is embellished with grapes and vines, supported on a slender twisted stem, above a spreading circular foot. Design number 263. *c.1918* 19cm (7½in) high **£2,000–3,000 SF**

FRENCH INFLUENCES

Regarding himself as an *orfèvre sculpteur* – a goldsmith sculptor – Jensen identified with the role of the French court goldsmith. Abandoning his earliest unornamented silver designs, he looked back to French silver of the 18th century and created simple, rounded silverware shapes that were embellished with sculptural, naturalistic decoration, such as bunches of grapes and bouquets of roses. Stylized handles and finials took the form of tendrils, while tureens and pots for coffee and tea perched on animal-paw feet.

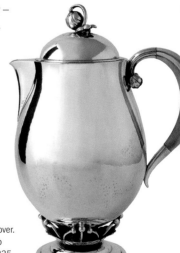

Silver chocolate pot designed by Georg Jensen, with a bud finial on the domed cover. Supported on a plant-form base. The loop handle is of fluted ivory. Design number 235. *20.5cm (8in) high* **£1,200–1,800 SF**

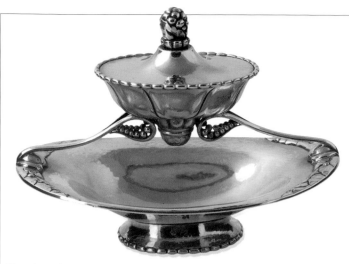

Silver cigar ashtray designed by Georg Jensen. The upper, smaller bowl has a cover and holds Vesta matches; it is supported on plant-like stems. Design number 22. *c.1910*

16cm (6¼in) long

£1,000–1,500   SF

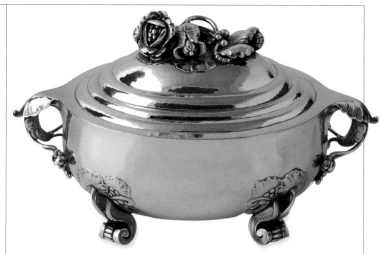

Silver bonbonnière designed by Georg Jensen. Scrolling feet join the body with floral motifs. The handles are foliate loops, and the stepped cover has a floral finial. Design number 262. *c.1915*

18.5cm (7½in) wide

£6,000–7,000   SF

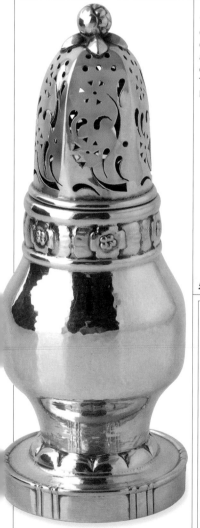

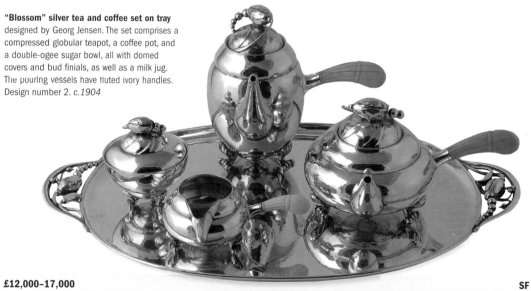

"Blossom" silver tea and coffee set on tray designed by Georg Jensen. The set comprises a compressed globular teapot, a coffee pot, and a double-ogee sugar bowl, all with domed covers and bud finials, as well as a milk jug. The pouring vessels have fluted ivory handles. Design number 2. *c.1904*

£12,000–17,000   SF

Silver-bellied sugar caster designed by Georg Jensen, embossed with a floral band. The bullet-shaped cover is pierced with foliate motifs. Design number 97. *c.1915*

16.5cm (6½in) high

£1,000–1,500   SF

A. Michelsen

Like London's Liberty & Co. and the Parisian jewellers and silversmiths Boucheron, the Copenhagen firm A. Michelsen manufactured large quantities of well-made Art Nouveau silver created by innovative, imaginative architects and designers. Among these highly influential artists were Thorvald Bindesboll, whose abstract designs featured undulating lines and motifs such as tadpoles or clouds; the painter and metalworker Mogens Ballin, whose workshop fostered the ambitions of the young Georg Jensen; and painter Harald Slott-Moller, whose designs were heavily influenced by the arts of Japan.

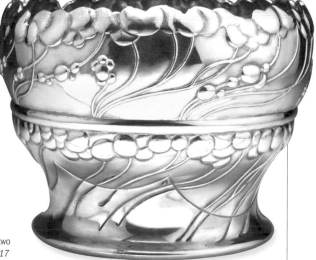

A. Michelsen silver vase of stylized blossom shape, made up of two sections, each embossed with plant forms on sinuous stems. *1917*

18.5cm (7½in) high

£2,200–2,800   Qu

French and Belgian Silver and Metalware

In France, many of the silversmiths working in the Art Nouveau style had initially achieved celebrity as jewellery makers. Established firms in the French silver industry took a cautious approach to the new style, but these artist-craftsmen created luxurious household accessories using unconventional materials. Horn, lacquer, mother-of-pearl, and enamels were married with precious and semi-precious stones and silver, gold, or base metals to create *objets d'art*.

Belgium's contribution to Art Nouveau silverware, though small, was nonetheless of superb quality, with Henry van de Velde and Philippe Wolfers creating lyrical, sculptural designs.

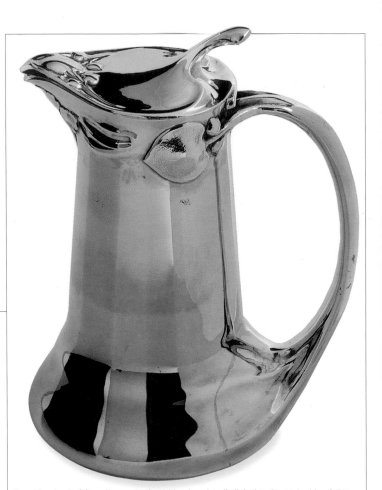

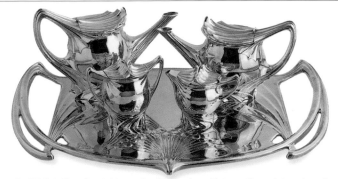

Rare Paul Follot silvered-metal tea and coffee service, with tray, coffee pot, teapot, sucrier, and cream jug. Each piece has sinuous fluted decoration. Signed "Follot". *c.1900*

Coffee pot: 20cm (7¾in) high

£26,000–42,000   **MACK**

Rare Maurice Dufrêne silver water jug with a loop handle linked to the neck with a foliate motif. The hinged cover has further foliage and a sinuous thumbpiece. Stamped "Leverrier".

20cm (7¾in) high

£9,000–13,500   **MACK**

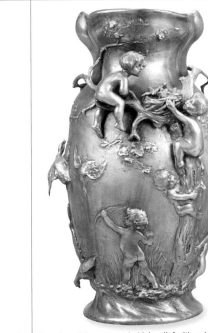

French pewter paper knife cast in relief with a mermaid holding a trident aloft in conflict with a sea monster. Signed "MMA". *1900*

24cm (9½in) long

£280–320   **Qu**

French metal vase cast in high relief with naked children climbing trees to reach birds' nests and shooting arrows from bows near pollarded willows. One of a pair with drop-in cylindrical liners.

35cm (13¾in) high

£300–400   **DN**

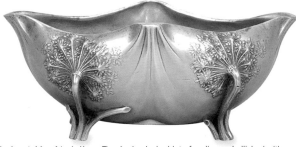

Elliptical metal bowl by L. Kann. The rim is pinched into four lips embellished with umbellifers, their stems forming feet. It is stamped with the artist's signature and founder's mark.

22cm (8¾in) long

£80–120   **DN**

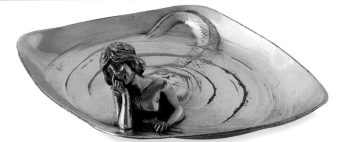

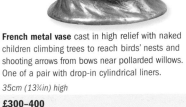

French silver-plated oval tray showing in high relief a pensive mermaid emerging from one edge of a pool, creating concentric waves. Her tail emerges at the opposite edge. *c.1900*

19.5cm (7¾in) long

£300–400   **Sty**

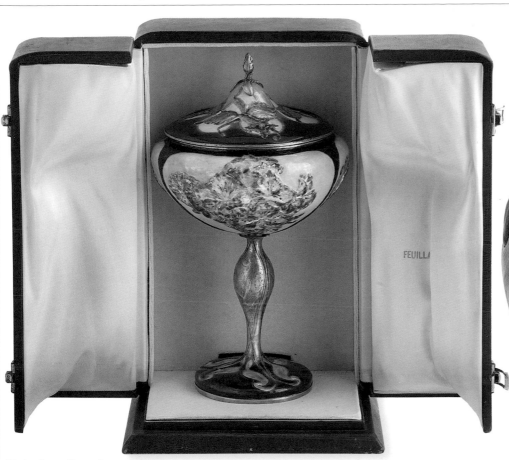

"Alzalees" rare silver and enamel pedestal cup and cover by Eugene Feuillatre with bud terminal and azalea decoration. The stem has a pale green enamel decoration. In original green-leather fitted box. *1901*

25cm (10in) high

£30,000–38,000 MACK

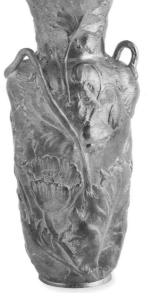

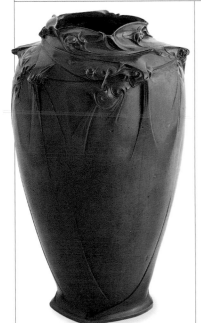

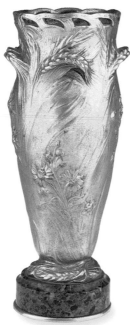

Rare bronze vase by Hector Guimard with vertical sinuous bands on the shoulders and rim in high-relief with whiplash curves and foliate fronds. Attractively patinated.

28cm (11in) high

£60,000–90,000 MACK

Gilt-bronze baluster vase by F. Barbedienne. Cast in relief with ears of wheat and autumnal flowers. With a pierced neck and marble base. Stamped "F. Barbedienne Paris". *1900*

20cm (8in) high

£500–700 Qu

Gilt-bronze baluster vase by Alexandre Vibert, cast in relief with dense foliage and poppy blooms. Signed "A Vibert" with the foundry mark for "Glisserei". *c.1909*

24cm (9½in) high

£1,800–2,600 MACK

Gilt-bronze vase by Alexandre Vibert, cast in shallow relief with peacock feathers with blue and green enamelled "eyes". Signed "A. Vibert" with Jallot foundry mark. *c.1900*

32cm (12½in) high

£6,000–9,000 MACK

181

KEY FEATURES

Decorative features inspired by Celtic art, such as Celtic knots and spear-headed entrelac symbols.

Pieces often lightly planished to created a handcrafted effect.

Innovative forms with strong lines give Tudric pieces in particular an architectural feel.

Cabochons of turquoise, lapiz lazuli, agate, or other semi-precious stones are often set into Cymric ware, along with panels of peacock blue and green enamelling.

Liberty & Co.

At the turn of the century, two distinctive ranges of Art Nouveau silver and pewterware – Cymric and Tudric – were added to the exotic jewellery, fabrics, and furniture sold at London's Liberty & Company.

By 1904, Liberty & Co. in Regent Street, founded by Arthur Lasenby Liberty in 1875, had become renowned for its collection of original Art Nouveau silver and pewterware. Among these was the innovative Cymric range of silver inspired by the designs and patterns of ancient Celtic art and the Arts and Crafts Movement. Finely hammered and simply decorated with enamels and semi-precious stones, the range included mantel clocks, boxes, inkwells, picture frames, jewellery, candlesticks, spoons, and cigarette cases.

Liberty's Cymric silver was machine-made, but it was finished by hand to give it a crafted appearance. Modern, architectural forms are decorated with motifs of stylized leaves, flower-heads, and interlaced tendrils known as entrelacs.

Liberty employed a talented range of designers, such as Jessie M. King, Archibald Knox, and David Veasey, to work on the Cymric silverware as well as the Tudric range of pewterware that was introduced shortly afterwards (*see box below*). However, intent on promoting its own name, Liberty refused to have the designers' names acknowledged and registered its own mark in 1894. Both the Cymric and Tudric ranges were made in collaboration with the Birmingham silversmiths William H. Haseler & Co. Other silverware was produced jointly with William Hutton & Sons of Sheffield.

Art Nouveau in Italy was known as *La Stile Liberty*, a reflection of the influence the famous London store came to exert on popular taste.

Above: Tudric pewter mantel clock by Archibald Knox. The shield-shaped body is embossed with stylized leaves and tendrils, and the round face has copper numerals and a floral design in coloured enamels. *1903-05. 21cm (8¼in) high* **£3,000-5,500 Qu**

THE TUDRIC RANGE

Liberty & Co.'s Tudric range, including chalices for domestic use, clocks, and vases, was made from 1903 onwards in pewter that contained a high percentage of silver. The Tudric range was created as a more affordable alternative to the silver Cymric range, using enamel cabochons and semi-precious stones for decoration. It was not, however, just a cheaper version of the silverware but a separate range in its own right, with its own innovative designs.

Liberty's most famous metalwork designer was Archibald Knox (1864–1933), who was passionate about Celtic art. He designed for both the Cymric and Tudric ranges, some pieces being of great complexity.

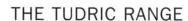

Tudric pewter vase by Archibald Knox. The three-footed bullet-shaped body is decorated around the neck with embossed Celtic entrelac symbols and blue and green enamelled cabochons. *c.1905. 29cm (11½in) high* **£1,500-2,000 TO**

Tudric pewter mantel clock by Archibald Knox, decorated with embossed buds, leaves, and stems. It has a blue enamelled clockface and cabochons, a copper dial, and brass hands. *c.1903. 20.5cm (8in) high* **£4,000-5,000 TO**

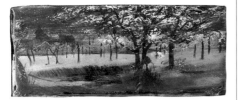

Many cigar and cigarette boxes in the Tudric range have inset panels with enamelled landscapes, mostly produced by Fleetwood Charles Varley.

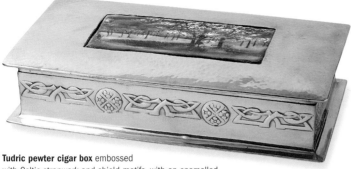

Tudric pewter cigar box embossed with Celtic strapwork and shield motifs, with an enamelled orchard landscape set into an overhanging lid. *c.1905*

31cm (12¼in) long

£1,500–2,500 VDB

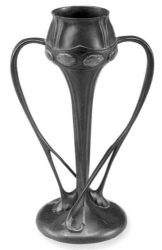

Stylized floral Tudric pewter vase with a band of enamelled oval cabochons. Two whiplash handles flank the elongated stem. Stamped "Tudric/029/4". *1903–05*

25cm (9¾in) high

£750–850 DRA

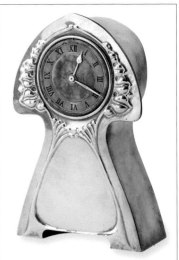

Tudric pewter mantel clock shaped like a Celtic entrelac symbol and cast with leaf motifs. It has an enamelled face, a copper dial, and black enamelled numerals. *1903–05*

20cm (7¾in) high

£2,800–3,400 WW

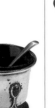

Three-piece silver cruet set made up of a pepper pot, a glass-lined lidded mustard pot, and a lined salt pot, all decorated with cabochons. Made in Birmingham.

5cm (2in) high

£350–550 L&T

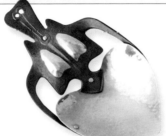
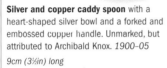

Silver and copper caddy spoon with a heart-shaped silver bowl and a forked and embossed copper handle. Unmarked, but attributed to Archibald Knox. *1900–05*

9cm (3½in) long

£300–350 WW

CORNERSTONE PIECE

Two trumpet-shaped silver Cymric vases designed by Archibald Knox. The vases' slender, tapering forms are supported by avant-garde splayed feet, the shape of which is based on Celtic motifs. Both vases are decorated with a ring of cabochons and have Birmingham silver hallmarks just below the rim. *c.1905*

Large vase: 22cm (8¾in) high

£20,000–25,000 VDB

Small vase: 16cm (6¼in) high

£15,000–20,000 VDB

Using simple turquoise cabochons here provides an effective hint of colour to the plain silver surface

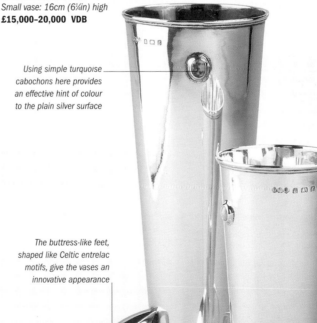

The buttress-like feet, shaped like Celtic entrelac motifs, give the vases an innovative appearance

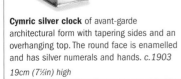

Cymric silver clock of avant-garde architectural form with tapering sides and an overhanging top. The round face is enamelled and has silver numerals and hands. *c.1903*

19cm (7½in) high

£1,500–1,800 VDB

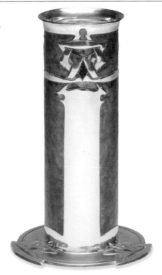

Rare tubular Cymric vase made from silver with panels of peacock blue-green enamel and a stylized coat of arms. The foot is embossed with Celtic motifs. *c.1903*

18.25cm (7in) high

£10,000–15,000 VDB

KEY FEATURES

Handcrafted appearance and high-quality workmanship are typical of all the Guild's pieces.

Visible hammer marks create an attractive rippled surface on much of the silverwork.

Wirework was a popular choice for loop handles, finials of muffin dishes, and toast racks.

Restrained use of naturalistic motifs was characteristic of the Guild's artist-craftsmen.

Guild of Handicraft

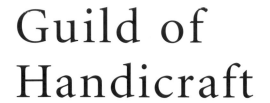

Reacting against the lamentable quality of mass-produced metalware, the designers and artists of the Guild of Handicraft attempted to breathe life back into the medieval tradition of handcrafted metal.

In both Europe and the United States, designers founded guilds that would foster the ideal of the artist-craftsman and provide a place where apprentices could gain experience in time-honoured handicrafts such as metalwork. A leading light of this movement was the British designer, architect, silversmith, and author Charles Robert Ashbee (*see below*), who founded the Guild and School of Handicraft in London in 1888. Here, Ashbee gathered together a burgeoning number of talented designers. Created as a working guild in the medieval and Renaissance tradition of masters training journeymen and apprentices, the Guild's artist-craftsmen practised metalwork, as well as woodwork, leatherwork, and jewellery making.

Much of the handcrafted metalwork produced by the Guild consists of small items of silver of the highest quality, such as church plates, jewellery, and glass vessels embellished with silver mounts. Other items include covered cups and bowls with curving loop handles reminiscent of ancient medieval metalwork designs. The finest pieces have been meticulously hand wrought and are often embellished with coloured stone cabochons and applied with enamelled plaques.

Above: Silver muffin and butter dishes by C.R. Ashbee. The muffin dish (*top*) has a domed lid with wirework and a beaded finial. The butter dish has a looped wirework handle set with a cabochon.
Muffin dish: *c.1900. 20cm (7¾in) wide* **£6,000–10,000**
Butter dish: *c.1904. 11cm (4¼in) wide* **£2,500–3,500 VDB**

CHARLES ROBERT ASHBEE

A champion of the Arts and Crafts movement and promoter of Art Nouveau in England, Charles Robert Ashbee's work combined an appreciation of traditional medieval forms, techniques, and materials with a contemporary slant. He created simple, distinctive designs for the Guild of Handicraft, including tea services, vases set with stone cabochons (*see left*), and silver bowls of medieval inspiration (*see below*). Although he promoted the idea of the self-taught artist-craftsman, Ashbee reluctantly accepted the use of industrial methods as an economic necessity.

Tubular silver vase by C.R. Ashbee. The main part of the vase is encircled by stylized tree-like motifs with garnet cabochons at their centres. The vase has a ring of bead moulding around the top of the base. *c.1900*
18cm (7in) high **£3,000–5,000 VDB**

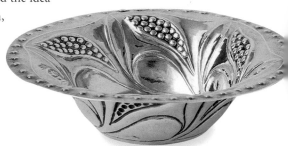

Medieval-style silver bowl (one of a pair) decorated with deep relief stylized leaf-and-berry motifs on both the interior and exterior. Marked "CRA London". *1900*
12.5cm (5in) wide **£2,000–4,000 (the pair) VDB**

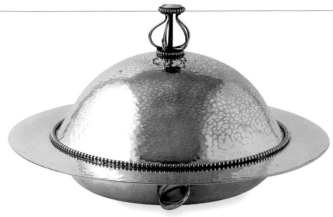

Lightly hammered silver-plated muffin dish by C.R. Ashbee, with a wire and beadwork finial, beadwork around the perimeter of the bowl, and a hot water reservoir in the base. *c.1900*

24cm (9½in) wide

£1,000–1,500 VDB

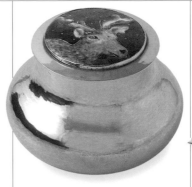

Small, bulb-shaped silver and enamel box with a round, flat lid inset with a polychrome-enamelled image of a reindeer. *1903*

7.5cm (3in) high

£2,500–5,000 VDB

Textured silver inkwell in a geometric shape, with riveted corner supports, flared feet, a glass liner, and a hinged lid set with a large, foiled blue enamel cabochon. *1906*

6.5cm (2½in) high

£1,300–1,500 WW

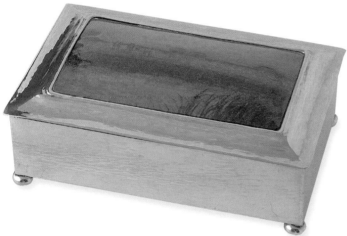

Rectangular silver and enamel box with bun feet. The lid has an inset, enamelled landscape panel created by the artist Fleetwood Charles Varley. *1904*

16.5cm (6½in) high

£7,000–9,000 VDB

Ornate silver toast rack by C.R. Ashbee. The ends have pierced, stylized foliate motifs edged with beadwork; the dividers and handle are made of silver wirework. *c.1899*

16cm (6¼in) long

£5,000–7,000 VDB

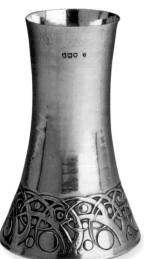

Silver inverted trumpet-shaped vase by C.R. Ashbee, decorated around the base with a band of entwining stems and berries. The vase is hallmarked below the rim. *1900*

18cm (7in) high

£2,500–3,500 VDB

CORNERSTONE PIECE

Silver bowl-shaped butter dish by C.R. Ashbee, with a (replacement) green glass liner, cut out around the perimeter to create a band of leaf motifs. The elongated, looped handle of the dish is characteristic of the Guild of Handicraft's use of silver wirework, as is the use of a cabochon highlight, in this case a teardrop-shaped piece of blister pearl. *1900*

20cm (8in) long **£3,000–5,000 VDB**

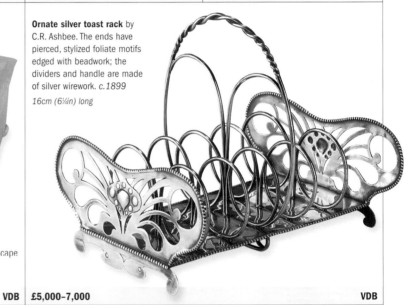

This is a piece of blister pearl but semi-precious stones were also used

Curvaceous, elongated wirework handles, handcrafted and of stylized organic form, are typical of Ashbee's work

Original glass liners are highly desirable. This replacement liner is of excellent quality, but reduces the value of the piece by approximately 20 per cent

British Silver and Metalware

In Britain, the aesthetic of the Arts and Crafts movement dictated the style of silver and metalware designs produced in the workshops of such pioneering artist-craftsmen as Charles Robert Ashbee, Gilbert Leigh Marks, Albert Edward Jones, and Omar Ramsden. Silversmiths spurned industrial methods and championed the importance of hand-craftsmanship, incorporating colourful enamels, mother-of-pearl, or semi-precious gemstones. Eventually, recognizing the need to reach a wider market, some designers accepted commissions from retailers and manufacturers to produce Art Nouveau silverware designs.

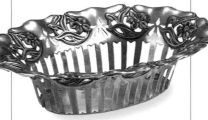

W.H. Haseler silver oval bonbon dish with pierced sides, embossed with floral and foliate roundels heightened with blue enamelling. Birmingham marks. *c.1905*

14cm (5½in) wide

£200–300 L&T

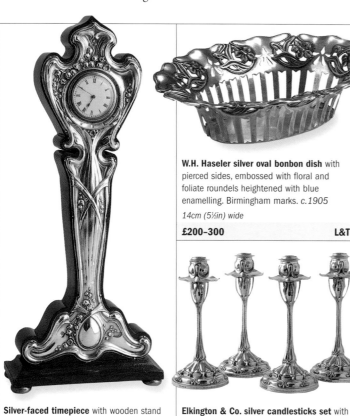

Silver-faced timepiece with wooden stand and framework of sinuous outline. It has a silver panel embossed with interwoven tendrils and florets. Birmingham date marks. *1910*

36cm (14in) high

£400–500 OACC

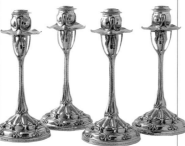

Elkington & Co. silver candlesticks set with bud-shaped sconces and foliate drip pans, on slender, naturalistically embellished stems rising from domed foliate bases. *1906*

32cm (12½in) high

£15,000–25,000 VDB

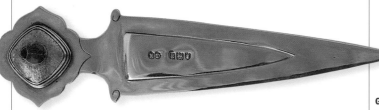

Edith and Nelson Dawson silver bookmark of dagger form surmounted with a lozenge-shaped plaque enamelled with a ladybird against pale green. Marked "N.D. London". *1905*

12cm (5in) long

£300–500 VDB

Gilbert Leigh Marks embossed silver vase of slender baluster form. It has applied roots at the base that form feet, and embossed stems that extend vertically and expand into leafy branches of dog roses, in relief against a planished background. It is signed "Gilbert Marks". *1899*

32cm (12½in) high

£15,000–20,000 VDB

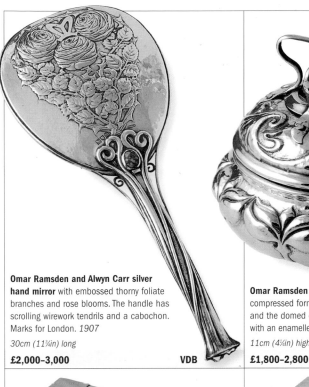

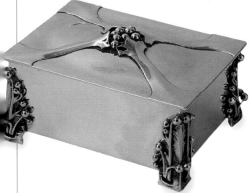

Omar Ramsden and Alwyn Carr silver hand mirror with embossed thorny foliate branches and rose blooms. The handle has scrolling wirework tendrils and a cabochon. Marks for London. *1907*

30cm (11¾in) long

£2,000–3,000   **VDB**

Omar Ramsden and Alwyn Carr silver box and cover of compressed form. The base is embossed with foliate motifs, and the domed cover with wave-like scrolling panels, centred with an enamelled plaque beneath a multi-looped finial. *1901*

11cm (4¼in) high

£1,800–2,800   **VDB**

Omar Ramsden and Alwyn Carr silver rectangular box with overall wave-like embellishment, and an enamelled plaque on the cover depicting a galleon in full sail. *1907*

9.5cm (3¾in) wide

£4,000–6,500   **VDB**

William Hutton & Sons Ltd. silver casket embellished at the corners in relief with beaded plant-form feet. The hinged cover is embossed with a similar motif. *1904*

13cm (5¼in) wide

£2,500–3,500   **VDB**

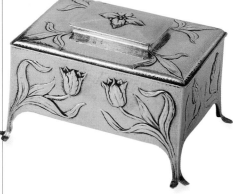

Gilbert Leigh Marks silver casket on splayed feet. Its side panels are embossed with tulips; the hinged cover with foliage and a floret. Signed and dated. *1898*

13cm (5¼in) wide

£5,000–7,000   **VDB**

Albert Edward Jones silver bowl supported on four feet with splayed ends. Its lower section has a planished surface, and its broad neckband is embossed with stylized rose blooms and foliate stems. It has marks for Birmingham. *1906*

17cm (6¾in) wide

£2,000–4,000   **VDB**

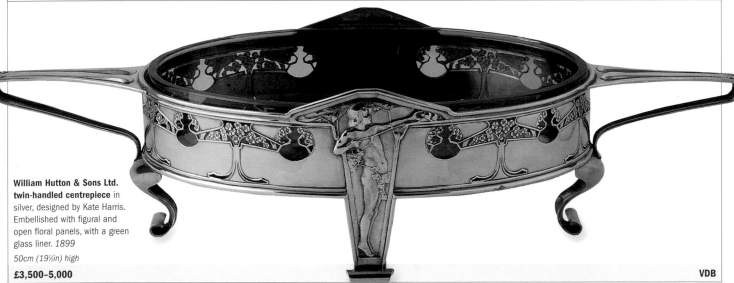

William Hutton & Sons Ltd. twin-handled centrepiece in silver, designed by Kate Harris. Embellished with figural and open floral panels, with a green glass liner. *1899*

50cm (19½in) high

£3,500–5,000   **VDB**

KEY FEATURES

Holloware pieces of silver are usually the most important, especially those with finely tooled designs in high relief.

Japanese-influenced designs and others from the aesthetic movement are very popular today.

Desk pieces and other bronze work from the Art Nouveau period are extremely well made.

The die-stamped Tiffany Studios designation should be clearly visible on the bronze pieces.

Tiffany

Tiffany & Co., led by Charles Tiffany, and the Tiffany Studios, run by his son Louis, produced some of the finest Art Nouveau metalware in the United States, under a name that has become synonymous with quality.

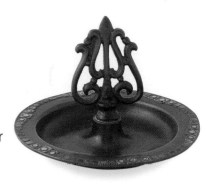

The firm established in 1837 by Charles Tiffany (1812–1902) and his partner Young, was named Tiffany & Co. in 1853. Fifteen years later, in 1868, it merged with the company of Edward C. Moore, which had been making silver exclusively for Tiffany's for over a decade.

With the influence of "Japonism" from the 1870s, silver pieces from this period were lavishly decorated in relief with oriental designs such as dragonflies, insects, and frogs, occasionally with details in other metals such as gold or copper. The emphasis, as always, was on fine craftsmanship and originality.

Charles's son Louis Comfort Tiffany was a very proficient artist and established his own business with colleagues in 1879, calling it Louis C. Tiffany & Associates. It was renamed Tiffany Studios in 1900. Primarily it was a prestigious decorating company and naturally lent itself to creating whole interiors, including the famous Tiffany leaded glass lamps (*see p.96*) and stained glass windows, and silver and metalware accessories.

Metalware such as stamp boxes, inkwells, pen trays, picture frames, and clocks are often found from the Art Nouveau period. These are generally cast in bronze with patterns such as Zodiac symbols or Native American motifs in shallow relief. Some pieces have pierced vine and glass trellis decoration revealing coloured marbled beneath. The most collectable pieces have a gilt or gold-doré finish.

Among the most desirable of the Tiffany Studios metal productions are the enamelled copper vases and bowls. These are often of organic form, sculpted in the shape of lush fruit, flowers, or foliage, and exhibiting the most vivid and exciting colours. The work required to produce these pieces limited the numbers made and, being easily damaged, means that perfect examples are rare.

Above: Enamelled bronze ashtray decorated with stylized flowers and foliage in coloured enamels with a scrolling central finial. With foundry marks and "307". *11cm (4¼in) wide* **£200–400 CW**

Tiffany & Co. silver baluster vase, rising from a spreading circular foot, etched and inlaid with copper, and showing fine floral blooms and highly stylized geometric tendrils. *1906–07 21.6cm (8½in) high* **NPA PS**

JAPANESE INFLUENCE

Edward C. Moore, the chief designer and head of the silver department of Tiffany and Co., was also a pioneer collector of Japanese art, which had become more easily available in the West since trade had been re-established in 1854. Moore was also especially interested in Japanese metalworking techniques, most notably that of *mokume* – the mixing of metals that when polished resembled woodgrain, previously used in Japanese sword making. The Tiffany craftsmen learned how to use this technique to perfection, and also applied natural motifs such as butterflies or gourds to silver vessels of Japanese inspiration. Examples of these were enthusiastically received when shown at the 1876 Philadelphia and 1878 Paris Exhibitions.

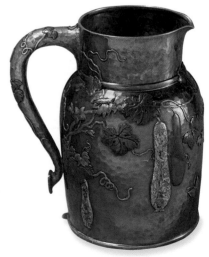

Tiffany & Co. Japanesque silver jug designed by Edward C. Moore. The surface is embossed and applied with mixed metal foliage and *mokume* gourds. *c.1880. 19.5cm (7¾in) high* **£60,000–80,000 BRI**

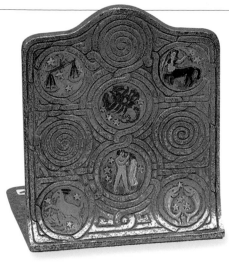

Pair of "Zodiac" bookends in gilt bronze with interwoven scrolls and roundels depicting the signs of the zodiac. Impressed with "Tiffany Studios, New York 1091".

15cm (6in) high

£1,500–2,000   JDJ

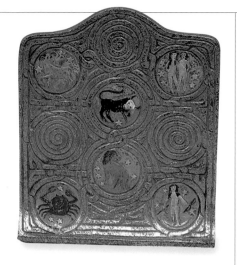

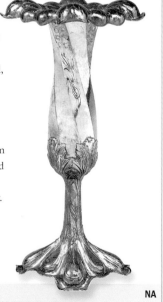

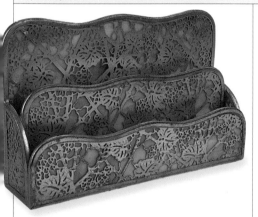

Gilt-bronze stationery rack with three shaped dividers pierced with vine decoration and enclosing marbled, honey-coloured glass panels. Stamped "Tiffany Studios, New York 1008".

25cm (10in) wide

£450–550   L&T

Bronze eight-light candelabra with bud-shaped tops and removable sconces supported on sinuous branches. The handle conceals a snuffer. Signed "L.C. Tiffany Studios, New York".

38cm (15in) high

£13,500–17,000   MACK

Pair of gilt-bronze candlesticks with bud-like tops and detachable sconces on slender, foliate branches extending from narrow stems. Stamped "Tiffany Studios, New York".

25.5cm (10in) high

£1,200–1,800   MACK

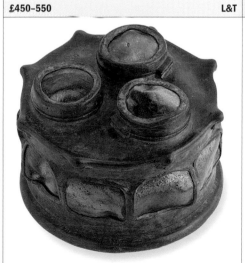

Bronze and "turtleback" revolving inkwell with reservoir covers set with glass plaques; the sides have further glass "turtleback" panels. Marked "Tiffany Studios, New York 4218".

17.5cm (7in) wide

£30,000–45,000   MACK

Gorham

The Gorham Manufacturing Company rivalled Tiffany & Co. as the most important manufacturer of fine silverware in the United States at the turn of the 20th century. Founded in 1815 in Providence, Rhode Island, to produce jewellery, the company embraced machinery early on to help with the manufacturing of a growing selection of items. Quality further increased with the move to sterling standard in 1868. In 1896, Englishman William C. Codman joined the company and designed the Martelé, or "hammered", range in the Art Nouveau style, earning Gorham lasting worldwide recognition. The Martelé range was formally introduced during the Paris Universal Exposition in 1900, but by 1910 sales had declined for several reasons, including expense and lack of practicality.

Gorham tall silver vase with spiralling sides embossed with lilies of the valley. The everted neck is embossed with graduated petals, the foot with further foliate panels. Retailer's mark "Spaulding & Co., Chicago". *1902*

39cm (14½in) high

£10,000–12,000   NA

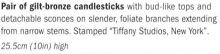

KEY FEATURES

Acid-etching was used in the later years of the factory; such pieces carry less cachet than the more "crafty" hammered ones.

Intended to be functional as well as decorative, Roycroft pieces were generally plainly designed according to American Arts and Crafts principles.

Hand-hammered copper surfaces are popular with collectors.

Roycrofters

Headed by the master soap salesman and visionary Elbert Hubbard, the Roycroft workshops and press operated in East Aurora, New York, from 1893 until 1938. The workers there were known as Roycrofters.

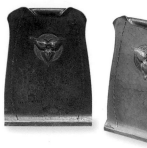

More a community than a factory, Roycroft developed its own interpretation of the Arts and Crafts movement in the United States, focusing its earliest efforts on book printing, having been greatly influenced by William Morris's Kelmscott Press in England. The company initially began producing furniture, lighting, and wrought metalwork solely to meet the needs of the growing campus, but by about 1910, such decorative items had become a large part of their stock, which they marketed nationwide in sales brochures.

While Roycroft's relatively small wood shop produced some of the best furniture of the period, the Roycrofters were most prolific in the manufacture and marketing of hammered metal objects, both decorative and utilitarian. Copper pieces, with lacquered copper patinas, remain the most popular. Other metals

used were brass and silver wash. Hammered surfaces are favoured by contemporary collectors. They also employed an acid-etched texture and, with later pieces, smooth sheet metal. Most desirable are early pieces of heavy-gauge copper that are augmented with the application of German nickel silver.

The factory's most desirable forms include the "American Beauty" vase – a tall, footed vessel with a long cylindrical neck – and other larger items such as ice buckets, wrought candlesticks, and lamp bases; the latter were often fitted with glass shades made by the Steuben Glass Works (*see p.98*).

Look for pieces with the company's earlier die-stamped mark, where the right leg of the "R" extends below the left leg of the "R". Original patina plays a critical part in both the value and collectability of all Roycroft work.

Above: Pair of patinated copper bookends of upright, almost rectangular, shape. They each have a curled edge, raised three-petal floral motif, green pigment, and impressed marks. *1909–25 13cm (5in) high* **£180–220 SI**

HAND-HAMMERED METAL

Roycroft had a preference for copper, and these pieces were mainly handcrafted in the workshops, with the occasional use of mechanical work on the less prestigious items. The action of hand-raising a piece from a flat sheet will result in the hammer marks remaining, and at Roycroft these were left or, indeed, "improved" in the finishing to enhance the overall handcrafted look. The effect is an outside surface covered with hundreds of delicate, light-reflecting indentations. Some pieces were produced by hammering a piece of metal into a pre-formed mould to give a relief "embossed" image of a flower – for example, on a pair of bookends. Later pieces were textured using acid-etching as a decorative "short-cut", and in a craft sense, these are less valid and of less interest to collectors.

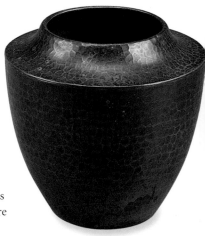

Hammered copper vase of broad-shouldered form with an overall hammered, textured surface with original patina. Impressed with the maker's orb-and-cross mark. *13.5cm (5¼in) high* **£450–550 CR**

Hammered copper table lamp with domed shade, bell-shaped harp, and candlestick base. Original patina. Impressed with the maker's orb-and-cross mark. *40cm (15¾in) high* **£1,800–2,200 DRA**

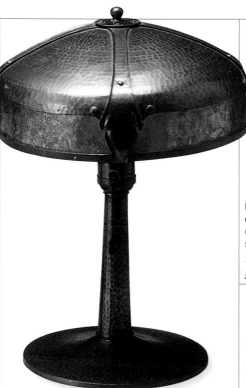

Hammered copper table lamp (one of a pair) in which the domed shade is riveted with acanthus straps and has original inset mica panels. It has a plain stem and spreading circular foot. Impressed with the maker's orb-and-cross mark.

25.5cm (14in) high

£6,000–7,000 (the pair) CR

Pair of brass-washed hammered copper candlesticks, each with cylindrical sconce and cup-shaped bobeche on slender tubular stems. Impressed with the maker's orb-and-cross mark.

17cm (6¾in) high

£5,500–6,500 CR

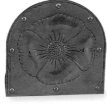

Pair of brass-washed hammered copper "Poppy" bookends with rounded tops and each embossed with a fully blown bloom. They are riveted around the edges. With original patina and the maker's orb-and-cross mark.

13.5cm (5¼in) high

£350–450 CR

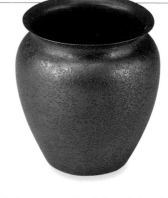

Acid-etched copper vase with a flaring neck rim and original patina. It carries the orb-and-cross mark as well as the word "Roycroft".

12.5cm (5in) high

£180–220 CR

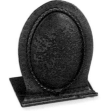

Pair of hammered copper oval bookends with an etched and rope-twist bordered panel, supported on fold-under rectangular bases. Impressed with the maker's orb-and-cross mark.

12.5cm (5in) high

£80–120 CR

Dirk van Erp

More than just a coppersmith, Dirk van Erp worked in San Francisco, California, from 1908 until his death in 1933, redefining the craft in several ways. While nearly every other metalsmith would reduce the size of the hammer marks with a repeated levelling or smoothing of the surface, van Erp would occasionally leave large copper "warts", turning the process into decoration. He also developed a series of rich, deep patinas to cover and protect his vessels. Nearly all van Erp pieces are marked with a distinctive "windmill" stamp. The two earliest marks (dating about 1909–13) – used during the Art Nouveau period – have van Erp's name in a rectangular box below the windmill; on the earliest, the name "D'Arcy Gaw" is above his.

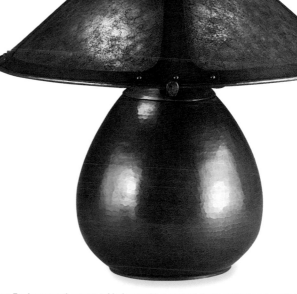

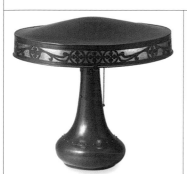

Dirk van Erp hammered copper table lamp with a shade pierced with quatrefoils and foliate scrolls over mica panels. New mica and patina. "Open box" mark and "San Francisco".

48.5cm (19in) wide

£8,500–10,000 DRA

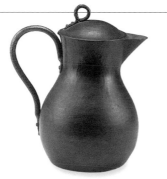

Dirk van Erp rare hammered copper ewer with sparrow beak spout and hinged cover. Original reddish-brown patina. "Closed box" mark with remnant of "D'Arcy Gaw".

30cm (11¾in) high

£3,000–4,000 CR

Dirk van Erp hammered copper table lamp with a conical shade pierced and applied with four original mica panels. With a newly patinated surface and an "open box" maker's mark.

45.5cm (18in) high

£8,000–10,000 CR

American Silver and Metalware

The Arts and Crafts movement, which celebrated handicraft traditions and rejected mass production, took root in England in the last quarter of the 19th century and its ideals soon spread to the United States. By the early 1900s, well-crafted, straightforward designs that drew inspiration from nature were being created by American metalware craftsmen. Silver and metalware companies, such as the Heintz Art Metal Shop and Roycroft, employed traditional craftsmen to create Art Nouveau lines of hand-wrought silver, copper, bronze, and pewter that were influenced by the Arts and Crafts style.

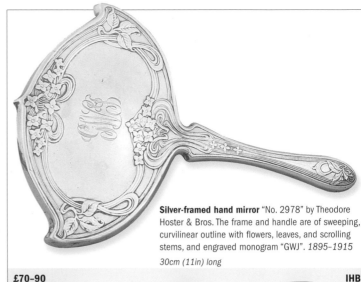

Silver-framed hand mirror "No. 2978" by Theodore Hoster & Bros. The frame and handle are of sweeping, curvilinear outline with flowers, leaves, and scrolling stems, and engraved monogram "GWJ". *1895–1915*

30cm (11in) long

£70–90   IHB

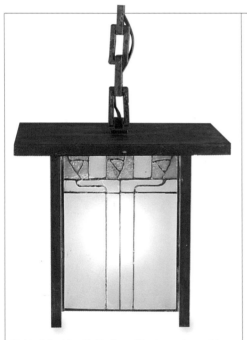

Prairie School hanging lantern with a bronze frame. It has an overhanging, convex sided top above four corner posts supporting frosted glass panels, which are decorated with Glasgow rose motifs with elongated, rectilinear trailing stems.

30.5cm (12in) high

£1,400–1,700   CR

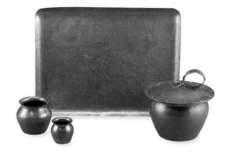

Jarvie smoking set comprising a humidor, matchbook holder, cigarette container, and rectangular tray, all in hammered copper with a lustrous mellow patina, and marked "The Jarvie Shop". The humidor has a riveted cover.

Tray: 40cm (15¾in) wide

£1,700–2,300   CR

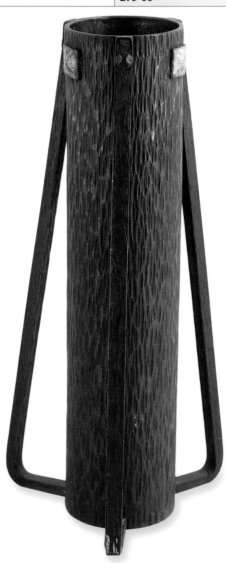

Roycrofters copper vase designed by Karl Kipp, with four buttressed handles attached to the base and rim, a tubular body with a hammered faux woodgrain and lacquered finish, and four, square silver highlights under the rim. *1908–10*

20.5cm (8in) high

£2,500–4,000   CR

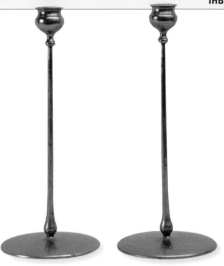

Jarvie bronze candlesticks, each with a candle cup of bulbous, ovoid form with a flaring rim. Set on a long, slender stem with a small ball knop under the cup, and flaring to a larger bulbous knop above a broad, circular foot.

34.5cm (13½in) high

£750–950   JDJ

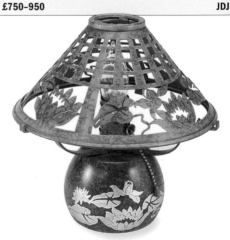

Heintz boudoir lamp in sterling-on-bronze. The bulbous base has an overlaid waterlily pattern, and the flared, circular shade has cut-out waterlily motifs and a trellis pattern (missing silk liner). The shade displays a heavy verdigris patina.

24cm (9½in) high

£1,600–1,800   CR

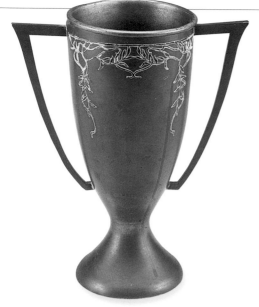

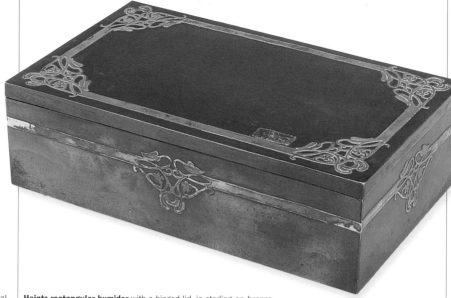

Heintz trophy cup in sterling-on-bronze. Its ovoid body tapers to a conical foot, flanked by slender, angular handles and decorated with scrolling, interlaced, and trailing vines. Stamped "HAMS" on the base with a patent.

28.5cm (11¼in) high

£100–200　　　　　　　　　　　　　　　　　　　　**CR**

Heintz rectangular humidor with a hinged lid, in sterling-on-bronze. The exterior of the lid and the sides are bordered with sinuously scrolling and interlaced flower, leaf, and stem imagery. The interior retains its original cedar lining. Stamped "HAMS" with a patent.

25.5cm (10in) wide

£180–320　　　　　　　　　　　　　　　　　　　　**CR**

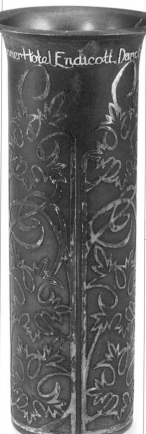

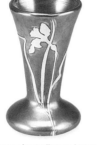

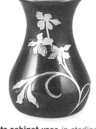

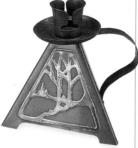

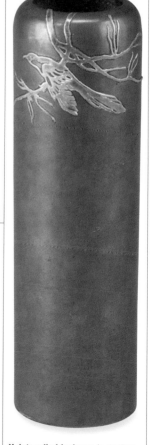

Heintz vase in sterling-on-bronze. Its brightly polished, trumpet-shaped body, with domed foot, is overlaid with a jonquil floral pattern.

16.5cm (6½in) high

£70–150　　　　　　　**CR**

Early Heintz chamberstick of pyramid form, with a floral-motif candle cup, a whiplash handle, and an overlaid landscape pattern.

10cm (4in) high

£400–500　　　　　　　**CR**

Heintz cabinet vase in sterling-on-bronze. The waisted ovoid body has an overlaid violet floral pattern. Stamped "HAMS" with a patent.

10cm (4in) high

£180–250　　　　　　　**CR**

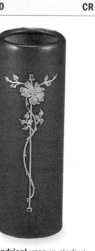

Heintz cylindrical vase in sterling-on-bronze, overlaid with scrolling plant forms, and inscribed "Winner Hotel Endicott Dance Contest". Some verdigris patina on rim.

25.5cm (10in) high

£400–500　　　　　　　**CR**

Heintz cylindrical vase in sterling-on-bronze, with flared and rolled rim and an overlaid bulrush pattern on verdigris patina.

15cm (6in) high

£250–350　　　　　　　**CR**

Heintz cylindrical vase with overlaid floral motifs with trailing stems, and some verdigris patina. Stamped "HAMS".

19cm (7½in) high

£200–275　　　　　　　**CR**

Heintz cylindrical vase in sterling-on-bronze, with a naturalistic overlaid climbing rose pattern, and a rich bronze patina.

15cm (6in) high

£300–400　　　　　　　**CR**

Heintz cylindrical vase in sterling-on-bronze with a mottled bronze patina and overlaid bird-on-a-branch pattern, under and over the rim. Stamped "HAMS" with a patent.

25.5cm (10in) high

£250–300　　　　　　　**CR**

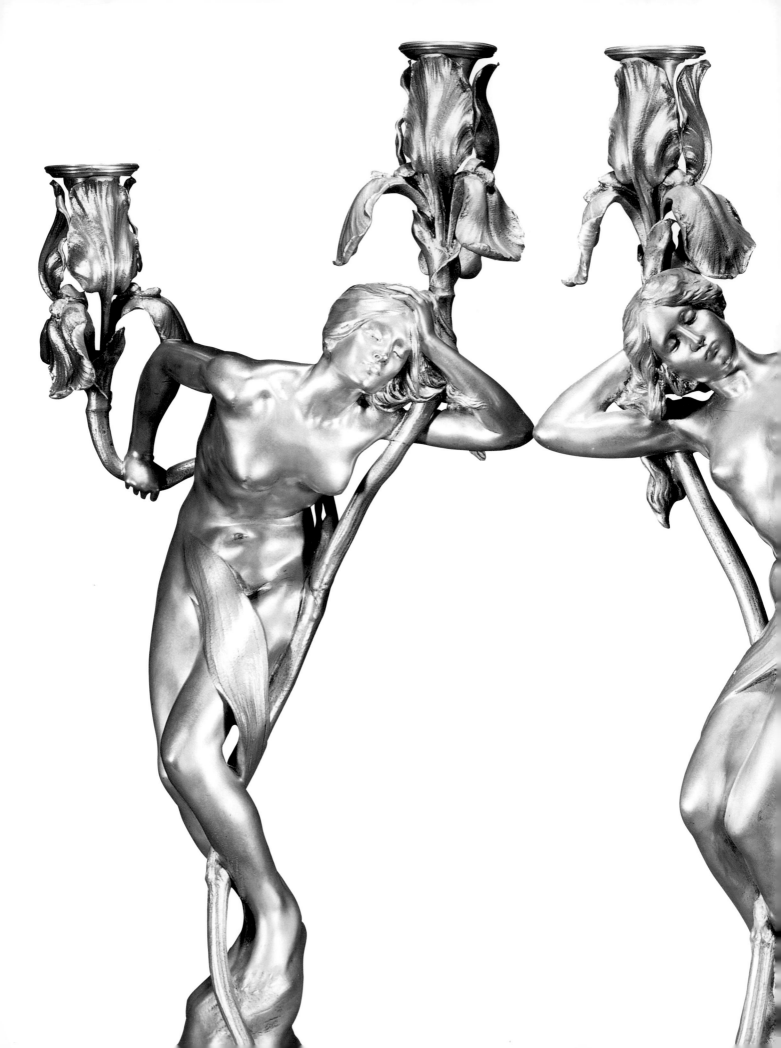

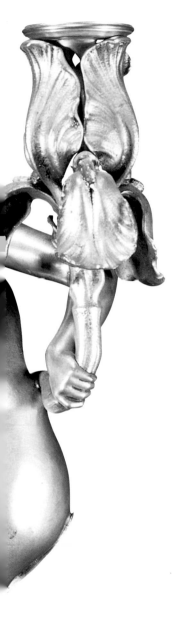

Sculpture

Until the late 19th century, French sculpture was dominated by traditional, classical forms and was usually commissioned to glorify the achievements of the State. The innovations in the decorative arts brought about by Art Nouveau, freed sculptors from the constraints of tradition, introducing new themes and materials, and made sculpture accessible to a far wider range of people.

Art Nouveau sculpture was mainly a French, and indeed Parisian phenomenon. By the 1890s, the French middle classes were looking for sculpture and other decorative objects to furnish their houses and show off their wealth, and they wanted pieces in the latest styles.

WINDS OF CHANGE

As the Art Nouveau style spread through Europe, sculptors began to adopt some of its themes, such as nature, symbolism, and the adoration of the female form, and translate them into their own work. Inspired by the innovative work in other areas of the arts, they broke away from the classical ideal of sculpture taught at the Ecole des Beaux-Arts in Paris and started to create sensuous figures and busts of naked or semi-clad maidens entwined with flowers and dancing women surrounded with billowing drapery.

IMPACT OF INDUSTRY

The invention of the pantograph in 1838 meant that statues could be reproduced in series, and in different sizes, bringing sculpture within reach of a much wider market than previously. One of the tenets of Art Nouveau was that artists should not restrict their output, but work in as many areas of the decorative arts as possible; sculptors responded to this by designing a wide variety of sculptural objects for the home. The increasing demand for sculpture was met with enthusiasm by foundries, which commissioned sculptors specifically to create work in the flowing Art Nouveau style.

The popularity of the archetypal figures of sensual maidens began to decline around 1910, but the female figure and its use as a decorative sculptural object formed the model for the stylized Art Deco pieces of the 1920s and 30s.

Maurice Bouval gilt-bronze candelabras entitled "Obsession" and "Reve", each with a partially clad female form flanked by stems that terminate with iris-bloom sconces. On spreading circular bases above black and green streaked onyx stands. *c.1898. 45.5cm (18in) high* **£14,000–16,000 CHR**

FEMMES-FLEUR

As in all the decorative arts, nature was one of the main inspirations behind Art Nouveau sculpture, taking form in swirling flowers with sinuous stems and voluptuous leaves, butterflies, dragonflies, and the crests of waves. A sense of movement was all-pervasive, conveyed by rhythmic lines and whiplash curves in characteristic Art Nouveau style.

However, the female form reigned supreme as a decorative theme, and remains the most celebrated image of Art Nouveau sculpture. From slender nymphs to sensuous, erotic versions of the *fin-de-siècle* femme fatale, she is portrayed dancing, rising from the waves, or swooning in a mysterious trance evocative of Pre-Raphaelite paintings and the Symbolist movement. She is often modelled metamorphosing from the blossom of a plant, a symbolic creature known as a femme-fleur (flower woman), who draws her strength from nature.

SCULPTURE IN THE HOME

The female figure was used not only as a decorative statuette or portrait bust but was also incorporated into a wide variety of sculptural household objects, such as inkwells, vases, candelabra, clocks, and especially table lamps. The invention of the electric light bulb gave sculptors a chance to design light fittings,

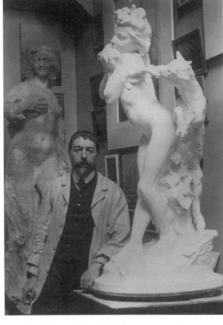

Raoul Larche was famed for his monumental architectural sculpture throughout Paris, and for his "salon" pieces sought by a burgeoning body of collectors.

creating a minor new art form. The figure of a nymph, or her robes, was often used to conceal the wires, light bulb, or mechanism of a lamp, and she frequently held the glass or shell lampshade in her hands, casting the glow of the lamp onto the modelling of her face or arms.

MATERIALS OLD AND NEW

The use of traditional materials combined with unexpected new materials was a hallmark of Art Nouveau sculpture. Bronze was the most popular metal, often gilded to make it brighter, but many sculptors also worked in marble, terracotta, porcelain, or stone, sometimes mixing several media together in one piece. Ivory was a favourite

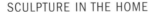

Louis Chalon "Sea Maidens" bronze vase of shouldered oviform cast with swirling waves from which emerge three maidens joining hands and wearing diaphanous robes festooned with aquatic foliage. *c.1900. 44cm (17½in) high* **£3,000–6,000 Soth**

DEFINITIVE STYLES

The Art Nouveau style of sculpture was predominantly naturalistic with a preponderance for the female form. Besides busts and models, we also see sculptural elements embellishing vases – for example, handles formed from lithe torsos. Figural lamps based on topical personalities, literary, or mythological subjects were fashionable, as reflected in Gurschner's formalized mermaid lamp that utilizes a natural shell as the shade (see right).

Charles Korschann gilt bronze desk lamp modelled as a young woman with robes flowing around her lower body onto a shaped pen tray that incorporates an inkwell. She holds an iris bloom that conceals the bulb. *c.1900 34cm (13½in) high* **£6,000–8,000 Soth**

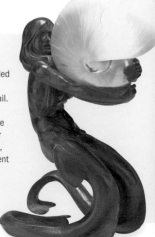

Gustav Gurschner bronze table lamp, sinuously modelled as the kneeling figure of a mermaid supported on her tail. She clutches a pale nautilus shell that acts as a decorative shade. It was made by Arthur Krupp, K.K. Kunst-Erzgießerei, Vienna, and has a replacement shell. *c.1900 26.7cm (10½in) high* **£5,000–6,000 Qu**

material with Art Nouveau sculptors, particularly Belgian ones, as it had become widely available after the opening up of the Belgian Congo in the late 1890s. Sculptors made the most of its sculptural qualities and luminosity, often combining it with bronze that had been patinated to provide a more striking contrast.

CAPITAL OF SCULPTURE

Aspiring sculptors from all over Europe were drawn to Paris. One sculptor, Raoul-François Larche, created table lamps featuring the American dancer Loïe Fuller, who performed dances with swirling veils at the Folies Bergères. The lamps, with their powerful sense of movement, soon became renowned as one of the best interpretations of the Art Nouveau style.

Other sculptors, such as Pierre Roche and the Belgian Agathon Léonard, also created pieces featuring dancers in long dresses. Maurice Bouval worked with many different foundries, creating busts, candelabra, and decorative objects featuring maidens draped with flowers and leaves or *femmes-fleur* emerging from plants.

When Siegfried Bing assembled the first exhibition of sculpture at L'Art Nouveau in 1895, he presented an international view of Art Nouveau, illustrating how sculpture had escaped the constraints of the classical tradition.

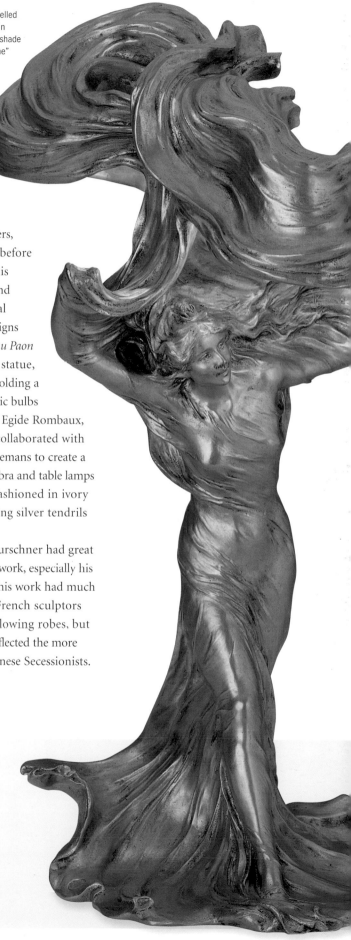

Raoul Larche gilt bronze lamp modelled as the dancer Loïe Fuller, swathed in diaphanous robes that form the lampshade above her head. Signed "Raoul Larche" with a Siot-Decauville foundry mark.
c.1900. 45cm (17¾in) high
£15,000–20,000 AKG

IVORY MAIDENS

In Belgium, Philippe Wolfers, who trained as a sculptor before becoming renowned for his jewellery, created bronze and ivory statuettes and figural lamps. His memorable designs include the celebrated *Fée au Paon* (Woman with a Peacock) statue, featuring a nude maiden holding a bronze peacock with electric bulbs illuminating the bird's tail. Egide Rombaux, also working in Brussels, collaborated with the silversmith Frans Hoosemans to create a series of decorative candelabra and table lamps featuring nude maidens fashioned in ivory and entwined within coiling silver tendrils and flower stems.

The Austrian Gustav Gurschner had great success with his sculptural work, especially his table lamps. Thematically his work had much in common with that of French sculptors and featured maidens in flowing robes, but his restrained use of line reflected the more geometric style of the Viennese Secessionists.

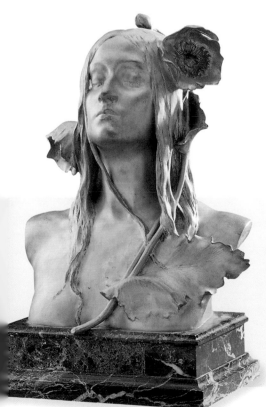

Left: Maurice Bouval "Ophelia" gilt bronze bust, modelled as the head and shoulders of a maiden with eyes closed as if in repose. Her hair is dressed with large full-blown poppies, mounted on a rectangular variegated marble base. Signed "M. Bouval" and stamped "E. Colin & Cie/Paris".
c.1900. 43.3cm (17in) high **NPA CHR**

KEY FEATURES

Household objects (including table lamps, ashtrays, inkwells, and cache-pots) boasting charming Art Nouveau sculpture that is integral to the design, are typical of the work of Raoul-François Larche.

Sumptuous materials are used, including gilt bronze, pewter, biscuit porcelain, stone, and terracotta.

Figurines portray a wide range of subjects: from dancing maidens inspired by Loïe Fuller, to groups of peasant girls; from sword-bearing young men, to sea nymphs and mythological deities.

Raoul Larche

Among the artists who championed the French philosophy of *L'art dans tout* – that household objects should be beautiful as well as functional – was the talented and prolific Art Nouveau sculptor Raoul-François Larche.

Having studied at the Ecole des Beaux-Arts in Paris before making his debut in 1881 at the Salon of the Société des Artistes Français, Larche took to heart the revolutionary idea that everyday objects should also be aesthetically pleasing.

Included in his oeuvre were lighting fixtures that incorporated his sculptural designs. Particularly famous was the gilt-bronze table lamp that made dancer Loïe Fuller – who used electric lights and billowing drapery in her shows at the Folies-Bergères – integral to the design (*see left and above*).

Larche worked in a wide variety of materials – pewter, bronze, biscuit porcelain, terracotta, and stone. A posthumous exhibition of his work revealed the dazzling dimensions of his talent, featuring figurines of youths brandishing swords, sea nymphs clasping shells, busts of mythological deities, and groups of charming peasant girls. A number of sculptures were executed during his tenure at the Sèvres Porcelain Factory at the turn of the 20th century.

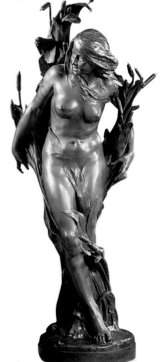

Above: Gilt bronze lamp, modelled as the dancer Loïe Fuller, swathed in diaphanous robes that form the lampshade above her head. Signed "Raoul Larche" with Siot-Decauville foundry mark. *c.1900. 45cm (17¼in) high* **£15,000–20,000 Soth**

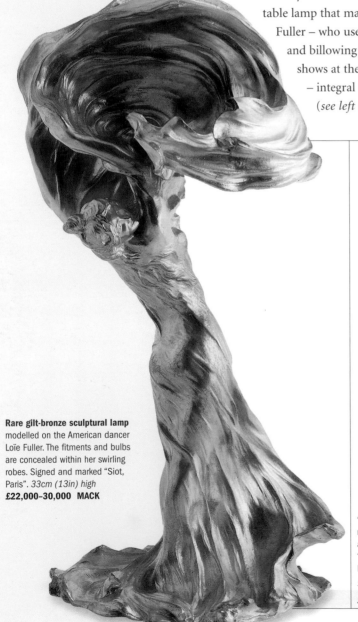

Rare gilt-bronze sculptural lamp modelled on the American dancer Loïe Fuller. The fitments and bulbs are concealed within her swirling robes. Signed and marked "Siot, Paris". *33cm (13in) high* **£22,000–30,000 MACK**

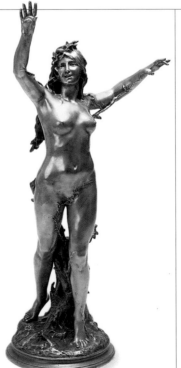

"La Sève" gilt-bronze figure modelled as the nymph Daphne, who, having spurned Apollo's advances, was turned into a laurel tree. Signed "Raoul Larche" with foundry marks for "Siot-Decauville Fondeur Paris".

95.5cm (37½in) high

£10,000–15,000	Qu

Nude in Rushes, a brown patinated bronze of a naked female nymph, emerging from tall branches of bulrushes that partly conceal her nakedness. *c.1900*

74cm (29in) high

£4,000–6,000	Soth

Maurice Bouval

One of the most memorable and easily recognizable images of Art Nouveau sculpture – the figures of women known as *femmes-fleur* – received considerable attention in the gifted hands of the sculptor Maurice Bouval.

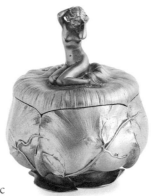

Maurice Bouval, whose work featured in exhibitions mounted at the Salon of the Société des Artistes Français and at the Goldscheider firm in Vienna, followed a more traditional path in his Art Nouveau designs for evocative bronze sculptures celebrating the female form. His sinuous, asymmetrical, semi-clad maidens with long, flowing hair drew inspiration from the Symbolist movement that percolated through art and literature in the 1880s. Many of his most successful designs featuring these voluptuous maidens – the bust of Ophelia with its heavy-lidded eyes or the enigmatic statuette known as "Le Secret", for example – are embellished with such naturalistic motifs as waterlilies, poppies, and lotus blossoms.

Bouval did not confine his sculptural designs to busts and figurines. Like many contemporaries, he embraced the *L'art dans tout* philosophy that had sprung up in 1890s France, stating that household objects should be both aesthetic and functional.

Above: Gilt-bronze covered bowl embellished with leaves and flowering stems. The cover has a nude female finial. Signed and marked "Jollet et Cie, Paris". *15cm (6in) high*
£5,000–7,000 MACK

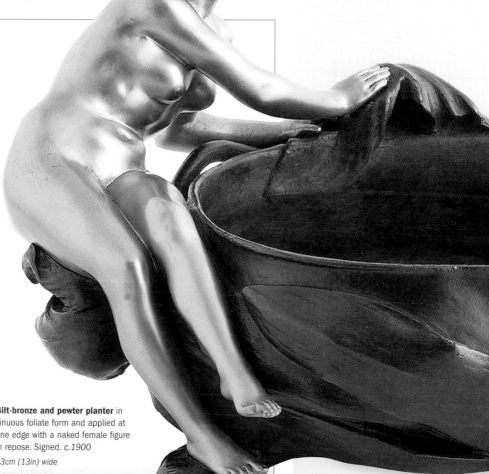

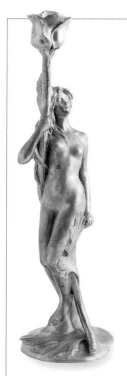

Gilt-bronze candlestick modelled as a naked maiden with leaves entwined around her. She holds the stem of a large flower, its bloom forming the sconce. Signed.
40cm (15¾in) high
£5,000–7,700 MACK

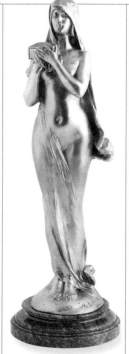

Gilt-bronze female figure (possibly Pandora), whose robes are parted to reveal her naked body beneath. On a stepped and striated green-marble base.
38cm (15in) high
£5,000–7,000 MACK

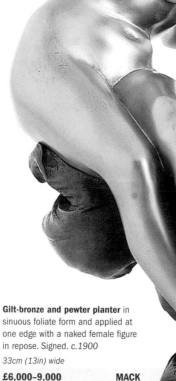

Gilt-bronze and pewter planter in sinuous foliate form and applied at one edge with a naked female figure in repose. Signed. *c.1900*
33cm (13in) wide
£6,000–9,000 MACK

French and Belgian Sculpture

In the late 19th century, French sculpture centred on Paris, where artists from across Europe gathered to study at the Ecole des Beaux-Arts and exhibit their work at the annual Salons. A small but pioneering band of Art Nouveau sculptors – including Maurice Bouval and Raoul Larche and, in Belgium, Phillippe Wolfers and Egide Rombaux – challenged the traditional classical idiom by creating statuettes and household objects in marble, stone, terracotta, and bronze, often inspired by nature. Drawing on the broad vocabulary of Art Nouveau motifs for both form and decoration, these innovative sculptors created a range of ornamental ware that boldly exploited the new art with originality and panache.

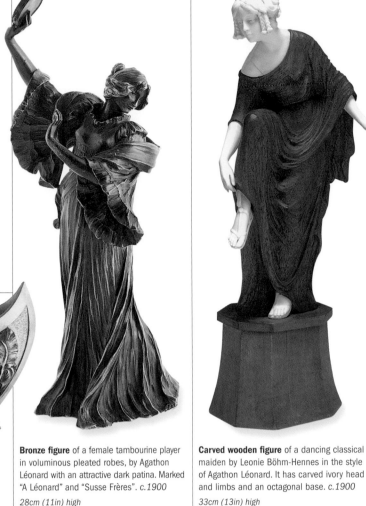

Bronze figure of a female tambourine player in voluminous pleated robes, by Agathon Léonard with an attractive dark patina. Marked "A Léonard" and "Susse Frères". *c.1900*

28cm (11in) high

£11,000–15,000   MACK

Carved wooden figure of a dancing classical maiden by Leonie Böhm-Hennes in the style of Agathon Léonard. It has carved ivory head and limbs and an octagonal base. *c.1900*

33cm (13in) high

£2,500–3,000   Qu

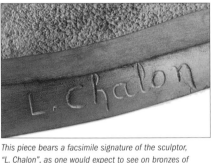

This piece bears a facsimile signature of the sculptor, "L. Chalon", as one would expect to see on bronzes of this quality from this period.

Silvered and gilt-bronze figural vase by Louis Chalon. It features a maiden, her hair dressed with irises and wearing a revealing diaphanous gown. She stands before a winged-shape vessel, embellished with further iris blooms. *c.1900*

40cm (15¾in) high

£9,000–13,000   MACK

"Carthage" by Theodore-Riviere: a bronze and ivory figure of Sarah Bernhardt as Salammbô, with her servant Matho at her feet. Inscribed "Theodore-Riviere" with foundry marks.

36cm (14in) high

£2,500–4,500   SI

Patinated metal mantel clock by A. de Ranier, with a circular enamel dial painted with flowers. The case is of organic form, embellished with leaves and dragonflies and flanked by a willowy maiden in diaphanous robes. It is signed on the base.

58cm (22¾in) high

£700–900 L&T

Bronze naked female figure by Fournier. She stands with an outstretched arm, on which a ball is balanced, above a black base of square section. Signed "Fournier". *c.1900*

37.5cm (14¾in) high

£600–800 VZ

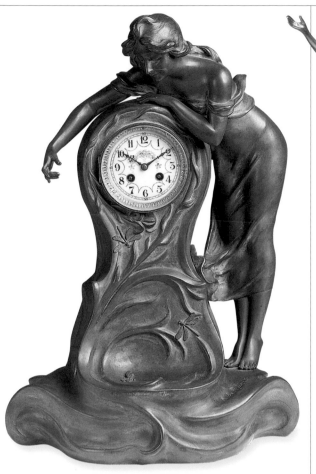

Silvered bronze bust of a maiden by Léopold Savine. The pedestal is embellished with peacock feathers with peacocks at the base.

39cm (15½in) high

£2,000–4,000 MACK

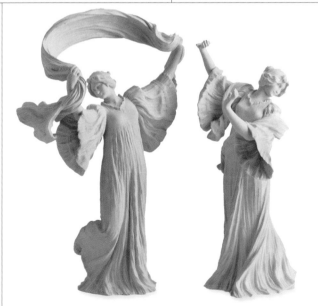

Sèvres bisque porcelain figurines by Agathon Léonard, depicting a tambourine player and a dancer, from a set consisting of 14 female figures dancing and playing music. Incised "Sèvres" and numbered "No.4" and "No.12".

Tallest: 36cm (14in) high

£4,500–7,500 (the pair) MACK

"Le Secret" gilt-bronze figure by Pierre Fix Masseau. A partially cloaked nude holds a mysterious box and, with finger to lips, enjoins silence. Signed and marked "Siot Decauville, Paris".

61.5cm (24¼in) high

£7,500–11,000 MACK

201

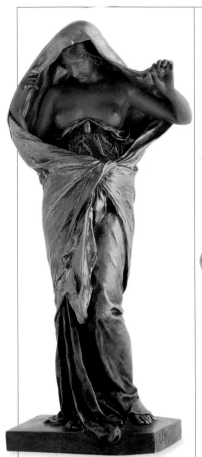

"Nature Revealing Herself Before Science" by Louis-Ernest Barrias. Partially gilt and silvered bronze of a young woman. Signed "E. Barrias"; produced by Susse Frères. *1893*

63.5cm (25in) high

£13,000–15,000   **DOR**

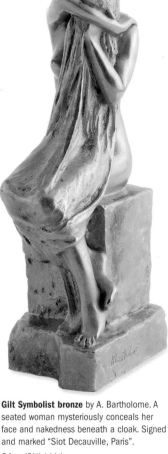

Gilt Symbolist bronze by A. Bartholome. A seated woman mysteriously conceals her face and nakedness beneath a cloak. Signed and marked "Siot Decauville, Paris".

24cm (9¼in) high

£2,500–4,000   **MACK**

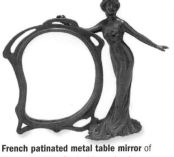

French patinated metal table mirror of sinuous outline, flanked by a slender woman in a long strapless dress. The mirror glass is probably a replacement. Unsigned. *c.1900*

18cm (7in) high

£600–800   **Qu**

Maillard Symbolist inkwell of silvered and gilded bronze, modelled as an oyster shell, revealing a naked maiden resting beside the ink reservoir. With a Jollet Paris foundry mark.

£2,800–3,500   **Sty**

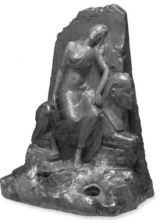

Bronze glazed earthenware classical female figure resting on a Sphinx, by Henri Louis Levasseur; produced by Emile Muller. Signed "H. Levasseur" and "E. Muller". *c.1895*

42cm (16½in) high

£800–1,200   **Qu**

Gilt-bronze bust by A. Cuenard depicting an elegant woman with an elaborate hairstyle and dress. Picked out with turquoises and red stone insets. Signed.

16.5cm (6½in) high

£1,500–2,250   **CALD**

"Reverie" bronze figure of a classical girl by Podany. Her hair is in a chignon, and she rests pensively on a rocky outcrop. Signed and marked on the base.

60cm (23½in) high

£9,000–13,500   **CALD**

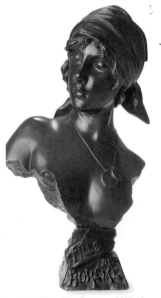

"Fille de Bohème" by Emmanuel Villanis. Bronze bust of a young girl wearing a head scarf and a necklace, with brown patination. Signed "E. Villanis". *c.1900*

47cm (18½in) high

£800–1,200   **VZ**

Gilded-bronze figural lamp by Victor Rousseau, of a young woman, possibly Loïe Fuller, with a billowing veil forming a shade. Signed "Rousseau". *c.1900*

42cm (16½in) high

£3,500–4,500   **Qu**

Gilt-bronze figural lamp by Antonio Bofill, modelled as a robed young woman holding a Japanese lantern (made of Daum glass). Signed "Bofill"; shade signed "Daum Nancy".

38cm (15in) high

£22,000–37,000   **MACK**

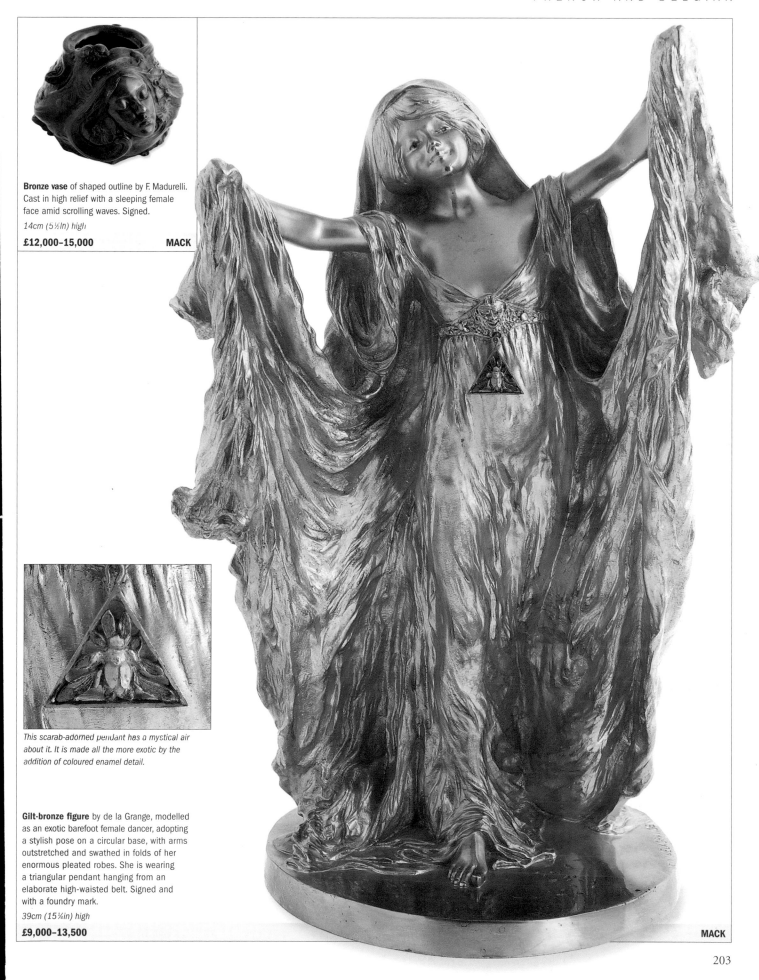

Bronze vase of shaped outline by F. Madurelli.
Cast in high relief with a sleeping female
face amid scrolling waves. Signed.

14cm (5½in) high

£12,000–15,000　　　　**MACK**

*This scarab-adorned pendant has a mystical air
about it. It is made all the more exotic by the
addition of coloured enamel detail.*

Gilt-bronze figure by de la Grange, modelled
as an exotic barefoot female dancer, adopting
a stylish pose on a circular base, with arms
outstretched and swathed in folds of her
enormous pleated robes. She is wearing
a triangular pendant hanging from an
elaborate high-waisted belt. Signed and
with a foundry mark.

39cm (15¼in) high

£9,000–13,500　　　　**MACK**

German and Austrian Sculpture

In the late 19th century, Paris was considered to be the unrivalled centre for Art Nouveau sculpture, enticing aspiring sculptors from throughout Europe. Elsewhere, Art Nouveau sculpture appeared only occasionally, with artists such as Gustav Gurschner in Austria or Germany's Thomas Theodor Heine in Munich bringing their unique vision to sculpture in the new style.

The popular Art Nouveau subject of a sensuous maiden – seen nude or dressed in a diaphanous gown – was a favourite for free-standing bronze figurines. Bronze was often combined with other materials, including glass or marble, and incorporated into decorative domestic objects, such as table lamps and inkwells.

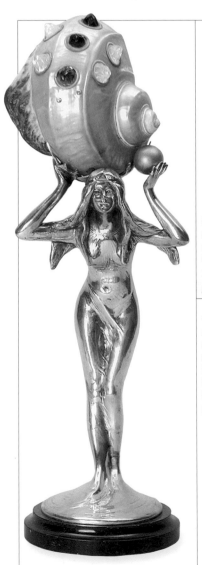

Austrian plated-metal figural lamp in the manner of Gurschner. The naked maiden holds an iridescent glass ball and conch-shell shade with art-glass jewels.
57cm (22½in) high

£3,500–4,500 JDJ

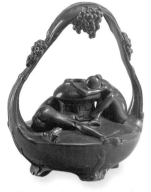

Franz Bergmann bronze vase, modelled around the rim with a naked man and woman, possibly Adam and Eve, with a loop handle embellished with grapes and vines. *c.1900*
16cm (6¼in) high

£700–1,000 HERR

Brown patinated bronze figure of a dancer by Rudolf Küchler. She is wearing a long sleeveless dress that swirls about her. The oval base is signed "R. Küchler". *c.1900*
59.5cm (23½in) high

£2,500–3,000 VZ

Gilt-bronze slender table lamp by Paul Tereszczuk, embellished in relief with a willowy maiden reaching towards two frosted-glass, flower-form shades. Signed. *c.1900*
52.5cm (20¾in) high

£2,600–3,200 Qu

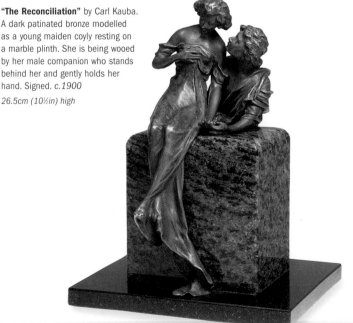

"The Reconciliation" by Carl Kauba. A dark patinated bronze modelled as a young maiden coyly resting on a marble plinth. She is being wooed by her male companion who stands behind her and gently holds her hand. Signed. *c.1900*
26.5cm (10½in) high

£500–700 BMN

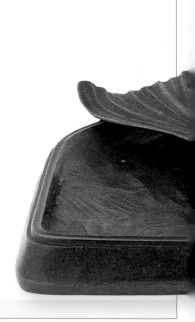

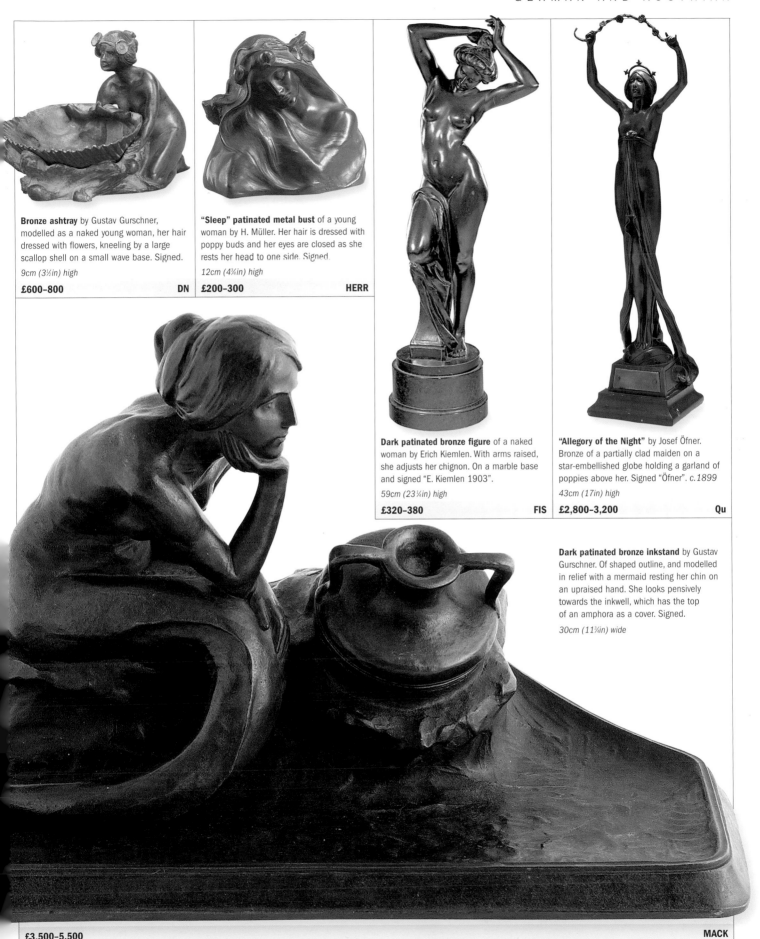

Bronze ashtray by Gustav Gurschner, modelled as a naked young woman, her hair dressed with flowers, kneeling by a large scallop shell on a small wave base. Signed.

9cm (3½in) high

£600–800   DN

"Sleep" patinated metal bust of a young woman by H. Müller. Her hair is dressed with poppy buds and her eyes are closed as she rests her head to one side. Signed.

12cm (4¾in) high

£200–300   HERR

Dark patinated bronze figure of a naked woman by Erich Kiemlen. With arms raised, she adjusts her chignon. On a marble base and signed "E. Kiemlen 1903".

59cm (23¼in) high

£320–380   FIS

"Allegory of the Night" by Josef Öfner. Bronze of a partially clad maiden on a star-embellished globe holding a garland of poppies above her. Signed "Öfner". *c.1899*

43cm (17in) high

£2,800–3,200   Qu

Dark patinated bronze inkstand by Gustav Gurschner. Of shaped outline, and modelled in relief with a mermaid resting her chin on an upraised hand. She looks pensively towards the inkwell, which has the top of an amphora as a cover. Signed.

30cm (11¾in) wide

£3,500–5,500   MACK

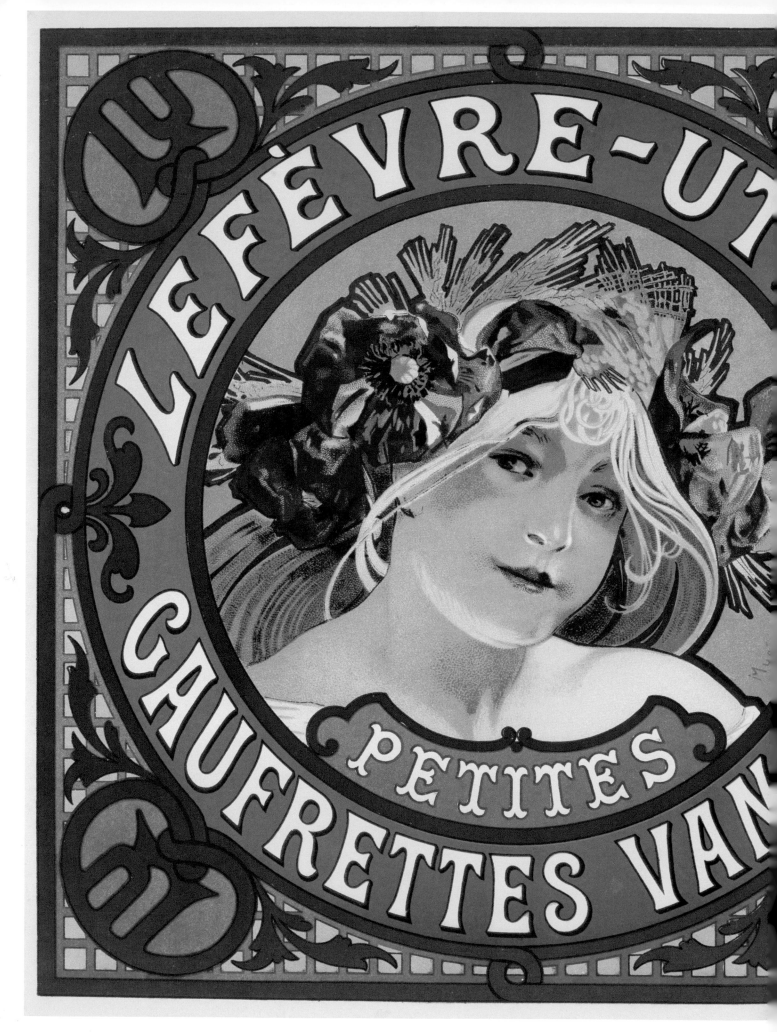

Posters and Graphics

From about 1890 to 1900, the general public was assailed by Art Nouveau posters splashed across hoardings and buildings. The posters ranged from bold, decorative images to a quieter, more reflective style. Although produced as a form of advertising, they reflected the artistic trends of the time and were just as much of an art form as any work on display in a gallery.

Posters and Art Nouveau came of age at roughly the same time, and it was through the medium of posters that the style was able to spread so quickly and with such enormous success.

STREET ART

Posters became a widespread art form in the late 1880s, after developments in colour lithography enabled artists and publishers to print large runs of a design. They soon became a hugely popular phenomenon. This art of the street was the first truly democratic art form, as it was available to everyone. It was also a great opportunity for artists, allowing book illustrators and unknown designers to create posters and make a name for themselves. This was an incredible break from the recent past, where art had been available only to a wealthy few. It soon became clear that the public could not get enough of these new, bold, colourful images, and posters

became an overnight sensation. Magazines were founded to follow the growing craze of poster collecting, and print dealers in Paris began offering posters for sale alongside fine art lithographs and other prints. According to some accounts, eager collectors would even run out into the streets under cover of darkness and soak newly hung posters off the hoardings with wet sponges.

AN INFLUENTIAL MEDIUM

A few years after they first appeared, posters became instrumental in spreading the Art Nouveau style. They were so popular that when Art Nouveau themes and motifs began appearing on them, the artists were assured of a widespread audience. In turn, this vast audience helped to spread the interest in Art Nouveau across the countries of Europe, and even across the Atlantic Ocean to the United States.

Alphonse Mucha "Lefevre Utile Gaufrettes Vanille", chromolithographic advertising retail label for the lid of a biscuit box. *c.1910. 18cm (7in) wide* **NPA COR**

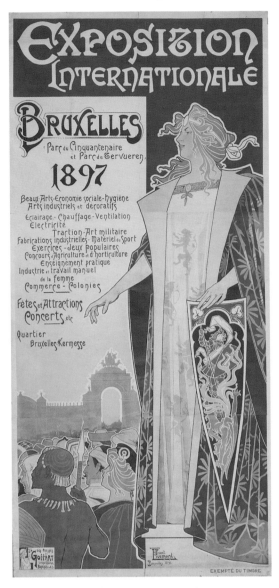

Poster for the 1897 International Exposition
in Brussels, designed by Privat-Livemont. It shows
a young woman with her long hair tied back, wearing
medieval costume with heraldic motifs. She is holding a
shield and overlooking a multicultural crowd entering the
exhibition. *275cm (107¼in) high* **£1,800–2,200 SWA**

A NEW ART FORM

Jules Chéret is generally accepted as the
"Father of the Poster". He refined the
lithographic method of transferring ink
from stone to paper, enabling posters to
be printed in a rainbow of colours. Aware
that, as a piece of advertising, the function
of the poster was to capture the public's
attention, Chéret's designs were
purposely vibrant, with eye-catching
imagery and arresting colours. Women
dominated his posters, and were always
portrayed as vivacious and lively. Much-
loved by Parisians, these radiant females
became referred to as "Chérettes", and
his posters were highly sought after
during his lifetime.

"LE STYLE MUCHA"

Many artists saw the poster as a new
form of artistic expression, and artists
such as Pierre Bonnard and Henri de
Toulouse-Lautrec were drawn to the
medium. However, it was the posters of
Alphonse Mucha, a relatively unknown,
Czech-born book illustrator, which are
today regarded as the quintessential Art
Nouveau posters.

Mucha designed a poster for
Gismonda, a play being performed by
the legendary actress Sarah Bernhardt.
This unexpected and revolutionary
image not only ignited the poster-
collecting community but, quite literally,
and accidentally, gave Art Nouveau
a visual spokesman in Mucha.

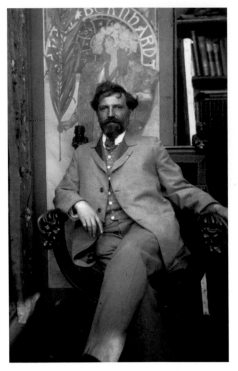

Alphonse Mucha, the celebrated Czech artist, sitting in his
studio before one of the theatrical posters he designed for
Gismonda featuring the actress Sarah Bernhardt.

Mucha's work is full of glorious patterns: he
could take the simplest items, such as the fold
of a dress, the smoke from a cigarette, or wheat
in a field, infuse them with a sensual liveliness,
and make them a central, decorative element of
a design. Mucha's style was so popular that Art
Nouveau was often referred to as *Le Style Mucha*.

THE PARISIAN CONTRIBUTION

But if Mucha was the visual spokesman for
the movement, the scholar was Eugene Grasset,
whose works reflected a Pre-Raphaelite
sensibility and the marked influence of William

DEFINITIVE DESIGN

*The first true art for the masses, posters began to be
produced by highly skilled graphic artists and proved
extremely popular from the 1880s onwards. They
became a hugely successful advertising medium
for a wide range of products: from fine art exhibitions
to light bulbs and from theatre productions to coffee.
Even the most ordinary, everyday products were
transformed into things of beauty at the hands of
the Art Nouveau poster designers – some opting
for the flowing female forms, while others worked
in the more rectilinear style.*

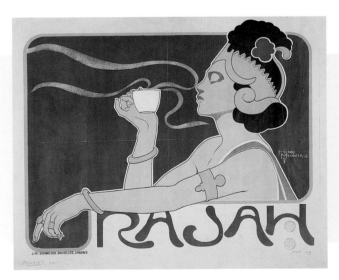

Poster for "Rajah Coffee", by Henri
Meunier, featuring the profile head and
shoulders of a South American priestess
savouring the aroma emanating from the
small cup that she holds. The colour used
for the background and typography is
indicative of the product's colour. This
classic example of Belgian Art Nouveau
poster art was considered at the time to
be the artist's best work, "A masterpiece".
1897. 65cm (25in) high
NPA V&A

Morris and the English Arts and Crafts movement. One of Grasset's passions was stained glass windows, and many of his posters reflect this interest. He was a master of heavily patterned and textured designs, and his figures often appear draped in unbelievably complex, decorative clothing.

Another Paris-based artist who contributed memorable designs to the movement was Paul Berthon, who used a soft pastel palette and took it to a representational, abstract level. Yet another was Georges de Feure, a Dutchman of Javanese descent. The women he portrayed were less sensuous than most Art Nouveau women and were often shown in isolation, yet adorned with the most elaborate dresses and hats.

BELGIAN ADVERTISING

The Parisian style of Art Nouveau poster spread to Brussels, where Privat-Livemont, a close follower of Mucha, created promotional illustrations. Although often compared with Mucha, his version of beautiful women with exaggerated flowing hair and his use of delicate shapes and ornamentation bore his own unique imprint. He used a predominantly green palette and gave his subjects a white outline, helping them to stand out from the rest of the design.

Also in Belgium, Fernand Toussaint created richly coloured, flamboyant posters with symbolic overtones, in which elements of Art Nouveau are clearly present.

Poster promoting L. Prang & Co's Holiday Publications, by Louis J. Rhead. It shows a young woman with flowing hair, sitting at a desk and holding Christmas books. *1895 56cm (21¾in) high* **£800–1,200 SWA**

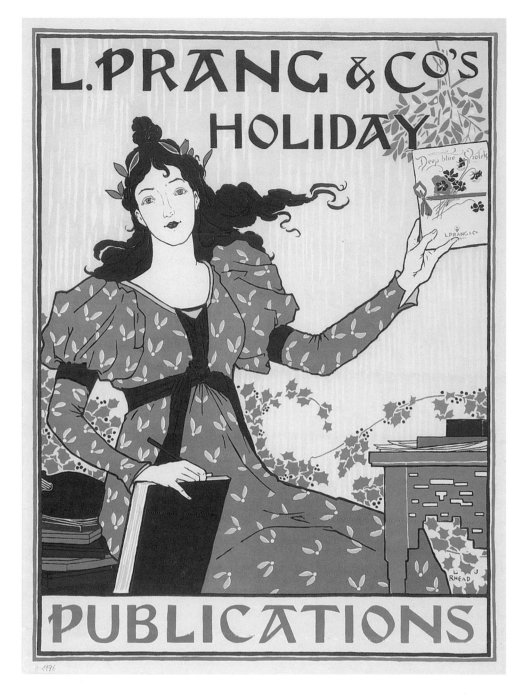

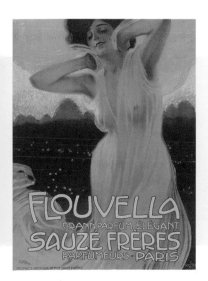

Poster advertising "Flouvella" perfume by the leading parfumier Sauze Frères, designed by Leopoldo Metlicovitz. The woman posing in a diaphanous gown is rendered in soft pastel colours, and is set against a stylized forest, under a pink sky. Such gently erotic promotional imagery is typical of Sauze and other French parfumiers such as Coty, D'Orsay, Bouchon, and Houbigant. *1911. 109.5cm (43in) high* **£2,800–3,200 SWA**

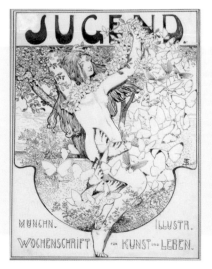

Illustration for the cover of *Jugend*, (an illustrated weekly magazine published in Munich) designed by Josef Rudolf Witzel. Framed behind glass, the lithographic composition in turquoise, black, pink, and yellow shows a young maiden or wood nymph sitting under a tree among wild flowers. She is draped with a garland of flowers, and surrounded by masses of fluttering butterflies. *1896–97. 114.25cm (45in) high* **£2,000–2,200 VZ**

VARIATIONS ON A THEME

The Italian Art Nouveau poster can be traced back to the work of one man, Adolfo Hohenstein. As the art director for the famed Italian printing house Richter and Company, he was able not only to produce masterpieces of his own, many of them posters for the opera, but also to help nurture and influence the talents of a host of important Italian designers, such as Leopoldo Metlicovitz, Franz Laskoff, Leonetto Cappiello, and Marcello Dudovich. By and large, Italian posters were not as ornately decorative as French ones. The design was straightforward (although by no means simple), with Art Nouveau elements beautifully and subtly combined with the rather realistic images. Italian posters were bolder than French posters, with a tendency towards the visually dramatic, and they utilized fewer colours, but their elegance and style is a powerful adaptation of the French model.

German and Austrian poster designs were more geometric in style than anything found in France. The Jugendstil and Secessionist posters adopted an austere, geometric style – characteristics displayed in all of their decorative arts – and artists tended to integrate more creative typography into their designs.

THE BRITISH STYLE

While recognizable Art Nouveau flourishes, such as patterned dresses and flowing, stylized hair, did appear in number of theatre posters (although never with the full force of design that was found in France), Britain's main contribution to the Art Nouveau poster came from two key artists whose work was tremendously influential in France and Austria: Charles Rennie Mackintosh and Aubrey Beardsley. Charles Rennie Mackintosh was primarily an

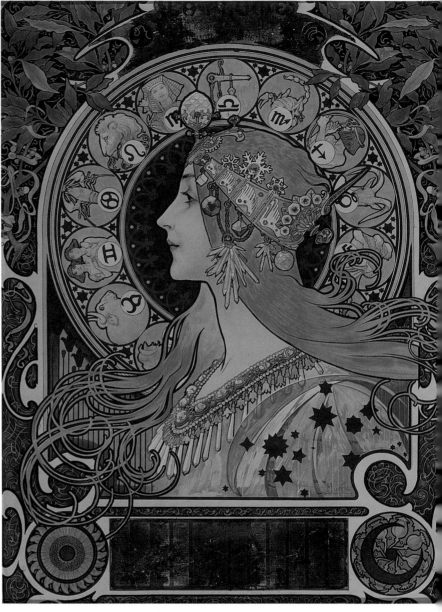

"Zodiac, La Plume" poster designed by Alphonse Mucha. It has the in-profile bust of a young woman with long, whiplashed hair flowing from under a bejewelled headscarf. It is circumscribed by a signs-of-the-zodiac ring, and surrounded by exotic flowers and foliage with scrolling stems, above sun and plant-form motif roundels. *c.1896. 64.75cm (25½in) high* **£3,000–4,500 SI**

GRAPHICS AND MOTIFS

As with all media of the Art Nouveau age, there were different interpretations across the globe. Mucha led the French style with flowing female forms, and his Art Nouveau poster work is perhaps the most well known of this genre. By contrast, the German approach utilized more formalized, figurative and natural imagery, as did Charles Rennie Mackintosh and Aubrey Beardsley in Britain. Typography was also revolutionized in this period, both complementing and adapting to the dramatic new designs.

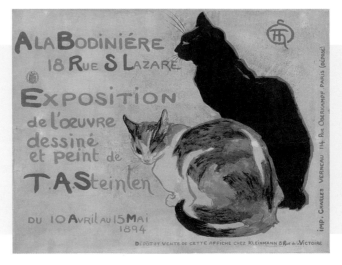

Poster for the 1894 Exposition à la Bodiniére, in Paris, designed by Theophile-Alexandre Steinlen. Animal imagery, especially of birds, dogs, and cats, was prevalent in Art Nouveau poster design. Here, the cats are crayoned in black and in naturalistic tabby colours, against a mottled, parchment-coloured ground. *75.5cm (29¾in) wide* **£3,000–4,000 SWA**

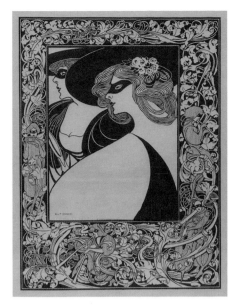

"Woman in Mask" poster by William H. Bradley in the style of Aubrey Beardsley. Two masked women are framed by a decorative border of scrolling flowers and foliage. *48.5cm (19in) high* **£350–400 SWA**

architect who only designed a few posters, each of which bears the linear, angular qualities characteristic of the Glasgow School, but their striking similarity to the posters of the Vienna Secessionists is a tribute to the strength and pervasiveness of his design.

Beardsley, while not received with open arms in Victorian England owing to his close association with Oscar Wilde, was nonetheless a tremendous influence on many of France's Art Nouveau artists, especially Alphonse Mucha. Beardsley's use of strong, controlled line to create graphic forms outlining contrasting areas of flat colour also had a strong impact on one of America's finest poster designers, William Bradley.

THE AMERICAN POSTER

The craze for posters spread from Europe to the United States, where the American poster enjoyed great popularity at the end of the 19th century. Maxfield Parrish was one of the first artists to gain recognition for his Art Nouveau-inspired posters, and designed covers for *Harper's*, *Life*, and *Scribners Magazine*. But William Bradley was America's first, true, home-grown Art Nouveau artist and was clearly influenced by Aubrey Beardsley's design principles, as well as by those of William Morris. His work was typically Art Nouveau, with dynamic sweeping lines and a strong use of colour.

On a trip to Paris, the British-born illustrator Louis John Rhead fell under the spell of the French Art Nouveau master Grasset, and took Grasset's pure French Art Nouveau style to the United States. Rhead's poster designs are characterized by a bold primary palette and daring colour schemes.

Whether in Europe or the United States, posters and Art Nouveau were in many ways a perfect match. Both the medium and the message were the perfect melding of art and industry. In the poster, Art Nouveau found a dynamic new form of artistic expression that lent itself to mass production and thus found true popularity with the public at large.

"Scottish Musical Review" lithographic poster designed by Charles Rennie Mackintosh. It shows a stylized central figure with linear representations of plant forms, flanked by the highly stylized images of swallows in flight. *1896. 230cm (90in) high* **NPA GM**

THE LITHOGRAPHIC PROCESS

The lithographic process is simply the transfer of an image from a stone or metal plate to paper. The artist draws on the plate using crayons or pencils with a high grease content. For each colour in the design, a separate plate is generally required. The printer then chemically treats the final drawing to prepare it for the printing process. Although lithography was invented in 1798, it was at first too slow and expensive for poster production. This all changed with Cheret's three-stone lithographic process. This was a breakthrough that allowed artists to achieve every colour in the rainbow with as little as three stones – usually red, yellows, and blue – printed in careful registration.

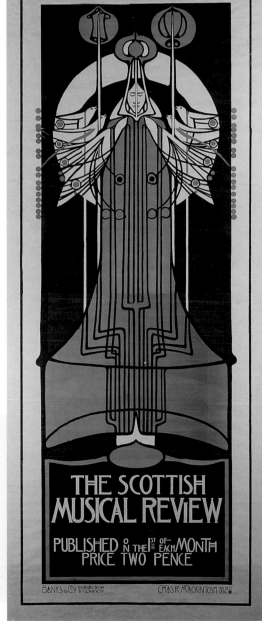

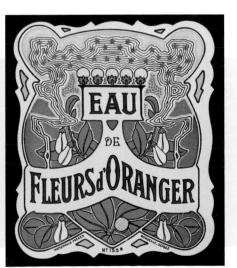

Chromolithographic advertising label for *Eau de Fleurs d'Oranger* (Orange flower water). The illustration features a stylized representation of the white flowers in bud, surrounded by green foliage, with sinuous, fine, star-speckled banding, probably indicative of the plant's aroma. The design is set within a shaped framework incorporating the name of the product. **NPA COR**

Alphonse Mucha

Mucha's poster designs came to epitomize the Art Nouveau style, becoming virtually inseparable from the term. So much so that Art Nouveau was often referred to in France as *Le Style Mucha*.

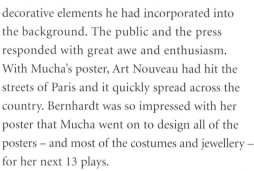

Czech-born Alphonse Mucha (1860–1939) trained as a set painter in Vienna and then studied art at the Munich Academy. In 1887, he came to Paris in search of work as a book illustrator. His explosion onto the Art Nouveau scene came almost as a complete accident and it happened on Christmas Eve, 1894. That evening Mucha was working late at a printing house, Champenois, when news came in that the actress Sarah Bernhardt, who was employing Champenois to produce posters for her current play, *Gismonda*, was very disappointed with the latest design. Mucha took up the challenge and when his design hit the streets less than a week later the results were revolutionary. His new poster broke all the traditions, from the tall, thin format of the poster, to the soft palette of colours used, and the decorative elements he had incorporated into the background. The public and the press responded with great awe and enthusiasm. With Mucha's poster, Art Nouveau had hit the streets of Paris and it quickly spread across the country. Bernhardt was so impressed with her poster that Mucha went on to design all of the posters – and most of the costumes and jewellery – for her next 13 plays.

Mucha's style became so popular that the printing house pressured Mucha to create more and more images to help satiate the public's growing demand for his beautiful women with flowing, ornamental hair. These decorative panels sold out almost as soon as they were printed.

Above: "Femme Aux Coquelicots" poster the lithographic composition is of a woman in a flowing robe and wreaths of foliage, seated behind a painting rack, in front of a ring of poppies. *1898 62.25cm (24½in) high* **£3,500–4,500 SWA**

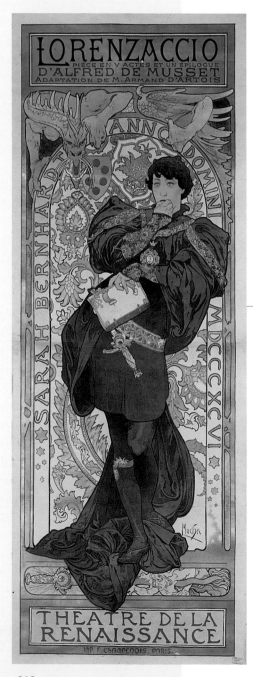

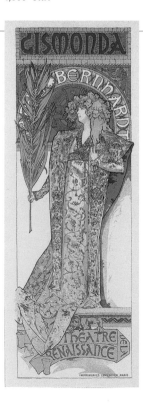

SARAH BERNHARDT

Sarah Bernhardt (1844–1923) was universally considered to be one of the finest actresses of her generation. She performed to glowing reviews in France, Britain, and the United States. Mucha's involvement with Bernhardt's artistic promotion began in 1895 (*see above*) and continued for six years, during which time he designed posters for the actress, as well as jewellery, costumes, and sets for her performances. It is fair to assume that Mucha's connection to the most famous actress of the era aided his meteoric rise to fame. Bernhardt also appeared in Mucha's works that were not advertising her theatrical performances, specifically in an advertisement for Lefèvre-Utile Biscuits (1903). Her image also appeared on a Mucha poster advertising *La Plume* magazine in 1896.

"Lorenzaccio" lithographic poster, in muted autumnal colours, for the play by Alfred de Musset, staring Sarah Bernhardt in the lead role, at the Theatre de la Renaissance, Paris. *1896 210cm (82¾in) high* **NPA AKG**

"Gismonda" lithographic poster for a production with Sarah Bernhardt. Its simplified draughtsmanship and muted colouring were both innovative and hugely influential. *1894 39.25cm (15½in) high* **£2,800–3,200 SWA**

DESIGNS FOR ADVERTISING

In addition to posters, Mucha created illustrations for many commercial products. Most accessible, and very collectable, are the labels he designed for tins of biscuits made by the French manufacturer, Lefèvre-Utile. Some are square in shape to fit the top of a tin, and others are made up of three horizontal panels that were printed to be folded around and pasted onto the top and sides of a rectangular tin. Most copies that have survived were ones that were never used by the factory (rather than soaked off from a tin) so their condition is usually extremely fine. As well as labels, Mucha also designed postcards, menus, bank notes, postage stamps, printed fabric, plates, and magazine covers.

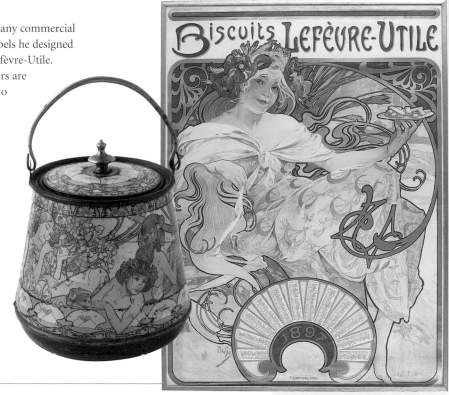

Right: Lefèvre-Utile biscuit tin with a barrel-shaped body and lid with polychrome printed imagery of young maidens and water nymphs in a woodland pond landscape. *c.1905*
16.5cm (6½in) high **£1,400–1,800 DH**

Far right: "Biscuits Lefèvre-Utile" coloured lithographic calendar depicting a maiden reclining under scrolled, interlaced, and whiplash stems and branches. Published in Paris by F. Champenois. *c.1897. 60cm (23½in) high* **£3,000–4,000 L&T**

Among the most successful of Mucha's panels were several distinct series each comprised of four lithographs: "The Seasons" (which proved so popular that Mucha redesigned it three times in 1896, 1897, and 1900), "Times of Day", "Precious Stones", "The Stars", and "The Flowers". Mucha also created designs for commercial advertising including beer, chocolate, champagne, and many other products (*see above*).

MUCHA'S MAIDENS

As public interest in the strictly decorative qualities of art was growing, Mucha's illustrations married the tastes of the present with those of the past, and his work was a huge success. The Victorians' idealization of womankind in art had made the female form an accepted and popular image. Mucha used the *femmes-fleur* motif to great effect, often depicting other-worldly, fairy-like women using flowing lines and sinuous curves. His abstracted and stylized interpretation of this traditional form fed people's hunger for the new and exciting, as the rigid Victorian attitudes gave way to a freer, more experimental mode of expression.

After the turn of the 20th century, Mucha spent some time living in the United States and then returned to his home country, Czechoslovakia,

to complete what he considered to be his life-long dream: a series of paintings commemorating the history of the Slavic people, which he called "the Slav Epic". Mucha also continued to design posters, although most of his later work, while bearing traces of his irrepressible Art Nouveau style, are strongly mixed with ethnic Czech styles and patterns. Mucha died in 1939 after being interrogated by the Gestapo.

Below: Stained glass panel made to the original Mucha poster design "La Plume". It features a woman's head and torso in profile, with a feather fan, centred in a formalized design of flowers and stems. *1899. 99cm (38½in) square* **£2,000–3,000 L&T**

INTERIOR DESIGN

Famous primarily for his posters, Alphonse Mucha also turned his hand to interior design. In Paris and Prague, he created Art Nouveau wonderlands for shops, municipal buildings, and exhibitions, incorporating sculptures, furniture, and stained glass designs.

FOUQUET JEWELLERY SHOP

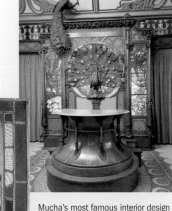

Mucha's most famous interior design work was for Georges Fouquet, whose jewellery shop in Paris (*above*) Mucha transformed with elaborate carved wood, glass, and metal, all in the swirling Art Nouveau style of his posters. Mucha also designed the Bosnia-Herzegovina Pavilion for the 1900 Universal Exposition in Paris, the Mayor's Hall in Prague, adorned with murals and window panes all designed by Mucha, and a stained glass window for St. Vitus, the largest cathedral in Prague.

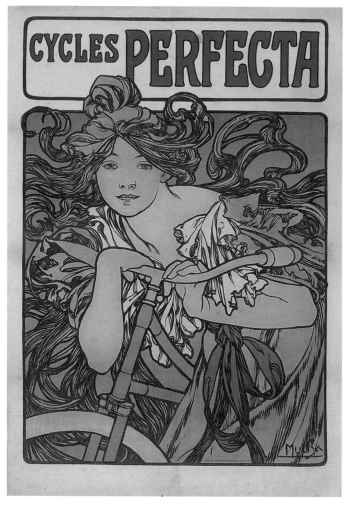

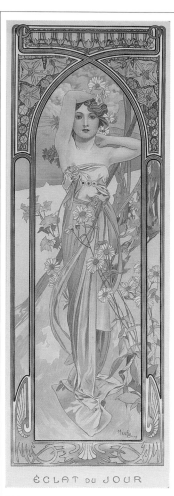

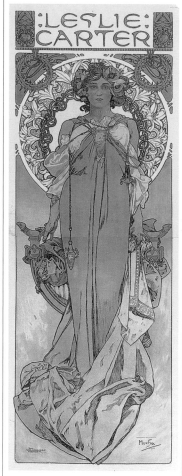

"Cycles Perfecta" poster with a lithographic image of a young girl with long, whiplash hair, in a loose-fitting robe, leaning over the handlebars of a bicycle. Rendered in reds, browns, bluish-green, and flesh tones, on white paper. This is one of Mucha's most graphic posters. *1902*

155cm (61⅛in) high

£15,000–18,000   SWA

"Eclat du Jour" lithographic framed poster. It depicts a young maiden among flowers, and is one of four panels that represent "Morning Awakening", "Daytime Dash", "Evening Reverie", and "Nightly Rest". *1899*

108cm (42in) high

£30,000–40,000 (the set)   SWA

"Leslie Carter" poster with a lithographic portrait of the American actress Leslie Cartier dressed for a Cincinnati production of the play *Kassa*. Stylistically, the design recalls Mucha's work for Sarah Bernhardt. *1908*

208cm (81¾in) high

£5,000–7,000   SWA

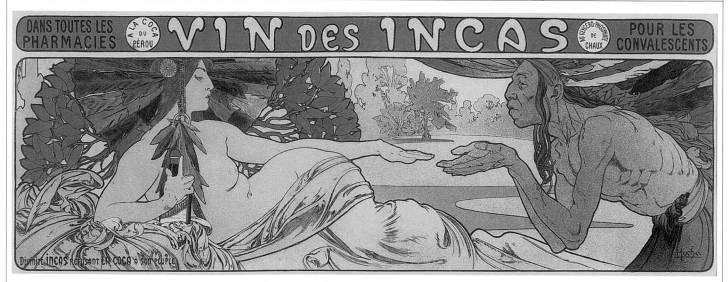

"Vin des Incas" lithographic poster designed to promote a cocoa-based tonic. It shows an elderly Native American man paying homage to a partly clad, voluptuous young woman or goddess, both in feather headdresses, and set in an idyllic rural landscape. *1897*

35.5cm (13¾in) wide

£3,200–3,800   SWA

PL.14

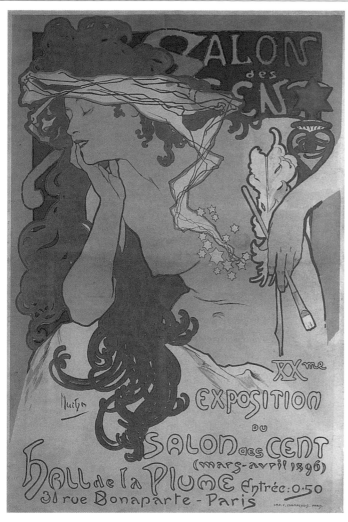

"Salons des Cent" poster with lithographic image of a partly clad girl. It promotes an exhibition at the Salon des Cents gallery on *La Plume* magazine's premises. *c.1896*

64cm (25¼in) high

£4,000–5,000 Qu

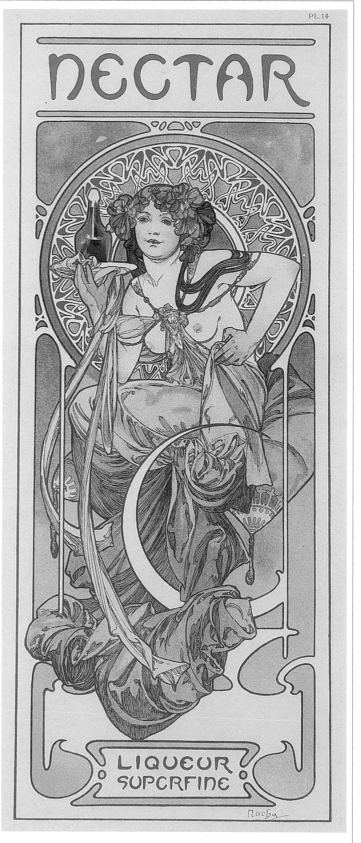

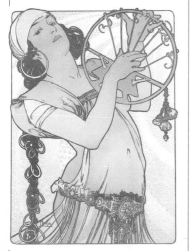

Polychrome lithographic panel depicting Salome dancing for Herod, in shades of gold and green on a mottled yellow ground. Mounted and framed behind glass. *1897*

33cm (13in) high

£800–900 Qu

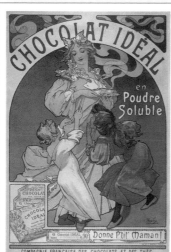

"Chocolat Ideal" colour lithographic poster for the Compagnie Française des Chocolats et des Thès. A young mother holds a cup of hot chocolate above her daughters. *1897*

85cm (33½in) high

£7,000–9,000 SWA

"Nectar" poster design for a mythical drink, created as an instructional example of advertising techniques for art students. Plate 14 from Mucha's "Documents Decoratifs", it depicts a partly clad woman holding the drink, in front of a medallion of flowers, and set within highly formalized plant-form motifs. The design was never made into a poster. *1902*

38cm (14¾in) high

£3,000–4,000 SWA

Chéret's brightly coloured, happy-go-lucky women were dubbed his "Chérettes".

Eye-catching and arresting, his sexy designs were frowned upon by puritanical factions in both Britain and the United States.

Men rarely feature in Chéret's poster designs, and if they do, they are in the background or obscured in shadows.

Uninterrupted colour in Chéret's posters was highlighted even further after 1890 when he stopped using black outlines on his images.

Jules Chéret

Widely regarded as "The Father of the Poster", French designer Jules Chéret (1836–1932) earned this well-deserved sobriquet as a result of his technical prowess and creativity, his exuberant style, and his prodigious output.

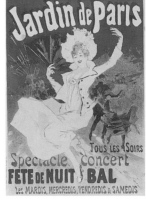

Jules Chéret designed over 1,000 posters during his career, which lasted from the 1870s until 1914. A pioneer in colour lithography, Chéret took the concept of transferring ink from a stone to paper and turned the technical process into an artistic one. He mastered the process of using three different stones for the primary colours and combining them to form a rainbow palette of shades and hues. A precursor to modern advertising, Chéret took the revolutionary step of using beautiful women to sell commercial products.

Chéret was the most prolific poster designer in Paris at the *fin-de-siècle*, and his brightly coloured, lively, and sexy posters, were among the first to ignite the curiosities and passion of the French public. This was the dawn of modern advertising and nothing was out of his reach; he advertised music halls, soaps, perfumes, lamp oil, books, performers, and skating rinks. In 1889, Chéret was awarded the French Legion of Honour for his work in "creating a new branch of art by applying artistic techniques to commercial and industrial printing". His work paved the way for future designers both stylistically and technically.

Above: "Fêtes de Nuit Bal" poster for the "Jardin de Paris" shows a young lady dancing beneath fireworks, and against the silhouettes of other revellers. *1890. 123cm (48in) high* **£2,000–2,500 SWA**

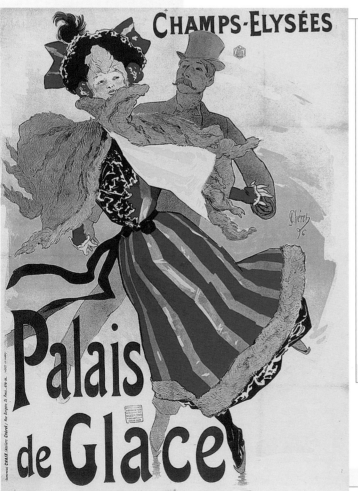

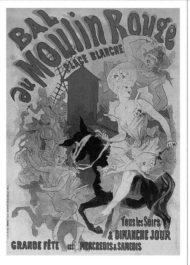

"Bal au Moulin Rouge" lithograph poster with a dancer in yellow, carrying a whip, and riding a horse in the foreground. Behind her are other riders and revellers. The vibrant red of a windmill is echoed in the red lettering. *1889 126.25cm (49¾in) high*

£3,500–4,500	SWA

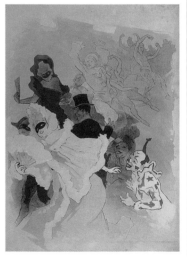

"Theatre de l'Opera Carnaval" lithograph poster showing a masked lady with a fan and a French clown, in the foreground, and a man and woman in black, with splashes of red. More revellers are sketched against a blue wash. *1894 121.25cm (47¾in) high*

£3,000–4,000	SWA

"Palais de Glace" lithograph poster depicts a characteristically lively young lady ice-skating in the foreground. She is wearing a vibrant red and gold dress, an orange and yellow cape, and contrasting black blouse, petticoat, belt, and shoes. She is attended by a top-hatted male skater who is rendered in shades of grey against a shadowy background. *119.5cm (47in) high*

£5,000–7,000	SWA

Eugène Grasset

Swiss-born Grasset was a scholar and theorist of the Art Nouveau movement as well as one of its most admired and influential poster designers. He is even attributed by some with having brought the Art Nouveau movement to America.

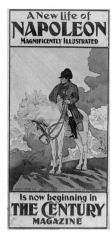

Having first studied architecture, Eugène Samuel Grasset (1841–1917) moved to Paris in 1871 and began work as an illustrator. Inspired by William Morris and the English Arts and Crafts movement, Grasset was also influenced by medievalism and attempted to instill his art with this ancient flavour and character. He was a multi-talented artist, who created furniture designs, book illustrations, jewellery, stained glass windows, and posters.

Although he produced fewer posters than some of his contemporaries, Grasset's importance to the Art Nouveau style cannot be overlooked. His influence ranged far and wide – he designed a room for the third Secessionist exhibition in Vienna in 1899, was instrumental in forming the style of American poster artist Louis Rhead, and was the professed role model of both Alphonse Mucha and Paul Berthon.

In 1894, he was chosen by American publishers to design a series of posters for *The Century Magazine*. The monumental, 2m (7ft) high poster of Napoleon he designed became so popular that it was recreated in stained glass by Tiffany and Co.

Above: Chromolithographic poster for *The New Century Magazine* showing the Emperor Napoleon at Austerlitz. Although the subject is historical, Grasset's treatment of the scene is contemporary. *1894 214cm (84¼in) high* **£1,300–2,000 SWA**

KEY FEATURES

Medieval influences, as well as the Arts and Crafts style, are evident in Grasset's work.

Grasset's colour palette consists mainly of bold blue, yellow, and green tones.

Less overtly sexual images than those of Chéret, meant that Grasset was a popular choice for puritanical American magazines.

Stained glass windows were also designed by Grasset, and many of his posters reflect this style.

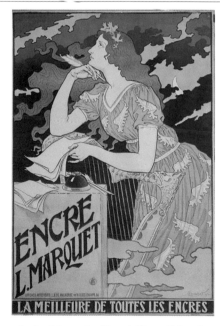

Lithograph advertising poster "Encre L. Marquet" for a French ink manufacturer, with an image of a woman leaning on a harp. *1892 116cm (45¾in) high*

£800–1,200 **On**

Lithograph panel for the Salon des Cents at *La Plume* magazine in Paris. One of Grasset's most striking images, the woman with red hair holds flowers, a pen, and a pad. Limited edition of 100, without lettering. *1899 62.75cm (24¾in) high*

£4,500–6,000 **SWA**

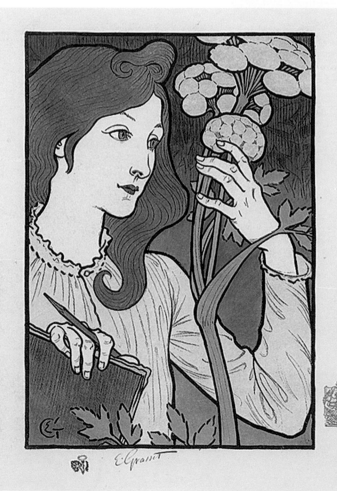

European Posters

While France was the leader in lithography, all over Europe artists began to see the potential of the poster as a valid form of artistic expression. The *femme-fleur* was a common feature in French posters and also came to be used by Belgian artists such as Privat-Livemont. The daily life of ordinary people also appeared in posters, reflecting the socialist ideals of their creators, and the influence in particular of the prolific French artist Henri de Toulouse-Lautrec. Many European Art Nouveau posters also reveal the influence of the Japanese style in their fluid forms and use of swirling organic lines, and in Austria and Germany the Secessionist movement led to the creation of posters with bold colouring and geometric motifs.

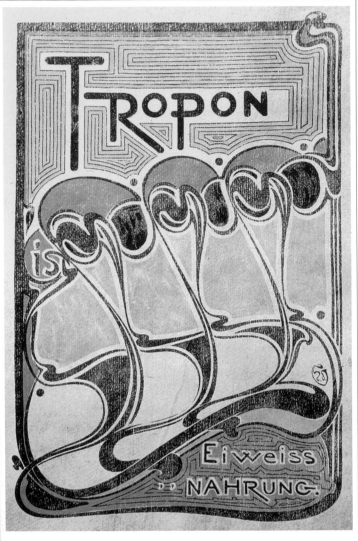

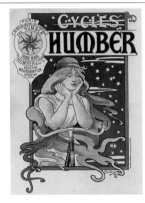

Henriette Bressler poster advertising Humber cycles, featuring a young girl in a headband with long whiplash hair leaning on handlebars against a night sky. *c.1900*

151cm (59½in) high

£2,200–2,800   **SWA**

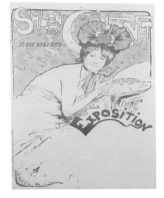

Lapierre lithographic poster promoting an exhibition at the Salon des Cent in Paris. It depicts a partly robed young woman perusing a collection of prints.

60.5cm (23¾in) high

£220–330   **DN**

Henry van de Velde lithographic poster, "Tropon", for a Berlin newspaper, with stylized and whiplash plant-form imagery. A reduced size collector's version issued by *Pan* magazine in 1898.

31.5cm (12½in) high

£450–550   **Qu**

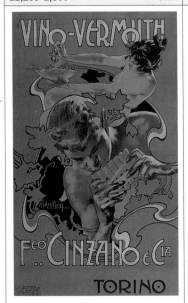

Adolfo Hohenstein poster advertising the Italian vermouth Cinzano with a lithographic image of the Roman god Pan playing his pipes in a rural setting. *c.1898*

169cm (66¾in) high

£2,000–2,500   **SWA**

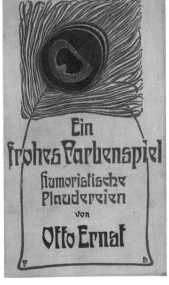

Hans Christiansen book cover with a stylized peacock-feather motif. From the cover of the novel *Ein Frohes Farbenspiel* by Otto Ernst with illustrations by Christiansen. *1903*

30.5cm (12in) high

£100–170   **Qu**

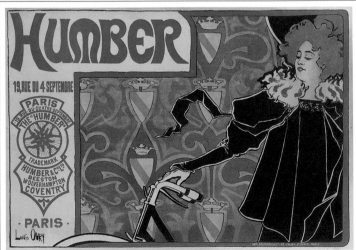

Louis Oury lithographic poster advertising Humber bicycles. It depicts a young woman in a black-and-green cape and hat holding the handlebars of her bicycle. Set against a red-and-grey background of shield and crown motifs within a stylized plant-form pattern.

157.5cm (62in) wide

£4,000–5,000   **SWA**

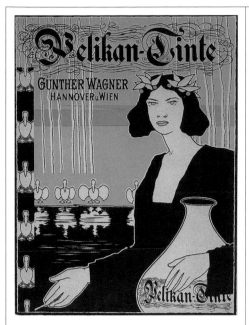

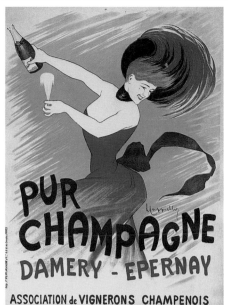

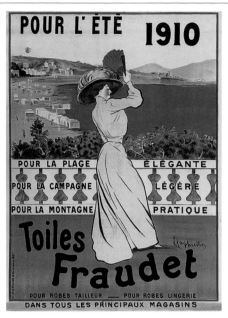

Georg Tronnier poster "Pelikan-Tinte", advertising ink and pens by Pelikan of Hanover, with a young girl holding a jar of ink, set against scrolling plant forms and German eagles. *1899*

73cm (28¾in) high

£1,200–1,800   SWA

Leonetto Cappiello poster "Pur Champagne", with a young woman dancing with a bottle and glass of champagne against a green, hatched background. *1902*

135.5 cm (53¼in) high

£3,000–4,000   SWA

Leonetto Cappiello holiday-advertising poster "Toiles Fraudet", featuring a young woman in a long dress holding a fan, with a beach and mountains in the background. *1910*

157.5cm (62in) high

£4,000–6,000   SWA

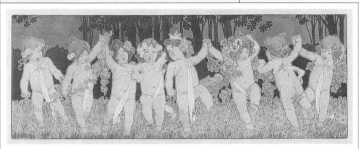

Privat-Livemont panel with a chain of cherubs, garlanded with pink flowers and dressed in white ribbons, cavorting in a field with trees in the background. *1903*

100.5cm (39¼in) wide

£1,800–2,200   SWA

Paul Berthon

A student and disciple of Grasset's, Paul Berthon (1872–1909) produced mainly *panneaux decoratifs* (decorative panels) that were hugely popular among the French public towards the end of the 19th century. Of all the Art Nouveau artists, Berthon's work is the most ethereal and dream-like, an effect achieved through his use of very light pastel colours and the distant-eyed, wistful maidens and nymphs who inhabit his romantic landscapes. Berthon was heavily influenced by both nature and the spirit of the Middle Ages, as he himself describes: "What we want is to create an original art without any model but nature, without any rule but imagination and logic, using at the same time the French flora and fauna as details and following very closely the principles that made the medieval arts so thoroughly decorative."

Paul Berthon poster advertising the novel *Sainte-Marie-des-Fleurs* by René Boylesve. It shows a sensuous lithographic image of a medieval- or pre-Raphaelite-style young woman, with long, flowing red hair, set against a formalized, green floral and foliate ground and caressing white blooms emerging from a planter, which is decorated with stylized, scrolling "beasts". *1898*

60.5cm (23½in) high

£1,800–2,200   SWA

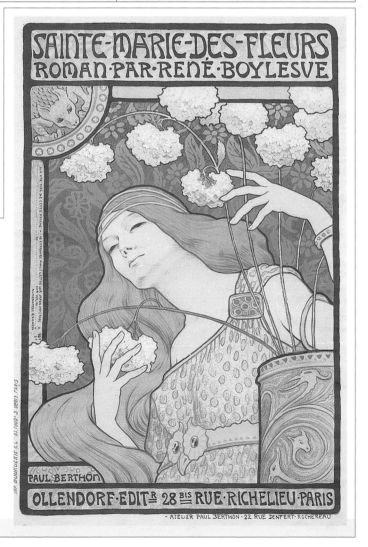

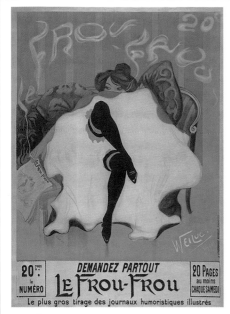

Lucien-Henri Weil poster for the risqué French magazine
Le Frou-Frou, with a young smoking woman in a provocative
pose with white petticoats and black stockings. *1900*

157cm (61¾in) high

£16,000–20,000   **SWA**

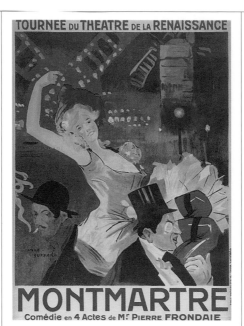

Ange Supparo poster promoting "Tournée du Théâtre de la
Renaissance, Montmartre", with a vibrant lithographic image
of a dancer on the shoulders of a man in evening dress.

159cm (62½in) high

£7,000–10,000   **SWA**

Jean de Paleologue poster "La Péoria", advertising luxury
American bicycles with a scantily clad girl emerging from
the sea, chasing a winged cycle across the beach. *c.1898*

157.5cm (62in) high

£2,800–3,200   **SWA**

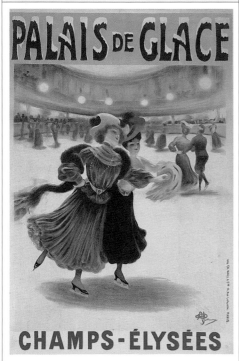

Albert Guillaume poster advertising the Palais de Glace on
the Champs Elysées. The lithographic image features two
nimble and lively female skaters in the foreground. *c.1896*

115.5cm (45½in) high

£3,500–4,500   **SWA**

Albert Guillaume poster promoting the revue *A Nous les Femmes* at
La Scala. The polychrome lithographic image is of female dancers and
singers; printed with black lettering on yellowish paper. *1900*

80cm (31½in) high

£350–450   **Qu**

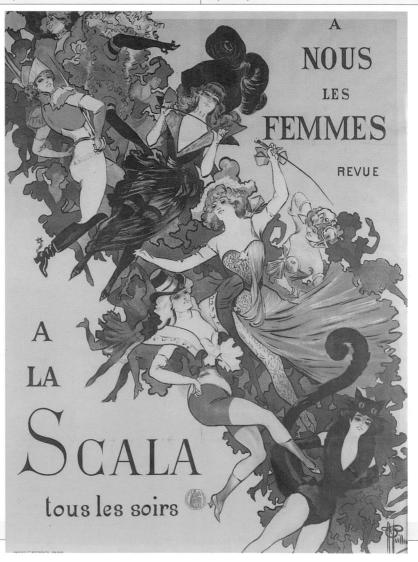

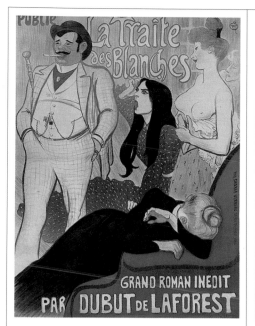

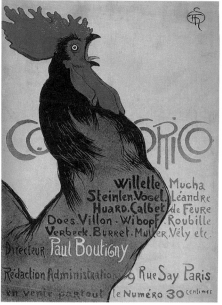

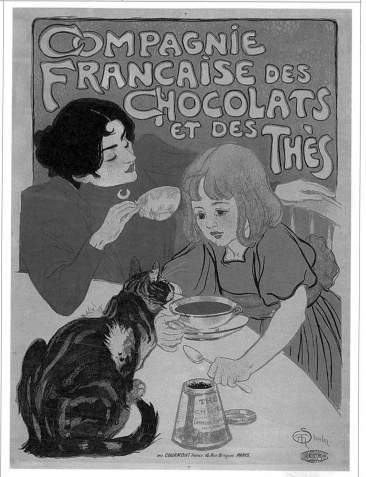

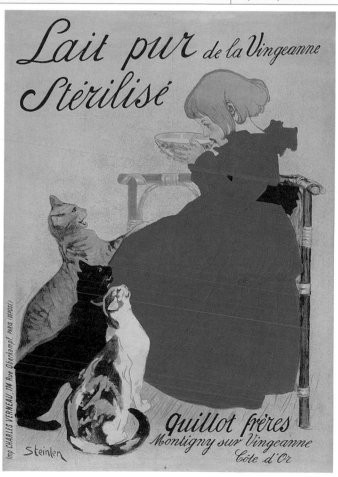

Théophile-Alexandre Steinlen poster of *Le journal: La Traite des Blanches*, with a lithographic image of three women and a man, in red, brown, yellow, black, and white. *1899*

153.5cm (60½in) high

£9,000–12,000   **SWA**

Théophile-Alexandre Steinlen poster for the Parisian arts journal *Cocorico*, with a lithographic image of a cockerel in red, black, and brown on a yellow background. *1899*

135.5cm (53¼in) high

£4,000–5,000   **SWA**

Théophile-Alexandre Steinlen poster advertising Clinique Chéron, a Parisian veterinary practice, and depicting a young woman surrounded by cats and dogs. *1905*

194.5cm (76½in) high

£16,000–20,000   **SWA**

Théophile-Alexandre Steinlen poster advertising *Lait Pur Stérilisé* (sterilized milk), and depicting the artist's young daughter drinking a bowl of milk, with three cats in attendance. *1894*

135.5cm (53¼in) high

£12,000–15,000   **SWA**

Théophile-Alexandre Steinlen poster advertising the Compagnie Française des Chocolats et des Thès, with a mother and daughter drinking tea and hot chocolate and a cat looking on. *c.1895*

80cm (31½in) high

£6,000–8,000   **SWA**

Used a primary colour palette and bold colour schemes that did not rely on the pastel shades so popular in Europe.

Depicted mainly women, clothed in intricately detailed patterned dresses.

Most famous poster designs by Rhead date from between 1896 and 1898.

Influenced by Grasset, whose style is apparent in Rhead's poster designs.

Louis John Rhead

Inspired by the work of French artist Eugène Grasset, English-born Louis John Rhead (1858–1926) took the pure French Art Nouveau style to the United States, where he became one of the country's most talented Art Nouveau poster designers.

Son of a Wedgwood pottery artist, Rhead studied painting in Paris as a boy. In the 1880s, he went to the United States and became art director for D. Appleton, a New York publisher. In 1891, he returned to Europe and while staying in Paris he visited a show at the Salon des Cent of the works of Eugène Grasset and immediately fell under their spell. He also met the artist himself, and it was as a result of these two events that Rhead was inspired to become a poster designer.

Rhead returned to New York, where he became a prolific designer, completing about 100 posters during the second half of the 1890s. That he was a devotee of Grasset's style was apparent in his work, and although he has often been derided for his adherence to this model, Rhead is actually the only artist to attempt to transfer pure the French Art Nouveau style to the United States. Most of his designs were for newspapers, various publishers and periodicals (*The Morning Sun*, *The Century*, *The Sun*, and *The Journal*), but he also designed posters for perfume, soap, and cigarettes.

Rhead became renowned for using a very bright, bold primary palette and daring colour schemes. His work was actually far more varied than Grasset's, as Rhead could alternate back and forth between a heavily-patterned intricacy and simple, bold, almost illustrative designs.

His design talents were well recognized during his lifetime: he was given a one man show in New York in 1895, was the gold medal winner at an International Poster Exhibition in Boston, and had a solo show at Paris' acclaimed Salon des Cent.

Above: "Scribners for Xmas" poster with an orange-haired woman in dark blue and black carrying an armful of holly along a snowy path through a forest of green trees. *1895*
50cm (19½in) high **£800–1,200 SWA**

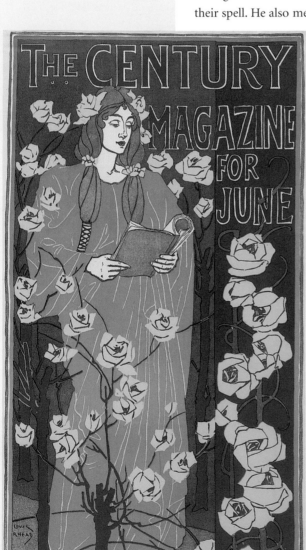

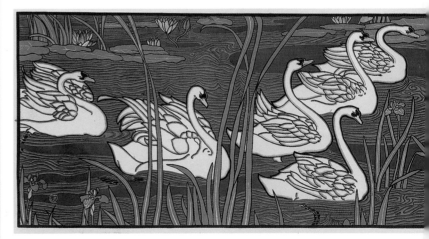

Left: ***The Century Magazine for June* poster** has a young woman with long, tied orange hair, in a blue medieval-style dress walking through an arbour of trees, surrounded by yellow roses. *1896*
53.5cm (21in) high **£1,000–1,500 SWA**

Above: Gaggle of Swans poster showing the black-and-white birds in a V-formation swimming across a blue pond with green waterlily pads and other aquatic plant forms. *1897*
154.25cm (60¾in) wide **£3,000–4,000 SWA**

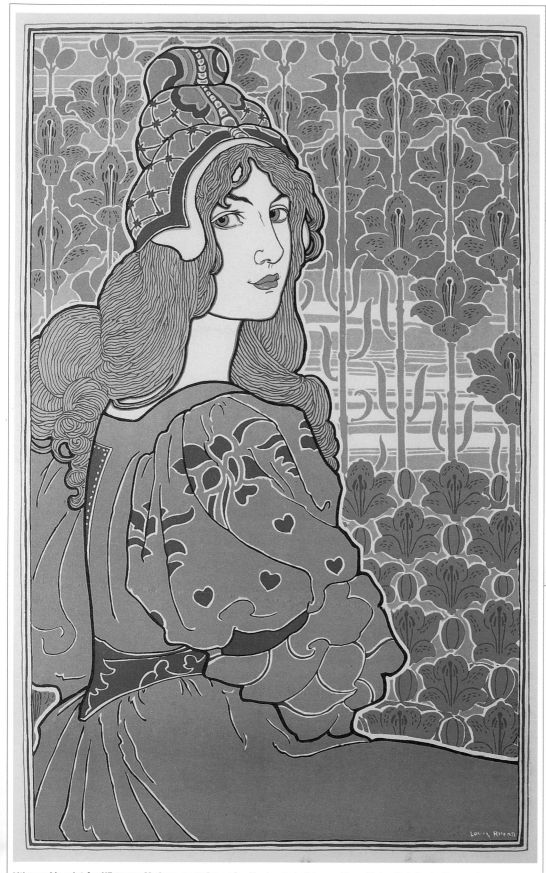

Lithographic print for *L'Estampe Moderne* magazine series. The image depicts a maiden with long hair flowing from under a domed cap, wearing a pleated dress, and sitting in front of stylized lilies, in shades of orange, red, pink, brown, blue, green, and white.

40cm (15¾in) high

£80–120 WW

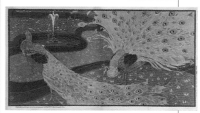

Peacocks in Paris poster. The lithographic image depicts a male peacock wooing a female with a full display of his tail feathers. Both birds are rendered in shades of pale green, blue, red, and pale brown. *1897*

153.5cm (60½in) wide

£3,000–4,000 SWA

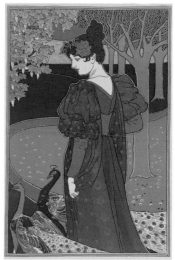

"Woman of the Peacocks" lithographic panel showing a classical young woman flanked by two peacocks within a woodland setting. Made for *L'Estampe Moderne*, signed in the print and with a blindstamp.

40cm (15¼in) high

£150–200 COR

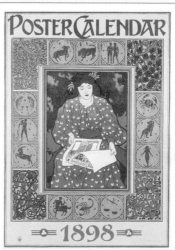

Poster Calendar for 1898, in vivid colours, showing a seated figure of a flame-haired woman examining a calendar. She is surrounded by a frame of seasonal foliage and signs of the zodiac.

NPA COR

British and American Posters

The majority of British posters in the Art Nouveau period reflect an illustrative and practical approach to advertising rather than an artistic one. Artists such as Aubrey Beardsley, John Hassall, and Dudley Hardy designed hundreds of posters for theatrical events, which are more bold and simple in style than elaborate.

In the United States, the first Art Nouveau posters were small window placards advertising literary magazines. The success of three artists in particular who had strong knowledge of European art styles, Edward Penfield, William H. Bradley, and Louis John Rhead, paved the way for the American design field to flourish.

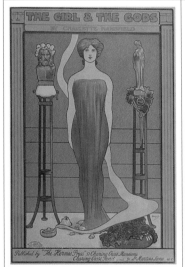

John Hassall poster for the novel *The Girl & The Gods* by Charlotte Mansfield. The hairstyle, clothing, and artefacts are classical in origin, but rendered in Art Nouveau style.

76cm (30in) high

£250–300   **On**

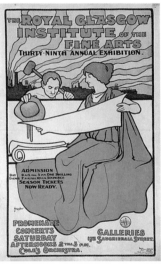

John Hassall poster for the Thirty-Ninth Annual Exhibition of the Royal Glasgow Institute of the Fine Arts. A woman, in flowing robes, peruses drawings before a blacksmith.

51cm (20in) high

£150–200   **On**

Charles Rennie Mackintosh

Chiefly known for his highly influential furniture design, interiors, and architecture, the father of the Glasgow School style Charles Rennie Mackintosh was also highly skilled as a fine and graphic artist. He produced only a few posters, which are now extremely rare and much sought after. His posters often show the influence of the linear aspect of Celtic art, as well as the clean lines and blocks of strong colour prevalent in Japanese graphic art. Mackintosh's illustrative designs are powerful in their imagery and reflect the recognizable elements of the unique Glasgow "look" he developed throughout his life. The other members of the "Glasgow Four" (*see p.44*), including his wife Margaret Macdonald, also produced graphic work and collaborated on a poster for the Glasgow Institute of the Fine Arts.

Charles Rennie Mackintosh's "Glasgow Institute of the Fine Arts" coloured lithographic poster, showing a young woman in a cape and flowing robe, standing beside a highly stylized flowering shrub. *1895*

NPA   **CHR**

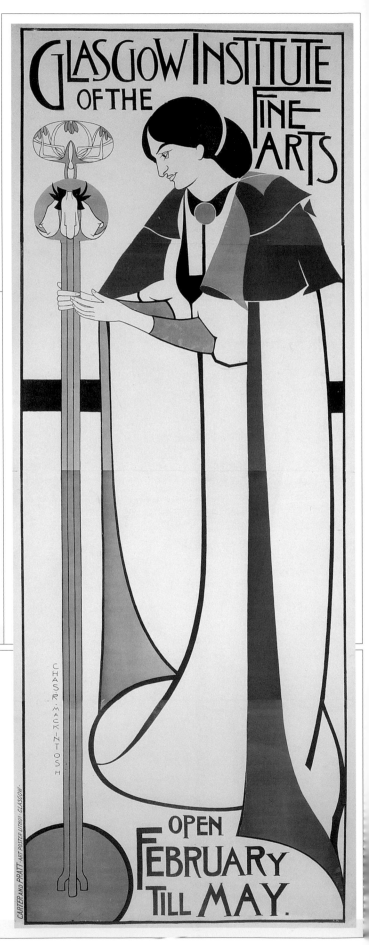

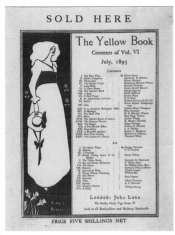

Aubrey Beardsley poster advertising the 1895 edition of "The Yellow Book", London. It has black lettering, and the figure of a young woman with long hair, dress, and bonnet.

37.5cm (14¾in) high

£500–700   **SWA**

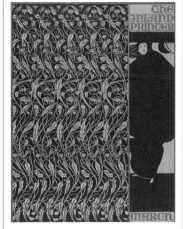

William H. Bradley poster of *The Inland Printer* magazine cover. A band of interlaced foliage abuts a woman losing her hat in the wind. *c.1898*

28cm (11in) high

£200–250   **SWA**

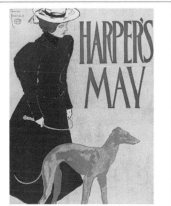

Edward Penfield poster for *Harper's May*. A woman in a long blue dress and white bonnet walks a brown hound, against a tan background, and with orange lettering. *1897*

46cm (18in) high

£500–700   **SWA**

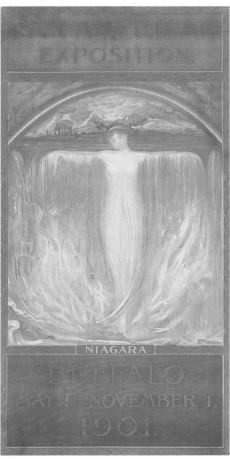

American poster for the 1901 Pan-American Exposition at Buffalo, New York. Based on the painting "Spirit of Niagra" by Evelyn Rumsey Cary, with the body of an allegorical female Niagra.

120.5cm (47in) high

£2,500–3,000   **SWA**

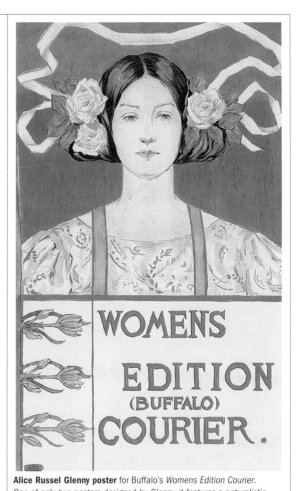

Alice Russel Glenny poster for Buffalo's *Womens Edition Courier*. One of only two posters designed by Glenny, it features a naturalistic depiction of a young woman, with halo-like, whiplashed ribbon. *1895*

68.5cm (27in) high

£1,500–2,000   **SWA**

Edward Penfield poster for *Harper's July*. A black and orange tabby cat, and an orange, black, and white calico cat sniff around a small tree in a green planter. Penfield's bull's-head logo monogram is applied to the base of the planter. *1898*

38cm (14¾in) wide

£800–1,200   **SWA**

Glossary

Acid-etching In glass decoration, a layer, or layers, of coloured glass is applied to a vessel and a design is blocked out with an acid-resistant material. When immersed in a bath of hydroflouric acid, the untreated areas are removed, leaving the image in relief.

Arts & Crafts A late 19th-century movement, based on the philosophy of William Morris, that advocated honest craftsmanship, using the natural beauty and quality of materials to artistic effect.

Astragal A narrow convex moulding often in the form of beading. The term often describes the wooden glazing bars dividing up a glazed door.

Aurene Ware A trade name for Steuben's iridescent glass developed by Frederick Carder in the United States. The name is derived from the Greek for gold.

Aventurine Translucent brown glass given a sparkling appearance by the incorporation of golden or copper flecks of oxidized metal. It can also be used as a glaze. The name probably derives from a quartz known in Italian as *Aventurina*, which has a similar appearance.

Baroque pearl From the Portuguese term *barroco* for a natural pearl that deviates from the usual, regular form. These pearls are generally less valuable than round pearls, but their organic shape is well suited to the Art Nouveau style.

Batik An Indonesian method where a textile is produced by applying a design in wax. When dyed, the waxed areas do not pick up the colour, and hence create a pattern on the fabric.

Belle-Epoque A French term for the prosperous time from the late 19th to the early 20th century, when graphics and the fine arts saw a surge of artistic creativity. Artists had the freedom to depict the less respectable elements of society as well as the more elegant side of life. Belle-Epoque imagery is typically bold and colourful.

Bentwood Furniture that has been created by bending wood into sinuous curves by steam processing. The Austrian firm of Thonet popularized this type of furniture.

Blindstamp An embossed mark devoid of ink applied to a work of art on paper to designate the creator.

Blister pearl A raised area of mother-of-pearl resembling a blister cut from the inside of a shell. The dark brown underside is sometimes left visible.

Blown glass A method of making glass where a glassmaker blows through a hollow rod, shaping a gather of molten glass at the other end. The glass can be either free-blown or blown into a mould to create a more uniform shape.

Briolette An oval or pear-shaped gemstone that is cut into triangular facets.

Brocatelle A durable decorating fabric, usually in silk or wool, with patterns in high relief.

Cabochon A term for a polished, rounded stone retaining the natural appearance of a pebble, with no faceting or cutting to its surface.

Cacateuse (or Caqueteuse) The name for a trapezoid-shaped chair seat with bowed arms, originally designed to accommodate voluminous skirts.

Cameo glass Glass made up of two or more separate, coloured glass layers. The top layer(s) is wheel carved or acid etched to produce a relief image and reveal the different coloured glass beneath.

Cane Used in furniture for making woven seats and backs, the material is from the rattan plant.

Canted (or chamfered) A furniture term for a surface that has been cut with a slanted edge for decorative effect.

Cartouche A panel or tablet in the form of a scroll with curled edges, sometimes bearing an inscription, monogram, or coat of arms, and used as part of the decoration.

Casting Creating a product by pouring molten material (e.g., silver, bronze, or glass) into a mould.

Celadon A distinctive grey-green or blue-green glaze. The technique imitates nephrite jade and has been used in China, South Korea, and Japan for over 2,000 years.

Chamfered *See* Canted

Chasing A method of improving the detail on an embossed metal object. The surface is carefully engraved with a chasing tool resembling a small chisel to add texture and pattern without removing any metal.

Chipped ice A technique used by Handel & Co. to give a frosted effect on the surface of glass, achieved by applying glue to the surface and heating it. When dry, the glue flakes off and creates a textured surface.

Chrysoprase A natural translucent bluish-green agate used in jewellery. The colour is derived from the presence of nickel. Some pale agates are stained green to resemble chrysoprase.

Cold enamelling Painting coloured enamels on ceramic, glass, and bronze without firing.

Cornice A decorative, moulded projection that crowns a piece of furniture, particularly tall cupboards or display cabinets.

Coupe A French term for a shallow bowl with a short stem.

Crackled ground A glazed surface on ceramics deliberately crazed and sometimes using a black stain to enhance the decorative effect.

Crewelwork Embroidery work using loosely twisted, worsted yarn in a free-flowing design, usually on a linen-based ground.

Crystalline A glaze suspended with zinc or calcium crystals created by a slow cooling kiln, which gives the effect of patches of colour.

Cuenca A Spanish tile-making process where soft, moist tiles are impressed with a design to create raised outlines. After firing, the resulting depressions are glazed.

Cultured pearl A pearl that has been "farmed". The pearl is generated by introducing foreign matter to the inside of the shell. To reduce the irritation caused, the mollusc coats the intruder with the same secretion it uses for shell-building and creates a pearl.

Cymric Silver and jewellery range introduced by English retailer Liberty & Co., which incorporated the use of Celtic motifs in many of the designs.

Demi-lune French term for a half moon shape.

Étagère A French term for a free-standing set of shelves, in two or three tiers.

Earthenware Low fired pottery made of a porous clay body that has to be waterproofed by a coating glaze. It has a porosity of more than 5 per cent.

Ebonized wood Wood that has been stained black in imitation of ebony. This technique was popular with German and Austrian Art Nouveau furniture designers as well as members of the Glasgow School.

Electroplated A film of gold or silver chemically deposited by electrolysis onto any object (usually metal) that will conduct electricity.

Embossed Decoration produced by raising a pattern in relief from the body of a piece.

Enamel A coloured, opaque composition derived from glass fired onto jewellery, metalware, ceramics, and glass as a source of decoration.

Entrelacs Interwoven sinuous tendrils used as an ornament (of Celtic origin). They are often used in jewellery making and were revived by the Arts and Crafts designers.

Eosin The trade name for a lustrous Zsolnay glaze.

Escutcheon A protective or ornamental plate, sometimes in the shape of a shield.

Faience The French name for tin-glazed earthenware of a buff or pale red colour covered with white enamel or glaze, which gives the appearance of porcelain.

Favrile A type of glass developed by Louis Comfort Tiffany, patented in 1894. The name comes from the German *fabrile* meaning handmade.

Femme-fleur A French term used to describe a hybrid of a female form and a floral bloom.

Fire polished A process where a glass piece is reheated to reduce any imperfections in manufacture, giving it a bright finish.

Fluogravure A technique devised by Müller Frères where a piece of glass is partly enamelled and partly acid-etched, producing contrasting opaque and transparent elements.

Foliate Shaped like a leaf. This was a popular motif in Art Nouveau decoration.

Gather (of glass) A mass of molten glass (sometimes called a gob) collected on the end of a blowpipe, pontil, or gathering iron.

Gilt bronze An object made of bronze that has been gilded, i.e., has a fine patination of gold applied to its surface for decorative effect.

Glasgow Style A style created by the "Glasgow Four" – Charles Rennie Mackintosh, Herbert MacNair, Frances Macdonald, and Margaret Macdonald. They developed a unique look that included innovative decorative forms. Bypassing many traditional historical references, they produced a rectilinear version of Art Nouveau that influenced German and Austrian designers. Their style paved the way for the later Art Deco period in the 1920s.

Glaze A coating for ceramics that can be transparent or opaque. In principle it is a thin layer of glass that strengthens and seals the surface and also makes it waterproof. Initially applied as a layer of powder, when fired in a kiln it vitrifies.

Gold-plated A metal item that has a very thin layer of gold deposited on it electrolytically. The thin layer is fragile and prone to wear when excessively cleaned. Also called gold-toned or gold-washed.

Goose-neck The neck of a piece of glass or ceramic that is curved to resemble the neck of a goose.

Guéridon A small and usually ornately carved and embellished stand or table.

Hammer-textured The effect achieved when metals are shaped by hand using a hammer and are left unfinished, leaving a textured, rather than a smooth, surface. Sometimes this surface is created purely as a decorative effect.

Humidor A chamber used for maintaining moisture levels.

Inro A Japanese portable container with a number of sections. Usually lacquered, it resembles a purse and is worn suspended from a belt.

Intaglio A sunken image that is cut into the surface of a glass vessel or gemstone. It is the opposite to relief decoration, which stands out from the surface.

Intarsio ware A type of ware produced by Foley, a British ceramics manufacturer, possibly to resemble a marquetry technique, using areas of flat colour.

Iridescence A surface effect that creates the appearance of rainbow colours caused by differential refraction of light waves, as is sometimes observed on an oil spill. It is produced by spraying a mist of metallic salts onto the hot ceramic or glass vessel.

Ivorine A trademark resinous substance resembling ivory and used as an ivory substitute.

Jugendstil Meaning "Youth Style", the term was used for the German strand of Art Nouveau. The Jugendstil style is generally more rectilinear than its French equivalent, and derives its name from the art magazine *Jugend*, which was first published in 1896.

Kayser pewter From the pewter factory of Kayser & Söhne near Dusseldorf, Germany. Pewter was mass produced here from 1885 to around 1904 and was used for many Art Nouveau wares. Pieces are marked "Kayserzinn".

Latticinio From the Italian word *latte* (milk), this is a term for the white spaghetti-like threads used for decoration in clear glass.

Lava glass Also known as volcanic glass, this is an iridescent gold glass often with a rough surface and dripping, lava-like decoration.

It was developed in the United States by Louis Comfort Tiffany.

Lithograph An image produced by the transfer of a design from a stone or metal plate, generally onto paper.

Lustre A surface effect that has similar properties to an iridescent surface (*See* Iridescence).

Majolica The name given to a ceramic ware created by the English Minton factory and first presented in 1851. It is an elaborately modelled earthenware with thick colourful glazes. The name is derived from the Italian name for tin-glazed earthenware (*maiolica*).

Marquetry A furniture decorating technique that involves the insertion of preformed pieces of wood exhibiting different grains or colours into a panel or piece of furniture.

Marqueterie-sur-verre A glass decorating technique developed by Emile Gallé, where hot pieces of coloured glass are applied to the surface of a glass vessel to form a decorative motif or pattern.

Martelé The French term for "hammer textured", a technique used by the Gorham Manufacturing Co. in the United States for a range they produced from 1897.

Millefiori Italian for "a thousand flowers", a technique where coloured canes (tiny, fused glass

rods, often in bold colours) are embedded in clear glass. This technique is often used for paperweights.

Mortise In furniture making, a hole that is made in the wood to receive a tenon.

Mullion An often decorative, slender vertical post that forms a division between units of a window, door, or screen.

Opalescence An effect usually seen in glass that emulates opal. It gives a milky blue appearance by reflected light, and an amber tint by transmitted light.

Openwork A decorative technique that has open elements created by piercing or wirework. It allows light to pass through the apertures.

Overlay A glass layer over the main glass body, which can be decorated by various techniques, e.g., carving, acid etching, or painting with enamels.

Parquetry A decorative process similar to marquetry, in which woods are inlaid into furniture or floors, often in a geometric pattern.

Pâte-de-verre A French term meaning "paste of glass" where ground glasses are mixed with a liquid to form a paste. It is then pressed into a mould and slowly heated to form the required shape.

Pâte-sur-pâte A French term meaning "paste on paste", where layers of slip are applied onto ceramics to produce a subtle relief image, sometimes with a degree of carved detail. Introduced by Sèvres in around 1850.

Patina A surface effect normally acquired over time. A manufacturer may sometimes give a piece the appearance of age with chemical treatments.

Pilaster A shallow rectangular column projecting slightly from a surface.

Planishing Hand-raising a metal object with the use of hammers to create the required shape. The by-product of this technique, if left unpolished, is a pleasing hammer-textured surface.

Plique-à-jour A jewellery technique creating a similar effect to stained glass, where translucent enamel is held in an unbacked frame allowing the light to shine through.

Porcelain A translucent ceramic made from china clay, quartz, and feldspar, first produced in ancient China, and then from 1709 in Europe, initially at the Meissen works.

Pressed glass Glass is given a preformed shape by pressing molten glass into a mould. The technique was developed in the United States from the 1820s.

Pyrography Creating patterns, generally on wooden furniture, using a red-hot poker or needle to burn decorative motifs onto the surface.

Repoussé A French term for relief embossing on metalwares, which is created by hammering the reverse side of the piece.

Reverse painted Painting an image in reverse on the inner surface of a glass vessel. This technique was popular on Art Nouveau lamps in the United States.

Rose cut A gem-cutting technique that gives a flat, circular base and small facets rising to a low point above. Viewed from the side, the gem resembles a small tent.

Runner A long, narrow decorative cloth cover for furniture. Also refers to a long narrow carpet.

Secessionist Now used as the term for Austrian Art Nouveau, it derives from an avant garde group who broke away from the Academy of Fine Arts in Vienna. Founded in 1897, the Vereinigung Bildender Künstler Österreichs – Wiener Secession (Association of Austrian Artists – Vienna Secession) promoted modern design under the chairmanship of the artist Gustav Klimt. Other leading members were Josef Hoffmann and Koloman Moser – the founders of the Wiener Werkstätte – and Joseph Maria Olbrich.

Selette A small, round side table.

Sgraffito From the Italian for "little scratch", a term for the technique of scratching a pattern through the overlaid slip of a vessel to reveal the colour of the clay underneath.

Slip A mixture of clay and water that is richer than the body of a piece of ceramic. It is used to smooth surfaces or to add decoration and colour. It can be used as a "glue" to join sections of clay together.

Stile Liberty The Italians named the Art Nouveau style *Stile Liberty* after the London shop Liberty & Co., whose textiles were particularly well known in Europe. The Italians also used the terms *Stile Floreale* and *Stile Inglese* to describe the Art Nouveau style.

Sterling Silver Metal where the alloy contains 92.5 per cent silver and 7.5 per cent copper. This standard measure was adopted in Britain from 1300, and is also used in the United States and Denmark.

Stoneware A watertight ware made with clay and a fusible stone such as feldspar. It has salt or lead glazes.

Stretcher A rod or bar extending between two legs of a chair or table.

Symbolism Believed by many to be the pioneers of Modernism, the Symbolist artists of the late 19th century avoided naturalistic representation in favour of fantasy and imagination. They drew inspiration from all areas of the arts including literature and music. Symbolism had a great impact on the work of the Art Nouveau period, where sensual images from nature and of the female form were recurring, popular motifs.

Tenon The tongue of a joint in furniture made to fit in the rectangular mortise.

Tube-lined decoration A decorative technique in ceramics where thin lines of slip are used as barriers between coloured areas. Tube-lining was used extensively by Moorcroft in particular.

Tudric A range of pewterware from Liberty & Co., made to complement the silver Cymric range. Each range had its unique designs.

Vaseline glass An opalescent glass with a greasy appearance, made by adding tiny amounts of uranium and metal oxides to the glass.

Vellum A prepared fine-grained unsplit lambskin, kidskin, or calfskin used in furniture.

Verdigris A green or bluish chemical deposit formed on copper, brass, or bronze surfaces.

Vereingte Werkstätte für Kunst im Handwork The United Workshops for Art in Handicraft was established in 1898 in Munich to promote modern, innovative design. Designers involved included Richard Riemerschmid, Hermann Obrist, August Endell, and Bernhard Pankok. The workshops embraced new technology in their approach to designing for modern life. They also aimed to price pieces reasonably to make them as accessible as possible.

Verre de soie From the French for "silk glass", the term is used to describe a silky appearance of glass.

Wheel carving A glass decoration technique where a piece is carved by a series of wheels varying in size, each giving a varied fineness of detail to the finished piece. Decoration of great subtlety can be achieved by this technique.

Wirework A technique where small items are crafted out of gold or silver wire shaped into a lattice.

Wiener Werkstätte The Vienna Workshop (1903–1932), founded by Josef Hoffmann, Koloman Moser, and Fritz Wärndorfer. The Wiener Werkstätte was an influential group, affirming the importance of the art of craftsmanship. Its output was vast, including furniture, silverware, jewellery, glass, and textiles. The theory of *Gesamtkunstwerk* was also key to their work, aiming to unite interior design, art, and architecture into one integrated whole.

Worsted yarn A smooth, compact yarn made from long wool fibres.

Zinn The German term for pewter or tin.

Key to Source Codes

Each piece of Art Nouveau shown in this book has an accompanying letter code that identifies the dealer or auction house that is either selling or has sold it, or the museum or picture agency where the image is held. It should be noted that inclusion in this book in no way constitutes or implies a contract or a binding offer on the part of any contributing dealer or auction house to supply or sell the pieces illustrated, or similar items, at the price stated. It should also be noted that the code PC, and any code ending in PC, denotes that the piece comes from an anonymous or named private collection.

AA
The Art Archive

AAM
Archives d'Architecture Moderne

ADE
Art Deco Etc
73 Upper Gloucester Road
Brighton
Sussex BN1 3LQ
E-mail: johnclark@artdecoetc.co.uk

AKG
AKG London

AL
Andrew Lineham Fine Glass
Stand G19,
The Mall Antiques Arcade
359 Upper Street
London N1
Tel: 020 7704 0195
Fax: 01243 576 241
www.andrewlineham.co.uk
E-mail:
Andrew@AndrewLineham.co.uk

ALA
Alamy Images

AR
Art Resource

ATL
Antique Textiles and Lighting
34 Belvedere
Landsdowne Road
Bath BA1 5HR
Tel: 01225 310 795
Fax: 01225 443 884
E-mail: joannaproops@aol.co.uk

BA
Branksome Antiques
370 Poole Road
Branksome
Poole
Dorset BH12 1AW
Tel: 01202 763 324/679 932
Fax: 01202 763 643

BMN
Auktionhaus Bergmann
Möhrendorfer Str. 4
91056 Erlangen
Germany
Tel: 00 49 9131 45 06 66
Fax: 00 49 9131 45 02 04
www.auction-bergmann.de
E-mail: kontakt@auction-bergmann.de

BonE
Bonhams, Edinburgh
65 George Street
Edinburgh EH2 2JL
Scotland
Tel: 0131 225 2266
Fax: 0131 220 2547
www.bonhams.com
E-mail: info@bonhams.com

BonLo
Bonhams, London
Picture Library
10 Salem Road
London W2 4DL
Tel: 020 7313 2729

BonS
Bonhams, Bond Street
101 New Bond Street
London W1S 1SR
Tel: 020 7629 6602
Fax: 020 7629 8876
www.bonhams.com
E-mail: info@bonhams.com

BRI
Bridgeman Art Library

CALD
Calderwood Gallery
1622 Spruce Street
Philadelphia, PA 19103-6736
USA
Tel: 001 215 546 5357
Fax: 001 215 546 5234
www.calderwoodgallery.com
E-mail: jc@calderwoodgallery.com

CFF
The Craftsman Farms Foundation

CGPC
Cheryl Grandfield Collection
Private Collection

CHR
Christies Images Ltd

Clv
Clevedon Salerooms
The Auction Centre
Kenn Road, Clevedon
Bristol BS21 6TT
Tel: 01934 830 111
Fax: 01934 832 538
www.clevedon-salerooms.com

COR
Corbis

CR
David Rago Auctions
333 North Main Street
Lambertville, NJ 08530
USA
Tel: 001 609 397 9374
Fax: 001 609 397 9377
www.ragoarts.com
E-mail: info@ragoarts.com

CW
Christine Wildman Collection
Private Collection

DH
Huxtins
11 & 12 The Lipka Arcade
288 Westbourne Grove
London W11
www.huxtins.com
E-mail: david@huxtins.com

DN
Dreweatt Neate
Donnington Priory Salerooms
Donnington
Newbury
Berkshire RG14 2JE
Tel: 01635 553 553
Fax: 01635 553 599
www.dreweatt-neate.co.uk
E-mail: fineart@dreweatt-neate.co.uk

DOR
Dorotheum
Palais Dorotheum
Dorotheergasse 17
A-1010 Wien
Austria
Tel: 00 43 1 515 600
Fax: 00 43 1 515 60443
www.dorotheum.com
E-mail: kundendienst@dorotheum.at

DRA
David Rago Auctions
333 North Main Street
Lambertville
NJ 08530
USA
Tel: 001 609 397 9374
Fax: 001 609 397 9377
www.ragoarts.com
E-mail: info@ragoarts.com

FIS
Dr. Fischer - Heilbronner Kunst - und Auktionshaus
Trappensee-Schlösschen
74074 Heilbronn
Germany
Tel: 00 49 7131 15 55 70
Fax: 00 49 7131 15 55 720
www.auctions-fischer.de
E-mail: KunstauktionenDr.Fischer@t-online.de

FRE
Freeman's
1808 Chestnut Street
Philadelphia
PA 19103
USA
Tel: 001 215 563 9275
Fax: 001 215 563 8236
www.freemansauction.com
E-mail: info@freemansauction.com

GorB
Gorringes, Bexhill
Terminus Road
Bexhill-on-Sea
East Sussex TN39 3LR
Tel: 01424 212 994
Fax: 01424 224 035
www.gorringes.co.uk
E-mail: clientservices@gorringes.co.uk

GorL
Gorringes, Lewes
15 North Street
Lewes
East Sussex BN7 2PD
Tel: 01273 472 503
Fax: 01273 479 559
www.gorringes.co.uk
E-mail: clientservices@gorringes.co.uk

GM
Glasgow Museums
The Burrell Collection
2060 Pollokshaws Road
Glasgow G43 1AT
Scotland
Tel: 0141 287 2595
Fax: 0141 287 2585
E-mail: photolibrary@clc.glasgow.gov.uk

Gul
Calouste Gulbenkian Museum, Lisbon
See "Museums" p.235

HA
Hulton Archive/ Getty Images

HERR
Herr Kunst & Auktionshaus W.G. Herr
Friesenwall 35
D-50672 Köln
Germany
Tel: 00 49 221 25 45 48
Fax: 00 49 221 270 6742
www.herr-auktionen.de
E-mail: kunst@herr-auktionen.de

Hor
Musee Horta, Brussels
See "Museums" p.235

IHB
Imperial Half Bushel
831 North Howard Street
Baltimore
MD 21201
USA
Tel: 001 410 462 1192
www.imperialhalfbushel.com
E-mail: ihb@imperialhalfbushel.com

JDJ
James D Julia Inc
PO Box 830
Fairfield
ME 04937
USA
Tel: 001 207 453 7125
Fax: 001 207 453 2502
www.juliaauctions.com
E-mail: jjulia@juliaauctions.com

L&T
Lyon and Turnbull Ltd.
33 Broughton Place
Edinburgh EH1 3RR
Scotland
Tel: 0131 557 8844
Fax: 0131 557 8668
www.lyonandturnbull.com
E-mail: info@lyonandturnbull.com

LGA
Leah Gordon Antiques
Gallery 18
Manhattan Art and Antiques Center
1050 Second Avenue
New York
NY 10022
USA
Tel: 001 212 872 1422
Fax: 001 212 355 4403
www.the-maac.com/leahgordon
E-mail: leahgor50c@aol.com

LynH
Lynn & Brian Holmes
304-6 Grays Antique Market
58 Davies Street
London W1Y 2LP
Tel: 020 7629 7327
Fax: 020 7493 9344
E-mail: holmes@grays.clara.net

MACK
Macklowe Gallery
667 Madison Avenue
New York
NY 10021
USA
Tel: 001 212 644 6400
Fax: 001 212 755 6143
www.macklowegallery.com
E-mail: email@macklowegallery.com

MEN
Mendes Antique Lace and Textiles
Flat 2 Wilbury Lawn
44 Wilbury Road
Hove
East Sussex BN3 3TA
Tel: 01273 203 317
Fax: 01273 203 317
www.mendes.co.uk
E-mail: antiques@mendes.co.uk

MEP
Mary Evans Picture Library

MET
The Metropolitan Museum of Art, New York
See "Museums" p.235

MW
Mike Weedon
7 Camden Passage
Islington
London N1 8EA
Tel: 020 7226 5319
Fax: 020 7700 6387
www.mikeweedonantiques.com
E-mail: info@mikeweedonantiques.com

NA
Northeast Auctions
93 Pleasant Street
Portsmouth
NH 03801
USA
Tel: 001 603 433 8400
Fax: 001 603 433 0415
www.northeastauctions.com
E-mail: neainfo@ttlc.net

NBlm
N. Bloom & Son Ltd.
12 Piccadilly Arcade
London SW1Y 6NH
Tel: 020 7629 5060
Fax: 020 7493 2528
www.nbloom.com
E-mail: nbloom@nbloom.com

On
Onslows
The Coach House
Manor Road
Stourpaine
Dorset DT11 8TQ
Tel: 01258 488 838
Fax: 01258 488 838
www.onslows.co.uk
E-mail: enquiries@onslows.co.uk

OACC
Otford Antiques and Collectors Centre
26-28 High Street
Otford
Kent TN15 9DF
Tel: 01959 522 025
Fax: 01959 525 858
www.otfordantiques.co.uk
E-mail: info@otfordantiques.co.uk

PC
Private Collection

PS
Photo Scala, Florence

Qu
Quittenbaum Kunstauktionen
Hohenstaufenstraße 1
D-80801 München
Germany
Tel: 00 49 89 33 00 75 6
Fax: 00 49 89 33 00 75 77
www.quittenbaum.de
E-mail: dialog@quittenbaum.de

RdM
Reunion Des Musées
Nationaux Agence
Photographique

RG
Richard Gibbon
34/34a Islington Green
London N1 8DU
Tel: 020 7354 2852
Tel: 020 7354 2852
E-mail: neljeweluk@aol.com

Rum
Rumours
4 The Mall Antiques Arcade
359 Upper Street
London N1 0PD
Tel: 020 7704 6549
Fax: 01582 873 561
E-mail: rumdec@aol.com

RV
Roger-viollet

S&K
Sloans & Kenyon
4605 Bradley Boulevard
Bethesda, MD 20815
USA
Tel: 001 301 634 2330
Fax: 001 301 656 7074
www.sloansandkenyon.com
E-mail: info@sloansandkenyon.com

SF
The Silver Fund
1 Duke of York Street
London SW1Y 6JP
Tel: 020 7839 7664
Fax: 020 7839 8935
www.thesilverfund.com
E-mail: dealers@thesilverfund.com

SI
Sloans
No longer trading

Soth
Sotheby's Picture Library
34–35 New Bond Street
London W1A 2AA
Tel: 020 7293 5383
Fax: 020 7293 5062

Stad
Stadtmuseum, Munich
Müncher Stadtmuseum
St.-Jakobs-Platz 1
D-803331 München
Germany
Tel: 089 233 22370
Fax: 089 233 25033

Sty
Style Gallery
10 Camden Passage
London N1 8ED
Tel: 020 7359 7867

SWA
Swanns Galleries
104 East 25th Street
New York
NY 10010
USA
Tel: 001 212 254 4710
Fax: 001 212 979 1017
www.swanngalleries.com
E-mail: swann@swanngalleries.com

TDC
Thomas Dreiling Collection
Private Collection

TEL
Galerie Telkamp
Maximilianstraße 6
D-80539 Münchenk
Germany
Tel: 00 49 89 22 62 83
Fax: 00 49 89 24 21 46 52

TO
Titus Omega
Shop 21, The Mall
Camden Passage
London N1 0PD
Tel: 020 7688 1295
www.titusomega.com

V&A
Trustees of the V&A, London
See "Museums" p.235

VDB
Van Den Bosch
Shop 1
Georgian Village
Camden Passage
Islington N1 8DU
Tel: 020 7226 4550
www.vandenbosch.co.uk
E-mail: info@vandenbosch.co.uk

VS
Von Speath
Wilhelm-Diess-Weg 13
D-81927 München
Tel: 00 49 89 2809132
Fax: 00 49 89 2809132
www.glasvonspaeth.com
E-mail: info @glasvonspaeth.com

VZ
Von Zezschwitz Kunst und
Design
Friedrichstraße 1a
D-80801 München
Germany
Tel: 00 49 89 38 98 93 0
Fax: 00 49 (0) 89 38 98 93 25
www.von-zezschwitz.de
E-mail:
info@von-zezschwitz.de

WKA
Wiener Kunst Auktionen -
Palais Kinsky
Freyung 4
A-1010 Wien
Austria
Tel: 00 43 15 32 42 00
Fax: 00 43 15 32 42 00 9
www.palais-kinsky.com
E-mail:
office@palais-kinsky.com

Wrob
Junnaa & Thomi Wroblewski
Box 39
78 Marylebone High Street
London W1U 5AP
Tel: 020 7499 7793
Fax: 020 7499 7793
E-mail:
echo.base@dial.pipex.com

WW
Woolley and Wallis
51-61 Castle Street
Salisbury
Wiltshire SP1 3SU
Tel: 01722 424 500
Fax: 01722 424 508
www.woolleyandwallis.co.uk
E-mail:
enquiries@woolleyandwallis.co.uk

Directory of other Dealers, Auction Houses, and Museums

UK

AS Antique Galleries
26 Broad Street
Salford
Manchester M6 5BY
Tel: 0161 737 5938
Fax: 0161 737 6626
E-mail:
as@sternshine.demon.co.uk

Beverley R. Ltd.
344 Grays Antique Market
58 Davies Street
Mayfair
London W1Y 2LP
Tel: 020 7408 1129
Fax: 020 8741 8904

B Silverman
4 Campden Street
Kensington
London W8 7EP
Tel: 020 7985 0555
Fax: 020 7985 0556
www.silverman-london.com

Christie's South Kensington
85 Old Brompton Road
London SW7 3LD
Tel: 020 7724 2229
Fax: 020 7321 3321
www.christies.com

The Design Gallery
5 The Green
Westerham
Kent TN16 1AS
Tel/Fax: 01959 561 234
www.thedesigngallery.uk.com

Fay Lucas Artmetal
Christies Fine Art Securities
42 Ponton Road
London SW9 5RA
Tel: 020 7371 4404
www.faylucas.com
E-mail: info@faylucas.com

Hall Bakker Decorative Arts
Span Antiques
6 Market Place
Woodstock
Oxfordshire OX20 1TA
Tel: 01993 811332
www.hallbakker.co.uk

Jacek Podlewski
356 & 121 Grays Antique Market
58 Davies Street
Mayfair
London W1Y 2LP
Tel: 020 7409 1468

John Jesse
160 Kensington Church Street
London W8 4BN
Tel: 020 7229 0312

Pruskin Gallery
73 Kensington Church Street
London W8
Tel: 020 7937 1994
Fax: 020 7376 1285
E-mail: pruskin@pruskingallery.
demon.co.uk

Sandy Stanley
58-60 Kensington Church Street
London W8 4DB
Tel: 020 7937 3450
www.sandystanleyantiques.com

Sotheby's
34-35 New Bond Street
London W1A 2AA
Tel: 020 7293 5000
Fax: 020 7293 5989
www.sothebys.com

Strachan Antiques
40 Darnley Street
Pollokshields
Glasgow G41 2SE
Scotland
Tel: 0141 429 4411
www.strachanantiques.co.uk

Tadema Gallery
10 Charlton Place, Camden Passage
Islington, London N1 8AJ
Tel/Fax: 020 7359 1055
www.tademagallery.com

Victor Arwas Gallery
Edition Graphiques Ltd
3 Clifford Street
London W1 2LF
Tel: 020 7734 3944
www.victorarwas.com

Zeitgeist
58 Kensington Church Street
London W8 4DB
Tel: 020 7938 4817
www.zeitgeistantiques.com

USA

Bonhams & Butterfields
220 San Bruno Avenue
San Francisco, CA 94103
Tel: 001 415 861 7500
Fax: 001 415 861 8951
www.butterfields.com

Frank Rogin Inc.
21 Mercer Street 5th Floor
New York, NY 10013
Tel: 001 212 431 6534
www.rogin.com
info@rogin.com

Galleria 733
733 West Lake Street
Chicago, IL 60606
Tel: 001 312 382 0546

Geoffrey Diner Gallery
1710 21st Street, NW
Washington DC 20009
Tel: 001 202 483 5005
Fax: 001 212 483 2523
www.dinergallery.com
E-mail: mdg@dinergallery.com

John Alexander
10-12 West Gravers Lane
Philadelphia, PA 19118
Tel: 001 215 242 0741
Fax: 001 215 242 8546
www.johnalexanderltd.com

JW Art Glass
8466 N Lockwood Ridge Rd, #252
Sarasota, FL 34243
Tel: 001 941 351-6759
www.jwartglass.com

Leo Kaplan Ltd
114 East 57th Street
New York, NY 10022
Tel: 001 212 355 7212
Fax: 001 212 355 7209
www.leokaplan.com
E-mail: leokaplan@mindspring.com

Lillian Nassau Ltd
220 East 57th Street
New York, NY 10022
Tel: 001 212 759 6062
Fax: 001 212 832 9493
www.lilliannassau.com

Miguel Saco
38 East 18th Street
New York, NY 10003
Tel: 001 312 777 5460
Fax: 001 212 254 2852

Rita Bucheit Ltd
449 N. Wells Street
Chicago, IL 60610
Tel: 001 312 527 4080
Fax: 001 312 527 3316
www. ritabucheit.com
E-mail:
info@ritabucheit.com

Robert Edwards
PO Box 238
Swarthmore
PA 19081
Tel: 001 610 543 3595

SPAIN AND PORTUGAL

Acanto
Passeig de Gràcia 55-57
Barcelona, Spain
Tel: 00 93 215 3297

Belle Epoque
Antonio Lopez 2
Cádiz, Spain
Tel: 00 95 622 6810

Centre D'Antiquris
Passeig de Gràcia 55
Barcelona, Spain
Tel: 00 93 215 4499

Gothsland
Consell de Cent 331
08007 Barcelona, Spain
Tel: 00 93 488 1922

Midge Dalton
Plaza del Mercat 20B
07001 Palma de Mallorca, Spain
Tel: 00 34 971 71 33 60
Fax: 00 34 971 72 14 92

FRANCE AND BELGIUM

Alain Chenel
Villa Printemps, 12 Montee
Desambrois, 06000 Nice, France
Tel: 00 33 4 93 13 48 72
Fax: 00 33 4 93 85 85 33

Amberina Antiques Antwerp
Kloosterstraat 2-4 & 30-32
B-2000 Antwerp, Belgium
Tel/Fax: 00 32 3232 4025
www.Amberina.com

Anne-Sophie Duval
5 Quai Malaquais
75006 Paris, France
Tel: 00 33 1 43 54 51 16
Fax: 00 33 1 40 46 95 12

b.v.b.a Romantica
Koningsbaan 74a
B-2580 Beerzel-Putte, Belgium
Tel. 00 32 1524 7365
www.Romantica.tk

Félix Marcilhac
8 Rue Bonaparte
75006 Paris, France
Tel: 00 33 1 43 26 47 36

Galerie Hopkins-Custot
2 Avenue Matignon
75008 Paris, France
Tel.: 00 33 1 42 25 32 32
Fax: 00 33 1 42 25 25 26

Galerie Yves Gastou
12 Rue Bonaparte
75006 Paris, France
Tel: 00 33 1 53 73 00 10
Fax: 00 33 1 53 73 00 12
www.galerieyvesgastou.com

Gallerie Sint-John
Bij Sint Jacobs 15a
B-9000 Gent
Belgium
Tel: 00 32 9225 8262
www.belgiumantiques.com

Jean-Jacques Dutko
13 Rue Boneparte
75006 Paris, France
Tel: 00 33 1 43 26 96 13
Fax: 00 33 1 43 29 21 91

L'arc en Seine
31 Rue de Seine
75006 Paris
France
Tel: 00 33 1 43 291102
Fax: 00 33 1 43 29 97 66

Louis Gauchet
20 Rue Ségurane
06300 Nice
France
Tel: 00 33 4 93 55 11 74
Fax: 00 33 4 93 55 11 74
www.closducouvent.com

Marcel Grunspan
6 et 8 Rue Royale
75008 Paris, France
Tel: 00 33 1 42 60 57 57
Fax: 00 33 1 40 20 95 50

Michel Souillac
6 Rue Antoine-Dubois
75006 Paris, France
Tel: 00 33 1 43 29 43 04
Fax: 00 33 1 43 29 43 04

Olivier Watelet
11 Rue Bonaparte
75006 Paris, France
Tel: 00 33 1 43 26 07 87
Fax: 00 33 1 43 25 99 33

Robert Vallois
41 Rue de Seine
75006 Paris, France
Tel: 00 33 1 43 29 50 84
Fax: 00 33 1 43 29 90 73
www.vallois.com

Veronique Bamps s.a.
Boulevard de Waterloo
1000 Bruxelles, Belgium
Tel: 00 32 2511 3804
Fax: 00 32 2514 4731

GERMANY AND AUSTRIA

Antiquitäten Grobusch
Kleinmarschierstraße 11-15
52062 Aachen, Germany
Tel: 00 49 241 36351
Fax: 00 49 241 40 70 46

Art 1900
Kurfürstendamm 53
10707 Berlin, Germany
Tel: 0049 30 8815627
Fax: 00 49 308815627
www.art1900.de

Bel Etage Kunsthandel GmbH
Michaela & Wolfgang Bauer
Mahlerstraße 15
1010 Wien, Austria
Tel: 00 43 1 512 23 79 99
www.beletage.com
E-mail: office@beletagecom

Dénes Szy
Königsallee 27-31
D-40212 Düsseldorf
Germany
Tel: 00 49 211 323 98 26
Fax: 00 49 211 323 98 26

Galerie Splinter
Sophie-Gips Höfe
Sophienstraße 20/21
D-10178 Berlin Germany
Tel: 00 49 30 285 98 737

Holzer Galerie
Siebenstrerngasse 16
1070 Wien, Austria

Jörg Schwandt M.A.
Keithstraße 10
10787 Berlin
Germany
Tel: 00 49 30 218 50 17

Kunsthandel Patrick Kovas
Rechte Wienzeile 31
1040 Wien, Austria
Tel: 00 43 1 587 94 74
Fax: 00 43 1 586 08 40 85
www.patrick-kovacs.at
E-mail: office@patrick-kovacs.at

Kunstsalon Kovacek
Stallburggasse 2
1010 Wien, Austria
Tel: 00 43 1 512 83 58
www.art-kovacek.at

Lichterloh Kunsthandelsges.m.b.H
Freisingergasse 1
1010 Wien, Austria
Tel: 00 43 1 532 09 00
www.licherloh.com

Marcel Wang Antiques
Spiegelgasse 25
1010 Wien, Austria
Tel: 00 43 1 512 41 87
E-mail: marcel@wang-antiques.at

MUSEUMS

UK

Glasgow School of Art
167 Renfrew Street
Glasgow G3 6RQ
Scotland
Tel: 0141 353 4500
www.gsa.ac.uk

House For An Art Lover
Bellahouston Park
10 Dumbreck Road
Glasgow G41 5BW
Scotland
Tel: 0141 353 4770
Fax: 0141 353 4771
www.houseforanartlover.co.uk

Mackintosh House Gallery

Hunterian Art Gallery
82 Hillhead Street
University of Glasgow
Glasgow G12 8QQ
Scotland
Tel: 0141 330 5431
www.hunterian.gla.ac.uk

The Royal Pavilion Brighton

Pavilion Buildings, Brighton
East Sussex BN1 1EE
Tel: 01273 290 900
www.royalpavilion.org.uk

Victoria and Albert Museum

Cromwell Road, South Kensington
London SW7 2RL
Tel: 020 7942 2000
www.vam.ac.uk

USA

Charles Hosmer Morse Museum of American Art

445 North Park Avenue
Winter Park, FL 32789
Tel: 001 407 645 5311
www.morsemuseum.org

Los Angeles County Museum of Art (LACMA)

5905 Wilshire Boulevard
Los Angeles, CA 90036
Tel: 001 323 857 6000
www.lacma.org

The Art Institute of Chicago

111 South Michigan Avenue
Chicago, IL 60603
Tel: 001 312 443 3600
www.artic.edu

The Metropolitan Museum of Art

1000 Fifth Avenue at 82nd Street
New York, NY 10028-0198
Tel: 001 212 535 7710
www.metmuseum.org

The Minneapolis Institute of Arts

2400 Third Avenue South
Minneapolis, MN 55404
Tel: 001 612 8703200
www.artsmia.org

Virginia Museum of Fine Arts

2800 Grove Avenue at the Boulevard
Richmond, VA 23221-2466
Tel: 001 804 3401400
www.vmfa.state.va.us

SPAIN AND PORTUGAL

Casa Museu Gaudi

Parc Guell – Carretera del Carmel
08024 Barcelona, Spain
Tel: 00 34 93 219 3811
www.casamuseugaudi.com

Museo Art Nouveau y Art Deco

Calle Gibraltar 14
Salamanca 37008, Spain
Tel: 00 34 92 312 1425
www.museocasalis.org

Museu Calouste Gulbenkian

Avenida de Berna 45a
Lisbon, Portugal
Tel: 00 35 1 21 782 3000
www.gulbenkian.pt

Museu d'Art Modern

Plaça d'Armes
Parc de la Ciutadella
Barcelona, Spain
Tel: 00 34 93 319 5728

FRANCE AND BELGIUM

Musée d'Art Moderne et Contemporain de Strasbourg

1 Place Jean Hans Arp
F-67000 Strasbourg, France
Tel: 00 33 3 88 23 31 31

Musée des Arts Décoratifs

105-107 Rue de Rivoli
75001 Paris, France
Tel: 00 33 1 44 55 59 26
www.ucad.fr

Musée des Beaux-Arts

3 Place Stanislas
54000 Nancy, France
Tel: 00 33 3 83 85 30 72

Musée de l'Ecole de Nancy

36-38 Rue du Sergent Blandan
F-54000 Nancy, France
Tel: 00 33 3 83 40 14 86
www.ecole-de-nancy.com

Musée d'Orsay

62 Rue de Lille
75343 Paris, France
Tel: 00 33 1 40 49 48 14
www.musee-orsay.fr

Musée Horta

Rue Américaine 23-25
1060 Bruxelles, Belgium
Tel: 00 32 2537 1692
www.hortamuseum.be

GERMANY AND AUSTRIA

Badisches Landesmusem

Schloss
D-76131 Karlsruhe, Germany
Tel: 00 49 721 926 6514
Fax: 00 49 721 926 6537
E-mail: info@landesmuseum.de
www.landesmuseum.de

Bröhan Museum

Schloßstraße, 1a
14059 Berlin, Germany
Tel: 00 49 30 326 906 00
www.broehan-museum.de

Hessisches Landesmuseum Darmstadt

Friedensplatz 1
64283 Darmstadt, Germany
Tel: 00 49 6151 16 57 03
www.hlmd.de

Hohenthor, Hagen

Stirnband 10
58093 Hagen, Germany
Tel: 00 49 2334 207-31 38
www.keom.de
E-mail: KEOM@hagen.de

Karl-Ernst Osthaus Museum

Hochstraße 73
58042 Hagen, Germany
Tel: 00 49 2331 207 31 38
www.keom.de
E-mail: KEOM@hagen.de

Museum Kunst Palast

Ehrenhof 4-5
40479 Düsseldorf, Germany
Tel: 00 49 211 899 2460
www.museum-kunstpalast.de

MAK- Österreichisches Museum für Angewandte Kunst

Stubenring 5, 1010 Wien, Austria
Tel: 00 43 1 711 36-0
Fax: 00 43 1 713 10 26
www.mak.at
E-mail: office@MAK.at

Museum für Kunst und Gewerbe

Steintorplatz,1
20099 Hamburg, Germany
Tel: 00 49 40 2486 2732
www.mkg-hamburg.de

ITALY

Museo del Bijou di Casalmaggiore

Via A Porzio 9
Casalmaggiore, Italy
Tel: 00 39 0375 42030
www.museodelbijou.it

Fondazione Regionale Cristoforo Colombo

Via all'Asila D. Garbarino 28R
16126 Genova, Italy
www.fondazionecolobo.it

Vetrate Liberty Museum

Cottage di Civetta
Villa Torlonia, Rome, Italy

EASTERN EUROPE

Mucha Museum

Kaunicky Palac, Panska 7
110 00 Prague 1, Czech Republic
Tel: 420 224 216 415
www.mucha.cz

State Hermitage Museum

Palace Embankment
38 Dvortsovaya Naberezhnaya
St Petersburg, Russia
Tel: 812 110 9625
www.hermitage museum.org

235

Index (Page numbers in *italics* refer to captions)

ACKNOWLEDGEMENTS

Acknowledgements

AUTHORS' ACKNOWLEDGEMENTS

Dorling Kindersley would like to thank Caroline Hunt and Angela Wilkes for editorial contribution, Karla Jennings and Dawn Young for design contribution, Scott Stickland and Jonathan Brooks for digital images coordination, and Pamela Ellis for compiling the index.

The Price Guide Company would like to thank Digital Image Coordinators, Cara Miller and Ellen Spalek, and European Consultant Martina Franke.

PICTURE CREDITS

DK Picture Librarians: Richard Dabb, Neale Chamberlain
Abbreviations key: t=top, b=bottom, r=right, l=left, c=centre.

2: Courtesy of Sotheby's Picture Library, London; 8: © Christie's Images Ltd (bl), Courtesy of Sotheby's Picture Library, London (tl); 8-9: Calouste Gulbenkian Museum, Lisbon, Portugal/ ADAGP/DACS 2004 (c); 10: AKG London/ Jurgen Raible (b), Corbis (kb), Courtesy of the Trustees of the V&A (tr); 11: Archives d'Architecture Moderne/ADAGP/DACS 2004 (l), Musee Horta, Brussels (br); 12: Alamy Images/Robert Harding Picture Library Ltd (bl), Courtesy of the Trustees of the V&A (tl); 13: Bridgeman Art Library, London/New York/Christies Images (tr), Courtesy of the Trustees of the V&A (bl), (br); 14: Courtesy of Sotheby's Picture Library, London (r), Stadtmuseum, Munich/Wolfgang Pulfer (bl); 15: AKG London (tr), Courtesy of Sotheby's Picture Library, London (bl); 16: AKG London, © Christie's Images Ltd/ADAGP/DACS 2004 (tl); 17: Courtesy of Sotheby's Picture Library, London (br), (t); 18: © Christie's Images Ltd (l); 19: Alamy Images/Fergus Mackay (l), Courtesy of Sotheby's Picture Library, London (cra); 23: Corbis (tl); 24: Courtesy of Sotheby's Picture Library, London (tl), (b); 25: © Christie's Images Ltd (bl), Réunion Des Musées Nationaux Agence Photographique/H Lewandowski/DACS 2004 (cr); 30: Réunion Des Musées Nationaux Agence Photographique/P. Bernard (tr); 31: © Christie's Images Ltd/ ADAGP/DACS 2004 (bc), (br), Réunion Des Musées Nationaux Agence Photographique/Jean Schormans (tr); 34: DK/Judith Miller Archive – Von Zezschwitz/ADAGP/DACS 2004, (bl), DK/Judith Miller Archive – Macklowe Gallery/ADAGP/DACS 2004 (br), DK/Judith Miller Archive/ADAGP/DACS 2004 (tr); 35: DK/Judith Miller Archive – Dorotheum/ADAGP/DACS 2004, (bl), DK/Judith Miller Archive/ ADAGP/DACS 2004 (cl), DK/Judith Miller Archive/ADAGP/DACS 2004 (tl), DK/Judith Miller Archive/ADAGP/DACS 2004 (c), © Christie's Images Ltd (bcr), Réunion Des Musées Nationaux Agence Photographique/P. Schmidt (br); 37: Courtesy of Sotheby's Picture Library, London (br); 44: © Christie's Images Ltd (tr), Courtesy of the Trustees of the V&A (bl); 45: Mary Evans Picture Library (tr), Courtesy of the Trustees of the V&A (cal); 48: Bridgeman Art Library, London/New York/The Fine Art Society, London, UK (tr), © Christie's Images Ltd (bc), Courtesy of the Trustees of

the V&A (bl); 49: Courtesy of the Trustees of the V&A (br); 53: Bridgeman Art Library, London/New York/Private Collection (br), The Craftsman Farms Foundation, Parsipanny, New Jersey (tr); 62: Bridgeman Art Library, London/New York/The Stapleton Collection (tl); 63: AKG London/Erich Lessing/Museum of Fine Arts, Budapest (tr), The Art Archive/Victoria and Albert Museum London/Sally Chappell (br); 70: Bridgeman Art Library, London/New York/Archives Charmet/Bibliotheque des Arts Decoratifs, Paris France/ADAGP/DACS 2004 (tr); 73: Bonhams Auctioneers, London (br), Hulton Archive/Getty Images/Museum of the City of New York/Archive Photos (tl); 74: Roger-viollet/Boyer (br); 75: Réunion Des Musées Nationaux Agence Photographique/P Schmidt (cr); 106: Corbis/Hulton-Deutsch Collection (tr); 144: Bridgeman Art Library, London/New York/Musee des Arts Decoratifs, Paris, France (tl), Réunion Des Musées Nationaux Agence Photographique/Hervé Lewandowski (tr); 145: Courtesy of Sotheby's Picture Library, London/ ADAGP/DACS 2004 (bl), Courtesy of Sotheby's Picture Library, London (br), Courtesy of the Trustees of the V&A/ ADAGP/DACS 2004 (r); 146: © Christie's Images Ltd (tr); 147: Courtesy of Sotheby's Picture Library, London (cr), (br); 148: Calouste Gulbenkian Museum, Lisbon, Portugal/ ADAGP/DACS 2004 (bl), (bc), (br), Courtesy of Sotheby's Picture Library, London ADAGP/DACS 2004 (tr); 149: © Christie's Images Ltd/ ADAGP/DACS 2004 (bl), (br); Courtesy of the Trustees of the V&A/ ADAGP/DACS 2004 (cb), DK/Judith Miller Archive – Dorotheum /ADAGP/ DACS 2004 (tc); 150: Courtesy of Sotheby's Picture Library, London/ ADAGP/DACS 2004 (tc), Courtesy of Sotheby's Picture Library (cr); 151: Courtesy of Sotheby's Picture Library, London (cr); 157: AKG London (bl), The Metropolitan Museum of Art/Gift of Sarah E. Hanley, 1946 (46.168.1) (br); 166: AKG London/Marion Kalter (tr); 167: Art Resource/The Newark Museum (bl); 168: AKG London (bl); 171: Courtesy of Sotheby's Picture Library, London (cra), Württembergische Metallwarenfabrik (tl); 174: Courtesy of Sotheby's Picture Library, London (bl); 175: Courtesy of Sotheby's Picture Library, London (cr), Courtesy of the Trustees of the V&A (bc); 188: Bridgeman Art Library, London/New York/Mazovian Museum, Plock, Poland (br), Photo Scala, Florence/Foto The Newark Museum/Art Resource (bl); 194: © Christie's Images Ltd; 196: Roger-viollet/Harlingue (tr), Courtesy of Sotheby's Picture Library, London (tl), (bl); 197: AKG London/Staatliche Kunstsammlungen, Kassel (r), © Christie's Images Ltd (bl); 198: Courtesy of Sotheby's Picture Library, London (tr), (br); 206: Corbis/Swim Ink; 208: Bridgeman Art Library, London/New York/Mucha Trust (tr); 208: Courtesy of the Trustees of the V&A/Given by Bertram Evans (bc); 211: Corbis/ Leonard de Selva (bl), Glasgow Museums; Art Gallery & Museums (br); 212: AKG London (bl); 223: Corbis (br); Corbis/Stapleton Collection (cr); 224: © Christie's Images Ltd. (r).

All other images © Dorling Kindersley and The Price Guide Company Ltd. For further information see: **www.dkimages.com**